Gift and the Unity of Being

VERITAS

Series Introduction

"... the truth will set you free." (John 8:32)

In much contemporary discourse, Pilate's question has been taken to mark the absolute boundary of human thought. Beyond this boundary, it is often suggested, is an intellectual hinterland into which we must not venture. This terrain is an agnosticism of thought: because truth cannot be possessed, it must not be spoken. Thus, it is argued that the defenders of "truth" in our day are often traffickers in ideology, merchants of counterfeits, or anti-liberal. They are, because it is somewhat taken for granted that Nietzsche's word is final: truth is the domain of tyranny.

Is this indeed the case, or might another vision of truth offer itself? The ancient Greeks named the love of wisdom as *philia*, or friendship. The one who would become wise, they argued, would be a "friend of truth." For both philosophy and theology might be conceived as schools in the friendship of truth, as a kind of relation. For like friendship, truth is as much discovered as it is made. If truth is then so elusive, if its domain is *terra incognita*, perhaps this is because it arrives to us—unannounced—as gift, as a person, and not some thing.

The aim of the Veritas book series is to publish incisive and original current scholarly work that inhabits "the between" and "the beyond" of theology and philosophy. These volumes will all share a common aspiration to transcend the institutional divorce in which these two disciplines often find themselves, and to engage questions of pressing concern to both philosophers and theologians in such a way as to reinvigorate both disciples with a kind of interdisciplinary desire, often so absent in contemporary academe. In a word, these volumes represent collective efforts in the befriending of truth, doing so beyond the simulacra of pretend tolerance, the violent, yet insipid reasoning of liberalism that asks with Pilate, "What is truth?"—expecting a consensus of non-commitment; one that encourages the commodification of the mind, now sedated by the civil service of career, ministered by the frightened patrons of position.

The series will therefore consist of two "wings": (1) original monographs; and (2) essay collections on a range of topics in theology and philosophy. The latter will principally by the products of the annual conferences of the Centre of Theology and Philosophy (www.theologyphilosophycentre.co.uk).

Conor Cunningham and Peter Candler, *Series editors*

Gift and the Unity of Being

ANTONIO LÓPEZ

FOREWORD BY
John Milbank

CASCADE *Books* • Eugene, Oregon

GIFT AND THE UNITY OF BEING

Veritas 11

Copyright © 2014 Antonio López. All rights reserved. Except for brief quotations in critical publications or reviews, no part of this book may be reproduced in any manner without prior written permission from the publisher. Write: Permissions, Wipf and Stock Publishers, 199 W. 8th Ave., Suite 3, Eugene, OR 97401.

Cascade Books
An Imprint of Wipf and Stock Publishers
199 W. 8th Ave., Suite 3
Eugene, OR 97401

www.wipfandstock.com

ISBN 13: 978-1-62032-667-1

Cataloging-in-Publication data:

López, Antonio, 1968–

    Gift and the unity of being / Antonio López ; foreword by John Milbank.

    xviii + 350 p. ; 23 cm. —Includes bibliographical references and indexes.

    ISBN 13: 978-1-62032-667-1

    Veritas 11

    1. Gifts—Religious aspects—Christianity. 2. Philosophical theology. I. Milbank, John. II. Title. III. Series.

BT751.3 .L67 2014

Manufactured in the U.S.A.

To David L. Schindler,
in friendship

Non per avere a sè di bene acquisto,
ch'esser non può, ma perchè suo splendore,
potesse, risplendendo, dir '*Subsisto*',
in sua etternità di tempo fore,
fuor d'ogni altro comprender, come i piacque,
s'aperse in nuovi amor l'etterno amore.

Not (for it cannot be) that he should gain
good for himself, but that, shining, his resplendence
might utter "I exist" beyond
all time in his eternity, beyond
confining space, as pleased him,
the eternal love opened into new loves.

DANTE, *PARADISO*, XXIX, 13–18

Contents

Foreword by John Milbank ix
Abbreviations xv

Introduction 1

I. Gift's Originary Experience 11
   1. Approaching Originary Experience 14
   2. Terminological Clarifications 16
   3. A Distinct Understanding 20
   4. The Inexorable Presence of the Sign 23
   5. The Experience of Being Given 28
   6. The Exigent Character of Life 35
   7. The Time of Gift 42

II. Concrete Singularity 51
   1. The Allurement of Anarchy 52
   2. A Radical Difference 59
   3. Giving Otherness 62
   4. The Gift of Existence 70
   5. Open Principles 77
   6. The Singular's Perseity 85
   7. Gift's Bodily Perseity 96

III. Reception and Reciprocity 100
   1. Giving Freedom 102
   2. Ordering Freedom 115
   3. Reciprocity as Recognition 122
   4. Human Action and the Gift of Self 128
   5. Orphans, at Last 135

IV. The Son's Gift of Self 148
1. On the Way of Being 150
2. Approaching the Figure of Christ 159
3. "You Have Given Me Your Name" (John 17:12) 164
4. Making All Things New 172
5. Gratuity's Owning 184

V. The Unpreceded Giver 191
1. Unpreceded Origin: The Father as Absolute Person 194
2. The Father's Unfathomable Light 196
3. A Father Like No Other 199
4. Hierarchical, Constitutive Order 210
5. Eternal Communion 218

VI. Gift's Unifying Memory 228
1. God's Fruitful Gift 229
2. *Donum Doni* 233
3. Divine Memory 238
4. Eternal Beginning 245
5. The Gratuity of the Divine Gift 249

VII. The Unexpected Gift 259
1. The Father's Giving 263
2. Restoration of Sonship 272
3. The Unity of Life (I) 279
4. The Newness of the Gift 286
5. The Unity of Life (II) 293

Envoi 305

Bibliography 311
Index of Names 329
Index of Subjects 334

Foreword

John Milbank

Today it would be difficult for any one theologian to write a complete, new *Summa*. Yet in this wonderful book, Antonio López offers us no less than a short, indicative *Summa theologiae* for our times, which points the way to a new theological and philosophical synthesis.

This synthesis pivots round the concept of "gift." This is no arbitrary, idiosyncratic choice on Fr. López's part, because today, to a remarkable degree, much academic and practical thinking is converging round this theme. Ever since Marcel Mauss, anthropologists, sociologists, and historians have come more and more to realize that human society as such is composed by gift-exchange before it is further cemented by state authority and economic contract. Increasingly it is acknowledged that this remains at bottom true for advanced and modern societies as well as for primitive ones. In consequence, both secular and Catholic social teachings have started to pay renewed attention to gratuitous exchange or reciprocity. It is realized that this unavoidable reality has been undermined by the impersonalism of much modern thinking, and that its recognition and restoration are crucial to solving our contemporary social and economic problems.

At the same time, modern philosophy has been much concerned with the "givenness" of reality and has sometimes understood this givenness as "gift," either in ontological or in phenomenological terms.

Yet here we can note a certain irony. Often the social discourse about the gift has been secular and has allowed that a gift, as a gift, may paradoxically require a return, rendering gift-giving something that always assumes a relational context. On the other hand, the philosophical and sometimes theological discussions of the gift have frequently insisted on a unilateral purism that denies that a true gift can, of itself, assume any return or even reception, nor exist genuinely within a context of preestablished relationship.

In consequence, the gift as "time" or as the ethical imperative is deemed to be at once a transcendental condition for all of reality, all of knowing and ethical action, and yet as "impossible" in terms of actual realization. Either this circumstance is regarded as a ground for postmodern skepticism, or else for a neo-Plotinian mysticism of that which lies supposedly "beyond being."

However, another group of theologians, less publicized in the Anglo-Saxon academy and including Benedict XVI, has developed an understanding of the gift in reciprocalist terms that can be much more related to the realism of the anthropological and sociological understandings of gift as gift-exchange.

Their efforts are brought to a new height of analytic sophistication in the current book, which is nevertheless commendably clear and accessible to a wide educated readership throughout. Because he begins his analysis with "the concrete singular," compounded of soul, body, and spirit and both physically and socially dependent, Fr. López refuses to endorse the idealism and abstraction of the theorists of purified donation. With a simple exactitude that might shame many would-be adepts of vaunted rigor, he rightly insists that a giver cannot give unless he is first already himself a recipient.

Equally he shows that the "impure" gift that is bound up with a reception and return more corresponds to the teaching of Christian theology. Created beings only exist as gift because in being "given to themselves" they are through and through a return of praise to God, even though this return is inadequate and not "needed" by God. The "nuptial" perspective upon Christology is precisely the recognition that the gift of the Incarnation would have been impossible without its reception by Mary and the Church. The traditional doctrine of substantive relations in the Trinity shows that the Father is in a crucial sense passive and receptive in his giving of the Son (as Hegel distortedly realized), while the necessary place of the Holy Spirit shows the essence of gift as reciprocity, while insisting on the asymmetry and non-foreclosure of further gratuity in the reality of relational union. In this sense there is always a "unilateral moment" in gift-exchange, which Fr. López fully incorporates.

Finally, were theology to deny the exchangist perspective on gift, then unilateral "mercy" would be divorced from justice, defined by Aristotle as all the proportional reciprocities that are shared by friends in the city. Then we would be left with a mercy without justice and worse, a justice without mercy. It could be added here that we would also be left with a generosity without economy and worse (just what neoliberalism has left us with today), an economy without charity. Those many recent thinkers who require a giving "outside the economic" need to reflect on how this abandons us to economic amorality and to an impotently formalistic ethics of "rights" (criticized at one point in this book) that proclaims the dignity of the isolated human being as such, but leaves people as situated in concrete biological, social, and vocational relations outside the sway of dignity altogether.

Christian thinking, instead of dreaming of a non-existent "aneconomic" realm, requires a re-rooting of the falsely disembedded amoral economy of today back in the divine *economia*. Then precisely defined contract would become subordinate to and guided by asymmetrical reciprocity and non-identical repetition of real personal relationships, always seeking the mutual good, even in monetary transactions.

Effectively, Fr. López sees the need to think gift in terms of the genuinely economic, so understood.

But his work has more fundamentally a much wider, metaphysical import. In developing his account of theological gift as reciprocity, he in effect treats gift as a "transcendental" in the medieval sense. This proves a natural intellectual move, since all the main categories and themes of Christian doctrine indeed concern gift at their heart: creation, incarnation, redemption, grace, the Church, the sacraments, virginity, and marriage. But more specifically one could say that this adoption of a new transcendental category achieves three things.

First, it allows one to transit readily from a philosophical concern with the givenness of being to a theological one with creation and grace. The gift character of reality that philosophy is able to ponder only receives an adequate clarification in terms of supernatural revelation.

Second, it allows Fr. López to reinstate a premodern realist and cosmological focus in metaphysics while incorporating what is valid in the modern "turn to the subject." Following the work of Mouroux, Giussani, and others, he realizes that modern subjectivism can only be undone by a kind of counter-subjectivism, not by any simple demand that we return to an objectivist ontology. This is because, for modern people, the meaning of "the objective" has already been determined by the turn to the subject as something meaninglessly given and manipulable. It no longer spontaneously suggests a meaningful donation. To recover this suggestion, we need to return to "an originary experience" that the older, objectivist metaphysics took for granted and so did not discuss. It is even the case, it is implied, that we must renew this experience in an unprecedentedly acute way, because the question must arise as to how it could ever have been lost sight of in the first place. In an ultimately "romantic" lineage perpetuated in our own times by German, French, and Italian Catholics like Guardini, Balthasar, Ulrich, Bruaire, and Giussani (all much cited), Fr. López insists that this experience has aesthetic, affective, and imaginative as well as rational dimensions.

In this respect he follows Giussani, who by no means peremptorily dismissed "liberal Protestant" concerns with religious experience, but instead transformed them so as to free them from any connotations of "foundational feelings." In the same spirit, Fr. López listens carefully to the insights of Husserl, Heidegger, and Marion, yet resists any notion of a pure phenomenological reduction to the sheerly given. Indeed, he sees that such an indubitably manifest reality cannot be the gift, because a gift involves always a personal, interpretative response to the relatively uncertain and even ambivalent. In consequence, any surd "given"—however ineffably "saturated" and not merely factual—cannot be a gift, but will remain thoroughly impersonal in character. It is near sophistry to try to associate this very impersonalism with the purity of the one-way gift. For such a gift, without recognizable giver, recipient, or content, can be of no social effect, including, therefore, no ecclesial or redemptive effect. To be sure, for Christianity gifts are given and received by the pure in heart, but any notion that this can be separated from the benefit of the materially poor is refused from the mouth of Jesus himself at the very outset.

Nevertheless, with a necessary generosity, Fr. López incorporates some of the insights of modern phenomenology and of modern linguistic philosophy and hermeneutics. In doing so he contrives to *balance* their respective emphases on the extra-linguistically "given" and on arbitrary linguistic construction or interpretation. For he insists throughout his book that *verbum* and *donum* go together—a point that has ultimately Trinitarian implications. Thus the world is given to us, but as signs that we must read and respond to if we want to receive it at all—including ourselves as gifts to ourselves. Conversely, we will misread these signs if we do not understand them as gifts, because then there would lurk no intention behind them. Merely apparent signs would reduce to the events of our reception of givens that are not gifts, and these events could only conceal an abyss. With an unfailing eye for the way in which Heidegger perversely ruined his own real and astonishing profundity by a kind of philosophical charlatanry, Fr. López shows that he after all closed the question of being by reducing it to the event of our ontic reception of existence. Elsewhere he is equally remorseless in exposing the continued subjectivism of Heidegger's postmodern heirs.

In the third place, and most crucially, the transcendentality of the gift permits a rethinking of the Thomistic metaphysics of act and being that renders it a fully Trinitarian metaphysics. The divine *actus* is already, as in the case of the Paternal origin, in a certain sense receptive in order that it may act at all; equivalently we cannot see any finite reality as an act unless we also see it as a received gift. Here Fr. López, drawing as he did in his first book on Claude Bruaire's "ontodology," makes use of modern idealism while purging it of what is invalid. Since a gift, in order to be given, must be received, if every being is a gift of itself to itself, then it can only exist as *reflectively* giving itself to itself. This means that consciously spiritual beings are the first and primordial created beings. There cannot be a cosmos without spirit, as indeed Aquinas like the Fathers taught, and equally every non-spiritual creature must exhibit this spirituality in some lesser, analogical degree. I find here a fascinating implication both that some kind of vitalism might be embraced by Christian metaphysics and that a genuine vitalism must derive from transcendence and not immanence, as Bergson and others have supposed.

If even God is receptive, then, conversely, even pure created recipients must be active: gratuitously generous on their own account to others and seeking the end of reciprocal union with others and with God.

It then follows not just that every being *qua* being is a gift and that God is eminent generosity, but also that every being is internally and externally involved in a gift-exchange of initiation, reception, and counter-giving that in God is Trinitarian relation—though Fr. López strenuously avoids any simplistic identification of the three divine persons with these three exchangist moments. Deploying great subtlety and suppleness of argument, he then associates this transcendental reciprocity with the "real difference" of being and essence in Aquinas's ontology; with the relation of Christ's divine being and his secondary and dependent created being; with the "nuptial" circulation between the historical/critical Jesus in his unity with the Christ of faith; and finally with the need for the third person in the Trinity.

Here the Son is indeed identified as the first Paternal gift, but were he not also the Logos who needed to be "remembered" and interpreted as word by the Holy Spirit, then he would not really be gift at all, since this requires a reception, and the Filial reception is identical to the Paternal outpouring. A closed mutuality of Father and Son would collapse into an impersonal, substantive egotism, were it not for their combined will to share the experience of being infinitely loved with Richard of St. Victor's *Condilectus*.

In this way, the Holy Spirit turns out to be at once supremely gift, reflexive spirit, the principle of life, and the ground of the unity of being. In order that the divine essence be not elevated over the persons or identified with the Father, it must be personally expressed as the Holy Spirit.

Thereby Fr. López caps his profound and yet most engaging reflections with the thesis that we cannot conceive of the metaphysical unity of being adequately as monistic act, but must conceive of it as the unity both emergent with and yet presumed by gift-exchange, in the sense of an exchange always already begun. This process only has a "beginning" in the infinite, which is properly speaking never begun at all.

The suggestion would seem to be that it is the revelation of the Trinity through the divine economy of times that alone allows us to complete our obscure philosophical intuitions as to the priority of gift for both being and human social existence.

I find all this thoroughly compelling in the way that the simple and manifest truth is self-evident as radiating forth. Reading this book confirmed me in the sense that the current Catholic intellectual project is by far the most coherent one available in the world today and actually the one that manages to make most sense of the best specifically contemporary intuitions and realizations. It gives me profound hope that in the current century this project will be able to recover and rethink the Western tradition in a way that could even (in the face of increasing global catastrophe) prove universally persuasive.

Abbreviations

Giussani's Works

AC	L'autocoscienza del cosmo
AVS	Un avvenimento di vita cioè una storia
GTSM	Generare tracce nella storia del mondo
IPO	L'io, il potere, le opere
JTE	The Journey to Truth Is an Experience
MO	Il miracolo dell'ospitalità
NFT	Se non fossi tuo
PLW	Is It Possible to Live This Way? (3 vols.)
ROE	The Risk of Education
RS	The Religious Sense
RVU	Alla ricerca del volto umano
SPVVC	Si può vivere (veramente?!) così?
TT	Il tempo e il tempio
"Tu"	"Tu" (o dell'amicizia)
USD	L'uomo e il suo destino
VNC	Vivendo nella carne
WTC	Why the Church?

Other Works:

AAS	Acta Apostolicae Sedis
An. post.	Posterior Analytics, Aristotle
C. Ar.	Orationes contra Arianos, Athanasius

Cat.	*Categories*, Aristotle
CCSG	*Corpus Christianorum, Series Graeca*
CCSL	*Corpus Christianorum, Series Latina*
Civ.	*De civitate Dei*, Augustine
DS	*Denzinger-Schönmetzer*
EE	*L'être et l'esprit*, Bruaire
Encyclopedia	*Encyclopedia of the Philosophical Sciences*, Hegel
ET	*Explorations in Theology* (4 vols.), Balthasar
GA	*Gesamtausgabe*, Heidegger
GD	*The Gift of Death*, Derrida
GL	*The Glory of the Lord* (7 vols.), Balthasar
GT	*Given Time*, Derrida
Haer.	*Adversus haereses*, Irenaeus
In Ioa.	*In Evangelium Ioannis tractatus*, Augustine
Metaph.	*Metaphysics*, Aristotle
In Metaph.	*In duodecim libros Metaphysicorum Aristotelis expositio*, Aquinas
In Nic. Eth.	*In decem libros Ethicorum expositio*, Aquinas
Or.	*Orationes*, Gregory of Nazianzus
OTB	*On Time and Being*, Heidegger
PG	*Patrologiae cursus completus. Accurante Jacques-Paul Migne. Series Graeca* (Paris)
In Physic.	*Commentaria in octo libros Physicorum*, Aquinas
PL	*Patrologiae cursus completus. Accurante Jacques-Paul Migne. Series Latina* (Paris)
De pot. Dei	*Quaestiones disputatae de potentia Dei*, Aquinas
PS	*Phenomenology of Spirit*, Hegel
SCG	*Summa contra gentiles*, Aquinas
I Sent. / IV Sent.	*Scriptum super libros Sententiarum magistri Petri Lombardi episcopi Parisiensis*, Aquinas
ST	*Summa theologiae*, Aquinas

TB	*The Texture of Being*, Schmitz
TD	*Theo-drama* (5 vols.), Balthasar
TDNT	*Theological Dictionary of the New Testament*, Kittel
TL	*Theo-logic* (3 vols.), Balthasar
Trin.	*De Trinitate*, Augustine
De ver.	*Quaestiones disputatae de veritate*, Aquinas
VPR	*Vorlesungen über die Philosophie der Religion* (*Lectures on the Philosophy of Religion*; 3 vols.), Hegel
WL	*Wissenschaft der Logik* (*The Science of Logic*), Hegel

Introduction

THE MYSTERY OF BIRTH fills our existence with joy, hope, and wonder, but it does more than this as well: it calls us to ponder the mystery of the positivity of being. There are several layers of meaning to the mystery of being born, and these layers, though intrinsically and circularly related, are distinct but not independent. The first meaning, perhaps the most obvious but not the least important, is the biological. Life, the fruit of the loving union between a father and a mother, is given to us with and through a corporeal, organic existence. Our very body continually refers us back to our birth insofar as our bodily being is truly ours—to be born is to be given to oneself. Simultaneously, the body reminds us at birth that our life is a life that is received. This reception has to do with both the moment of conception and also with the entirety of our historical existence. Just as we cannot give birth to ourselves or completely manipulate this bodiliness at will, so we cannot exist without receiving the light, the warmth, and the language that enable us to see, create, and speak.

Our corporeality reflects in its particular mode the second, ontological meaning of the mystery of birth. We come into existence from a dual, nuptial union and, as was also the case for all who went before us, our own being remains distinct from this origin. In an additional reflection of its origin, our being is itself a dual unity. Our "to-be," our existing, is unique to us and at the same time is common to everything that exists. We soon come to learn what we are. At the same time, we never cease to grapple with what seems to be the truest and most beautiful mystery about us: *that* we are. *What* we are is not deducible from the mystery *that* we are, and this mystery of the irreducibility between *what* we are (our essence) and *that* we are (our *esse*) brings to a quick end the temptation to believe that what we are lies simply at the disposal of our reason and will.

The mystery of birth also has a spiritual meaning. Ours is in fact the birth of a spirit; that is, of someone who becomes aware of him or herself in a free and affective response to the other. The finite spirit grows insofar as it listens to, discourses with, and freely dwells in the source that generates it. This process takes place through the riches of life as well as through its dangers, failures, and tragedies. To be born is to be given to ourselves, to be free, with the task to contemplate the mystery of our being and to be what we are. This spiritual sense also reveals that birth encompasses both a historical circumstance (the temporal beginning of life) and a permanent dimension of existence. All the so-called rebirths we experience after having been born, such as falling in love, becoming a father or mother, being forgiven, and so on, are expressions of and a new flourishing of our own birth. These events, in fact, connect us to the origin of life in a way that is as novel and unprecedented as it is ancient and familiar.

The spiritual meaning of birth opens up the fourth layer, the theological meaning. This aspect, which is perhaps the most difficult to perceive, is illuminated if we recall the surprise that greets the news of a new child coming into existence. This surprise is, at its core, a signal of the relationship with the ultimate source from which it is given to the child to be. The justice of pointing to this theological meaning (as opposed to forcing an interpretation on a neutral event) is underscored when we reflect that the child is a new person, a new spirit, who is irreducible either to his own parents or to the biological process through which he came into being. Births that do not come from a genuine act of love between a man and a woman do not call into question this experience of wonder; they presuppose it. Moreover, the light of a new existence has within it the capacity to correct from within the meager measure behind its conception. Irreducible to parents or biological laws, the child is born into a solitude that no human companionship, not even that of his own parents, can eliminate. The solitude of this twofold irreducibility is not one of loneliness, however; it is rather a sign of a deeper communion. The child is placed in a dialogue with the ultimate origin of existence, which theology has always expressed through the term "God." This irreducibility, forming a constitutive element of the person, also indicates that the relationship with God is at the chronological beginning of our existence and also at every moment thereafter. We are not our own. The theological meaning of birth grounds not only the ontological and spiritual meanings, but also, to return to the beginning, the somatic meaning. The body, while expressing the difference from God who is pure spirit, also reveals the divine, original generosity. From within its own finitude, the body reflects divine life through the interpersonal relationships of man and wife, parents and children. Furthermore, our historical existence, precisely as existence in time, images the unmoving movement of the eternal being. Rather than an arc stretching from nothingness to the unknown void, corporeal and historical existence is a movement towards the original giver that contains the hope that our finite "be-ing" may be confirmed in the relation with that giver. Birth, both as the inception of life and a permanent dimension of existence, provides a stance for thinking about the whole: a mystery that illuminates the positivity of finite existing and of being as such.

When we look at the fourfold dimension of the mystery of birth—biological, ontological, spiritual, theological—the complexity and paradoxical nature of the unity of our being emerges. It is complex because we come to be ourselves as the fruit of a nuptial union and, while remaining distinct from our relations with God, parents, and others, we do not exist apart from them. This complexity is present in all four dimensions of the mystery, but we may particularly consider our ontological structure, a dual unity of being and essence. The unity of being is paradoxical because, as we are born into a communion that precedes us, we are born in and to the promise of being, which is fulfilled through a relation with what we are not. The mystery of our being, which is truly given to ourselves and yet incomprehensible without the constitutive relation with the giver, instills in us the desire for the unity we have been given, that is, for the unity of our own being what we are in time, and for the union with those to whom we are entrusted and to whom we are called to entrust ourselves. Thus our ontological structure grounds our desires to know and be known, to love and be loved, to build and to endure. These desires are prompted by and are an expression of our nature: of being born in and to a unity of being that both precedes us and deepens anew through us. Human existing seeks a form that gathers all its various elements into a unity, which, however, it cannot give to itself.

The mystery of birth holds out the possibility of understanding the unity of our being, and of being as such, in terms of gift. Our positivistic culture's widespread idea that birth, and so finite existence, is merely the fruit of chance or necessity cannot account for the surprise that is proper to the sheer existence of life; the existence of the spirit and its irreducible wholeness. Yet, the meaning of gift is not obvious. To suggest that the unity of our being has the form of gift means that we are not our own, that our "to-be" owes itself most deeply to another. Today there is a great need to retrieve the meaning of creation. Nevertheless, gift as the form of the unity of being means more than the fact that concrete singular beings are created, although this is both important and true. The positivity of being concrete singulars requires examining in what sense being, man, and God (the ultimate source of our birth) are gift; that is, in what sense God is gift in himself and in what sense being and man participate in the divine gift-ness.

Our inquiry cannot stop at considering only the singular being and God in terms of gift. The concept of gift also extends to the spiritual, transitive relation between the original giver, the gift, and the receiver. To examine in what sense being, man, and God are gift requires seeing in what sense the bond that ties them together—while simultaneously preserving their difference—can also be accounted for in terms of gift. If gift indicates the form of unity, unity indicates the permanence of the gift. This permanence is the source and significance of the negation within the term "indissolubility." In this light, the relation between original giver, gift, and receiver can be viewed in terms of being if it is also viewed in terms of time. Here the modern temptation to juxtapose time and eternity arises, in response to which we can say that if the unity of the concrete singular reveals the permanence of the gift, it is because eternity is the very center of time. The permanence of the gift proper to God, which we call eternity, is the ground of the permanence that is proper to the concrete singular. Rather than the "conditions of possibility" for something to happen, the spatial term "ground" points to the occasioning, sustaining, and ordering in being of the concrete singular. The hoped-for, final confirmation of the singular gift does not appear then as a leap out of time into eternity, but rather as the gratuitous, unexpected, victorious re-giving of the gift of being. Hence, to think of the unity of being as the permanence of the gift permits the relationship between the original giver, the gift, and the receiver, between time and eternity, to emerge in the light of asymmetrical indwelling. The giver makes it possible for the gift and the receiver to be, and it is also up to the giver, not without the participation of the gift/receiver, to confirm the original donation. To remain in being, in the unity of being, is to dwell in the unceasing donation of the gift that God is. Time and eternity are bound up with being because each is the enduring of the gift of being: while eternity is its own beginning, time is the permanent letting the concrete singular be and become itself.

We can now try to formulate what we would like to ponder in this book: gift is the form of the unity of being and unity is the permanence of the gift of being. One point that helps to avoid reducing the horizon of this investigation is that any reflection on the gift from the aspect of action, important as it is, rests on the human being's capacity to give himself. An account of the act of giving something, whether from God to man, man to God, or among men, calls for some explanation of how the concrete singular, permanently given to itself, participates in the original gift of self not only by further giving but through its very ontological constitution. Given our cultural context, marked as it is by the atheistic claim that fragmentation is more primordial than unity, to fail to give an account of the relationship between *esse* and essence, between God and the world, and between men in terms of gift would collapse the act of giving into either a technological interpretation of causality and human making or a philosophical hypostatization of human giving. Gift, instead, brings all its richness to bear on the question when it is first thought of as a principle, rather than a "present" that is offered to someone. In other words, to root ethics in ontology allows us to perceive the real newness that an act of giving represents with regard to the ontological gift-structure of the concrete singular.

In these pages, therefore, gift is considered primal. The term "primal" has a twofold meaning: *arche*, the "permanent principle of origination and ordering," and the temporal aspect of being "first" in time. Gift, on the one hand, is a permanent source of originating, ordering, and restless rest. Reading the second connotation in light of the first we can say that gift is, on the other hand, an ever-new beginning—and not simply the commencement of being. Although this perception of gift and of the nature of the unity of being in terms of gift is radical and comprehensive, it does not propose a system built on a concept (gift). As the Hegelian project demonstrates, the attempt to elevate a concept as adequate to the whole is liable to end up on the shores of nihilism despite the best of intentions. The following reflections wish to offer, then, rather than a system, a synthesis of the type of unity that is proper to man, being, God, and the relations among them. The term "gift" reveals the sense in which God and the concrete singular are placed together (*syn-thesis*).

Three methodological criteria specified by the subject itself deserve mention. First, the present work attempts to keep the integral mode of being of the concrete singular and of God, as well as their analogical relation, clearly at the forefront. The opening remarks on the meaning of birth, which will come up again later, were not a rhetorical overture. The concrete singular requires its interlocutor to approach it in its entire, multifaceted wholeness. It is the concrete singular that "is," and not the principles that account for its being. *Esse* and essence, matter and form, act and potency, are principles of the singular being whose physical or spiritual self-standingness (*substance*) carries the ontological memory of its belonging to the whole. The constant temptation in the attempt to examine the positivity of the unity of being is the desire to possess the object of thought and to make a definitive pronouncement about the *logos* of the object and its existence. The haste to give an account for things can lead to overlooking the inexhaustible wealth of the concrete singular and to simply eliminating various aspects that do not fit easily into a given schema. It is tempting to take the concrete singular as either the starting point or the conclusion of a reflection. Yet to lose sight of the concrete singular during the process of thinking turns thinking itself into a unilateral exercise. To consider the unity of being requires the poverty of acknowledging that one does not possess the measure of being, and of never wearying of seeking and receiving the wealth of being that has been communicated, however inchoately. The claim to have a firm grasp on the wealth of being at the beginning, and its twin, the claim to take and give the measure of being (which views the beginning as a sheer undetermined void), both lead to an abyss of contradiction. When the integral mode of being takes on only a minor or supporting role, the claim seems to emerge that the real essence of donation is contradiction (for example, matter-form, act-potency, body-soul, parents-children, etc.) and that dialectics is its anointed method. Gift is understood in either univocal or equivocal terms and precludes reflection on either the distinction or the unity between the giver, the gift, and the receiver. The integral mode of being always leads back to the mysterious wholeness of the singular: both in its permanent being given and in its being gift.

The concrete singular in its integral mode of being brings us to the second methodological criterion. The point where anthropology, metaphysics, and theology meet in all their distinction to shed light on each other offers the privileged place for contemplating the gifted unity of being. Anthropology provides an entryway to being in one sense because the human person recapitulates in himself the cosmos and has the task of uniting it to the ultimate source. In another sense, being is most perfect at the level of the person, not at the level of substance. At the same time, metaphysical reflection grounds the anthropological approach and dispels the specters both of an ever-present romantic, neopelagian understanding of morality (which identifies the person with a self-determining freedom blind to its own having been given to itself) and of the psychological reductions of the person. Mutually illuminating as they are, anthropology and metaphysics remain incapable on their own of accounting for the positivity of being that is constantly brought forward by human experience and the mystery of birth. By becoming flesh, the eternal Logos of the Father not only pronounces himself within the parameters of the concrete singular. He, the concrete universal, to speak with Cusanus, also reveals the ultimate meaning of God, the world, and man as gift. The hypostatic union of the two natures in the person of the Logos, who intends the radical offering of himself to the Father on the Cross, is not an instance of philosophical gift-giving, but rather represents the archetype of gift. Christ's "eventful" existence confirms the positivity of being that is suggested by human experience by bringing it to a new, unforeseeable depth. As John Paul II wrote in *Fides et ratio*, philosophy and theology must not be isolated in self-enclosed castles; they must rather encounter each other and acknowledge the enriching circularity that unites and distinguishes them.[1] This circularity is possible precisely because man's reasoning is open to and constantly seeks the divine mystery that unforeseeably took

---

1. John Paul II, *Fides et ratio*, nos. 73–74, (AAS 91 [1999], 61–62).

flesh in Mary. Two simultaneous poles guard against collapsing theology into philosophy or reducing philosophy to a stepping-stone toward theology: (1) the unity of being and gift revealed in the person of Jesus Christ (1 John 4:8 and 16), in which all are called to participate (John 17:22), has its speculative measurement in the ontological difference between *esse* and essence; and (2) the revealed theological insight regarding the coextensiveness of being and love is the ultimate ground of the ontological structure of the concrete singular. The ontological is open to the theological order and finds therein the fulfillment that renews it. In light of this, the "place" from which to examine the mystery of being and its gifted unity has in a sense a twofold center. It is first the human being himself, as he is engaged with all of his own self, with all of reality, and with the triune God who is the center of both. Yet the center is also Christ, in whom all things consist and who holds everything in being.

The twofold center from which to examine the unity of being as gift helps clarify a third methodological aspect. The circularities touched upon so far (the ontological structure of the singular and its action, metaphysics and theology, unity and gift) are more than the regular swing of a pendulum or unconscious redundancies. Circularity here means a reciprocal, perichoretic illumination and a continual deepening into the subject matter. These circularities grant a vision of what is new by permitting it to flourish at a new level, not by opposing one element to another. Novelty, in this sense, is a re-acquaintance with the whole. Newness, recapitulating what preceded it, discloses more fully the mystery of being. To express this fullness, thought finds its greatest ally in paradox. Paradoxes, rather than contradictions, allow us to see the complex unity of the whole without letting go of its inexhaustibility. If we turn to look again at the three circularities already mentioned, we see first that the gift-ness of the ontological structure is reflected at the level of human reciprocation of the original gift. The human being can give gifts or give himself because his very being shares in its having been given. This reception and reciprocation, however, rather than the payment of a debt, represent the coming into being of something new: the receiver is himself by being one with and in the giver, without ceasing to be himself. Second, the relation between being and action reflects at its own level the incomprehensible mystery of the divine act. As we shall see, God is one in being a triune communion of persons and vice versa. The unity of the gift is not just a matter of piecing elements together; it is a whole that is present from the beginning and that, as a whole, is something other than its parts. Lastly, the relation between Christology and anthropology allows us to understand who the human person is and leads to a reflection of God that is irreducible to his image. Christ's renewal of the gift of being does not resolve the human drama or silence every question. On the contrary, it allows the encounter of the divine and human freedoms—this encounter is what we call drama—to take place anew by fleshing out in history the dialogue with the Father in the Spirit that constitutes him as the eternal, beloved Son. From this place, the concrete singular can contemplate the mysterious inexhaustible wholeness of God, can become like him in affirming its radical otherness, and can let everything that is called into existence be and remain in the communion for which it was created. This new place, as we shall see, endlessly intensifies and deepens our questioning and contemplation of the whole.

A brief presentation of what follows is now in order. In order to justify looking at the unity of being in terms of gift, the first chapter examines the structure of man's originary experience. Originary experience represents the most comprehensive and concrete approach to the reality of gift. This approach permits an elucidation, in the second chapter, of the structure of the singular being in terms of gift. Benefitting from the Aristotelian and Thomistic tradition, we will attempt to show how, in contrast to Derrida's thought, the Entity of a concrete singular participates in its being given. This ontology of gift and a non-technological perception of causality enables chapter 3 to inquire into the adequate response to the original giving. A foray into the meaning of reciprocity results in an exploration of the irruption of nothingness introduced into history by the free rejection of the gift. Chapter 4 turns to the archetypal role that the hypostatic union of the two natures in the person of the Logos plays in an adequate understanding of the nature of gift. The christological illumination of the unity of gift enables us to see the continuity and discontinuity between philosophy and theology. The question of Christ's human experience of his divine filiation guides the attempt in chapter 5 to approach the mystery of the person of the Father as the origin of all giving. The chapter goes on to consider in what sense (in contrast to Hegel) the Father's giving is an absolute donation: he is the unpreceded giver, the source of the communion of love that is the triune God. To look at the unity of the gift in God requires seeing in what sense the giving and the receiving are one in him and, furthermore, what it means for the gift of God to be gratuitous. The pneumatological reflection of chapter 6 takes up these two questions. The last chapter considers God's unexpected response to the original rejection of the gift. Giving anew the gift of being, forgiving, the triune God communicates unexpectedly the permanence of the gift of being, and thus the permanence of his union with the concrete singular. The eternal permanence of the gift renews from within the original donation and causes the concrete singular to be.

While this book is born from a dialogue with many authors of diverse and sometimes contrasting philosophical and theological positions, I owe special thanks to Luigi Giussani (1922–2005). Although what follows is not a systematic presentation of his thought and the responsibility for this book's content and flaws is mine, this attempt to ponder the unity of being in terms of gift could not have taken place without his immensely rich and profound work.

I. Gift's Originary Experience

ORIGINARY EXPERIENCE OPENS UP a seldom pursued but uniquely fruitful path for pondering the form of the unity of being. In part because of the troubled history of the concept, and partly because of the contemporary use of the term "experience," originary experience may seem a doubtful starting point. "Experience," in fact, has been described as the "most deceitful" and "most obscure" of terms.[1] Nevertheless, if by originary experience we mean the engagement of the whole of our being with the whole of reality and with God, who is their innermost and transcendent center, originary experience, despite its difficulties, can help us perceive from within life itself the unity of the concrete singular and its dynamic unity with and difference from God. Originary experience represents an encounter with truth that takes place beyond the dualism between subject and object. It involves, as John Paul II illustrated, objectively informed subjectivity.[2] The person knows himself in knowing finite beings and their respective link with God. Experience therefore opens up access to the truth of self, world, and God without abstracting the person from what gives itself to be known or the act itself of knowing, and without the knower absorbing or being fully measured by what is known.

Originary experience also allows us to see that the unity and difference within the concrete singular and its intrinsic relation with God is a gift. In

---

1. The first adjective is from Whitehead, *Symbolism*, 16. The second is from Gadamer, *Truth and Method*, 346ff.

2. See, for example, Wojtyła, *Acting Person*, 3–22. John Paul II's reflections on the nature of human love are built upon this understanding of experience. To him, there are three original experiences: original solitude, original unity, and original nakedness. These are three inseparable dimensions of the person that have to do with the discovery of what is specifically human through one's encounter with the world and the human other. For John Paul II, "original" is intended in the twofold sense of "in the beginning" and at the source of every human being's daily experience (John Paul II, *Theology of the Body*, 146–78). See also the fine introduction of Anderson and Granados García, *Called to Love*.

this sense, originary experience grants access not only to the truth of the unity of being but also to the perception of its goodness as gift. The singular being is not only good in itself; it is a gift. Its goodness, in other words, bears the memory of its origin from another and also the intimations of its destiny, its being for someone other than itself. The term "gift" offers a synthesis of what we learn through our originary experience: first, that our origin lies permanently with another, and so in a certain sense we belong to that other; second, that we can enjoy our own being and give of ourselves because, within that prior having been given, we are truly our own; third, that the relation with the permanent origin of our being is constitutive of our nature. Finally, since it is primarily through our own originary experience that we learn what gift means, this knowledge is not an abstract reflection; it is rather a lived awareness of oneself, the world, and God that involves all of our history.[3] As historical lived awareness, originary experience allows us to savor the beauty of being given since the truth and goodness of being are radiated through one's own concrete existence.

This approach to the nature of what is by way of man's originary experience rests on a crucial methodological decision: rather than an analysis of being that considers all singular beings equally (meta-*physics*), we begin here with an exploration of the human person. Anthropology will lead to ontology. A note on a difference introduced since the advent of modern science can serve to justify this anthropological starting point: for modern man, physics is no longer what the Greeks intended by the term but is rather the science of the material world. Contemporary science, with its technological understanding of reason, relates to the world, that is, considers and manipulates it, in a way that presupposes a thorough reconfiguration of the world's own nature. If at first early modern thinkers reinterpreted "nature" to mean blank, finite matter, sheer data that was open to manipulation, it is now the case that the "restlessness" of science, as Hans Jonas shows, understands matter as "an always reopened challenge for further penetration," a theoretical and practical pursuit that can only be accomplished if science generates "an increasingly sophisticated and physically formidable technology as its tool."[4] The concept of nature (*physis*) as having an intrinsic,

---

3. Rather than approach the meaning of gift from a sociological (Mauss, Godelier, Weiner), phenomenological (Heidegger, Marion), ethical (Seneca), or deconstructionist (Derrida, Schrag) point of view, I would like to present the relation between being and gift through an examination of "human originary experience." Incidentally, John Milbank's reflection on gift begins with an examination of evil (see Milbank, *Being Reconciled*).

4. Jonas, "Toward a Philosophy," 195. Jonas writes further: "In brief, a mutual feedback operates between science and technology; each requires and propels the other; and as matters now stand, they can only live together or must die together" (ibid., 195).

non-manipulable goodness in itself must be dispensed with if humanity is to progress ever onward. Since this scientific worldview deeply informs our thinking inasmuch as it has transformed thinking itself into a way of making, we cannot retrieve an adequate concept of nature and being without reexamining the grounds for our mastery over nature. This is not an easy task. On the one hand, the justification of our mastery simply through an unreflective appeal to evolution is merely another expression of our contemporary view informed by science. On the other hand, the issues raised by the scientific mastery of the world cannot be dismissed by a facile rejection of the role played by speculation and the human spirit in the constitution of singular beings. Clearly we cannot attempt to examine the nature of being as though contemporary science had nothing to offer here; that way leads to anachronisms and simply false conclusions. While the claim of modern science and philosophy needs not to be embraced acritically, it still raises a legitimate issue. In our current cultural context, reflection on the nature and unity of what is seems doomed if it halts at considering the human being as just one being among others. The human being, unlike other concrete singulars, has a unique mastery over being.

To take up and understand this mastery over nature depends on the human being's attention to his own enigmatic makeup and his centrality in the cosmos. His makeup is enigmatic because the human being is, and yet he does not come from himself; it is given to him to be. His "power" and mastery over nature emerge within this mystery of his existence having been given. His centrality in the cosmos is due to the fact that his person is a unity of body, soul, and spirit. Through his own body, which is more than a receptacle for the soul or a neutral tool for obtaining ends determined by the soul, the human being recapitulates the cosmos within himself. That the form of his body is given by the soul indicates that the human person, endowed with the capacity to desire, to reason, and to be free, unlike other creatures, is affectively aware of his own position in the cosmos. From this original place, the human being discovers himself to be limited, bodily, and yet capable of receiving the whole. This capacity for the infinite indicates that the human person not only recapitulates the world, he also transcends it. Because the human person is spiritual, his transcendence of the cosmos is a relation with the one who can ultimately account for his existence. Our encounter with nature and the world, therefore, takes place within this twofold mystery: our being given to ourselves to live the relation with the origin. Human making takes place within the human person's constitutive and prior being given to himself and is informed by a way of thinking that recognizes the gift-character of the concrete singular in wonder and permits it to be. Proceeding from the human person through the existential analysis of originary experience holds out the possibility of an ontological discourse on the gift-form of the unity of being that can correct our contemporary perception of nature without the loss of any speculative rigor.[5]

A final twofold clarification about methodology will be helpful. To take the path of originary experience in order to approach the nature of what is, rather than anthropomorphizing ontology, enables us to grasp the gift-character and wholeness of the singular being. Furthermore, if understood correctly, originary experience protects against an objectivization of God—as if he were an object that could be encompassed by human feelings or reason—and against the tendency to relegate God to the position of a subject alongside the human being. In the face of all our attempts to confine God, the original giver, within the narrow boundaries of our transient emotions or our limited capacity to know, originary experience continues to reveal a structural disproportion between God and us. Within our experience, God naturally reveals himself as other and as calling us to respond to him. Starting from an anthropological reflection, originary experience leads us to the ontology of the concrete singular as gift and invites us to await the unexpected fulfillment of being and the human person in the Incarnate Logos who unites, without confusion or separation, the concrete singular and the divine (1 Tim 2:5; Heb 9:15).

While subsequent chapters will deal more specifically with the ontological structure of the concrete singular, its response to the original giver, and what the renewal of the gift reveals of the nature of the original giver, the present chapter attempts to illuminate the meaning of gift as revealed through our originary experience. Following the insights of Luigi Giussani, we begin with the meaning of originary experience and how it reveals the unity in difference between God, the human being, and the world; then follows an indication of the characteristics of gift that guide our reflection; and finally we will see how our originary experience invites us to perceive the historicity of the concrete singular.

1. Approaching Originary Experience

Because a word is not neutral to its historical and cultural development, it is therefore helpful to examine the main elements that constitute the full meaning of the term "experience" by looking at its etymology. The Latin root (*experior*), derived from the Greek (*peiraw*), indicates that experience

---

5. This approach is also proposed by Hans Urs von Balthasar and described by him as meta-anthropology. See, among others, Balthasar, *GL*, 5:653; Balthasar, *Love Alone Is Credible*. See also Bieler, "Meta-anthropology and Christology," 129–46.

has to do with the acquisition of knowledge by trying. We become experienced by testing something repeatedly (Greek *peiraw*), as, for example, after having treated many patients, a doctor can recognize and treat a specific illness based on very few symptoms. The German word for experience, *Erfahrung*, offers another interesting aspect. Here experience is the process of learning that consists in traveling (*fahren*) around and seeking to discover the unknown by trying out different things. During this process, the traveler exposes himself to the possibility that unexpected discoveries may radically change him. To experience requires an openness to being affected by something whose origin remains beyond the control of the person.

Before making further attempts at the meaning of experience, a word about its content is in order. When we talk about "originary" experience we indicate that fundamental dimension of our human existence that becomes actual in every discrete experience. "Originary," besides its chronological connotation of beginning in time, points to a sourcing and guiding by means of ordering. Originary experience does not, then, refer to the events of infancy. It points rather to the actual living out of existence considered as a whole and, as this experience brings to light what is specifically human, its relation with the underlying mystery that makes all of being intelligible. The "content" of the originary experience is the whole of life as engaged in every circumstance with the ultimate meaning.

Pondering all these elements together, we see that experience refers to the entire human person: historical bodiliness, freedom, affection, desires, reason, being with others. More radically, it means that what is at stake is the person as such and his destiny. Our common experience teaches us that we truly see only when we put ourselves at risk. This risking is not embraced out of a love of danger but in the desire to discover what one does not yet fully know, namely, who one is and what being is. In fact, since what is sought in whatever one seeks is the meaning of oneself and all that is, it is clearly all of the human person that is risked. Traveling to a foreign land (*Erfahrung*), one hopes to grow, to know oneself by "recognizing the divine that is within us," as Plato said.[6] That there is risk and the possibility of changing indicates also that the content of what one experiences remains larger than what one can comprehend. Experience is not coextensive with life. That there will always be more to discover is indeed an indication of life's greatness; and this ever-more is a sign of the presence of the infinite mystery.

---

6. In this regard, the knowledge acquired through "experience" can be approximated to the classic understanding of wisdom (*sapientia*): the knowledge of oneself that requires acknowledging that one "does not know" and that one's own self is comprehensible only with the relation to the divinity (Plato, *Apology* 23b; Plato, *Alcibiades* 132c–135b).

To discover something new through experience suggests further that "originary experience"—man's engagement of all of himself with all of reality and its center, God—has a twofold dimension. It implies a receiving and a capacity to create. In order to discover, one needs to be actively searching. Distracted, ideological, or bored spirits are not available to find anything. At the same time, the traveler discovers because what he seeks comes to him first. The priority of the receptive over the creative, rather than a diminishment of man's greatness, indicates his true stature. The traveler begins to walk because, in a certain sense, he has already been given what he has yet to find. The initiative to look for the meaning of one's own enigma is a response to the invitation of the land where one hopes to find the sense of existence. In fact, after having gained some experience, one realizes both that he has been put on the path and that existence itself is always this already-being-on-the-path. For this reason, although one is involved in the discovery, the *logos* of what is seen is not imposed externally by the traveler. The content of experience is greater than the experience itself; rather than being produced or predetermined, this content is also welcomed.

The unity of the receptive and creative dimensions of experience, on the one hand, and the engagement of one's entire self with a reality that remains always greater than what one can experience, on the other, brings us to a deeper layer of experience. To experience means to encounter the truth in which one becomes aware of the totality of reality. More precisely, a person becomes aware of himself in his relation to the world and to the ultimate guarantor of reality's and his own goodness. Yet, since the priority of receiving is to be retained with respect to the creative aspect of experience, this dawning awareness grows, not as the fruit of conquest or the intake of a given *datum*, but out of the lived acknowledgment of oneself and the world as given. Experience, then, is not the stockpiling of information but rather the relation of all of oneself with the divine; it is lived awareness of the whole as an inexhaustible given.[7]

2. Terminological Clarifications

To understand better what "originary experience" means and how it grants access to the unity of being as gift, a brief presentation of the cultural development of the semantics of the term will be helpful. As we shall see, because

---

7. For further development of this, see the famous work of Jean Mouroux, *L'expérience chrétienne: Introduction a une théologie* (Paris: Editiones Montaignes, 1952). English translation: *Christian Experience*, 24. See also Ratzinger, *Principles of Catholic Theology*, 346–50.

what is at stake in every experience is our relationship with the whole, the history of the concept of experience tends to overemphasize one or another particular aspect. Yet the neglect of other aspects results in confusion and hinders the growth in truth that is the desire of wisdom. Early Greek philosophy does not seem to attribute much importance to what one acquires through experience. For example, Aristotle considers experience to be that degree of knowledge between the simple sensible perception of finite beings and the proper sciences. "Experience knows the particular, whereas science (art) knows the universals."[8] Experience is an acquired skill, the synthesis of memories that prepares theoretical and practical knowledge.[9] This sense of experience, according to which *nihil in intellectu nisi in sensu*, was adopted by Aquinas, although he also speaks of a knowledge by connaturality in which, through experience, one is attuned to the whole of being as, for example, the chaste knows what chastity is by experience and not by what he may have studied of this evangelical counsel.[10] It is true that experience also has, at its first level, the connotation of searching for the truth and the acquisition of forms through sense knowledge. Nevertheless, the meaning of this search is more fully elucidated within the context outlined above.

Through the Middle Ages, "learning by trying" was still seen as part of a path that both presupposed and yielded recognition of an ultimate origin, a final cause. Physics, metaphysics, and theology formed a differentiated unity. The origin was seen as the ever-present, initiating, and guiding *telos* of one's own inquiries. It was God who was sought in whatever one was learning. This, of course, did not mean that theology trumped science. Although, as many have shown, the perception of God guided scientific inquiry, the latter had its own integrity and methodology. This does not intend to say that the sciences were conceived independently from God, but that they represented a further exploration into the mystery of the whole. Independently of how it was used and accounted for, experience had to do with one's own organic encounter with truth. It took into account both the whole person and the way in which knowing took place.

---

8. Aristotle, *Metaph.* 981a15–16. For Aristotle, experience does not offer knowledge of the reasons for things; it is only science that studies the universals that can grant this knowledge: "Men of experience know that the thing is so, but do not know why; while [those who possess scientific knowledge] know the why and the cause of the facts" (ibid., 981a28–30).

9. Ibid., 980b25–981b9.

10. *ST*, II-II, q. 45, a. 2, c; *ST*, I-II, q. 26, a. 2; *ST*, I-II, q. 29, a. 1. This connotation of experience as the acquisition of knowledge is also found in more recent authors such as Bernard Lonergan, for whom experience has four different senses that must be properly distinguished: biological, aesthetic, intellectual, dramatic. Besides these, he also speaks of religious experience (Lonergan, *Insight*, 182–91).

Modernity's progressive rejection of fourfold causality, however, gradually began to account for beings as if God did not exist.[11] Detached from their ultimate ground, concrete singulars became tools at the disposal of our technological endeavors and hence mirrors to serve the solipsistic perception of human existence. This epistemological strategy, as is well known, was the fruit of modernity's attempt to ground reasonableness (and hence truth) in reason alone, that is, in the identification of the act of thinking with its content.[12] This identification, with its undergirding separation of reason from experience, so it was hoped, was to yield absolute certainty. Modernity gradually separated the different elements that constitute human experience.

The Cartesian claim to ground truth in thought, without the presumed necessary reference to something other than the human mind (ultimately God), not only inaugurated the so-called transcendental turn to the subject and the methodical experience of empirical reality; it also introduced a separation between reason and its object that still haunts much of today's thought. The Cartesian claim, however, revealed itself as unable to reconcile the pursued immediacy of the subject to itself with the inescapably mediated character of human subjectivity. While idealism claimed to overcome this separation between reason and its object, and to retrieve via dialectics (Hegel) the role of mediation for a truth that attempts to account for difference within itself (thus eliminating both the Enlightenment's claim of immediacy without presuppositions, and the positivistic reading of being), it did not succeed in preserving the integrity of difference throughout the theoretical or practical process of the constitution of the absolute. Knowledge gained through experience aimed ever more decisively at the acquisition of power and at the manipulation of nature for the sake of a perennial progress. Phenomenology's pursuit of the originary experience that precedes the opposition of subject and object comes to a halt (at least in Heidegger) because its reading of metaphysics as onto-theology finishes by hypostasizing the appearing of being in an event of reciprocal belonging that represents the end of being and of *Da-sein*.[13]

11. Grotius, *De iure belli*, prolegomena 11.

12. Of course, this concept of reason and truth is only one aspect characterizing "modernity." Robert Spaemann, for example, indicates the following as the primary aspects: understanding freedom as emancipation; the myth of necessary and endless progress; progressive mastery of nature; objectivism; homogenization of experience; hypothesizing reality; naturalistic universalism (Spaemann, "Ende der Modernität?," 232–60).

13. Gadamer's attempt to continue the phenomenological reflection through hermeneutics still accentuates the separation between ontology and history. See Gadamer, *Truth and Method*.

I. GIFT'S ORIGINARY EXPERIENCE 19

The modern perception of experience also affected the understanding of religious experience, that is to say, of man's relation with God. Christian dogmas, for example, rather than the expression of the truth revealed through the person of Jesus Christ, are perceived as historical, relative truths. Although at first one could claim the need in faith to obey these truths, once they lose their intrinsic, universal value, any remaining moral force quickly disappears under the dominance of relativism. Religious experience, as seen in the different forms of Protestantism, is relegated to emotions whose validity is determined by their intensity since historical mediation is no longer acceptable. Schleiermacher's emblematic account of religion in terms of a feeling of absolute dependence falls back into the attempt to eliminate conceptual and historical mediation and seeks to ground the perception of truth in an ineffable, incommunicable, interior experience that yields no volitional or cognitive content.[14] In this regard experience is revelatory of a knowledge that is unable to transcend the subjective sphere of the person and so be communicated.

The philosophical and theological understanding of experience is both prompted by and responsible for the contemporary scientific concept of experience. As Robert Spaemann argues, for modern science, the acquisition of knowledge through experience is equivalent to "planned, homogenized experience, i.e., experiment."[15] The aspect of receiving in experience is interpreted as sheer passivity or simply set aside. Nowadays, to experience something is tantamount to verifying a hypothesis through an experiment that remains under the control of the scientist. An experience is a controlled experiment. To learn by trying has come to mean to experiment with things or, more crucially, with oneself—as biotechnology enables us to do in unprecedented ways. The encounter with truth offered by the scientific understanding of experience no longer leaves room for discovery as the unexpected fruit of a patient search that demands putting oneself at the disposal of what is given to be known. To understand experience as undergoing an event, circumstance, etc., which is deprived of intrinsic meaning, is yet another expression of this reduction of experience to experiment. It is left up to the human person to construct meaning by imposing a relative sense on a given event.

That experience seems to be trapped either by sheer subjectivism or by a technocratic interpretation of knowing is a revealing witness to the fact that when one sets aside God as the ultimate giver and *telos* of all that is, one is left with the illusion of a mastery over reality that can only fragment the

---

14. Schleiermacher, *On Religion*; Schleiermacher, *Christian Faith*, 3–128.
15. Spaemann, "Ende der Modernität?," 240.

human person out of existence, as the tragic events of the twentieth century and the servitude of man at the hands of the technical manipulation of his own life illustrate. Experience requires the whole of the human person as always already engaged with all of reality and with the common center of both, God.

3. A Distinct Understanding

While an empirical conception of experience emphasizes only the receptive side of experience, and the idealist and scientific views hold up experience as the manifestation of the constructive capacity of the spirit, experience in the sense we are unfolding here is beyond the Enlightened separation of the receptive from the creative aspects.[16] When dealing with experience we need to realize first that we are talking about a living whole, that is, the concrete historical existence of someone who is engaged, with all of his being, with the antecedent and ever-greater mystery as the mystery freely gives himself to be discovered in the human path towards wisdom. Second, contemporary entanglements with the term "experience," as outlined in the previous section, emerge from a misconstrued anthropology that grants man's central role in the cosmos while ignoring the fact that this dignity has been given to him. In other words, it is an anthropology that claims to have transfigured itself into a theology. Whereas prior to Christianity man could understand himself either as part of the cosmos and doomed to disappear with it, or as possessor of a tragic nobility that was always aware of the temptation of hubris, with the Judeo-Christian tradition the dignity and centrality of man emerges through the covenant and creation in Christ. After this revelation occurs in history, it is not possible to return to earlier anthropologies and cosmologies. Man either conceives himself as given to himself and, bearing the image of the divine, as invited to live a dramatic relation with God, or he replaces God.[17] In the latter case, desire, reason, freedom, will, bodiliness, history, the world, and God are seen as disconnected fragments that the human person is free to reassemble at will. The problem is that one cannot define the meaning of all these fragments beforehand. The meaning has to be discovered as they play themselves out in experience. Detached from experience, Giussani contends, one comes up with a concept of reason as

---

16. Mouroux, *Christian Experience*, 9–15.

17. "O man!" Gregory of Nyssa wrote, "realize what you are! Consider your royal dignity! The heavens have not been made in God's image as you have, nor the moon, nor the sun, nor anything to be seen in creation. . . . Behold, of all that exists there is nothing that can contain your greatness" (cited in de Lubac, *Drama*, 20).

the measure of being. Thinking, reduced to measuring, becomes a species of willing.

Originary experience regards man's capacity to grasp the meaning of something, its "objective link to everything else," and the awareness of this link.[18] Giussani's absolutely innovative concept of religious, elementary experience—or originary experience as we have translated it here—allows us to ponder the enigma of the human person as given to himself in order to acknowledge the totality of the gift of being.[19] For Giussani, originary experience is neither one way of knowing among others, nor a practical implementation of a theoretical ideology, nor a neutral instrument with which to gather information whose value and meaning are then assessed through heuristic, extrinsic criteria. Rather, "experience is reality's emerging into man's awareness; it is the becoming transparent of reality to man's gaze."[20] The fact that reality "emerges" into man's awareness shows that what is at stake in originary experience is the unity of the numerous factors already indicated: the reality that precedes the traveler and gives itself to be known, the traveler who seeks to discover the meaning of things and of himself, the distinction without separation of the two as they are held together by their link, their union with the ultimate mystery. What becomes transparent to man's gaze is the character of the concrete singular as a sign, that is, as a reality given to itself, which, carrying the memory of the giver, brings the beholder to their common origin.

Giussani offers this precious synthetic definition: "elementary [or originary] experience tends to indicate totally the original impetus with which

18. "Experience demands an I, an object, a relationship between the I and the object; but this is not enough: [these three elements are to be perceived] within an ideal horizon that colors in different ways the relation that God establishes between me and the thing. This is the mortal sin from Descartes onwards: to speak of reason forgetting that from which one extracts the concept of reason: experience. Doing this one fabricates, pre-fabricates the concept of reason and with it judges the concept of experience. In this way one confuses everything" (Giussani, "*Tu*," 84; *ROE*, 98–102, at 99). This chapter of *ROE* was originally published as Luigi Giussani, *L'esperienza*. For an approximation of Giussani's concept of experience, cf. Scola, "Esperienza cristiana," 199–213; Scola, "Esperienza, libertà e rischio," 71–89; Sani, "L'educazione," 5–27, at 21–23; Konrad, *Tendere*.

19. For Giussani, *esperienza originale* (here translated as originary experience), *esperienza elementare* (elementary experience), and *esperienza religiosa* or *senso religioso* (religious sense) are synonymous terms. Although familiar with the solitary work of Jean Mouroux on experience and well-versed in North American Protestant theology, Giussani contends that his understanding of experience is "totally original" (Giussani, "Seminario," 134). For a comprehensive bibliography from 1951–1997, see Giussani, *Porta la speranza*, 205–60. For a historical development, see Montini and Giussani, *Sul senso religioso*.

20. Giussani, *USD*, 107.

the human being reaches out to reality, seeking to become one with it. He does this by fulfilling a project that dictates to reality itself the ideal image that stimulates it from within."[21] Originary experience speaks therefore of our dynamic encounter with reality in all its complexity: on the one hand reality emerges before man and dictates "an ideal image" that the concrete singular carries within itself, that is, its own *logos* and its unique relation with God and the world. The "ideal image," in this regard, is an echo of "the Word of Another."[22] Man's original encounter with truth is always already offered to him by the objective and historical self-presentation of being, whose full disclosure requires the entire person. This is why, on the other hand, and simultaneous with the self-presentation of the concrete singular, the human being "reaches out" with an "original impetus" and "seeks to become one with reality."

The "impetus," which is always a response to the emergence of reality, brings something new into existence. It does so by fulfilling a project that was first elicited by the ideal image hidden within the reality itself. This ideal image is given back to the reality itself now unfolded anew in a unity that includes both the reality and the person in their relation with their common giving origin. Fulfilling the project entails bringing about something new because the becoming transparent of the concrete singular in man's consciousness is the fulfillment of the former in the latter and a more intense radiance of the latter with the light of the singular being. That the human person "seeks to become one" with what gives itself to be known reveals that the ontological unity with what gives itself to be discovered and embraced requires an ordering towards the origin of both the person and the concrete singular.

For Giussani, therefore, every original human experience is either a religious one or it is not an experience in the first place: ultimately, experience is the living affirmation of God as that "unitary meaning which nature's objective and organic structure calls the human conscience to recognize."[23] Experience, therefore, has to do with the dynamic unity of the encounter between reality and all of man, whose *telos* (and fulfillment) is the affirma-

---

21. Giussani, *RS*, 9.

22. Giussani, *ROE*, 99.

23. Ibid. Giussani therefore is not proposing either a naïve realism or a critical idealism as an understanding of man's access to truth. His concept of experience has little to do with Rahner's, for whom man's experience of God and of himself is passive, transcendental, non-thematic, and non-reflexive. For Giussani experience does not have to do with "conditions of possibility" but with actual understanding in which history never comes at a second moment, nor is it seen as history of God. See Rahner, "Experience of Self," 122–32.

tion of God. Let us first look at how originary experience allows us to perceive finite beings as gift and then at the involvement of the human person.

4. The Inexorable Presence of the Sign

One can never stress enough that experience implies "an encounter with an objective fact that is independent from the experience that the person has."[24] Finite beings send man into a state of ongoing wonder, presenting themselves attractively (beauty), carrying their own *logos* (truth), and introducing him to the perception of and response to the good. Finite beings therefore are not sheer data, material that is infinitely open to manipulation by the subject. "Being," Giussani writes, is "not some abstract entity"; it is "a presence that I do not myself make, that I find. A presence that imposes itself on me."[25] Being is given to the person; it is a gift. Thus for Giussani, in some similarity with Balthasar, originary experience represents the perception of the concrete analogy of being through its transcendental determinations and not through an abstract reflection on being.

In an attempt to overcome the positivistic understanding of finite being (and reality as a whole) mentioned earlier, Giussani does not speak of the concrete singular in terms of an object lying before a knowing subject, but rather of "presence." With this term, he wishes to illustrate the interiority of finite beings and their relation with the knowing person (primarily man, but ultimately God). Let us look at what this term, "presence," entails.

"Presence" indicates, first of all, that something is present to someone. That is, as "present," it is another, irreducible to the one before whom it presents itself. What is present comes from some other who is distinct from both what is present and the beholder. For being to be "present" means further that it addresses the one to whom it comes. The coming into being of concrete singulars aims at man's welcoming of the irreducible, inexhaustible alterity of the singular gift. Taking traditional metaphysics as a starting point would have meant stopping at the acknowledgment of the creatureliness of a finite being. We would miss the fact that concrete singulars, in being themselves, are also present to someone, that is, they are themselves inasmuch as they address someone. This reference to another, which is proper to being-gift, grounds the subsequent ethical reflection.

Another aspect of "presence" has to do with belonging. To be present to someone is to be given to someone, and in a certain sense to belong to that person. Finite being, we could say, operates the claim of the beautiful

24. Giussani, *RE*, 130.
25. Giussani, *RS*, 101.

on the one who is called. The otherness of the concrete singular represents a gift because the claim of its beauty is to let its own light illumine and shine in the beholder so that this one can come to see and desire the source. To belong to another does not have a univocal meaning and depends on a free giving to the beholder. Yet, even at its most basic level, to speak of belonging indicates that gift, being as presence, is not a self-enclosed reality; it is always already with other beings. It contains the memory of the origin, and it exists within a communion of beings.

Being as "presence" arrives at its full meaning in man when his awareness reaches its fullest form, when it offers, that is, recognizes, the divine mystery as the ultimate consistency of all that exists.[26] This characterization of being as presence is a way of expressing a unity of that which is present and the one to whom it is present. This unity is not a static, topographical face-off. It is a free belonging to each other that preserves their difference because the one to whom singular being is given acknowledges the origin and *telos* common to both.

Giussani clarifies further that the condition for perceiving the gift-character of being and its irreducible alterity is the passionate, insistent, and complete observation of reality and of oneself in action. This observation has to be "complete" in order to make room for all the factors of reality, without censoring for any ideology or dividing what is separate only in thought. It has to be "passionate" because freedom and reason are co-originary. There is no such thing as a simple rationalistic observation of the nature of beings. The one who does not love does not discover.[27] Finally it has to be "insistent" because the temptation to ideology is always lurking.

The other part of the condition is that one's engagement be with the whole of reality and its center. Without engaging the whole, instead of knowledge one would end up, once again, in an ideological account of oneself and of being—an account that attempts to fit the whole to the particular of one's choice. Grasping the unity of being as gift is an arduous exercise that requires paying attention to oneself in action. We could even say that experience and action are two sides of the same coin. Action, which is not simply "production" or "making," is the concrete, dramatic dialogue in history between God and man, a dialogue in which circumstances are as much

---

26. For an account of the ontological movement of beings, see Pseudo-Dionysius, *Divine Names*, 3.8–9 (PG 3:704D–705B).

27. Giussani, *RS*, 3–33. The circularity between freedom and reason can also be found in, e.g., Benedict XVI's *Caritas in veritate*: "Intelligence and love are not in separate compartments: *love is rich in intelligence and intelligence is full of love*" (no. 30; AAS 101 [2009], 665).

the stage on which the action takes place as the content of this drama.[28] The perception of being as gift is never the necessary or automatic outcome of a logical process but requires the engagement of the human person. The gift must be received in order to be seen. When the human being is engaged thus, it is possible for him to discover the positivity of what he encounters and of himself in three aspects: the fact that beings are given (are present to him); that finite beings are not simply opaque objects but signs with which the human being is united; and that he, along with the concrete singular, is constantly generated by the source.

The perception of being as gift disclosed by man's original relation with the other and revealed in experience opens a further dimension of intelligibility. That being is gift indicates that gift is also a *logos*, "a word, an invitation," that speaks of another. In fact, "the gift whose meaning is not also given is not really a gift."[29] Gift, in other words, carries its own intelligibility. This means not only that reality's own light enables man to see it as gift but also that this gift is the word of another, a mystery always present and ever greater that speaks to man. It is important to realize, first, that to say that the gift has its own *logos* not only means that truth and goodness are coexistent in the singular as it is given to itself and to another. It also means that originary experience, to discover the meaning of any given being or circumstance, must listen carefully to the *logos* that speaks within and through the gift. Man must not impose an aleatory meaning on his own experience. Just as life is larger than our experience of it, so the *logos* that speaks in the gift cannot be enclosed in a human concept. The fact that originary experience bears its own meaning does not imply that one will understand or grasp that meaning. The inseparability of gift from its own *logos* indicates that the mystery pronounces himself to man in infinitely different ways without repetition. Every finite being-gift is a whole, an integral singular being, a word infinitely other than the mystery and yet a word that communicates this mysterious other on which it constitutively depends.

Giussani speaks of *sign* as the dual unity of gift and *logos* discovered through originary experience: "The sign is a reality whose meaning is another reality, something I am able to experience, which acquires its meaning by leading to another reality."[30] Finite being is a sign, a word-gift that brings man to the transcendent ground of both reality and the human being.

---

28. Maurice Blondel's work is in fact one of the main sources of Catholic reflection on experience. See his *L'action* (1893).

29. Giussani, *JTE*, 71. Translation modified. The text continues: "And we would not be able to recognize that life and the cosmos are gift if we did not await the revelation of its meaning."

30. Giusanni, *RS*, 111.

While some of his christological writings treat "sign" and "sacrament" as synonymous, Giussani does not use the term "symbol" to refer to the dual unity of gift and *logos* that characterizes finite beings.[31] "Symbol" does not indicate the intrinsic link between gift and *logos* as clearly as "sign" seems to do. "Symbol" can be easily understood as a reality whose meaning is culturally determined and hence imposed on human experience. In this sense, "symbols" would be historically conditioned and so would have no claim to universality or ontological depth. This understanding of symbol easily leads to conclusions such as those of M. Lawler, for whom "experience and not ontology makes reality."[32] For Giussani, instead, the sign is "a word that shakes up because it is through the sign that the presence of the transcendent *touches* the flesh."[33] Whereas the culturally determined understanding of symbol leads to endless interpretations, for Giussani, experience is "bumping into a sign, an objective reality that moves the person towards his *telos*, towards his destiny."[34] The sign, therefore, indicates the concrete way in which the mystery gives himself to the human being, so that, through the flesh, once it is received, the sign moves the human being to recognize and assent to the source that generates everything.

It is in the experience of the encounter with the inexorable presence of finite beings that one discovers oneself as given to oneself. Giussani says that "there was a time when the person did not exist: hence what constitutes the person is a given (*datum*), the person is the product of another."[35] Our birth, more than a biological beginning whose only meaning is chronological, reveals something very important about finite human being: not originating with oneself is the sign that one has been given to oneself. The existence of freedom, limited though real, and of self-awareness prevents us from reducing the human being to his historical and biological antecedents. The human being is an incarnate spirit that transcends nature. "One cannot deny," Giussani insists, "that the greatest and most profound evidence is that I do

---

31. Giussani, "Ogni cosa." See also Giussani, *TT*, 11–35; Giussani, "Mistero e segno coincidono." For his understanding of sacrament, see Giusanni, *WTC*, 179–200.

32. Lawler, *What Is*, 48. Karl Rahner does have an interesting theology of symbol, which nonetheless remains problematic because it does not integrate his Trinitarian ontology with Christology. See Rahner, "Theology of the Symbol," 221–52; Rahner, *Church and the Sacraments*.

33. Giussani, *RVU*, 114.

34. Giussani, *AVS*, 351.

35. Giussani, *ROE*, 98. That man depends, that he is "the product of another," is "the original condition that is repeated at all levels of the person's development. The cause of my growth does not coincide with me but is other than me" (ibid.).

not make myself, I am not making myself. I do not give myself being, I do not give me the reality that I am; I am 'given.'"[36]

To welcome the evidence of one's own constitutive givenness reveals the unity binding the self together with its mysterious and permanent source: God, the ultimate source at the origin of both the sign and the human being. Since the origin revealed in the sign is the one from which one's own self and every sign is ultimately continuously begotten, the mystery may be called "father." Unlike a human father, however, the mystery is "Father at every moment. He is begetting me *now*."[37]

Although paternal, the mystery remains mystery. Any attempt to define the face of the mystery inevitably becomes ideology.[38] This will remain the case even when, in Christ, the mystery lets himself be seen. "God is father, but he is father like no other is father. The revealed term carries the mystery further within you, closer to your flesh and bones, and you really feel it in a familiar way, as a son or daughter."[39] Human experience does give us an intimation of what the Incarnation of the Logos reveals, apart from which we could never fathom this: the mystery is Father like no other father. Because of the dialogical aspect of the mystery's self-manifestation (through the sign that is both gift and *logos*), Giussani also designates the mystery with the second personal pronoun. Both reality itself and, as we shall see, man's own dynamism attest to the existence of the mystery, that "Thou" who speaks to man. Once again, although to speak in terms of dialogue presupposes ascribing personhood to the divine mystery, this "Thou" remains "inexhaustible, evident, and not 'demonstrable'"—that is, beyond man's comprehension.[40]

To sum up, we can say that originary experience allows us to discover both finite being and oneself as gift at whose respective centers is the divine mystery. Since the nature of being is gift and the divine mystery addresses himself to the human person, the truth of this claim about originary experience cannot be seen if it is detached from the engagement of freedom. When Giussani says that originary "experience" enables us to perceive the *evident* nature of the sign's dual unity of being-gift and *logos* he does not have in mind a certainty that does not require freedom. "Evidence" does not mean logical (univocal) or empirical evidence. It is thus neither the result of physical observation nor a necessary deduction from certain premises. Rather,

---

36. Giussani, *RS*, 105; Giussani, *GTSM*, 77ff.
37. Giussani, *RS*, 106.
38. Ibid., 95–97, 132–40.
39. Ibid., 145.
40. Ibid., 161.

"evidence" indicates the peculiar ontological and epistemological nature of truth, according to which truth presents itself offering the meaning for which man is searching and calling for the decision of man's freedom. The relation with truth is always a dramatic event. The self-presentation of truth offers meaning and invites man to receive it. While truth's self-presentation is unequivocal, being's meaning as gift cannot be seen until it is embraced. Reason and freedom are co-originary. "Evidence," therefore, means "to become aware of an inexorable presence." To perceive the evidence is to "open my eyes to this reality which imposes itself upon me, which does not depend upon me, but upon which I depend; it is the great conditioning of my existence—if you like, the given."[41]

5. The Experience of Being Given

We have mentioned that originary experience indicates the engagement of all of oneself with all of reality and its center, God. Man's engagement with the whole, or his lived awareness, acknowledges that both the human person and other concrete singulars have been made, are given to themselves and to each other. The encounter with the gifted irreducibility of the other can be accounted for in many different ways. Yet, rather than imagining what we have described so far as a solitary individual contemplating a beautiful starry night, or a sudden realization in the midst of life—but in a sense also apart from it—that one is not one's own, it is more helpful to realize that the gift character of being involves first and foremost the personal encounter and the common life that takes place within the family. To be sure, acknowledging being's utter positivity also happens in many other circumstances. Still, since both knowing and loving have the form of a personal encounter, a look at the nature of familial relations will enable us to give a more complete account of the main characteristics of gift.[42] I will thus sketch out the existence of the human person from its beginning to its end with an eye toward indicating the main features of gift.

Giussani referred constantly to the event of one's own birth to indicate the gift-character of finite being.[43] For him, the crucial cultural problem

41. Ibid., 101. "Man depends, not only in an aspect of his life, but in everything: whoever observes his own experience can discover the evidence of a total dependence on Another who has made us, is making us, and continuously preserves us in being" (Giussani, "Paternità," 1–4, at 1). See also Giussani, *GTSM*, 77.

42. For the personal nature of human knowing, see Nédoncelle, *Personne humaine*; Nédoncelle, *La réciprocité*; Nédoncelle, *Vers une philosophie*.

43. "Try to imagine a baby who has just come to life in the womb of its mother, just conceived. To make an unimaginable paradox, if that small fetus knew that all that he

today is the retrieval of the meaning of birth. "Every evil," he said in an interview, "originates with the lie according to which man theoretically and practically attempts to define himself, forgetting, erasing from his memory his own birth."[44] Birth expresses primordially the gift of being. We have already alluded to the fourfold mystery of birth as that which more than anything else puts us in the way of seeing being's nature as gift. We can now return to this mystery to see that it first indicates an exuberance of the gift. The child is the fruit of a loving union of a man and a woman. Birth, in this regard, is a radically non-democratic event: the child has no say in his own birth and the parents cannot force his personal existence into being. Certainly, scientific progress can facilitate the manipulation of the begetting of a child, but science can never overcome the fact that it always operates with preexistent material that it did not and cannot create.[45]

The existence of gift requires a giver, who gives without claiming a return; a receiver—which in our case also coincides with the gift itself; and a dynamic, loving relation between them. This relation constitutes in different degrees a dwelling place. The child is loved into existence and comes as a gift within a home. It is rather difficult today to understand what a home is. Technology has left us homeless and has forced us to think unilaterally of "place" in terms of time and hence as empty space. A dwelling place is now seen as a stopping point in the path of time, and time is no longer viewed as the confirmation of the gift that grants indwelling and unity. Pushing the human being to do more and better, to try different things, and to master nature, the technological mindset and the tools it creates project the human being ahead in the future, preventing him from living the present and from being some-where. Tragically, since the future is not yet and the past is no longer, by preventing his dwelling in the present, the technological mind-set places the human being no-where. Because he is no-where, technology

---

is, everything, each tiny drop of blood, each cell from its newly begun structure, everything in him, comes from the body of his mother . . . if this small fetus could be aware, he would feel everything flowing from the organism of his mother. . . . Think of the kind of total dependence—total in the absolute sense of the term—his self-awareness must be" (Giussani, *PLW*, 3:25). This example is also used to clarify the nature of morality.

44. Testori, *Il senso*, 38.

45. A rather lucid example of this opposing view was written by Gregory Stock: "IVF still accounts for fewer than 1 percent of live births in the United States. Improvements, however, may transform the procedure enough to integrate it into routine procreation. With a little marketing by IVF clinics, traditional reproduction may begin to seem antiquated, if not downright irresponsible. One day, people may view sex as essentially recreational, and conception as something best done in the laboratory" (Stock, *Redesigning Humans*, 55). See also Ratzinger, "Man between Reproduction and Creation."

cannot but consider the human person as an individual, that is, a holder of rights who determines himself through his action—now understood as making. Yet, in this way, technological thinking quantifies the subject. It abandons man to laws and policies that accentuate his homelessness. Because of this quantification of the person, even at home, social life turns out to be a sequence of individual encounters that not only leave the person radically isolated but, more intensely, force the relationship with others into an exercise of power and instinct. The home into which a child is born is the place that love generates by allowing people to participate and dwell in it. In this sense, the home, with the shared life it entails, is not only where one is born but also the place that continuously helps the person rediscover his own constitutive childlikeness. The home is the continual, living reminder of one's own having been begotten, of the gift-ness of life, and of the task of existing. The gift is never a monad: it exists only within a communion.

As a fruit, the child always arrives as a surprise. Although he cannot come into being without the parents, he is another spirit, who is irreducible both to his parents and to the biological laws. The child is a gift because he is given to himself. Yet the origin remains present in the child as other. The child belongs to this origin, yet is truly given to himself and can enjoy his very being (as the child's joyful play reveals). The gift is not simply the correct array of gift, giver, and receiver. The giver remains present in the gift (the child), but as other than the gift. This is true both somatically and, more importantly, spiritually. Let us look at this more closely.

The parents' embrace of the child—expressed both by the physical embrace and by the existence of the home and life together—represents the certainty that allows the child to grow, precisely because each parent images (differently) the ultimate paternal origin from which the child comes. The father is the sign of God's absolute otherness, and as father, he is always oriented towards the begotten child and the child's destiny. The human father therefore is rightly seen as the reminder of one's own origin *and* as he who accompanies one on one's own path and leads one to fulfillment. Fatherhood is as much about origin as it is about *telos* and accompanying the child in moving toward his *telos*. The mother is the sign of God's gratuity. The gift does not count the cost of how much it gives. It gives all of itself without regard for what is left for itself because it knows that it is itself only when it gives itself completely and embraces what it receives in giving itself. Paternity and maternity, although different expressions of the same love, are not interchangeable roles. As Balthasar says, "In love and in fidelity the woman has an easier time of it. . . . The woman is not called to represent anything that she herself is not, while the man has to represent the very source of life, which he can never be."⁴⁶ Fatherhood and motherhood, however, image the totality of God's love only *together*. The father can be father (and so represent the origin and its fecund, accompanying authority) only in responding to the wife's incarnation of love's gratuity. The mother can be mother (the icon of divine gratitude and creaturely reception of divine love) only as a response to the husband's representing the origin. In this way, as the educative task illustrates, the mother helps the child to face life with the certainty of being loved (hence complementing the task of the father), and, as the father responds to the gratuitous love that the wife incarnates, he helps the child to face existence, to grow free in becoming personally responsible for his own destiny. This asymmetrical reciprocity that is fruitful in a third person expresses the nature of gift at the anthropological level.

Experiencing the fatherhood and motherhood of his parents is essential to the child's discovery of the positive sense of dependence on God and of the positivity of existence, for it is through his parents that the child can discover the utter positivity of God's fatherhood. Thus, without fatherhood and motherhood, dependence (and hence sonship) would be slavery, finitude an unbearable limit, and life's positive destiny dissolution in the One. The home is the place in which one can discover the truth of the freedom of the gift: autonomy (*autexousia*) and indebtedness.

The education to the truth of the gift that the father and the mother are to give begins by accepting the child as other. The gift is not a gift until it is received. This is the case first of all for the parents: they are to accept the child as a gift to them from another. The reception of the child requires them to affirm joyfully their own finitude, that is, their not being the ultimate origin of the child. If the parents were to present themselves as the only origin, the child would perceive himself to be just a reiteration of that human origin, and the gift of his very self would lose its freedom and novelty. If the parents were to distance themselves completely from the ultimate origin and deny that they are a sign of the divine giver, the gift, as F. Ulrich writes, "would be absolutized; it would be consumed in the things that are and coincide with them."⁴⁷ To receive the child as a gift entails the constant acknowledgment that the child is given to them and that they are a true origin precisely because the gratuitous and ongoing gift of their substance is a real sign of the divine love. The child thus needs to be set free if he is to discover being's gift-ness.⁴⁸

---

46. Balthasar, *New Elucidations*, 221.
47. Ulrich, *Mensch als Anfang*, 140.
48. We refer to the child in the singular, but we include within this reference the relation among siblings. The multiplicity of children is, in fact, an important sign of the fecundity proper to love (beyond its quantitative value), because every child is an

When the parents avow their relativity to God and to the child, when they teach the dynamic of the gift that is to elicit the personal response of the child to God by witnessing their own, the home is revealed to be a sign of the difference in unity that, as we shall see, constitutes being as such. Precisely because originary experience allows man to perceive the constitutive dependence of any finite being-gift (sign) on its mysterious source, it also shows that the mystery's presence not only guarantees finite beings their proper alterity, it also suggests that being is communion. The home is a sign of this ontological "evidence." Undoubtedly, this perception of being as communion revealed in experience is only reached thanks to divine revelation. Nevertheless, the dogma of the Trinity clarifies and strengthens what man's experience witnesses to: the positivity of being and the unity of the many, which is at the root of that surprising experience that the more one loves and affirms another, the more one affirms oneself.

Within the home, the child is called to receive the gift of himself in its entirety. This reception means acknowledging one's own being given to oneself and calls one to respond to the human and the divine givers. The fatherhood and motherhood of his parents constantly call forth the child's personal responsibility. This responsibility, before being a duty, takes the form of a gift, because the original gift of himself to the child seeks to be reciprocated gratuitously. Within the context of the family we can see that, rather than through an abstract dialectics of freedom and nature, the reception of the gift is better accounted for as a loving response that gratuitously recognizes the other as other and wishes to be one with it. When, at home, parents codify every response, the gratuity of the original gift dries up and with it the response itself. Instead, the obedience that a rule of life demands is an incarnation of love. The "rule" is the ordering of the life together in light of its origin and its *telos*. Thus, the "rule," as an incarnation of love into which all the members of the family are called to enter, purifies the reciprocation of the gift from undue attachments to oneself precisely because in requiring obedience in what may contradict an instinct, it ensures the gratuity of the gift. The difficult years of adolescence are in fact the growth into the truth of the gift; that is, the belonging to the giving source must become truly one's own, fully free and conscious. One is called to discover what it means that "youth" is a true belonging to the source.

The gift that childhood represents would not be gratuitous if, besides being given to himself, the child were not endowed with the capacity to give. Generosity includes the giver's giving to the gift the capacity not only to

---

expression of the novelty and similarity proper to otherness—both because every sibling is a new expression of the same love and because each one has a different task and unique relation with the same origin.

respond but also to give further. This is why the sexually differentiated body is nuptial: it is the way that enables us to dwell in the memory of our coming from another and of our continuous dependence on something we are not in order to be ourselves. Rooted in the memory of having been given, one can thus discover one's true self in the gratuitous gift of self.[49] The gift (child) remains filial inasmuch as he gives himself to others and becomes fruitful through the nuptial union with another of the opposite sex, exercising his given capacity to give further. Therefore, fecundity is not only the begetting, but also the maturing of the child. To give oneself is also to entrust oneself to others in search of the mysterious origin, the permanent source of one's own being—a dangerous process since the gift of self to another may be rejected. In addition to marriage, giving further also has the form of friendship and work. Giussani's synthetic definition of originary experience is also a description of the meaning of work: man's activity as the fulfillment of a project is, in fact, the mystery of becoming one with reality in the transfiguration of the latter according to the ideal image that is suggested to the human being by reality itself, and dictated to reality by man through his creative capacity. Fruitful giving and receiving—as, for example, in teaching, healing, and building—has to do with a spiritual communication without loss. The giver (teacher) communicates himself to the receiver (student) through the gift without imposing himself on the receiver and in so doing collaborates in bringing something new (understanding) into existence.

The relation between the parents, and that between them and the child, reveals another crucial aspect of the logic of the gift: donation is not unilateral. It is not simply the case that one gives and the other receives, and then the one who receives will give further at a second moment. Thinking of the exchange of gifts in terms of passivity and activity could preclude seeing that giving entails a receiving in the giving itself, while the receiving entails a giving in the receiving itself. It is important, however, not to lose sight of the priority of the giving and the receiving in either case. While there is a receiving in the giving, it remains a giving, and while there is a giving in the receiving, it remains a receiving. To read the relation between the giving and receiving as purely reciprocal or interchangeable is tantamount to reading the logic of gift through the lens of a power that forgets its own having been given to itself. Equality between the giver, the gift, and the receiver is preserved only when the order and the difference are respected. Otherwise, gift would be ontologically inferior to the giver, and hence, not really a gift but a "fall" from the giver. In spousal love, the husband gives himself and,

---

49. John Paul II, *Theology of the Body*, 429–32; Granados García, *La carne*; Scola, *Nuptial Mystery*.

in giving himself, receives his wife, who, in receiving the husband, gives herself. Through the parents, the child is given to himself, and in so doing they accept him as given to them. The child receives the gift of himself in giving himself to the parents and others. Since the original evidence of being given to oneself remains the permanent determination of the gift that the person is, one does not grow out of childhood. To be sure, infancy fades away in adolescence, which disappears in adulthood. Yet childhood, as indicating the identity of the gift that acknowledges the priority of its being given, grows ever deeper. Leaping out of childhood not only represents a denial of the gift but also calls forth its opposite: chaotic being. We shall return to this later.

Recapitulating what has been said so far, the singular is a gift because it is given to itself from another that remains present in the gift without absorbing it into itself. The gift is called to reciprocate the gift to the giver with the same gratuity that characterized its being given to exist. In this dialogue that opens the possibility to respond, although never completely, in thankfulness, one discovers that one is with others in a home, whose existence is the sign of the ultimate source that calls every finite singular to be. The fruitful response is as much giving further (work, begetting) as it is personally responding to the destiny that the original giver prepares for everyone and that unfolds gradually through the historical existence of the person. Throughout this itinerary the person has constant negative and positive intimations of death. The negative encounters are all those instances in which the risk of giving meets an ungrateful rejection of the gift or a denial of further giving. But the risk of giving does not derive simply from possible negative outcomes. Giving always requires the detachment of the giver from the gift and the receiver so that they can be themselves and respond to the giver gratuitously. The giver's detachment is not a withdrawal, but, endowed with the form of giving, is a waiting for the response to come and to do so gratuitously. The "risking" indicates the totality of the giving that respects the irreducible otherness of the gift and thus waits for a gratuitous response that may not come.

The positive intimations of death can be perceived if we realize that death, beyond its meaning of biological extinction and interruption of the original giving, reminds the person of the gift of his own existence. Death reminds the receiver of the constant being allowed to be. In this regard, death reveals anew the truth of birth: finite gift's ontogenic dependence on the source that begets the human being at every moment. One advantage of lived time is that it affords the possibility to see the unity of existence as a gift under the never-ending light of the mystery—even if most of the time this unity passes unnoticed. Perhaps more forcefully than birth itself, death discloses that life is a gift that calls for further giving, but a giving that in reality, since it is a response to the presence that calls, coincides with permitting oneself to be taken. Our contemporary culture holds up sudden death as the ideal way to die. Yet, while in some cases death may occur abruptly, normally speaking one is called to receive it, that is, to learn to give oneself over to the origin of one's own existence. Through death, one is asked to give oneself over completely. This could seem an unacceptable expropriation if we lose sight of the fact that the logic of gift that sustains existence is one of love. In love, one wishes to give oneself over completely to the beloved. Death, of course, has the flavor of a punishment and threatens to be the last word on existence. Yet it also brings us to the truth of the gift: the complete entrusting of oneself to the paternal origin. If giving were not ultimately an allowing to be taken, an offering, it would be determined by a limited, self-imposed measure that, as has often been lamented, undoes the gift from within. The wealth of the gift is to give itself completely—a donation that can be described as utter poverty. In order to be true the gift has to be complete; it cannot admit any measure. This is also why previous, discrete moments of giving were perceived as true only when one abandoned oneself in the giving. Those moments also taught that to hand oneself over to the other, as in marriage, has the unexpected though desired fruit of being given back along with the one to whom one has entrusted oneself. This is why in dying, too, one permits oneself to be taken and hopes that this ultimate gift may be finally confirmed. In this regard, death encompasses both moments that must be viewed in and through the other: giving oneself and allowing oneself to be taken. Understanding death in this way, we discover a new sense of limit. Limit, or finitude, which after Christian revelation is no longer a sign of perfection, emerges not as an end and total solitude, but as relation with the paternal origin. If originary experience allowed us to see the gift-ness of the person and of what is present, we now need to ask how recognition of the original giver, and hence the unity with and difference from him, takes place.

6. The Exigent Character of Life

The previous sections attempted to show, with the help of Giussani, that originary experience touches on the encounter with the presence of the other, a sign that is the unity of *logos* and gift. The gift of the singular sets man on the path toward the affirmation of the transcendent giver of the gift, of whom the sign is a word. As the analysis of gift through the reality of the family indicated, the person comes to recognize through his own experience that the origin of his existence cannot be fully identified with his progenitors or the natural biological mechanisms. Originary experience leads man to discover from within life itself a "structural disproportion" between him, the sign, and the ultimate giver, which, in light of such disproportion, cannot but be acknowledged as the divine paternal mystery. Before examining this further, there is a methodological implication to note: the human person's call to acknowledge the original giver means that the core of the doctrine of the analogy between God and finite being—which will be developed formally in the next chapter—consists in the dramatic relation between God and the human person. If the gift is freely given to itself so that it can be itself in responding to the giver, the analogy of being between God and the concrete singular takes place within the horizon of what can be called, with Balthasar, an *analogia libertatis*. This analogy of freedom, having its apex and condition of possibility in Christ, contains an *analogia personarum* according to which each person discovers his or her unique face in the response to the call of the paternal giver.[50]

The encounter with truth, which we call here originary experience, takes the concrete form of the encounter between the wonder-causing self-presentation of being in the sign's dual unity (gift-*logos*) and the original needs that constitute the human heart. Giussani says that originary experience invites us to perceive the presence of being, but in addition, that experience also reveals what constitutes the gift of one's being: the "heart," that is, "a complex of needs and 'evidences' which throws man into comparison with all that is."[51] Giussani orders the original evidences, needs, and exigencies that constitute the human heart in four fundamental categories: truth, justice, happiness, and love.[52] The first category of truth is man's search for the meaning of everything; that is, for the idea or form that gives things their identity and relation with the whole, with the ultimate: "the need for truth always implies singling out the ultimate truth, because one can only define a partial truth in relation to the ultimate. Nothing can be known without a quick, implicit comparison, if you like, between the thing and totality. Without even a glimpse of the ultimate, things become monstrous."[53] Giussani places great importance on this first category, to the extent that it is the ground for his understanding of reason. Here again, it is experience that

---

50. See Balthasar, *TD*, 3:206–14, 220–29.

51. Giussani, *RS*, 7. Translation modified.

52. It is perhaps clear now that "desire" for Giussani does not mean an *élan*, a Schellingian force that drives the human being forward without having been initiated by anything, nor does it mean just any type of desire. It is inappropriate, for example, to identify desire here with cupidity.

53. Giussani, *RS*, 113.

yields the adequate nature of reason: "reason is that singular event of nature in which it [reason] reveals itself as the operative need to explain reality *in all its factors* so that man may be introduced to the truth of things."[54] The totality indicated here is not quantitative. It regards the *ultimate* meaning of all that exists, a meaning that the concrete singular itself is not. Thus the need for meaning, awakened by the sign, always opens to the threshold of the infinite mystery.[55]

Without the affirmed perspective of the divine origin as "the unitary meaning which nature's objective and organic structure calls the human conscience to recognize," human justice is impossible; love becomes sentimental, barren possessiveness; and happiness *(satis factus)* is a momentary illusion.[56] Positively stated, the original needs of truth, love, justice, and happiness always seek a totalizing response, a response that does not stop short of the ultimate. They therefore root man in the relation with the mystery of which the constitution of reality, and indeed of man himself, speaks. Originary experience reveals that the gift of our being has the task of affirming the ultimate mystery, the all-encompassing meaning that gives man and the cosmos to themselves.

Giussani does not speak of man's needs and exigencies in the search for the ultimate in terms of "rights" or of a "claim" on God. Man is interiorly ordered to the vision of God in whom alone he finds fulfillment. Nevertheless, these needs, precisely as needs, do not present a claim on this vision. Man is not on an equal footing with God, who remains other. Giussani contends that the original needs express themselves as questions, not claims. These questions seek a "total answer, an answer which covers the entire horizon of reason, exhausting completely the whole 'category of possibility.'"[57] Man's needs seek a totality that is other than the sign, the human person, or the

---

54. Ibid., 97.

55. It is important to see that Giussani is proposing a renewed sense of mediation, which brings together truth's particular evidence and man's access to it without confusion. Through the encounter with the dual unity of the sign (gift and *logos* in a third) and through one's own original needs, it becomes clear that "the proper characteristic of man's being is that of being transparent to himself, aware of himself and, in him, of the horizon of the real" (Giussani, *RS*, 97).

56. Ibid., 99.

57. Ibid., 47. The four categories are not drawn from any anthropological or eschatological system that might tend to downplay the integrity of human nature for the sake of shoring up the primacy of God's salvific will. Nor are they an expression of Rahner's supernatural existential; they do not indicate an original bestowal of grace. The "needs" delineate human nature's twofold being given and openness to the mystery. The human end of seeing and being in communion with God does not lead Giussani to reduce history to the categorial, or religious anthropology to an athematic orientation toward God.

unity of both. Furthermore, the fact that Giussani calls them "needs" and "exigencies" does not imply that God's definitive self-revelation in Christ is demanded by man's given structure. There is no forced arrival of grace. Giussani reminds the reader that the opening line of Augustine's *Confessions*—*fecisti nos ad te*—means that God has created man already turned to him.[58] This being turned toward God ("*ad*") is part of the gift of human nature.[59]

The gift of human being, for Giussani, is thus a call to live in a vertiginous existential condition, that is, in a tension between poles due to the paradoxical human nature (to speak with de Lubac): man cannot give himself that which he needs and without which he cannot live. In concrete human experience, both worldly goals and eternal striving leave the original needs unsatisfied; what these needs seek is an inexhaustible response. Giussani indicates, then, that the human being always experiences a sense of "structural disproportion" at a finite response to the totalizing human needs. The sign always leads the human person beyond what reason can grasp. Reason, in faithfulness to experience, shows that the exhaustive response to the ultimate question lies beyond the horizon of one's own existence. If man's encounter with the world is this interplay of "sign" and original needs, which are awakened and set in motion by the sign, we can say, according to Giussani, "that the world 'demonstrates' something else, demonstrates God as a sign 'demonstrates' that of which it is a sign." God's existence is implied in the dynamic proper to human experience. With a remarkable trust in human nature's capacity to perceive the evidence, Giussani continues that "the answer exists because it cries out through the constitutive questions of our being, but experience cannot measure it. It exists but we do not know what it is."[60] While revealing himself within our originary experience, God remains beyond human grasp. Since there is a structural disproportion between the need for total meaning and the sign whose *logos* speaks of the giver, the perception of God through experience cannot be reduced to a feeling of his presence. Since God gives himself to be known through the mediation of the sign's gift-character, originary experience does not propose a direct intuition of God (ontologism). Consequently, what this means for man and his constitutive needs is that both remain beyond understanding until man is encountered by God. What man really needs is discovered only in Christ.

---

58. See also Aquinas, *ST*, II–II, q. 68, a. 4.

59. The ground of Giussani's treatment of Augustine and Aquinas on man's constitutive desire to see God—a theme we cannot explore here—is creation in Christ.

60. Giussani, *RS*, 116. Translation modified.

It is then that he realizes that he is thirsty because, incomprehensibly to him, God is more profoundly thirsty for him.[61]

The encounter between the sign and the constitutive needs of the heart comes to expression in a judgment, that is, as a knowledge in love, which acknowledges God to be the ground of the sign and, at the same time, discovers the correspondence of both the sign and the ground to the human heart.[62] Because the transcendentals are coextensive, all that exists co-responds to a certain extent to man's original needs. That is, through this judgment man acknowledges that reality responds with and in man to the ultimate source. Originary experience therefore reveals a *unity* between man, reality, and the whole. For Giussani, elementary experience is true if it "throws us into the rhythm of the real, drawing us irresistibly toward unification with the ultimate aspect of things and their true, definitive meaning."[63] It also discloses that "to understand" does not mean to comprehend something in the sense of completely grasping its meaning. It is rather to acknowledge the integrity and the fullness of presence.[64] To acknowledge this fullness, to know, involves all of the human person. The criterion for judging the truth of any thing has to be independent of the judger's wishes and limited cognitive capacities and, at the same time, it has to be truly his. To emphasize the latter without the former leads to subjectivism; to affirm the former without the latter leads to alienation. For Giussani, the criterion for judging given to man is not outside of him. It is given to him and, as such, it is his; it coincides with him. Yet since it is given to him with his own nature (in a sense it is his own nature), the criterion is greater than he is, and so is never subjective. The infallible criterion is the array of inextricable needs that constitute the human heart. To say that the original needs are the infallible criteria man is given—"infallible as criteria not as judgment"—attempts to liberate man from alienation, that is, to keep man from jettison-

---

61. Benedict XVI, *Church Fathers*, 86. The discontinuity between revelation and man's affirmation of the mystery is also why the original needs by which man judges the truth of everything should not be understood as *potentia oboedientialis*. Indeed, they indicate man's creaturely dependency. As Balthasar says, "obediential potency" does not give God the priority that is proper to him, and it would be better to dispense with this term. See Balthasar, *ET*, 3:40. It is better, then, not to think of the original needs in abstract terms (nature's capacity to receive grace) but rather in personal ones, i.e., these needs are an expression of the relation between God and man that is always initiated by God and within which man's existence (and nature) comes to be understood.

62. The expression "knowledge in love" is from Augustine, *Trin.* 9.10.15 (PL 42:969). This *cum amore notitia* is also expressed by Aquinas as *sapida scientia*. See Aquinas, *ST*, I, q. 43, a. 5, ad 2.

63. Giussani, *ROE*, 99.

64. Giussani, *VNC*, 20–22.

ing the responsibility of "seeing for himself."[65] Given the dimensions of the original needs, what responds adequately and totally to man's exigencies and original needs would be a sign that coincides completely with the mystery. This is why, Giussani says, only "something exceptional corresponds," that is, only Christ, the sacrament of the Father, the one in whom mystery and sign coincide, adequately responds, that is, addresses and fulfills without satiating the needs of man's heart.[66]

It is important to note that the judging, as knowledge in love, that acknowledges the gift-character of the singular, and so God as the singular's ultimate, takes place in collaboration with man's affection and freedom. The way reason knows something is not by processing information as a computer does; it requires being touched by the sign (gift-*logos*) and being moved to know. Giussani, rejecting the Enlightenment claim of an isolated reason unimpaired by any form of mediation, stresses further the unity of affection and reason and states that "without evidence we would not be moved, and without being moved, there would not be evidence."[67] Bearing in mind the twofold connotation of affection—first the passive sense, to be touched, to be struck; then the active sense, to love something—we can say that reason desires to know: it is provoked and moved to know and it loves what gives itself to be known. There is another dimension, however, of the need to welcome in freedom, to re-cognize, what reason sees and what the affections love. "To know (*conoscere*) is to recognize (*riconoscere*) what exists in the comparison with one's original needs."[68]

Freedom, however, can and does come between reason and affection to separate them. In this separation, freedom negates the ultimate and evident meaning of things, that is, the source that gives them to themselves. The alternative between affirming the gift or rejecting it that is offered to human freedom is never, for Giussani, a choice between two equally relevant options. The positivity of being (one's own being and that of reality) requires

---

65. He writes that "without religiosity man is used by man and destroyed by man. The power that operates in this way is not only the power of multinational companies or well-known dictators: it is mainly the power of man over woman, of woman over man; it is the power of parents over children, and of friends over friends" (Giussani, "Esperienza cristiana e potere," 18). If understanding means to grasp the link between something and reality, Giussani means "the whole of reality." Since this wholeness is always beyond man's grasp, to understand something means to begin "a very long search in order to reach that threshold from which—participating in the eye of Another, in the heart of Another—one can see and love everything" (Giussani, SPVVC, 59).

66. Giussani, SPVVC, 36–49. In this regard, Giussani's understanding of judgment (and therefore reason) has its truth in faith.

67. Giussani, AC, 277; Giussani, SPVVC, 58–64.

68. Giussani, "Per lo sviluppo," 39.

reason to acknowledge the priority of being over nothingness. The fact that one *is* indicates that there is a meaning and that one is made for and so exists always in a movement towards this meaning. Only the affirmation of the "evident" corresponds to being's self-presentation and its specific anthropology. To separate reason from the affective adhesion to the mystery is the form of freedom's reluctance to embrace the "evident." Experience makes it clear that just as reason cannot resist identifying the mystery of the whole with a particular—a reduced sense of unity that ideology quickly conflates with totalitarianism—so freedom's fear of affirming being simply because it is cannot be overcome by man's energies alone. Although the milieu of the community is not a guarantee, Giussani says that without it freedom cannot say its yes to "the possession of the link that binds one thing to the other and all of the things together."[69]

It is possible now to see that if, in contradiction to the unity between God, man, and the world as disclosed by originary experience, one separates them into three fragments, the result is an arsenal of false understandings of experience. If experience is understood as "sheer trying out, proliferation of initiatives, and undergoing," it results from having lost the link between experience and judging. If experience is seen as "mere reaction to circumstances and events," there has been a loss of the sense in which the impact with reality always invites freedom to recognize the ultimate ground. Experience understood as an "experiment" at man's disposal loses sight of the fact that man and reality are always being held in existence and confuses conversion and novelty with power and repetition. To "insist on one's own plans and ideas," instead of embracing the true novelty that takes place in experience, is to abandon oneself to the fear of affirming being for what it is. It is a rejection of the risk of oneself that is constitutive of the dramatic existence of man. To reduce experience to a subjective, indisputable, or even "graced" event, is to overlook its integral relation with the objective, transcendent side of experience (sign, authority, tradition, God). To circumscribe experience to the limits of one's own sexuality is to neglect the meaning and universality of the original needs and evidences. Finally, to separate meaning from experience and consider the former imposed on the latter through cultural mediation is to neglect the dual unity of gift and *logos* that characterizes all that is.

---

69. Giussani, *JTE*, 20.

7. The Time of Gift

Treating of gift as the form of the unity of being, examined by way of man's originary experience, also demands taking up the topic of time. To experience, we noted, is to travel around (*Erfahrung*) and to discover that gift characterizes the form of being's unity and permanence. Both aspects presuppose an idea of time, which we must now make explicit.

The association of experience with time, of course, is nothing new. One opinion says that experience is fundamentally static, since it has to do with our awareness of the relation between God, man, and the world, an awareness that, as we just saw, is expressed through the person's knowing in love (judgment). The lack of history and growth would indeed be the case if by "awareness" we meant "feelings" or "emotions" (as William James understood religious experience), or if awareness spoke of the possibility of direct knowledge of God (as if sign, mediation, and thus authority were secondary to originary experience), or, finally, if the content of this awareness were the "knowledge" of a limited object (that could also be called God). This "limited object" is incapable of changing the human person or setting him on a path toward the truth of himself, either because the relation between God and the human being is conceived in strict katalogical terms, or because, according to our technological culture, finite beings are only nominalistically related to God and so have no power to bring the human person upwards (*analogia*) to the original giver.[70] Others take an opposing view and identify experience with time, or more precisely, history. Experience, in this sense, would represent the Heraclitean river through which nature makes itself. Here the traveler would construct his own nature through his wandering in existence.[71] The preceding reflections clarify why originary experience is not static in these various senses, but it remains to say a word on the concept of history that many common accounts of experience presuppose and build upon.

The development of modern sciences and the hermeneutical reflection that followed Husserl's phenomenology inverted the premodern worldview that accounted for movement in terms of *energeia* and *entelecheia*. Consequently, experience is now understood as meaning more or less the same thing as time, while the combination of the two create an understanding of time as history. "For most contemporary thinkers," writes K. L. Schmitz, "the timeless is a deficient and static mode found (if at all) in abstract

---

70. James, *Varieties of Religious Experience*; Calvin, *Institutes*.

71. Much of feminist and liberal theology presupposes this understanding of time and history. See, for example, Firestone, *Dialectic of Sex*; Johnson, *She Who Is*.

human thought, and movement is unconditionally necessary."[72] Motion is nobler than rest—now identified with boredom and inactivity. The meaning of movement, however, is currently reduced to its topographical sense, or, more importantly, accounted for in terms of "possibility" and "will." Depending on this latter idea of movement, time becomes the measure by which to observe man's accomplishments. In this sense, for our contemporary culture, time is almost exclusively read in terms of a history that is no longer a context larger than the individual. History is not that "collective life of man," as G. Grant says, that totality in light of which one's own existence and works were seen as an indispensable but small contribution to a larger whole. History has become, as Grant writes, "the orientation to the future together with the will to mastery. Indeed the relation between mastery and concentration on the future is apparent in our language. The word 'will' is used as an auxiliary for the future tense, and also as the word that expresses our determination to do."[73] The "present" counts only inasmuch as it is history in the making; that is, as it is potentiality for a better future.[74] The primacy of the will in a technocratic culture makes the human being believe that he can completely master himself, either by manipulating his very nature (as biotechnology claims to do in ever new and ever more effective ways) or by creating his own rights and values. This view of history is consistent with the idea of progress mentioned earlier because for both there is no longer an objective order of the good (no perception of the coextensiveness of being and gift) into which one enters. The perception of order and good is built by the few and embraced by the rest through democratic consensus—which generally reveals itself to be the submission of the majority to an anonymous oligarchy. It is this view of movement and time (as history) that considers any discussion of ontological principles such as gift or being as an archeological exercise, irrelevant for anyone familiar with the development of thought in the last centuries.

To perceive history as the collective life of man into which one enters and offers his great or small contribution requires a retrieval of rest as *entelecheia*. This, however, calls for recuperating the link between time

---

72. Schmitz, "Human Nature," 126. See also Oliver, *Divine Motion*; Oliver, "Motion," 163–99.

73. Grant, "Time as History," 21.

74. "We North Americans," writes Grant, "whose ancestors crossed the ocean were, because of our religious traditions and because this continent was experienced as pure potentiality (a *tabula rasa*), the people most exclusively enfolded in the conception of time as progress and the exaltation of doing that went with it. We were to be the people who, after dominating two European wars, would become the chief leaders in establishing the reign of technique throughout all the planet and perhaps beyond it" (ibid., 24).

and eternity that was severed by modernity. Modernity's identification of experience with time transforms history into an immanent reality. History now refers only to two dialectically opposed dimensions of movement, becoming and stasis, where the former takes priority. To clarify the relation between the two requires no reference to a transcendent horizon in order to render history comprehensible. History, as "orientation to the future together with the will to mastery," is self-sufficient; it is a self-enclosed reality whose measure can be made to fit man's stature. As Heidegger puts it, "The philosopher does not believe. If the philosopher asks about time, then he has resolved *to understand time in terms of time* or in terms of the *aei*, which looks like eternity but proves to be a mere derivative of being temporal."[75] We now need to look back at the nature of gift as disclosed by originary experience in order to indicate its relation with time and eternity. In this way we will be able to assess why the sketched perception of time and history is based on a false or at least misconstrued anthropology.

There are three implications that arise from this discussion of the concrete singular being given to itself. First, as given to itself, the concrete singular does not coincide with itself. It is not its own origin. The fundamental evidence of being-made-now calls forth the awareness in the person as a singular being that his being and what he is, although inseparable, are not identical. He is a whole that is different from his being and his essence but is nonetheless constituted by the dual unity of essence and *esse*. The existence of the concrete singular, in its dual unity of *esse* and essence, is always already oriented towards its paternal origin. It thus exists only as a dramatic relation with the origin. The ontological difference, or *real distinctio* in Aquinas's terms, is not a static description of the structure of a finite being whose activity can be cleanly detached from its ontology. The ontological difference reveals the singular's specific temporality. As we saw, the human person comes to be at a moment not of his choosing, that is to say: he is given to himself. He has to receive his own being in order to be—and this reception, as we shall see shortly, has both an ontological and ethical connotation. The concrete singular's historical existence includes the continuous movement (action, *entelecheia*) of receiving himself from and entrusting himself to others in the loving affirmation of their unknown, common origin. To exist as gift means that one enjoys a continual growth in the truth of what gift means. Finally, this growth reaches its resting point when the concrete singular's destiny is fulfilled.[76]

75. Heidegger, *Concept of Time*, 1–2.

76. Euthanasia is an affirmation of what it sets out to deny, i.e., the insurmountable difference between oneself and the giver of one's own being. If I were the origin of myself, the principle of life would rest within me. Since I am not, the ultimate

The second implication relates to the gift as truly given: it remains other from and irreducible to the giver. The giver remains present in the gift but does not identify himself with it. It would be impossible to account for the meaning of the singular being's existence if the difference from the original giver were not preserved, or if this difference were reduced to a simple separation. The singular being would be a "fragment" that never belonged to any totality. It would not even be possible to talk about its "whatness," or, if attempted, it would simply come down to indulging in linguistic games. Time, reflecting the non-subsistence of finite beings, separates finite beings from God. Yet it does so not by denying God, but by imaging him. Because the giver remains present in the gift without losing his transcendence, time, as finite gift's mode of being, images eternity, the eternal giver's mode of being. Plato famously states in the *Timaeus* that since "it is not possible to bestow eternity fully upon anything that is begotten . . . [the Father] began to think of making a moving image of eternity, moving according to number, of eternity remaining in unity."[77] Time images eternity precisely in its continuous movement. Of course, for Plato the moving image meant above all circular movement. Yet, as Gregory of Nyssa explains, it is possible to think of the image's movement (time) as a continuous becoming like the source as a result of the relation with that source. Time is coming into existence from and returning to the source while growing ever more like it, but without relinquishing the gift's finite nature. The passage of time, because already sharing in the source, promises a unity with the source in which the finite gift is confirmed in the gift of being. From this point of view, the passage of time is a turning in desire towards the source, which, infinite itself, cannot but fulfill man's desire without ever satiating it.[78] Eternity does not simply lie before the beginning of time or wait at its end. It is, to speak with Bulgakov, "the *noumenon* (eternity) within the phenomenon (time)."[79] Eternity is the truth of time that, in manifesting itself through time, distinguishes itself from time.

---

self-contradictory act of euthanasia is in reality a denial of the good of death (allowing oneself to be taken). This is also why euthanasia is a form of suicide. Suicide attempts to get rid of *bodily* existence because the body is the continual reminder of the difference (and similarity) between oneself and God—and since the denial of this difference is the denial of oneself, the act tragically affirms what it attempts to escape: that I am not the origin of myself.

77. Plato, *Timaeus* 37c5–d9. This passage was used by Plotinus to explain time. See Plotinus, *Enneads* 3.7.

78. Gregory of Nyssa, *Commentary on the Song of Songs* 1.51, 6.127–29, 12.217–18 (PG 44:780, 885–89, 1021–24).

79. Bulgakov, *Lamb of God*, 135.

Third, the singular gift is totally given to itself in its own distinct unity; it is a "self." Since it is irreducibly a "self," even though its being and essence are not coextensive, the gift, from the point of view of the giver, cannot be taken back. It is crucial not to lose sight of the totality of the gift; otherwise we would think that gift relies only upon the power to give. The potentiality to give, however—or "gift," considered as a verb—is only one aspect. "Gift" is also a noun and, as such, describes the nature of the concrete singular. In addition to the inseparability of these two aspects of the word "gift," there also exists a proper *taxis* between them. The singular's capacity to give or to be given rests in its being given completely to itself. It is true that the gift is to grow in the truth of its being, yet this is a growth into what has already been given: participation in being. The totality proper to the singular being, therefore, also contains a promise of more, that is, of being confirmed in being and of participating in a being with others that knows no end. The promise is not made, however, because the beginning of the singular's existence is an empty void waiting to be filled. The promise of more is, rather, an increase of what has already been given. This promise is not a movement from sheer potency to actuality, but an indwelling of the latter. An inquiry into the meaning of substance in what follows will explore in what sense the connotations of gift's actuality and potentiality are not dialectically related, and why the need to grow in the gift does not threaten the concrete singular's being. It suffices here to note that to think of time without relation to eternity is to give potentiality priority over actuality. Taking as primordial the verbal sense of gift as potency grounds the claim that history is all-encompassing.[80] This claim, however, looks at the concrete singular from its historical end (death) rather than from its inception, and holds up the future rather than the present as time's fundamental category. The human being is indeed oriented towards the future, but this is because the fullness of the present opens him to it. How is the "present" then to be understood?

Heidegger, who attempted to think of "being (*Sein*) without regard to metaphysics" and, in order to do so, had "to leave metaphysics to itself," said in his famous lecture *Time and Being* that "from the dawn of Western-European thinking until today, Being (*Sein*) means the same as presencing (*Anwesen*). Presencing, presence (*Anwesenheit*) speaks of the present. . . . Being is determined as presence by time."[81] There is a sense in which this

---

80. A well-known exponent of this claim, which enjoys a great ascendency in theology, is Alfred North Whitehead. See his *Process and Reality*.

81. Heidegger, *OTB*, 24 and 2. For his understanding of *Sprung* (leap), see his *Contributions to Philosophy*, §117. Heidegger dedicates §§115–67 to defining the meaning of *Sprung*. In a very different context, Hegel wrote: "Absolute timelessness is distinct from duration; the former is eternity, from which natural time is absent. But in its Concept,

1. GIFT'S ORIGINARY EXPERIENCE 47

Heideggerian affirmation is correct. We mentioned earlier that originary experience invites us to account for being in terms of a presence (being as gift and *logos*) that imposes itself. Presence, we saw, presupposes a threefold movement of the concrete singular: its coming from another to call the human being through beauty to freely let himself and the sign (the concrete singular) be united with God, the sourcing giver and *telos* of both, in the historical return of both to him. This coming to, being with, and going towards is also time—although not identical with it.[82] Time is therefore not the receptacle in which the being of gift is given or contained. The question will be whether what we described as presence is what Heidegger intended.

The methodology adopted here—the anthropological starting point that moves from the human being to being in general and the divine giver—enables us to see that there is a reciprocity between being's presence (gift-*logos*; sign) and the human being. In a deceivingly similar way, Heidegger writes that the human being is "standing within the approach of presence, but in such a way that he receives as a *gift* the presencing that It gives by perceiving what appears in letting-presence."[83] Presence, according to him, means "the constant abiding that approaches man, reaches him, is extended to him."[84] As is well known, Heidegger calls *Ereignis* the belonging together of what gives itself and the one it claims in giving itself to it. Of course there can be no pretense of attempting to give here a full explanation of what Heidegger means by this complex term. It will be helpful for our purposes, though, to indicate first the main differences in the sense of "presence" and hence "time," and second, how dialogue with Heidegger helps us understand time's threefold dimension of past, present, and future.

Ereignis (event) is neither a historical occurrence nor a phenomenon presupposing a god to give a gift of a finite being to the human being and the latter to the former. *Ereignis* is a reciprocal belonging that "is a giving as destiny, giving as an opening up which reaches out. Both belong together, inasmuch as the former, destiny, lies in the latter, extending opening up."[85] This opening of the open takes place on the basis of a concealment, not because the giving (*Es gibt*) is the action of a god who remains hidden, but

---

time itself is eternal; for time as such—not any particular time, nor Now—is its Concept, and this, like every Concept generally, is eternal, therefore also absolute Presence" (Hegel, *Encyclopedia*, §258, *Zusätze*, 36. English translation slightly modified).

82. Aristotle already explained that time is the complex whole that is both inseparable from movement but not identified with it. See Aristotle, *Physics* 217b29–224a20.

83. Heidegger, *OTB*, 12. Emphasis added.

84. Ibid.

85. Ibid., 19. For the concept of *Ereignis* in Heidegger, see Heidegger, *Beiträge zur Philosophie*, GA 65. See also Heidegger, *Pathmarks*.

because the withdrawal proper to giving—which determines the modes of giving as sending and extending—belongs to what is proper to *Ereignis*.[86] Contrary to Heidegger, the belonging together of presence and the human being, however, must also keep in view the fact that, as originary experience discloses, both finite beings and the human being come from another. To eliminate this third in the totality of being and time by hypostasizing the event, as Heidegger seems to do (the event events, *Das Ereignis ereignet*), is tantamount to making human finitude the prime analogate for the whole.[87] This metaphysical decision, however, overlooks the constant discovery of experience that one is still being made and held in existence. The wonder that being's presence elicits in the human being precludes any burning of the bridges between metaphysics and the experience of time. It is true that the present, as Heidegger says, cannot be a simple "now," understood as the instant measurable by the clock. But beyond what he grants here, the present includes the presence that bears both the continual reminder of the passage from nothingness to being given, and the ongoing movement towards the ultimate source of being.

If the present is a gift in which the source gives itself in distinction from the gift while remaining its innermost, as the originary experience of being in the world and of childhood discloses, then perhaps we can adopt Heidegger's understanding of past and future as true with a correction from the metaphysical reading of gift, which is open to the transcending Eternal that constitutes it. This can account for the union as well as the distinction between time and eternity and so lead to a deeper understanding of the mystery of donation. "That which is no longer present," Heidegger says, "presences immediately in its absence—in the manner of what has been and still concerns us.... But absence also concerns us in the sense of what is not yet present in the manner of presencing in the sense of coming toward us."[88] Heidegger explains further that it is "nearhood (*Nahheit*) that brings past, present, and future near to one another by distancing them. For it keeps what has been open by *denying* its advent as presence."[89] Through *Nahheit*, Heidegger sees future as the withholding of presence, and past as the refusal of presence. Certainly the past and the future are not the present, though they remain within it. Contrasting Heidegger's account, however, they do so not as a denial of the present but as part of its constitutive gift. The past remains in the present as past in the form of tradition and memory, a hand-

---

86. Heidegger, *OTB*, 22.
87. Ibid., 24.
88. Ibid., 13.
89. Ibid., 15. Emphasis added.

ing over of and to the gift. The content of this tradition is not a sterile mass of doctrine. It is rather, on the one hand, human nature with its exigent character and all of the cosmos, and on the other hand, the cultural and historical inheritance that enables the human being to understand the present and the task laid out for him. In light of the perception of gift elucidated here, rather than "withholding," the future is a coming, as Heidegger also mentions, but more so it is a coming that ratifies the promise that constitutes the gift of the present. Hence the future is not present because it is withheld, but because it is promised. In this sense, it is God, rather than *Ereignis*, who accounts for time's fourth dimension: the unified givenness of time.[90]

Without the promise contained in the present gift, time would lack its *logos* and history would collapse in competing worldviews or shrivel down to an open space at man's disposal. Furthermore, if the positivity of the present did not include difference within itself and from God, the present would let go of the past and forestall the future possibilities. In other words, if the gift were a sheer, *univocal* repetition of the gift—as seems to be the case in Heidegger's understanding of being—there would be neither past nor *telos* to tend towards. The originary experience of time, instead, requires an analogical concept of being as gift.[91]

The mystery of death could emerge here as an ultimate objection to time as the presence of the gift that, enriched by its past, awaits fulfillment. But to grant this objection would mean identifying the mystery of death with biological death—thus losing sight of what death reveals of the nature of gift as indicated above—and, more importantly, denying that the continual coming from another, as witnessed by originary experience, presupposes the creative call to be that is capable of begetting where before there was "nothing." In our account, by contrast, the future is opened up by death in a far more radical way than if finite gift were its own origin or confined within a self-enclosed historical horizon. Since the present is a gift, the fulfillment of the promise is not a necessary, mechanical payment of something that is due. It is, instead, a gratuitous and overabundant gift that surpasses the exuberance even of the surprising origin of finite existence.

The unity and difference of the gift of being and time enables us to say that the distinction of past and future from the present also engages the

---

90. "The unity of time's three dimensions consists in the interplay of each toward each. This interplay proves to be the true extending, playing in the very heart of time, the fourth dimension, so to speak—not only so to speak, but in the nature of the matter. True time is four-dimensional. But the dimension which we call the fourth in our count is, in the nature of the matter, the first, that is, the giving that determines all" (ibid., 15).

91. It is possible now to understand why Giussani wrote that "experience is time inasmuch as it identifies itself with a present event" (Giussani, *AC*, 50).

freedom proper to the gift. The gift is asked to receive itself and the whole from the source—in this sense its past—and to welcome the fulfillment of the promise—its future. Originary experience calls for the recognition of a real, created, finite freedom that is itself (autonomous) because it is given to itself (indebted). The difference and unity of past, present, and future reveals man's finitude as relation with the original giver, whose presence in the gift represents also the call to make the gift like itself but, *pace* Hegel, without denying the concrete singular gift.[92] What follows attempts to ground the assertion that what constitutes the gift of the present as gift is the fact that it is in the present time that all of the gift is given, received, and awaited.

---

92. "If God is all sufficient and lacks nothing," asks Hegel, "why does He disclose Himself in a sheer Other of himself? The divine Idea is just this: to disclose itself, to posit this Other outside itself and to take it back again into itself, in order to be subjectivity and Spirit. . . . God is subjectivity, activity, infinite actuosity in which otherness has only a transient being, remaining implicit within the unity of the Idea, because it is itself this totality of the Idea" (Hegel, *Encyclopedia*, §247, *Zusätze*, 14–15).

II. Concrete Singularity

THE ENGAGEMENT OF THE whole of ourselves with the whole of reality, and with the center of both, who is God, calls us to recognize the positivity of all that is. With all its dramatic tensions, originary experience reveals that being itself is good *qua* given, that it is good to exist with others, and that the task for life is given with our destiny. It also reveals how every concrete singular is thus bound together in a complex, manifold unity in which each is fully itself.[1] The preceding chapter's anthropological

1. I would like to refer to self-standing being-gifts in terms of "concrete singularity"—an expression that has already been used in the previous chapter. In this context "concrete" indicates the physical or spiritual self-standingness of a singular being that always carries within itself the ontological memory of its belonging to the whole (*concrescere*). "Singularity," however, does not have only a quantitative meaning, as is the case for Aristotle, who sees the "singular" as the "individual" member of a species. "Singularity" is not limited to the qualitative sense either, as in Hegel's work, where "singular" refers to a subject, and subjectivity is just one moment in the constitution of the individual, not itself constituting an actual, self-standing being. As we know, for Hegel, the "singular" is a moment of the universal's path towards its own absolute determination, a process throughout which the universal gathers within itself the singular and the particular. Lastly, the concrete singular is not the empirical particular, always docile to technological manipulation. The concrete singular, as Schmitz indicates, "is that which takes the commonality of the universal and the determinacy of the particular" (Schmitz, "Postmodernism," 247). Thus, "concrete singularity" wishes to indicate the complexity of the ontological gift-ness of created beings in their irreducible uniqueness. The term thus reflects the difference from and similarity with God in a twofold sense: first, in creatures' own constitutive distinction between *esse*—which should not be too quickly explained away as "existence"—and Entity, and, second, in creatures' always already being part of the communion of beings—a communion that imperfectly images the unity of the paternal source without being absorbed by him. As we shall see in this chapter, "concrete singularity," although it does acknowledge the role of the negative, illuminates the relation to the universal in non-dialectic terms (as opposed, for example, to the terms "finitude" and "infinity"). "Concrete singularity" also resists thinking of the relation to God in a univocal sense—as is common in the different nominalistic interpretations of being. It conceives the relation with the universal analogically; that is, as it preserves the singular's openness to, and hence distinction from, the universal in the singular's dynamic self-transcendence towards the source. "Concrete singularity" indicates the "dynamic" sense of being without diluting each being's what-ness in a

reflection now opens up into a path to see in what sense "gift" is able to account for the form of the concrete singular's unity in its relation to and difference from others and with God, the primordial giver. We begin our ontological exploration by addressing the postmodern attempt to dethrone the category of unity and the primacy of philosophical principles in order to ward off the yoke of totalitarianism (section 1). We will see that this representative exponent of the contemporary, fragmented worldview, as thematized in the postmodern understanding of gift, seems to fall short by not thinking radically enough of the difference between God and the world (sections 2–3). Viewed in light of the radical gift of creation *ex nihilo*, it is possible to perceive the constitutive gift-ness of concrete singulars with respect to their existence (sections 4–5), their essence (section 6), and their finite *perseity* (section 7).

1. The Allurement of Anarchy

To characterize a historical epoch without losing its richness and variety is always a difficult enterprise. Moreover, it may be simply presumptuous even to make the attempt when one is still living within the epoch to be described. One aspect of our own culture, however, may be indicated without the risk of platitudes. The technological understanding of reason enshrined in the West (thinking understood in terms of willing) seems to have destined our age to a pervasive fragmentation. This radical disunity appears at every turn: sciences treat wholes as heaps of fragments in order better to use them for the advancement of progress and societal well-being; individual rights, understood increasingly in terms of freedom from coercion, transform persons into individuals who view each other as potential enemies; bureaucracy, intended to serve a well-ordered society, alienates citizens from government while it quantifies and treats them as numeric instances of problems to resolve; families appear as transient congregations of isolated individuals; not infrequently work, family life, and play—now reduced to entertainment—are loosely connected for economic but not organic reasons; sexuality is severed from fecundity and both from spousal union; gender is redefined as a cultural category that is not necessarily connected

---

Heraclitean river, a dilution that would mean deprivation of both source (*arche*) and destiny (*logos*). Lastly, "singularity" also includes a reference to the specificity of the *human* spirit (not to be interpreted as *animus* or *Geist*) without, however, proposing a totalizing system or exalting subjectivity. The term "concrete singularity" opens up the possibility of perceiving created realities without getting lost in the justification of knowledge or in a static ontology that needs constant support from a theory of action and is unable to account for being itself as flourishing.

II. CONCRETE SINGULARITY   53

to somatic features; fleeting and competing feelings define, if only for the moment they last, the identity of the human person.

This panoramic description of disintegrated wholes has found in some postmodern thinkers a theoretical elaboration that expresses the opposite view from originary experience. Jean-François Lyotard, elucidating the meaning of postmodernity, wrote that "we have paid a high enough price for the nostalgia of the whole and the one, for the reconciliation of the concept and the sensible, of the transparent and the communicable experience.... The answer is: Let us wage war on totality; let us be witnesses to the unpresentable [which is not another obscure name for God or source]; let us activate the differences and save the honor of the name."[2] It is important to underscore that this account both interprets unity in terms of totalitarianism—which itself is a political reading of unity in terms of power—and proposes to overturn it by means of, once again, power. In their attempt to leap out of the metaphysical discourse, postmodern thinkers present the philosophical reflections that preceded them as the inevitable succession of great narratives. Nevertheless, "the grand narrative," Lyotard writes, "has lost its credibility, regardless of what mode of unification it uses."[3] To underscore the radicality of the rejection of the grand narrative, it is worth recalling that Jacques Derrida, responding to David Tracy's adoption of the metaphor of fragments to depict our postmodern spiritual situation, rejected his being labeled a postmodern. Even though Tracy acknowledged that "there are only postmodernities," Derrida noted that postmodernity is yet another "attempt to periodize the totality of history within a teleological scheme."[4] Derrida clarified further that "what is going on today—in religion, in art, in philosophy, in thinking—is a way of inventing gestures which are not subject to totality or to a loss of totality, to the nostalgia and work of mourning for totality. Of course, this is impossible. We cannot simply stop mourning and nostalgia, but then something else is perhaps at work, but this 'perhaps' is not in tune with 'postmodernity' or with the 'fragment.'"[5] To bring this claim forward inevitably requires postmodern thinkers to reject the subjective humanism that begot the perception of "unity" they so sternly contest.[6] The subject is to be let go without remainder and unity replaced

---

2. Lyotard, *Postmodern Condition*, 81–82. It is worth noting the emphasis placed on will and violence in this description of postmodernity.

3. Ibid., 37. The violence generated by the totalitarian systems (national socialism, fascism, Marxism, capitalism) during the twentieth century is perhaps one of the main reasons for this unsettling awakening. Derrida, *Of Grammatology*, 3–5.

4. Caputo and Scanlon, *God, the Gift, and Postmodernism*, 182.

5. Ibid.

6. Derrida, *Margins of Philosophy*, 109–36; Heidegger, "Letter on Humanism";

by a never-ending multiplicity of origins whose reciprocal supplementarity undermines the very names of "origin" and "unity."⁷ Western culture seems to have fallen prey to the allurement of anarchy, that is, to that radical lack of principles that does not even have to conceive of itself as opposed to God. Derrida signals this "something else that is perhaps at work" in many different ways, including the unthinkable, polysemic, and equivocal "unname": gift. Let us now consider briefly what he means by "gift."

Derrida's reflection on gift is offered as a contribution to the destruction of what Heidegger considered one of the basic assumptions of Western thought: the identification of being with presence (*parousia*).⁸ Gift, so Derrida contends, rather than accounting for presence as we saw earlier, undercuts it without replacing it with another more basic ground. "Gift" creates difference between the gift, the giver, the receiver, space, and time. For Derrida, therefore, the term "gift" refers to the unpresentable, the unnamable.⁹ As such, it is not possible to move away from the undecidability with which, according to him, the coexistence of the existence and nonexistence of gift leaves us. Gift plays a "fundamental" role. In fact, it is an "open infrastructure" that enables him to elucidate the meaning of time, space, and interpersonal relations. It is important to bear in mind, however, that his exploration of the meaning and relation between gift, giver, and receiver is built upon the presupposition that the logic of gift requires both the absolute purity of the giver's and the receiver's intentions and the utter neutrality of the gift with respect to both. More precisely, gratuity presupposes for Derrida the a priori elimination of the subject (both the giver and the receiver). For this reason, Derrida casts gift within what he describes as the logic of the economy, which both requires and precludes gift.

Taking Mauss's famous work on gift as a starting point, Derrida's *Given Time* contends that "gift" belongs to the logic of the economic circular exchange—a logic that could be expressed as *do ut des*, I give so that you may (have to) give, or *do quia dedisti*, I give because you have given first.¹⁰ For "gift" to be, there has to be a giver who hands on a gift (a "present," we could say, taking advantage of this feature of English) to a receiver, who is thus put

---

Sartre, *Being and Nothingness*; Nietzsche, *Will to Power*.

7. This fragmentation can be seen in realms as different as art (Picasso, Pollock, etc.), literature (Joyce, Beckett), and contemporary music.

8. Derrida, *Margins of Philosophy*; Heidegger, *Being and Time*. This has also been indicated by Oster, *Mit-Mensch-Sein*, 155.

9. Derrida, *GT*; Derrida, *GD*; Caputo and Scanlon, *God, the Gift, and Postmodernism*; Gasché, *Tain of the Mirror*; Milbank, "Can a Gift Be Given?," 119–61.

10. Mauss, "Essai sur le don," 145–279. See also Hénaff, *Le prix*; Weiner, *Inalienable Possessions*.

in the position of reciprocating the first donation with a greater (excessive) gift *after some time*. For the donation to be truly gratuitous, however, it has to break away from the necessity to reciprocate, or to give in the first place. Thus, the giver cannot be aware of himself as giver. A giver must radically let go of the memory of the intention that triggers his giving if he is to truly give and not seek something in exchange. Any intention to give a gift that is not immediately thrown out into the most absolute oblivion spoils the gift and reduces the donation of the gift to pure commerce.[11] The human being, so it seems for Derrida, is irremediably egotistic, always turning the gift into a profit of sorts. The gift (a present), to be such, cannot disclose its gift-ness because it would impose its own measure upon the giver or receiver; that is, it would require reciprocation. Lastly, Derrida claims that if the receiver knows himself to be a receiver, he is put in a position of having to show his gratitude and reciprocate the gift, even if simply by receiving it. For the reception of the gift to be true, therefore, the receiver must neither see the gift nor respond to the giver.

Derrida's other well-known essay on the nature of gift, *The Gift of Death*, gives the same account of gift from the point of view of ethics and offers, among many other things, an elucidation of the meaning of responsibility in light of gift. The protagonists in this case are God, Abraham, and Isaac. This book, a relentless critique of a distorted perception of Christian ethics, contends that responsibility to God—the *mysterium tremens* that sets Abraham before the utterly irresponsible content of the request to murder his own son—is possible only "on the condition that the good no longer be a transcendental objective . . . on the condition that goodness forgets itself, hence a movement of infinite love."[12] The giver has to respond and "at the same time efface the origin of what one gives."[13] God, in this regard, is the name for the possibility to keep this secret, that is, to forget the gift.[14] For Derrida, donation requires absolute secrecy: the gift (in the threefold "unity" of giver, receiver, and gift) cannot be present. The gift therefore remains unthinkably polysemic and indescribable.[15]

That the gift is both necessary and impossible entails that, for Derrida, "gift" does not belong to practical reason, nor does it indicate the

---

11. For an alternative and more balanced reading of the economy see, e.g., Berry, *Way of Ignorance*; Bandow and D. L. Schindler, *Wealth*.
12. Derrida, *GD*, 50–51.
13. Ibid., 51.
14. Ibid., 108.
15. Derrida, *GT*, 76–77.

"essence" or the "presence" of a phenomenon.[16] To give, rather, is to open up the difference of time and space. "The gift is such only inasmuch as *it gives time*.... Where there is gift there is time."[17] In *Given Time*, Derrida uses Baudelaire's story "Counterfeit Money" to illuminate his understanding of this "trace" he calls "gift" and of the difference that gift introduces between giver, gift, and receiver on the one hand, and of time and space on the other hand. Exiting a tobacco shop, so the very short story goes, two friends encounter a beggar. One gives him what later turns out to be a false coin. The giving, Derrida indicates, establishes a difference between giver, gift, and receiver. This difference is first of all time: "the given thing requires or takes time."[18] In order for the gift to be true, the receiver cannot respond immediately. He must receive the gift and reciprocate it *later* with another gift. Derrida suggests that the gift of one's own life for another is perhaps the clearest illustration of this assertion that giving gives, above all, time: to die for another, says Derrida, does not eliminate the other's death. It simply delays it. The gift reveals in this way that time's present—in both the subjective and objective connotations of the genitive—is always postponed and hence time cannot be understood as "presence."

Derrida argues that gift clarifies the meaning of time because it forces us to think of it apart from the category of the present. Just as with the gift that requires a present (gift) with neither memory (of the intention that gave the present) nor promise (of a return), the present time cannot be considered in terms of a "now" coming from a past and open to the arrival of an imminent future. Derrida would concur with Heidegger when the latter writes that "to giving and sending there belongs keeping back—such that the denial of the present and the withholding of the present, play within the giving of what has been and what will be."[19] For Derrida, time is not the Aristotelian measure of movement or the Augustinian psychological extension, but rather the passing away without trace and expectation of reciprocation. As such, time, and hence being (*parousia*), eludes the framework of presence and absence. Time is a "play" without origin or *telos*.[20] Play, reminiscent of Wittgenstein's language games and de Saussure's theory of language, is not the grateful, bold enjoyment of having been given existence. Rather, here it is the lively but joyless fight where there is no "other"

---

16. Ibid., 156, 28–29.
17. Ibid., 59–60.
18. Ibid., 62.
19. Heidegger, *OTB*, 22.
20. Derrida, *GT*, 36–37; Derrida, *Margins of Philosophy*, 29–67.

to respond to or speak to.²¹ As gift, time plays and conceals "itself" like a forgotten secret. Time, rather than speaking of the unity of the gift, points us to its irretrievable dissemination.

For Derrida, it is this temporization that ties gift and time to a narration, to a text. With this he does not mean that the story has to be told. The text is not simply a conveyance of content. Rather, giving and temporization appear only in a discourse.²² It is important to realize that Derrida's insistence on the relationship between the gift-giving and its written account does not come from the inseparability of gift and *logos* alluded to earlier. He is not seeking an origin of the gift that would have no grasping intention. He is rather signaling that there is no "origin" from which the gift is given. What happens (*Ereignis*), therefore, happens to both the narrator and the narration, "*as if* the narrative produced the event it is supposed to report."²³ It is the text that makes giving possible in the first place. "The narrative gives the possibility of the recounted thing . . . and by the same token the possibility of the impossibility of gift and forgiveness."²⁴ For Derrida, what is guiltlessly and inevitably false in Baudelaire's text is not simply the counterfeit coin given to the beggar, but the text itself. In this sense, the text itself also shows that gift is not possible.

Besides time, according to Derrida, gift speaks of yet another difference: that of "spacing." Space, for Derrida, is not the indwelling of the gift that our examination of originary experience yielded. In his view space does not have anything to do with indwelling. For Derrida, "gift" differentiates as "space" that simultaneously unites and, more importantly, separates. Here again, the emphasis rests on difference rather than on unity. In Baudelaire's story, as explained by Derrida, when the "giver" tells his friend the real "value" of the coin, the narration-gift drives a wider distance between all the characters. The gift separates the two friends because the one does not give and the gift of the other turns out to be deceptive. The gift also separates itself from the giver, since it shows that he has not been true to his own gifts and position in society.²⁵ His gift reveals him to be de-centered. Furthermore, the gift causes the beggar's status to plummet further down the social scale, while the apparent magnanimity of the giver heightens his

---

21. For the concept of "play," see Derrida, "Différance," in *Margins of Philosophy*, 1–28; Wittgenstein, *Philosophical Investigations*, 23. It is interesting in this regard to refer to Foucault's reflections on the relationship between author and text. See Foucault, *Archeology of Knowledge*; Foucault, *Order of Things*.

22. Derrida, *GT*, 119.

23. Ibid., 120.

24. Ibid.

25. Ibid., 167–69.

superiority.²⁶ Lastly, since the text is what enables the story to be narrated, the distance also affects Baudelaire's reader—at least in Derrida's account. The donation of the false coin, as in the case of the betrayed friend, detaches every engaged reader from the story. This distance, opened by the gift of the counterfeit money, signals the "absolute heterogeneity" proper to space.²⁷ The gift reveals further, as with time, that space is made both possible and impossible by the giving of the difference. Derrida calls this differing "spacing," which, as R. Gasché clarifies, "is the discrete synthesis of (1) the movement by which the self-identity of an entity is interrupted and (2) the passive constitution by inscription as habitation."²⁸ Gift gives time and space, that is, it differentiates being by postponing the present and forestalling indwelling.

The circularity of time, space, and gift—aimed at the elimination of the metaphysical understanding of being as presence—could seem to define gift as the ruling principle that orders the Derridean "system." Yet Derrida's "gift" does not designate a giving origin. To understand what "it" is, it may be helpful to acknowledge that, for him, gift and *différance* are synonymous. Like *différance*, gift temporizes and spaces. Like *différance*, gift—in its simultaneous possibility and impossibility—is more originary than contradiction is; it is understood through the written text; and it sets itself forth as absent in what is present. In this regard one could define gift simply as *différance*: "the non-full, non-simple, structured and differentiating origin of differences. Thus the name of 'origin' no longer suits it."²⁹ In other words, both *différance* and gift—without being an "it"—displace being as presence and eliminate any unified whole by proposing a perception of time as event in which event differs from itself. Derrida claims that the simultaneous possibility and impossibility of gift is not an oxymoron. Paradox and contradiction still presuppose unity. The simultaneity of the possibility and impossibility of the gift reflects the "unpresentable": *equivocal* origins that ongoingly supplement and undo each other.³⁰

The analysis of originary experience prompts the question of whether "gift" necessarily leads to the dissemination of origins or subjectivity indicated by Derrida's empty, abstract *différance*. Is it not rather the case that Derrida's conclusion results from his abstract account of the difference between gift, giver, receiver, time, and space, an account that systematically

26. Ibid., 134.
27. Ibid., 156.
28. Ibid., 120; Gasché, *Tain of the Mirror*, 200.
29. Derrida, "Différance," 11.
30. Derrida, *Of Grammatology*, 303–4.

neglects the concrete singular's integral mode of being and hence, a priori, excludes the role of the body and the community from consideration?[31] If the previous examination of originary experience is valid, we may ask further: is it not the case that gratuity, which is required for both the donating and the reciprocating of the gift, is better thought of through the lens of *agape*, rather than through the purity of a subjectless, objectless intention? The experience of being given, as it appeared earlier, reveals "giving" as an event in which one desires union with the other without absorption. If, as originary experience suggests, this is how difference is to be conceived, does it not appear then that Derrida's equivocal account of gift rejects unity and the *tout autre* (God) precisely because he does not accept that the concrete singular, in this case the human person, is not the absolute other? If this is the case, then perhaps postmodernity—in its numerous forms, Derrida's included—is the epitome of the subjectivity that it attempts to deconstruct; that is, a subject that does not wish to deal with itself, the world, and God because it cannot account for its own finitude from and by itself.

2. A Radical Difference

Giving has indeed a paradoxical nature: the finite giver's gratuitous donation must be total and free; yet the donation is also a response to a preceding sign. The gift is both a sign of and irreducible to the source, hence, it is simultaneously transparent to the giver and other than the giver—the child, as we saw, is not a mechanical repetition of the parents. The receiver's response is gratuitous when it reciprocates without closing itself off to the giver, that is, when it affirms the giver and is open to further giving. This paradoxical structure of the gift requires taking up two related factors. First, in contrast to the view that the gift is both possible and impossible, as Derrida believes, the paradoxical structure of the gift can be explained through the primordial giving known as creation *ex nihilo*. In fact, to claim that the gift cannot presuppose anything, that it must give all of itself to another who remains other, that it gives time and space, and that it must generate a free, gratuitous response, is to describe creation. Only creation allows an understanding of difference and unity that does not conclude by hypostasizing the giving and receiving of being—as is the case with Heidegger's *Ereignis*—or breaking the whole into fragments from whose relation their identities are carved out—as in Derrida's work. The substitution of creation with reflections on "ground" or "differentiating origins" in order to avoid dealing with the gift *ex nihilo* that creation is, and hence to avoid grappling with both

---

31. Pickstock, *After Writing*, 33–37.

the nothingness and real being proper to finite beings, leaves Derrida's philosophical reflection on gift at an unresolved, aporetic level. Creation *ex nihilo* reveals that the exchange of gifts is a free participation in the original, creative gratuity that brings singular beings into existence and whose gratuity constitutes their very nature. Second, to account for gratuitousness it does not suffice to invoke a purity of intention, particularly one that ends by evacuating the giver, the receiver, and the gift of any identity or content for fear of losing the gift. It is necessary to consider the dimensions of love expressed in the terms *eros, agape,* and *koinonia*. What follows will consider the difference that creation *ex nihilo* introduces and how the negative aspect is to be perceived, beginning with this threefold dimension of love.

To start with an obvious but important point, we must recall that creation *ex nihilo*, while a legitimately philosophical concept, presupposes a difference between God and the world that is not available to unaided human experience. Creation requires the possibility that the world could have not been and that God's greatness would have been unaffected by the lack. As Sokolowski describes it, the Christian difference, that is, the difference between a world created *ex nihilo* and its transcendent God, was unknown to the Greeks.[32] Greek tragedies taught that however the gods excelled human beings and historical affairs, their dwelling place was on Mount Olympus, and their eternal history was inescapably tied to human history. Although corrected on many crucial points, the worldview underpinning Greek mythology remains intact for the great philosophers. Sokolowski also notes that Aristotle's unmoved mover or self-thinking thought, Plato's Good, and even Plotinus's One are part of the cosmos. Plotinus's One, despite its extreme otherness, cannot be without the Spirit and the Soul; Plato's Good, although separated by an abyss from finite beings (becomings), does not exist independently of them; Aristotle's self-thinking thought, regardless of whether it is aware of it, shares a necessary existence with those finite beings that never fully reach the unmoved mover and that imitate it either through eternal circular movement or through continual reproduction.[33] Once philosophy welcomes the intimation of divine revelation, it is possible to see that creation accounts for what human experience perceives as the truth of the gift: a complete, gratuitous donation that awaits, without demanding it,

---

32. Sokolowski, *God of Faith*, 12–20. See, e.g., Aeschylus, *Orestia*.

33. Schmitz, *Creation*, 13; Von Ivánka, *Plato christianus*; Brague, *Aristote*. For Aquinas, creation is not just an article of faith; it is scientifically demonstrable. He claims that only creation in time is not demonstrable by reason. As is well known, Aquinas attributes the doctrine of creation to Aristotle. See, for example, Aquinas, *In Physic*. 8.3.21. Full bibliography in Aquinas, *Aquinas on Creation*.

a free response. For there to be the gift of the concrete singular at all, this radical difference between the world and God is needed.

Without pondering the meaning of *nihil*, one could claim that what originary experience considers a gift is simple necessity, and that the cosmos does in fact enclose the divine within its own horizon. Since Hegel's attempt to integrate within the absolute spirit the difference between God and the world established by the creative *nihil* and Heidegger's claim regarding the equi-primordial nature of truth and nothingness, we are inclined to think that we enjoy a panoptic vision of nothingness. Nothingness tends to be perceived as a concept synonymous with biological death. As a verb, "nothingness" is an exercise in contradiction. Nothingness is thus pictured as an "absent being" or an "enabling void" waiting to be filled by being's presence. *Nihil*, however, is not a crypto-being that human reason can handle. Just as being is not a mere concept that the human mind can encompass, so *nihil* is not the dialectical partner of being. Nothingness is not a primordial poverty (*penia*) longing to be enriched by fullness (*poros*). It is not Hegel's power of the negative, or even the negation of the negation through which the syllogistic logic of absolute spirit moves from "Logic" to "Spirit" through "Nature." Both structures presuppose being. As C. O'Regan describes it in his account of why Hegel's system ultimately rejects a creation *ex nihilo*, the *nihil* of creation is an *oukontic*, absolute one.[34] If it is no-thing, then the coming of beings from God cannot be a Plotinian emanation or a production that benefits from some pre-existent material. Creation is not another kind of movement or the prototype of becoming—although it makes both of them possible. In this regard, creation is not another exemplum of human efficient causality. If it were simply another human making, the radical difference required to account for the positive existence of concrete singulars would still be lacking. Creation *ex nihilo* is the one act in which God communicates his *esse ad extra* to what he is not and what was not there before the original donation. It is, in other terms, the positing of an authentic multiplicity of singular beings that remain other from the source while not weakening or transforming that source.[35]

Creation's radical *nihil* alone accounts for the being of concrete singulars without their confusion with the divine source or their reduction to pieces broken away from it. That beings are "from nothingness" entails that

---

34. The *oukontic* (absolute or Parmenidean) sense of negation is the common way Christianity has understood creation from nothingness, starting with Irenaeus's *Haer.* 2.10ff. It is not the relative negativity (*meontic*) that may be found in Spinoza or Hegel. See O'Regan, *Heterodox Hegel*, 147. There is, of course, a sense in which the relative sense of negation needs to be accepted in order to give an account of becoming.

35. Aquinas, *ST*, I, q. 45, a. 1; Aquinas, *De pot. Dei*, q. 3, a. 1, ad 12 and ad 13.

they are given to themselves, hence, that they are irreducible to the origin. The difference that creation introduces between the original giver and the concrete singular, since it indicates that the concrete singular being does not have consistency in itself, also requires the presence of the source in the singular-gift. The giver is present in the gift without absorbing it into himself.[36] How are we to think then of this presence of the divine giver in the gift? Besides the similarity between the giver and the gift, it indicates that the concrete singular is relation with the source. Aquinas clarified that if creation is neither a change nor a movement, because both change and movement presuppose the existence of something (even if this something is primal matter), then creation indicates relation with the source.[37] The positing of this relation is coincident with the inception and endurance of the concrete singular's existence. Yet since the giver is present in the gift, the "relation" the original giver intends toward the gift/receiver is one of indwelling. Obviously, this "indwelling" varies according to the specific nature of each concrete singular. Nevertheless, it is analogically the case for each that having been given to itself entails being itself in another. This indwelling preserves the radical difference between God and concrete singulars because it affirms the radical *oukontic* negation. To claim the contrary would concede the relation between the divine giver and the gift to be one of pantheism. Yet if pantheism were the correct view of the relationship between God and the world, what sense could we make of our own bodies? Indwelling perpetuates this negation—negation is also a verb, "noughting," as W. Desmond indicates—because it makes the original giving as a return to the source *as other* possible.[38]

3. Giving Otherness

The foregoing reflection on the radical nature of the gift in terms of creation *ex nihilo* considers creation to be a unique type of giving that speaks of a primordial act of love on the part of the original giver. While creation *ex nihilo* will enter again into the discussion later, at this point a few words on

---

36. Augustine, *Confessions* 3.6.11 (PL 32:687–88). See also Aquinas, *ST*, I, q. 8, a. 1.

37. Aquinas, *De pot. Dei*, q. 3, a. 2; Aquinas, *ST*, I, q. 45, a. 2, ad 2. Aquinas states: "This relation is an accident, and considered in its being (*esse*), inasmuch as it adheres to a subject, is subsequent to the thing created: even so an accident both logically (*intellectu*) and naturally is subsequent to its subject. If, however, we consider it *secundum suam rationem* from the point of view of its arising from the action of the agent, then the aforesaid relation is after a fashion prior to its subject, because like the divine act (*actio*) itself it is the proximate cause thereof" (Aquinas, *De pot. Dei*, q. 3, a. 3, ad 3).

38. Desmond, *Being and the Between*, 292.

the relation between gift and love are in order. As we saw with Derrida, the gratuitousness of the gift and the unity between the giver, the gift, and the receiver depend on what we mean by love and gift. Clearly it is beyond our purpose here to summarize the intricate debate on the nature of love. In light of the richness of the tradition we will limit ourselves to a suggestion of how to understand this term.[39]

To characterize creation as a giving could give rise to an understanding of the nature of God, the original giver, in terms of the transcendental *bonum*, the Good. Much of Greek thought, particularly in Plato and the neoplatonic tradition, already pondered the nature of the ultimate, the One, in terms of goodness. From this Good, they said, proceeds all that is. Every concrete singular receives from the eternal goodness form, being, light, and goodness, and some receive life. The ancient philosophers knew full well that the more perfect a being is, the more it communicates; *bonum diffusivum est sui*. This communication meant that the cosmos moved towards the One by means of love.[40] Yet this communication is not seen as the One's love for the singular; it happens without the free and conscious decision of the Good itself.[41] Furthermore, what comes forth from the Good, though participating in its fullness, is always less than the Good. The love that moves the cosmos and the stars knows only an upward movement. It is the cosmos that loves the Good, not vice versa. This is why for Plotinus, for example, the name of "good," rather than indicating what the One is, has to do with its relation with the other hypostases.[42]

Through Christian revelation, God presents himself as a mystery of love. God not only gives creation to itself; he loves it and does so to the utmost. This understanding of God as absolute love fulfills the revelation of God as being (Exod 14:4; John 8:28) and transforms the Greek understanding of the Good. There is of course a sense in which the Good and love are synonymous. Love too, as revealed by Jesus Christ (1 John 4:8 and 16), regards the very essence of God. However, they do not coincide fully. Let us note three aspects of what love unfolds of the nature of God.

39. For further exploration on this term see, among others, Prieto, "*Eros* and *Agape*," 212–13; Giuliodori, *Intelligenza teologica*; Pérez-Soba Díez del Corral, "*Amor es nombre*"; Mouroux, "Eros et Agape," 23–38; De Rougemont, *L'amour et l'occident*; Scola, *Identidad y diferencia*.

40. Aristotle, *Metaph.* 12. For an understanding of the One as good, see Plato, *Republic* 505a–e.

41. This is the context within which we can grasp Plato's prophetic answer: "Let us state the reason why. He [the maker and father of the universe] was good, and one who is good can never become jealous of anything. And so, being free from jealousy, he wanted everything to become as much like himself as was possible" (*Timaeus* 29e).

42. Plotinus, *Enneads* 6.9.6; 6.7.41; 5.3.11.

First, the identification of love with the divine *esse* permits a vision of love as witnessing to the transcendentality of the transcendentals, rather than as a simple synonym for goodness. Love grants a dynamic unity and intensification to the coextensiveness of being, oneness, truth, and beauty. In his being absolute love, God is one, true, good, beautiful, and living. This transcendental absoluteness can be seen in the self-revelation of himself to himself as the eternal communication of the totality of oneness, unity, good, truth, beauty, and life to the other.[43]

The second aspect that love unfolds is the personality of the Godhead. God is not only the fullness of being and goodness in the objective sense. He is superabundant being, goodness, wisdom, and life because he is also a personal being—that is, a being who exists as an infinite relation of love in which one has always already given himself over to the other completely. Due to the inseparability of love and *logos* in God, divine revelation does not lead to an understanding of the concept of "person" as marked by a random, arbitrary will, but rather as a mystery of dialogue and constitutive relation with another. Personhood, in light of revelation, is recognized as the perfection of being, first in God and analogically in the human being. God's self-communicating goodness always exists as a communion of persons. The eternal communication of his own goodness (*Deus Trinitas*) is, analogically speaking, a loving, ever-greater, eternal encounter of the divine persons.

Third, the relation between love and person also means that God's communication of his own being is accompanied by fruition. God not only communicates his being; he takes delight in doing so and, moreover, desires that the other participate in both the giving and the delight of loving and being loved by the other. There is no love without the delight of being loved and sharing this delight with the other. The love that is at the origin of creation *ex nihilo* is not an ornamental cloak over an exercise of power. When we say that God loves the world into existence we mean that he communicates his own goodness and being to what he is not.

While love unveils these three dimensions of the nature of the Good and so gives rise to a reading of the *summum bonum* as *summa caritas*, love is also a gift given (in God and from God). There is a circularity between love and gift that prevents us from reading love simply as a faculty of the will, and gift as an object of that love. Love is gift, and gift, in its highest expression, is love. Love is not just one gift given among others. Love is what makes gifts be gifts and not mere exchanges of property. It is love that ensures the purity of the giver's and the receiver's intentions. Alexander of Hales, describing the properties of the Holy Spirit, writes that love is what is

---

43. Chapter 5 deals with this issue in depth.

given in whatever is given.⁴⁴ Love, says Aquinas, "has the nature of the first gift, and through it all gratuitous gifts are given."⁴⁵ What love gives is itself, that is, it gives being with all the incomprehensible ever-greater unity of its transcendentals. It gives it so that the other can be. Creation *ex nihilo* is God's absolute affirmation that generates another, one that is identical to the origin (the Son), and another that is what he is not.⁴⁶ This communication is an expression of his love for the world, and it is given so that the concrete singular may experience from within, taste, and take delight in his love.⁴⁷

Human love has its roots in the creative affirmation of the singular, according to which God says to the creature: it is good for you to be (Gen 1:31). Willing man's ultimate good, God wishes the creature to participate in his life, to dwell in him. Because of this divine love, every true lover wills the good of the beloved.⁴⁸ In light of the circularity between gift and love we can suggest now that gift is the mystery of the communication of love whose unity is also one of ever-greater differentiation.

To express the mystery of unity and difference in a third specific to love, and so to better understand the gratuity proper to the giving and the receiving of the gift, we need to look briefly at the two indissociable terms that come together in the name love, that is, *eros* and *agape*. Love has an oblative, *agapic* dimension and a desirous, *erotic* dimension. *Eros*, a god for the Greeks, has an ambiguous nature. The offspring of *poros* (wealth) and *penia* (poverty), *eros*, so Plato recounts, indicates need and precariousness and, at the same time, impetuousness, the desire for wisdom.⁴⁹ *Eros* is not a self-motivated impulse. It is awakened by beauty. This beauty is first the corporeal beauty, which attracts and entices the lover out of himself because it is the overflowing of the eternal beauty in a concrete form. We thus find the first connotation of *eros*: the beginning of desire lies in a certain *given* participation in beauty. *Eros* is moved by something else, in which it seeks the fullness of what it has foretasted. Receiving the form of beauty, *eros* en-

---

44. Alexander of Hales, *Doctoris irrefragabilis* 4, l. 3, Pars 3, inq. 1, Trac. 1, q. 2, a. 2, sol 1. 4 (n. 609), 959.

45. Aquinas, *ST*, I, q. 38, a. 2.

46. Bonaventure, *Collationes in Hexaemeron*, 161–62. Also in Aquinas we see this affirmation of the relation between the Trinity and creation: *De pot. Dei*, q. 2, a. 6; *ST*, I, q. 45, a. 6, ad 2; *ST*, I, q. 45, a. 7.

47. Because the original giver is both transcendent and immanent, he cannot be considered another object or being, even if the most excellent one. God is not a genus; he is giver like no other. See Aquinas, *ST*, I, q. 3, a. 5.

48. This is Aquinas's classic definition of the nature of love: "in hoc enim praecipue consistit amor, quod amans amato bonum velit" (Aquinas, *SCG*, bk. 3, c. 90 [no. 2657]).

49. Plato, *Symposium* 201a–204d.

gages the whole of the person, including his body, and drives the person to transcend himself. Desire tears him away from his own limitations. This, then, is the second connotation: *eros* not only indicates the need to receive; it also draws the person to seek unity with what he still does not possess. Seeking unity with love itself, *eros* moves the lover upwards to the root of beings. Love "thirsts," so to speak, for the beauty that comes to it first. This is why *eros* has been described as the ascending dimension of love.

We can say further, and apart from the neoplatonic tradition, that, anthropologically speaking, *eros,* as the desire of unity with the other, includes physical, conjugal union. Yet the union that desire seeks is better perceived in its highest degree: spiritual indwelling. *Eros*, again, is the desiring dimension of love that seeks unity with the other. Undoubtedly, *eros* tends to be burdened by its own ambiguity, which, as Benedict XVI says, is that the *erotic* force can overpower reason. *Eros*, separated from *logos* (truth, reason), can become a sort of "divine madness,"[50] which results in self-destructive excesses. If united to truth (*logos*), *eros* seeks a union that does not reduce the good of the other to the satisfaction of one's own whims.[51]

It is important, at this point, to correct a common misunderstanding. The fact that *eros* separate from *logos* becomes an irrational, maddening desire does not mean that the yearning for unity with the other, the need both for the other and to be received by the other, is in itself negative. One does not understand the nature of conjugal union, for example, by starting out from instances of sexual degradation and violence; in the same vein, *eros* goes equally misunderstood if greed or lust is taken as its complete form. If *eros* and *agape* are two inseparable dimensions of love, this desire is in itself a perfection. In fact, as Aquinas says, every creature yearns for God according to the degree proper to its own participation in being.[52] Thus *eros* reveals that the perfection of oneself is not in oneself. The lover desires to be one with the beloved, who already somehow dwells in the lover. The lover desires, needs, and implores that the beloved let him be part of her as she is in him. *Eros* indicates that the lover cannot give to himself that of which he already has a foretaste; it must be given to him gratuitously. This is the radical poverty of *eros*: not that it does not know love, but that it puts itself at the disposal of the other's gift, orienting itself towards a reception whose occurrence and measure does not lie at its disposal. Of course, hu-

---

50. Benedict XVI, *Deus caritas est*, no. 4 (AAS 100 [2008], 220).

51. In this regard, we can say with Sallust that friendship is to want the same and to reject the same, only if, however, by the "same" we mean the *logos* of love. In this case friendship will be communion in the good. Sallust, *Catiline's War* 20.4.

52. Aquinas wrote "non solum homo vel angelus, sed quaelibet creatura plus amat Deum quam seipsam" (Aquinas, *Quodlibetum*, I, q. 4, a. 3).

man desires are always in need of purification. The desire for unity tends to become possessiveness. Yet to consider the poverty proper to *eros* as an imperfection presupposes a negative anthropology, according to which all desires are taken a priori as sinful.[53] A love that does not desire is a love that cannot suffer and, as such, is a love that cannot find joy in being welcomed by the other. The giving of a gift is an expression of love (*eros*) inasmuch as it is both a response to a preceding gift and a yearning for a response, a gratuitous unity with the receiver.

If the *erotic* dimension of love acknowledges the exigence to receive the other and the search for unity with the other, the *agapic* dimension highlights the oblative gift of self. To love another is to love its good. To love its good, however, always requires surrendering oneself to the other, living for the other's sake, giving oneself to the other. *Agape* represents love's *katalogical* movement. Just as it is proper to love to ask (*eros*), it is also a perfection of love to kneel (*agape*). The lover who is intent only on seeking the unity turns the beloved into a means for self-satisfaction. Instead, the true lover, that is, the person whose *agape* is true, spends himself for the sake of the beloved. He wishes to affirm the beloved with the radical gift of self. The love that keeps too close an eye on what it has done, acquired, or sacrificed for the sake of the beloved suffocates both parties. This is why *agape* purifies *eros*. It ensures that the desire to be one with the other is for the other's sake and not for one's own profit. *Agape* helps *logos* give form to *eros*. At the same time, *eros* is intrinsic to *agape* because the love that gives without receiving or being permanently open to receive from the other is, in reality, a denial of self. *Eros* without *agape* becomes egotism—in this case, the gift will crush the receiver. *Agape* without *eros* is a denial of self. A self-effacing offering of oneself without the simultaneous delight in and plead to be received by the other, that is, without an awareness of what one receives in giving and gives in receiving, is yet another form of egotism, this time under the form of piety.[54] The gift without the giver is no longer a gift.

Eros and *agape* are two dimensions of the same form of love. From the point of view of the unity between the giver, gift, and the receiver, we can now see that whereas *eros* emphasizes the unifying aspect of love, *agape* underscores the difference between them. Love posits another who is different

---

53. It is not a coincidence that Nygren's famous elucidation of the meaning of *eros* and *agape* presupposes Luther's anthropology. Nygren, *Agape and Eros*.

54. Benedict XVI wrote that "were this antithesis [between *eros* and *agape*] to be taken to the extremes, the essence of Christianity would be detached from the vital relations fundamental to human existence and would become a world apart, admirable perhaps, but decisively cut off from the complex fabric of human life" (Benedict XVI, *Deus caritas est*, no. 7 [AAS 100 (2008), 223]).

from itself, in order that this other might be (*agape*). Love, in doing so, also seeks to be received within the other itself to dwell in it (*eros*). Love does not want to be received by the other in order to disappear in or use the other, but rather to enjoy a gratuitous and, in a term that will be explained later, virginal unity with the other (*agape*).

The *agapic* dimension of love is perceived as a perfection of love thanks to Christian revelation. While the Aristotelian unmoved mover or the Plotinian One does not care for the world, the God of Jesus Christ does. Love is what is most proper to God. He alone, without losing himself, can give himself to what he is not because, in himself, he exists as a tripersonal communion of love. It is at the level of the three divine persons that the relation between *eros*, *agape*, and *logos* indicated earlier finally becomes clear. The perfection of love, where the beloved without regard for himself gives all of himself to the other, all the while desiring to be loved by this other, is protected from egotism through the third that both unites them and preserves their distinction. Love gives itself, a relation of personal indwelling in which everything is given and shared. As we saw with childhood, and as it will reappear with the mystery of gift's gratuity when we ponder the role of the third hypostasis, this relation does not collapse into the giver or the receiver because of this third, who represents at the personal level the objective unity between the giver and the receiver. The complete form of love is marked by the giving and receiving known as *koinonia*. In this communion, as Christian revelation confirms, the third is both fruit and summit of the love that binds the lover to and distinguishes him from the beloved. This *koinonia*, when referred to God, describes both the unity of love and its preservation of the difference of giver, gift, and receiver.

Before proceeding further, there is a mysterious, difficult implication to consider, even if only briefly. If *agape* and *eros* are two dimensions of love, and both are perfections, there is a sense in which, as Benedict XVI suggests, *eros*, and not only *agape*, is proper to divine love.[55] Most of the Christian tradition, as, for example, in the seminal work of Origen, perceives the relation of *eros* and *agape* in terms of an analogical and katalogical movement.[56] As we mentioned, *eros* represents the movement of the soul upwards, seeking union with the primordial giver. *Agape* represents the downward movement from God to man, which purifies and preserves man's *erotic* search for beauty and transforms it into *agape*. Dionysius the Aereopagite, however, offers a different account. Instead of the vertical axis, Dionysius speaks of God's love (*eros*) in terms of ecstasy, yearning. Love can go outside itself and move, so

55. Benedict XVI, *Deus caritas est*, no. 9 (AAS 100 [2008], 225).
56. Origen, *Song of Songs*, part 1, prol., 2.20–25.

to speak, in any direction: upwards, downwards, or towards another at the same level. God is enticed away to become one with his creatures.[57] Dionysius, who, like Origen, was free of the contemporary dualistic reading of *eros* and *agape*, indicates that love is what moves one towards the other. The tripersonal God comes out of himself (*ek-stasis*), without abandoning himself, in order to dwell in the creature and so bring the communication of divine life to its perfection in that creature.

It is of course the case that, as Dionysius shows, *eros* has no ambiguity in God: in him there is no separation between love and *logos*, nor does the existence of a yearning dimension to God's love mean that the world dictates his response. Yet, part of the unfathomable mystery of creation is that God creates (*agape*) because he wishes (*eros*) a relation with the world. Overemphasizing divine freedom as having the possibility of not creating (*agape* without *eros*), while it intends to preserve God's transcendence, fails to do justice to his immanence and his original creative intention: incarnation and recapitulation in Christ. To emphasize the *erotic* dimension of love over and against the *agapic* is to transform God into an empty, monadic, undetermined absolute, unable to create another different from itself because it stands in need of the finite to fulfill itself. Only the complete form of the dual unity of *eros* and *agape*, *koinonia*, allows us to see *ex nihilo* as the expression of God's loving freedom in the communication of *esse*.

The gift of creation, therefore, is the giving of the creature to itself without the possibility of claiming it back (*agape*).[58] The creature has its own integrity and time, for time begins with the creature. Giving the creature to itself entails furthermore that both the creature's openness to the transcendent source and search for unity with it echo the source's *erotic* love that seeks to unite itself with the gift without annihilating it (*agape*).[59] The

---

57. Pseudo-Dionysius, *Divine Names* 4.13 (PG 3:712B).

58. Etienne Gilson, following Aquinas, indicates that existence rests in the created being as a perpetual donation that can be revoked if the giver wishes. Nevertheless, it will never be revoked because "since non-existence has no direct cause, God cannot cause a thing to tend to non-existence, whereas a creature has this tendency of itself, since it is produced from nothing. Indirectly God can be the cause of things being reduced to non-existence, by withdrawing His action therefrom" (Gilson, *L'être et l'essence*, 99). See also Aquinas, *ST*, I, q. 104, a. 3, ad 1. Aristotle also expresses the impossibility for the gift to be taken back in his *Topics* 4.4.125a18.

59. In light of this we could say theologically that both are asymmetrically true: creation is for the sake of the covenant, that is, it is already an expression of the covenant of the triune God with man that has its fulfillment and truth in Christ; and the covenant presupposes creation. Ratzinger, *"In the Beginning. . ."*; Ratzinger, *Principles of Catholic Theology*, 153–71. The circularity between the covenant and creation does not represent the elimination of natural theology. It rather prevents us from adopting a dualistic conception of the relation between nature and grace.

radical contingency of singular beings disclosed by creation *ex nihilo* is not subject to irrational randomness (a-*logos*), because, as Aquinas says, the gift of creation reflects God's being.[60] The dual unity of *eros* and *agape* in the one God prevents us from interpreting *exemplar* causality and the reflection on gift in terms of onto-theology and from elucidating the nature of God, as Ockham did, in terms of absolute, illogical will.[61] In the present context, therefore, the opposite of "randomness" is "gift" and not logical necessity or the ascription of a self-explanatory nature to singular beings. The "necessity" of the form of singular beings is, in this view, the expression of the ontology of gift, the formal inverse of the gratuity of the gift. The reflection on the radical difference (*ex nihilo*) leads us now to consider the gratuity of a singular being's existence and its ontological structure.

4. The Gift of Existence

Created *ex nihilo*, concrete singular beings are gifts because they are brought into existence in one act of absolute divine liberality. Since they are created from nothingness, their gift-ness marks their ontological structure. Ontologically speaking, the affirmation that the concrete singular is gift would not be complete if the finite being were not given to itself, that is, if it did not participate in its own being given. Gift relates to the concrete singular's *actus primus qui est forma*, as Aquinas would say. If gift did not reach the level of the first act, we would equate being's gift-ness to accidental existence. This, however, fails to account for the positivity of finite beings, and, in our view, for the unity proper to each one. This does make a rather tantalizing option for the modern mind, interested as it is primarily in "essence." Being's actual existence, not forming part of the definition of any being, tends to be perceived as indifferent to both our knowledge of it and to the being of the singular. Accordingly, "existence" would be relevant for religious reflections on the relationship between God and the human person, for obsolete metaphysics of creation, or for ethical reflections that seek a social transformation of an economy of self-interest into one capable of integrating principles of solidarity or subsidiarity. Reacting to this rationalistic approach, though retaining the abstraction from originary experience that gave rise to it,

---

60. This is the Thomistic doctrine of the divine ideas. Divine ideas are the way in which God understands himself as capable of being imitated by a creature. Aquinas, *ST*, I, q. 15, a. 1, ad 3; *ST*, I, q. 15, a. 1, ad 2; *De ver.*, q. 3, a. 2. As mentioned, God's exemplar causality needs to be seen together with the fact that God is a triune being. Aquinas, *ST*, I, q. 44, a. 3; *ST*, I, q. 45, a. 7.

61. William of Ockham, *Scriptum Sent.*, vol. 1, d. 1, q. 6.

philosophers like Kierkegaard and Sartre privileged existence over essence. In this view, freedom includes the capacity to generate its own nature, and, as we saw, time is reduced to history.

Separating essence from existence results in a poor understanding of both. When considered apart from its relation to existence, essence tends to be perceived as a concept closed in on itself—and so with no transcendent relation to the *logos* it images—whose meaning can be encompassed by human reason. This abstract essence views existence as an unnecessary though desirable supplement. Severed from essence, existence is wrongly ascribed the capacity to produce meaning. Yet since it is the concrete singular that is created, both existence and essence are given, and this givenness can be perceived in each as well as in their asymmetrical relation. *Esse* and *essentia* are the two distinct, inseparable principles of a concrete singular being and cannot be rightly construed in abstraction from it. Though we will revisit the category of substance at a later point, our current task is to ponder the meaning of *esse* as gift. To enter into the mysterious perfection of all perfections, *esse*, we will turn to Aquinas's conception of *esse* and its deepening of the Aristotelian account of form. We will see first Aristotle's dealing with *esse* and then Thomas's rereading of it in light of creation *ex nihilo*.

For Aristotle, being (*to on*), simply speaking, is an equivocal *pros hen* whose primary instance is form (*morphe, eidos*, or *idea*).[62] What it means for something to be itself can be expressed as accidental being, as truth, as the categories, and as being-potential and being-at-work (*energeia*).[63] It is the same being that can be expressed in this fourfold manner. As is known, the sense that accounts for the others is *ousia* (Entity).[64] *Ousia*, according to

---

62. "Being is meant in more than one way, but pointing toward one (*pros hen*) meaning and some one nature rather than ambiguously" (Aristotle, *Metaph.* 4.1003a32 passim). For Aristotle, things are equivocal that have one name in common, but different definitions as denoted by the different name in each case (Aristotle, *Cat.* 1a1–6). The term "equivocity" in the first section referred mainly to its logical connotation—which better respects Derrida's thought and its absence of reference to concrete phenomena. For Aristotle, as Owens explains, terms refer to things, not to concepts. The equivocal is a property of language only because it is a property of the thing itself. Language, in Aristotle, respects being's proper ontology: things can be said in many ways. Rather than seeking clear and distinct Cartesian precision, one needs to learn beings' capacity to mean/be different things. Owens's study, to which we are much indebted, helps readers to grasp Aristotle on his own terms—inasmuch as that is possible—and corrects anachronistic or idealistic readings of Aristotle (Owens, *Doctrine of Being*, 107–31).

63. Aristotle, *Metaph.* 6.1026a33–1026b2.

64. The common translation of *ousia* is "essence" or "substance." Augustine reserves *essentia* for God's being to preempt the possibility of thinking that accidents could be added to him. He reserves *substantia* for created beings. With Boethius's work, "substance" becomes the common translation of *ousia*. Yet essence tends to be understood

Aristotle, is either matter, form, or the composite of matter and form. Form is the most proper instance of Entity, and its most fundamental meaning is reducible to act (*energeia, entelecheia*), a principle that can be pointed at but not defined in terms of anything more comprehensive.[65]

To grasp the ontological depth of gift, it suffices for our purposes to indicate how the circularity of form and act clarifies the issue of the concrete singular's existence. For Aristotle, form accounts for both the cause of a singular being (it is thus: *to ti en einai*—what-was-being) and for its intelligibility (*logos*).[66] Form is that principle, internal to a thing, thanks to which a concrete singular is a whole and not merely a heap of characteristics. For Aristotle, unlike Plato, form is in a sense identical with the particular being and different from it, but only in thought.[67] Form is separate in notion (not abstracted) and exists as separate from matter only in human thinking. This is why, although form is the principle of the definition, it is not a universal. For Aristotle, form is thus the principle that accounts both for this singular being and for its universal meaning. It is a *this* (*tode ti*) without being singular. Form is a *this* that causes a particular being to be itself. To know the form therefore is to know both, for example, "this horse" and "horse." For Aristotle, as Owens clarifies, form is "prior to and act of both composite Entity and logical universal."[68]

Form is an active principle and not an archetype that is received by finite beings. It is act, that is, being-at-work-staying-itself (*entelecheia*).[69] The form of a horse does not simply account for its horse-ness; it is also what is responsible for its neighing, galloping, grazing, breeding, etc. This "being at work" (*energeia*) therefore has no end outside of itself. The purpose of act, in other words, is the enjoyment of being. Like seeing and contemplating, *entelecheia* rests in itself. This is primordially the case for the unmoved mover, which is self-thinking thought.[70] Of course, the actuality (*energeia*)

---

as opposed to existence, and substance as Locke's *substratum* that undergirds accidents. Neither of these terms respects what Aristotle had in mind when he coined the term *ousia*. For him essence and existence cannot be separated. To avoid these common misunderstandings, J. Sachs prefers to translate *ousia* as "thinghood," and Owens, perhaps with a more felicitous expression, as "Entity." We follow the latter translation here.

65. Aristotle, *Metaph.* 9.1048a25ff.
66. Aristotle, *Metaph.* 7.4–6, 17.
67. Aristotle, *Metaph.* 8.1042a28–31.
68. Owens, *Doctrine of Being*, 393.
69. Aristotle, *Metaph.* 9.1047a30. This is J. Sachs's translation of *entelecheia*.
70. "And the course of its life is of such a kind as the best we have for a short time. This is because it is always the same way (which for us is impossible), and because its being-at-work is also pleasure (which is what makes being awake, perceiving, and thinking the most pleasant things, while hopes and memories are pleasant on account

of concrete singular beings is always imperfect. A single instance (a horse) never embodies its entire pattern (horse-ness). This is why every sub-lunar being, for Aristotle, is constituted by these two principles: actuality and potency—which is the possibility for actuality to be present. The "material" can become a single being if it receives the form from an already actual being. Once it receives the form, potency, while limiting the act of one being, is also the ability, the capacity, to live up to the form. Inasmuch as a singular being continues being what it is, both act and potency, form and matter, remain present in the actual existing being. Potency thus indicates both the limiting of a form and the capacity to live up to it, without being able to identify itself fully with the form.[71]

The unmoved mover is ultimately what is responsible in Aristotle's understanding of form, whose primary instance is act. Self-thinking thought is the guarantor that there has always been and will always be form and order in the cosmos. Thus, to adopt this concept of form entails conceding the eternity of the world. Every being is necessary: the unmoved mover and the singular beings that imitate the unmoved mover precisely by having form and by being ordered.[72] This view of form and its relation with act prevents Aristotle from having to give an account of the existence of single beings. Aristotle's reflection is not open to the consideration of the first level of givenness of the concrete singular, that is, its existence as gift. In Aristotle's metaphysical view of the cosmos, there is no real distinction between *esse* and essence. Let us see why.

As his treatment of accidental beings shows, existence is not reducible to form and so it does not yield scientific knowledge, which is the goal of the collection of books grouped under the name *Metaphysics*.[73] Existence has

---

of this). And the thinking that is just thinking by itself is a thinking of what is best just as itself, and especially so with what is so most of all. But by partaking in what it thinks the intellect thinks itself, for it becomes what it thinks by touching and contemplating, so that the intellect and what it thinks are the same thing. . . . So if the divine being is always in this good condition that we are sometimes in, that is to be wondered at; and if it is in it to a greater degree than we are, that is to be wondered at still more. And that is the way it is" (Aristotle, *Metaph.* 12.1072b15–28).

71. For the different senses of potency, see Aristotle, *Metaph.* 12.1019a15ff.

72. Aristotle, *Metaph.* 12.1072b3–30. Self-thinking thought causes motions by being loved, hence it does not move. As the act of thinking, it is responsible for the unity of the cosmos.

73. Aristotle, *Metaph.* 7.1017a12–13. The question regarding how a form can be present in different individuals is Platonic, not Aristotelian. Aristotle does not begin with a one, e.g., the Good, that allows other finite beings to participate in its goodness. If this were the case, form would be passive, not active. But form, as mentioned, accounts for both the singular and the universal. Aristotle instead begins from the eternal coexistence of the unmoved mover and finite beings.

no place in contemplation, and therefore there is no need to account for it. It is true that some passages of the *Metaphysics* indicate the difference between what something is and its existence.[74] Nevertheless, when looked at in the presupposed, broader context of the *Posterior Analytics*, the inquiry regarding the facticity of a being ("if-it-is") does not demonstrate the "existence" of a particular essence.[75] "To ask whether there is an eclipse or not," Aristotle writes, "is . . . the same as asking whether there is an account (*logos*) for it, i.e., the moon is eclipsed; and if this condition actually exists, we assert that it also actually exists."[76] As Owens indicates, Aristotle deals with the universal and necessary connections between the elements that form part of the definition and not with the existence of a thing. If the connection is accidental, then we are to conclude that there is no fact (e.g., a centaur). In the case of an evident indemonstrable, one can ask what it is. If it is a fact but it is not evident or indemonstrable (as the case of the lunar eclipse observed from the earth rather than the moon), one can inquire further what it is. For this reason, Owens concludes that for Aristotle "the '*if-it-is*,' is a quasi-generic knowledge of the thing sufficient to establish it as a Being. The '*what-it-is*' is the specific knowledge obtained through the addition of the proper difference."[77] Thus, there is no need to account for existence, nor is this "lack" a deficiency. Perfection is contained within the limits of the singular, not the infinite. Aristotle does not seem to wonder before the miracle of being given; he rather admires the intrinsic, ever-lively necessity of the order of the world.

Aquinas, benefitting from the doctrine of creation *ex nihilo*, revisits the Aristotelian principles and argues that the fundamental difference

74. Aristotle, *Metaph.* 6.1025b16–18, 1.981a29, 7.1041a10–b5.
75. Aristotle, *An. post.* 2.89b23–94.
76. Aristotle, *An. post.* 2.93a31–35
77. Owens, *Doctrine of Being*, 288–93, at 292. Owens discusses the conclusions of Suzanne Mansion's *Le jugement d'existence chez Aristote* and, although he criticizes her methodology, indicates that her interpretation agrees with his. Mansion, Owens clarifies, only argues that "the 'existence' indicated in the *if-it-is*, though that of an individual, is understood in an abstract and undetermined state. . . . It is not something contingent to the essence (her book, 261)," (ibid., 262–65). He then quotes further from her book: "Aristote n'a pas songé à séparer la possibilité des essences de leur existence, parce qu'il ne possède pas une idée précise de la contingence métaphysique (273)," (ibid., 294). That Aristotle does not possess a precise idea of the metaphysical contingency of finite beings is further verified in several other instances of the *Metaphysics*: (1) form, as we saw, accounts both for universality and singularity; (2) Aristotle's efficient causality is explained as reducible to form, and it does not take into account existential act (*Metaph.* 8.1050a30–31, 9.1066a27–34); (3) nor when dealing with Entity as truth does there seem to be a grasp of the existential act (*Metaph.* 9.1051a34–b9). In light of all this, trying to find an *esse*/essence distinction in Aristotle seems anachronistic.

traversing every singular being is not so much between form and matter, or act and potency, but between what they are and their *esse*.[78] The difference between *esse* and the *Entity* of any singular being can help us to explore the first level of givenness: the meaning of the existing of beings as gift. Numerous authors have clarified that Aquinas does propose a real distinction between *esse* and essence in singular beings.[79] Benefitting from their work, it suffices to recall two arguments that illustrate the gift-ness of the "to be" of every singular being. The first clarifies that everything that "is in the genus of the substance is composite with real composition."[80] Whatever is a substance has an existence of its own. Yet there are many different members that belong to the same genus. The difference, then, indicates that in each existing being, its being (*esse*) and the thing itself must differ. Whereas in Aristotle form is responsible for both the essence and the singularity of a being, in Aquinas the "to be" of a thing no longer depends on the form—when the being is considered as a single, self-standing creature. Leaving aside other arguments that do not necessarily presuppose the proof of the existence of God, *ipsum esse subsistens*, if we turn to those that do, it becomes clear why there is, according to Aquinas, a real distinction between *esse* and essence in concrete singular beings.[81] Aquinas contends in one of the latter arguments that every being causes an effect that is proper to its essence and that the effect images the essence: fire, for example, communicates light and heat; the architect communicates the form of the house he has in himself to the heap of material that can receive this form. At the same time, they also communicate an effect that is not directly proper to their own essences since they all give this other effect: heat makes something *to be* hot, and the builder *gives being* to a house. The communication of *esse* can be explained only thanks to that being the immediate effect of whose essence is *esse* itself: God. It is only God who is the simple, self-subsisting being whose essence is

---

78. *Esse*, infinitive present of the verb "to be," functions both as noun and as verb. It is normally translated as "existence." Given the commonly assumed separation between essence and existence, to prevent false presuppositions I leave the Latin term untranslated.

79. Besides the works of Owens and Gilson already cited, see Wippel, *Metaphysical Thought*; Fabro, "Dall'essere di Aristotele"; Geiger, *La participation*.

80. Aquinas, *De ver.*, q. 27, a. 1, ad 8. This is the main text used by Gilson. For Wippel, this argument, taken in itself without the support of other arguments, does not suffice. See his *Metaphysical Thought*, 161. See also Aquinas, *ST*, I, q. 3, a. 5; *SCG* 1.25.3.

81. According to John Wippel's lucid explanation, other arguments include the controversial chapter 4 of Aquinas's *Ente et essentia*; the argument based on participation (*De ver.*, q. 21, a. 5); and those based on the limited character of individual beings, such as *I Sent.*, d. 8, q. 5, a. 1, *sed contra*.

his *esse*, whereas all the others are given to participate in *esse* and, thanks to this participation, can also communicate *esse*.[82]

The difference between *esse* and what a being is affects every created being, regardless of its being composed of matter and form or its being a spiritual being. Even in the latter, according to Aquinas, it is still possible to find the distinction between being (*esse*) and what is (*quod est*).[83] Finite beings, from the lowest to the highest, participate in *esse*. With this distinction, Aquinas separates the two main characteristics of form proposed by Aristotle. For Aquinas, form accounts for the intelligibility of a singular being and *esse* for its actuality. Form is no longer the highest principle of actuality. Form has to receive *esse* (act) in order to be the principle of being for the substance. "Nothing has actuality (*actualitatem*) if not inasmuch as it is: hence existence (*ipsum esse*) is what actuates all things, even their forms. Therefore it is not compared to other things as the receiver is to the received; but rather as the received to the receiver."[84] For Aquinas, Aristotle's account is accurate when form is regarded as belonging to intraworldly causes, but in itself it is not the ultimate source of *esse*; it rather receives *esse*. Form is responsible for *esse* at the level of substance, but it is able to give it because it has received it. Form, although it keeps the necessity of its *logos*, no longer entails the necessity of its own existing. Form, for Aquinas, is thus endowed with a certain potentiality that is not the potentiality of matter. To synthesize Gilson's account, when thinking of the relationship between *esse* and essence in that which is (*ens*), form is a potency that, without being matter, receives *esse*, which is an act that is not a form.[85]

Aquinas's profound and indispensable ontological account of the structure of the concrete singular arrives at the threshold of the perception of *esse*, the first act, in terms of gift. This does not mean to imply, of course, that he did not see or account for the positivity of being. Rather, the exploration of *esse* in terms of gift was not needed at a time such as his when being's positivity was commonly assumed, though explained in many different ways. More deeply, perhaps, Aquinas's dependence on Aristotelian

---

82. Aquinas, *De pot. Dei*, q. 7, a. 2; see also Aquinas, *ST*, I, q. 3, aa. 3–4; *I Sent.*, d. 8, q. 5, a. 1; *SCG* 2.52.7–8. It is important to note that Aquinas is saying that it is God's *esse* that is his essence, not the other way around.

83. Aquinas, *SCG* 2.52.1.

84. Aquinas, *ST*, I, q. 4, a. 1, ad 3. See also Aquinas, *De pot. Dei*, q. 3, a. 4, ad 7: "A form may be considered in two ways. First, in so far as it is in potentiality: and thus God cocreates it with matter, without any concurrent action of nature for the disposition of matter. Secondly, in so far as it is in act, and thus it is not created, but is educed by natural agency from the potentiality of matter: wherefore there is no need of dispositive action on the part of nature in order that a thing be created."

85. Gilson, *Être et l'essence*, 114–23.

metaphysics prevented further development of his own original metaphysical reflection. Even acknowledging the primacy of *esse* as gift, which creation *ex nihilo* discloses, Aquinas still interprets the priority of act in a too Aristotelian way. That is to say, although he does speak of a reception at the level of first act, he does not account this owing oneself to another, this being affected by another that the gift of *esse* reveals, as a perfection that also constitutes the nature of act.[86] Let us examine this a little more closely.

5. Open Principles

Creation *ex nihilo* shows the creature's absolute ontological dependence on the primordial giver. This dependence is reflected in the fact that even form receives *esse*. To speak of receiving *esse*, however, requires seeing how the priority of act, without denying its priority, includes within itself something like reception. In doing so, we do not lose sight of the miracle of being: not only does God posit a concrete singular being where before there was nothing; in this very act of communicating his *esse* to the singular, God enables the singular to participate in the gift of self. The creature's participation in the gift of self does not eclipse the priority of God's creative act. God does everything. He posits a whole, a concrete singular, and not a collection of random pieces that come together at a certain point. The wholeness of the creature is reflected in the fact that the giving of the gift coincides with the positing of the receiver, the concrete singular being. The very wholeness of the concrete singular being speaks of its coming to be from another all at once. The singular participates in its being given precisely within its prior coming from God (*esse ab*) and its depending completely on him. At the same time, because God truly gives, the communication of his *esse* is coincident with the singular's participation in its being given and in giving, the first form of which is reception of the gift. Creation allows a sharing in the creator's act of sharing, yet does so without this sharing making the created *esse* identical with the divine *esse*.

What does this participation in giving mean at the level of the first act? We know that giving requires the receiver's reception of the gift in order for the gift to be complete. To participate in giving, before it is "doing" something for others or for oneself, is to receive the gift of oneself. We also know that the giver always runs a risk in giving: the receiver could reject the original gift. Whereas at the level of the second act this rejection could take the

---

86. This is true of his metaphysics, but not of his Trinitarian theology. What we indicate here is that Aquinas's metaphysics does not take advantage, for the notion of act, of what is clear in his elucidation of the triune God.

form of, for example, possessiveness, or hatred toward the giver, at the level of the first act, where the receiver is posited by the gift, the possibility of not receiving and hence of not reciprocating the gift still exists. What could it mean for a receiver (first act) to reject the gift? At this level, it is possible for not-being to penetrate the deepest structure of the concrete singular. What tradition calls ontological evil, the imperfection of the creature, can illuminate the mystery of the singular's involvement in the reception of its own gift of being at the level of the first act. Since there is no concrete singular before the communication of being, no whole before it is totally given to itself, the acceptance of the gift takes place with the very reception of it. Creation *ex nihilo* does not allow us here to think of a before and an after. There is no such thing as a created *esse* that, so to speak, "has the time" to think of what to do with itself. At the same time we cannot project a human freedom at the level of the first act and imagine that this purported independent being decides to receive itself. K. L. Schmitz, a student of Gilson, concurs here with Ulrich, Balthasar, Schindler, and others, when he states that "we must understand the acceptance as expressed by its subsistent self-reference (*per se*) and within its primordial ordination towards the Source of the being communicated to it without which there would be no self (*autos*), so that its original reception is communicated to it in its very institution."[87] To speak spatially where there is no body, at the level of the first act, inasmuch as it is allowed to participate in its own gift-ness, we can acknowledge a fourfold dimensionality of *esse*: (1) its having been given to itself (*esse ab*); (2) its own self-affirmation, its being-itself (*esse per se*); (3) its orientation to the source (*esse ad*); and (4) its being received not just by one concrete singular but by a community of *esse* with which every concrete singular is in relation. Act is therefore a complete principle that, as Schmitz suggests, is also open, though not in the Derridean sense.[88]

Here an aspect of the foregoing anthropological analysis of gift serves to dissipate a recurring objection. Gift indicates both a reception and an action. In giving, we mentioned, one receives, and in receiving one gives. This non-unilateral understanding of gift forestalls identifying giving with action and receiving with passion. Receiving is not passivity; it is a form of giving. In this regard, Schmitz also says that "there is more than passivity in reception: there is also self-possession and orientation towards the good. *Esse* as the supposit of the secondary activity already possesses the integral mode of potency and act in the form of an integral ordination towards (*esse-ad*)."[89] If

---

87. Schmitz, *TB*, 120–28; Schmitz, "Created Receptivity," 364ff.
88. Schmitz, *TB*, 127–29. He refers to Aquinas, *ST*, I, q. 75, a. 2, ad 1.
89. Schmitz, *TB*, 365.

II. CONCRETE SINGULARITY   79

the communication of being is an expression of love, as we saw in the previous section, and if this communication is desired, then this perfection also regards the reception of the gift. If, contrary to the Greeks, desired giving is a perfection of love (*agape*), then receiving is no less a perfection of love. Reception understood in terms of passivity and imperfection is contrary to the revealed data that the one who gives, who is pure act, is a Father begetting the Son and, with and through the Son, spirating the Holy Spirit. Act is received act, first and foremost, as we shall see later, in the triune God, and, analogically speaking, by participation also in the concrete singular.

It is important to realize further that the first act as a received act does not mean either that everything is already decided at the ontological level, reducing human freedom to the simple iteration of this original reception or, more starkly, that action is irrelevant. Rather, the newness that takes place in human action is genuine because the wholeness of the concrete singular being represents an inexhaustible newness in its very being. The ontological newness is its being created from nothingness; yet its irreducibility to the source (its being given to itself) is not fully explained by reference to a divine generous act. For the concrete singular to be itself irreducible (*per se*), it also needs to participate in the giving. Otherwise, how could we defend the assertion that the concrete singular is not a tool required by the divine for some inscrutable purpose? Furthermore, if the concrete singular were not "original," that is to say, if it were not somehow at its proper level a giver in receiving the gift of its own *esse*, could there actually be a human action in which God is recognized as all in all?

To indicate more fully what we mean by "received act," let us unfold further, with the help of Aquinas, what *esse* means and what kind of unity it maintains with the essence of the singular.[90] *Esse*, Aquinas explains, is neither a genus nor a difference; it is not part of the essence but is really distinct from it. If *esse* is not an essence, one could claim that *esse* would have to be an accident of the essence. For Aquinas, however, *esse* is neither an *ens*, a subject of being, nor an accident, though it can be described as an accident.[91] *Esse* is participated in by the singular being as something that

---

90. For the sake of clarifying the gift-ness of the concrete singular, we will continue to refer to *esse commune* and not to *ens commune*. *Esse commune* as participated in by singulars is called by Aquinas *ens commune*. *Ens commune* is the proper object of metaphysics. For Aquinas, *esse commune* is being considered universally, in its fullness and not yet received by a participant. Wippel, *Metaphysical Thought*, 123.

91. Referring to Aquinas's *Quodlibet* 12, q. 4, a. 1 and *In Metaph.*, 4, lect. 2, no. 558, Wippel explains: "Given this, one must distinguish the question *an est* ('Is it?') from the question *quid est* ('What is it?'). In fact, Thomas even goes so far here as to say that since anything not included within the essence of a thing may be described as an accident, the *esse* which answers to the question *an est* is an accident. He does not mean by this

is not included in the essence of the participant. For lack of a better word, Aquinas refers to *esse* with the term *aliud*, but it does not have a *quidditative* content and hence *esse* cannot be defined. It could seem that *esse*, not being a some-thing, is no-thing. Did not Kant's critique of the ontological argument indicate that existence is indifferent to both the reality of a concept and our understanding of it? Although there is a sense in which it could be stated that *esse* is not (since it does not subsist in itself), for Aquinas *esse* is not a mere *ens rationis*. It has, in a certain respect, priority over essence. Essence, in fact, relates to *esse* as potency to act.[92] "*Esse*," Aquinas states in wonder, "is the most perfect, the actuality of every act and the perfection of all perfections."[93] Only if this depth of *esse* is acknowledged does it become possible to indicate in what sense it does not exist.

As the actuality of every act, *esse* is *common* to all finite beings, although it cannot be predicated univocally since "received acts are diverse."[94] This entails two crucial points: first, as "the first of created things" and being present in all existing beings, *esse* has a quasi-unity of its own.[95] Whatever is created *is* and, as we saw earlier, in causing their proper effects, finite beings also give *esse*. If *esse* did not have a quasi-unity, it would lose its priority and become an accident of essence. Furthermore, it would be difficult to say why, contrary to what we learn from originary experience, essence is not the cause of its being if it were true that *esse* proceeded from it. Second, and here we see the priority of essence over *esse*, this *quasi*-unity does not exist independently, floating, so to speak, between God and beings, as the broken mast of a ship floats free on the surface of the ocean. If it were a unity in its own right, *esse* would be a subject of being and not being itself. And since, in itself, *esse* is not limited nor can limit itself, if it were a proper unity, *esse commune* would be nothing but *ipsum esse subsistens*.[96] The gift of being is a real, albeit limited, participation in the divine *esse*.

Aquinas explains that finite beings participate in the divine *ipsum esse subsistens* but not by means of formal causality. God is not the *esse* whereby each singular being exists.[97] Whereas God's *esse* is being in such a way that nothing can be added, *esse commune* for Aquinas is something

that *esse* (the act of being) is a predicamental accident, but only that it is not part of the essence of any creature" (Wippel, *Metaphysical Thought*, 106).

92. See, e.g., Aquinas, *SCG* 2.53.
93. Aquinas, *De pot. Dei*, q. 7, a. 2, ad 9.
94. Aquinas, *ST*, I, q. 75, a. 5, ad 1.
95. Aquinas, *De causis* 4. See also, e.g., Aquinas, *SCG* 2.52.
96. Aquinas, *SCG* 1.43; *ST*, I, q. 7, a. 1; *I Sent.*, d. 43, q. 41, a. 1; *SCG* 2.52; *De pot. Dei*, q. 7, a. 2, ad 9.
97. Aquinas, *SCG* 1.26.

II. CONCRETE SINGULARITY   81

to which nothing is added but to which something could be added.[98] The *nihil* of creation, as we saw, prevents us both from interpreting God's creative donation in pantheistic terms and from adopting an epistemology that would grant direct contemplation of the divine essence. God is only known through the sign (presence-gift). *Esse commune* therefore cannot be confused with the divine *esse*. Rather, *esse commune* is the divine being as participated in by creatures—and so distinct from them—by means of *exemplar* causality.[99] Within a *maior dissimilitudo*, finite beings resemble God's being. For Aquinas, concrete singular being images God's being in its being (*esse, unum*), essence (*logos*), and dynamic order (*amor*) towards God the source.[100] With a unique insight, Aquinas clarifies the similarity and difference between God's *esse* and created *esse* in these terms: whereas God is *ipsum esse subsistens*, *esse commune* signifies "something complete and simple but not subsistent."[101] *Esse*, therefore, can only be predicated analogically from God and singular beings.[102]

The foregoing reflection on the asymmetrical reciprocity of *esse* and essence in Aquinas helps us to think afresh the *unity* proper to the concrete singular in terms of gift and to deepen the meaning of the internality of receptivity in act.[103] The union of *esse* and essence is a mystery of gift precisely because they are given to each other and subsist in the reciprocal gift to each other. In the creative act, God co-creates *esse* and essence in giving one to the other so that the singular being may be.[104] While remaining distinct from and ordered to each other, they are equally responsible for the being of the singular. As Aquinas says, since it does not limit itself, *esse commune* exists only as limited by essences. To "limit," however, does not mean that essence has the capacity to possess the perfection of *esse* in its fullness. As we mentioned, the fact that *esse* remains a quasi-unity does

98. Aquinas, *De pot. Dei*, q. 7, a. 2, ad 6; *ST*, I, q. 3, a. 4, ad 1.

99. Aquinas, *In librum beati Dionysii De divinis nominibus expositio*, c. 5, l. 2, 658–60.

100. Aquinas locates here the *trace* of the Trinity in every being. Because every creature subsists in its own being (*esse*), the creature shows (*demonstrat*) the Person of the Father; since it has a form and species, it represents the Son; as it has a relation of order towards God, it represents the Holy Spirit (*ST*, I, q. 45, a. 7). See also Aquinas, *ST*, I, q. 104, a. 1; *SCG* 2.54. Augustine, says Aquinas in the same question, sees unity (*unum aliquid est*) as representing the Father.

101. Aquinas, *De pot. Dei*, q. 1, a. 1.

102. Aquinas, *ST*, I, q. 75, a. 5, ad 1.

103. For the following account of being in terms of gift, I am indebted to the works of Giussani, Balthasar, and, among others, Bruaire, *EE*; Ulrich, *Homo abyssus*; Walker, "Personal Singularity."

104. Aquinas, *De pot. Dei*, q. 3, a. 5, ad 2.

not mean that essence comes from it or that *esse* is the ultimate subject of being. At the same time, just as *esse* does not exist without essence, so essence cannot be itself without *esse*. Therefore, neither is separated from the other or comes from the other: *esse* is not a proper accident of essence, nor is essence produced by *esse*. Thus, they do not enjoy independent existences, and they come together to form a specific finite being.[105] Since *esse* is *given* to essence as act to potency, the *compositum* is not a union *per accidens* (like a horse and its rider) but a substantial one. They are both principles of the one being. Wippel accurately puts it as follows: while *esse* "actualizes . . . essence . . . , simultaneously the essence principle receives and limits the act of being. . . . Each enjoys its appropriate priority in the order of nature . . . with respect to its particular ontological function within a given entity."[106] The reciprocity of *esse* and essence does not eliminate the proper priorities of each principle. The difference and the order remain and are what make an inexhaustible whole.

If with Aristotle we acknowledge that the "to be" of a singular being involves a limited participation in act (being-at-work-staying-itself) and, with Aquinas, that form receives *esse* while at the same time essence limits *esse*, then the "to be" of every being is this ongoing communication of *esse* that makes an essence be while, at the same time, *esse* is received by the essence that *esse* causes to be. The unity of essence and *esse* that constitutes every created being is a gift given to the concrete singular that remains in being inasmuch as it ontologically participates in its own being given—this is also why the "singular" gift is perceived in its wholeness only when its relation with God is affirmed. Here we can return to the understanding of act as a complete and open principle. *Esse* and essence, Schmitz clarifies, are "radically open to each other in the constitution of a *single* entity. They do not achieve this unity by themselves. If God's creative act is left out of the picture, it is impossible to explain how a non-existent and merely possible essence can determine the creature's act of existence." Each principle is incomplete in itself. It needs the other to be in one concrete singular. Thus, Schmitz concludes, "Each principle is inherently implicated in the other through the causal activity of the First Cause, and by a subordination of the one (potency) to the other (act) rather than by a reciprocity of two complete principles."[107]

---

105. D. L. Schindler, *Ordering Love*, 350–82.

106. Wippel, *Metaphysical Thought*, 129–30. My presentation of Aquinas is indebted to the work of Wippel and Owens.

107. Schmitz, *TB*, 129.

II. CONCRETE SINGULARITY 83

Interpreting the singular's unity in terms of gift as the relation between *esse* and essence requires acknowledging a certain dependency of act on potency. Is it not the case that this relative "dependency" of act on potency, or, in the earlier expression, the "received act," eliminates the principle of act? Do the mutual dependence of *esse* and *essentia* and their asymmetrical reciprocity—that *esse* is limited by essence, and so receives it in itself, and that essence is actualized by *esse* while limiting it—jeopardize act altogether? Hegel, in fact, contended that what we here consider an asymmetrical reciprocity between *esse* and essence, rather than expressing the gift-ness of the concrete singular being, is merely an expression of the law of contradiction. Contradiction, according to Hegel, is abhorred by common thinking. It thus tends to disguise contradiction under "the process of relating and comparing."[108] Yet Hegel claims that everything is "inherently contradictory." Not by chance, contradiction plays a pivotal role in Hegel's system: if in the first part of his *Science of Logic*, the logic of being, contradiction is presented as infinity, in the second, the logic of essence, it is contradiction that illumines the livingness of anything, and hence of the spirit as such.[109] The universal, "abstract self-identity is not as yet a livingness" because life is the "power to hold and endure the contradiction within it."[110] Without contradiction there is no movement, only dead identity. "Only when the manifold terms have been driven to the point of contradiction do they become active and lively towards one another, receiving in contradiction *the negativity* which is the indwelling pulsation of self-movement and spontaneous activity."[111] To the terms Hegel uses (e.g., infinite-finite, father-son) we could add act-potency, *esse*-essence. The gift-ness of the concrete singular and its sheer dynamic, in his view, would not be anything but the denial of one by the other. Contradiction, Hegel contends, does not indicate imperfection or a defect to be eliminated. On the contrary, it is that which permits absolute activity. While it is undoubtedly fundamental that, as Hegel indicates, in a certain sense a relation always goes both ways—and hence there has to be what we call asymmetrical reciprocity—what is contrary to our view is that the unity's liveliness of the singular is owed not to the singular's nature as gift but to the power of the negative. Hegel claims that every thing and notion "is essentially a unity of distinguished and distinguishable moments, which, by virtue of the *determinate, essential difference*, pass over into con-

---

108. Hegel, WL, 439. English translation in Hegel, *Science of Logic*. See also WL, 375–77, 385.
109. Hegel, WL, 137–57.
110. Ibid., 440.
111. Ibid., 442.

tradictory moments."¹¹² The resolution draws the negated moments into a new sphere in such a way that the spirit reaches its fullness. On this path to its own completeness, one discovers that "the truth is that the absolute is, because the finite is the inherently self-contradictory opposition, because it is *not*."¹¹³

Hegel indeed ponders deeply the "noughting" that creation *ex nihilo* indicates. Nevertheless, by making negativity the pulsating center of the movement of the absolute spirit, as the theological a priori of his philosophy requires, he seems to fall into the unilateral thought he so strenuously criticizes. In Hegel, the movement of the absolute spirit is simply *erotic* and not *agapic*. That is to say, absolute spirit, beginning with the emptiness that contains the promise of a fulfillment, posits from itself the difference that is then absorbed by the unity of the absolute Idea. From the beginning, all the way to the Cross, and back to the absolute spirit by means of the spirit within the absolute spirit, absolute spirit does not know an *agapic* love, that is, the affirmation of the other's irreducibility. Contrary to Hegel, we can say that the gift of the singular being, its very identity, is perceived in its wholeness when the difference that traverses every being—and which allows us to say that, before God, creatures are indeed nothing—is the expression of a fullness that does not need another to be itself. For Hegel, instead, difference is the progressive and necessary fulfillment of an empty beginning. The fullness of the creative origin, as we see it, since it is the union of *eros* and *agape*, can and does decide against existing for itself alone. Difference—in the singular beings and between them and God—should thus be thought of as the gift's availability to receive and to give. This availability is a permanent dimension of act.¹¹⁴

If our understanding of gift is correct, we can note with F. Ulrich that the difference the gift of being establishes between God and the world does not reside so much in the difference between divine "*esse*" and *esse commune*, for the latter also remains simple and complete, but rather, as Aquinas says, in the "non-subsistent" character of *esse commune*. What this adjective reveals of the dual unity of the created singular (*esse*-essence) is precisely its constitutive relation with the primordial giver. Non-subsistency points to

---

112. Ibid.

113. Ibid., 443.

114. The circularity of act and potency at the created level expresses ultimately divine actuality. Undoubtedly, there is no potency in God. If that were the case, God could not claim responsibility for the world as is. With this, we do not mean to say that Aquinas and Aristotle—who would agree that, at the created level, act's relative dependency on potency is required to account for the difference between God and the world—are then rightly characterized by Hegel's law of contradiction.

the mysterious, ineffable wonder of being given to be, of depending on and belonging to the source. The positive understanding of the difference between God and the cosmos, which does not eliminate the difference or read it as contradiction, depends on the underlying idea one has of God, man, and the relationship between them. If absolute act is conceived according to the ideal that is perfect, self-contained, self-thinking thought, potency will always remain a deficiency, and the human being will always be trapped in the attempt to imitate an imaginary, self-subsistent God. If, instead, the one God is, as we saw, the richer unity (*koinonia*) of *eros* and *agape*, capable of creating another who is different from itself, then potency, rather than "something" left behind once *esse* is given and potency actualized, becomes the singular's ongoing availability to be confirmed in being.

6. The Singular's Perseity

The previous sections attempted to show how the category of gift can explain the dual unity of *esse* and essence in the concrete singular, while it also reveals the asymmetrical reciprocity between the two poles, thereby offering an account of both the contingency and the necessity proper to each created being. We need now to ponder how the perseity (*esse per se*, *ousia*) of the concrete singular can be considered in terms of gift. This reflection on substance and its relationship to the other categories that intrinsically inhere in it (traditionally called quantity, quality, relation) intends to show that the singular is both completely given to itself (*esse ab*) and at the same time, receiving itself, is dynamically oriented to (*esse ad*) the paternal origin.

Bearing in mind the ontological distinction required by creation *ex nihilo*, Aquinas rereads Aristotle's characterization of substance, "to be by nature self-subsistent (*kath'auto pephukos*)," as "that to whose quiddity it belongs not to exist in another."[115] With this distinction, Aquinas is not rejecting the conception of substance as "to be in itself." He is rather indicating that a created singular stands *in itself (per se, kath'auto*) not so much because it is the source of its own existence—this would be the case if *esse* were an accident of essence—but because it is given to it to be. Thus, for Aquinas, the definition of substance must include the essence (*quiddity*) and not only *esse* as in Aristotle (to be by nature self-subsistent).

---

115. Aristotle, *Metaph.* 7.1028a20–29; Aquinas, *I Sent.*, d. 8, q. 4, a. 2. See for example: "substantiae nomen non significat hoc solum quod est per se esse: quia hoc solum quod est esse, non potest per se esse genus, ut ostensum est (in c). Sed significat essentiam cui competit sic esse, idest per se esse: quod tamen esse non est ipsa eius essentia" (Aquinas, *ST*, I, q. 3, a. 5, ad 1).

Considering substance, that to whose quiddity it is given not to be in another, from the point of view of the singular's gift-ness, we could say that the mystery of being's singularity requires a perseity that is both absolute and relative. It is "absolute" because otherwise it would not be an actual, existing singular; it would not be a self, but only an appendage of the divine *esse*. As absolutely given to itself ("it belongs"), the singular-gift is *other* than its source; it has the capacity to be in itself and to be what it is for as long as it is.[116] In light of this we can also say that, as Aristotle explains, besides being the principle of intelligibility, a substance has no contraries.[117] In our understanding of being as gift, this means that a substance is either given or it is not at all. To say, in fact, that there is no contrary to "man" means that man either is or is not at all. Furthermore, if the singular gift were to admit variations or degrees, the gift would not be complete; it would be undetermined.[118] Aristotle, as is known, also indicates that the substance is itself because, while remaining itself, it is intrinsically open to receiving contrary qualities without itself changing.[119] The gift of the substance is also "relative": it possesses itself inasmuch as it has received itself. It finds itself possessing itself (*per se*), so to speak, as having received itself, and it continues to receive itself. Perseity has a foreign origin.

The relative dimension of the gift clarifies two implications of the substance's capacity to receive contrary qualities. First, the singular substance is originally open to receiving other qualities and other beings because it has received itself from the transcendent source. This is intended ontologically and not simply chronologically; that is, it is not that the substance exists first in itself, independently from any quality that it might receive at a second moment. The "openness," as well, is not merely epistemological, as though gift-ness were simply a condition of possibility for change. The fact that to be given to oneself coincides with having received oneself and being oriented towards the source means that the substance is always already receiving contrary qualities. The positivistic account of the singular in terms of data, or the technological account of it as heaps of material at our disposal, account for change, if at all, ultimately in terms of necessity or self-preservation. Both miss, however, the wonder of the enjoyment of being that change represents.[120] What the substance receives, in our view, is

---

116. Aristotle, *Cat.* 1a24.

117. Ibid., 3b25.

118. Ibid., 3b34–35.

119. Ibid., 4a10, 5b16–19. "One and the same individual at one time is white, warm or good, at another time black, cold or bad." Aristotle considered this receptive capacity to be the main characteristic and the one that enabled him to account for change.

120. As we mentioned earlier, if there were no distinction in God, it would not be

not simply, for example, a new temperature or a different color, but through them a participation in the infinite variety of being. The reception of contrary qualities is an openness that the different ways of knowing (sensible, intellectual), for example, are able to express. One is given to receive another and to grow in being. The liveliness borne by natural change expresses the dynamic and inexhaustible character of the gift of being. Yet to be part of nature does not mean that openness to and actual reception of otherness (acts, forms, and other beings) is automatic or mechanical. To be given to be also means that one is *given* to see, know, and tend to the good at every moment. If we look at the reception and intrinsic openness of the singular's perseity from the point of view of the particularity of the human being—the recapitulation in himself of the world while transcending it—the depths of this reception and openness become clearer. Just as, for example, the sun's light at dawn permits a rediscovery of the infinite richness of each singular being and its unity with the whole, so the four seasons are not given in order to be merely a cyclical reiteration, but rather as the reminder that the singularity of being is always offered the possibility to begin again. Both the beginning of a new day and the changing of seasons unfold the mystery of being given to be and of having one's self be made anew by receiving another. Nature expresses the novelty of the gift as the necessity of beginning again in order for the gift to be what it is. Novelty, in this regard, is not simply the coming to be of what did not exist before. Novelty means to be the same, anew. This wonder is possible only because the giving and receiving of being is never the reiteration of the same but rather a mediated relation with the ultimate source. "Necessity" does not bring in a mechanical inevitability but rather serves to highlight the priority of the giver in the gift. This priority of the giver in the gift makes novelty possible because the original giver always gives the possibility of returning to him, the source, and so to be one's self anew.[121]

Second, the openness is not a free decision to come forth from an initial state of purity. On the contrary, the singular is approached without its permission. As Aquinas says, following Aristotle, accidents are affections of the substance, without some of which the substance could not be itself.[122]

---

possible to account ultimately for why openness to receiving others is constitutive of substance.

121. As we mentioned earlier, substantial change, called death for higher beings, does not represent the denial of "growth" but, in its positive meaning, the totality of the gift. We shall return to this when we take up the subsistence of the singular.

122. Since, unlike creatures, God's *esse* is his essence, Aquinas's rich and complex understanding of the relationship between substance and accidents is always careful to show the distinction between the creator and his creatures. In this same concern, the

This relativity of the substance, rather than portraying a weakness, suggests receiving to be a continuous enrichment. What is received does not undo the perseity of the singular; it rather makes it be. Created substances are both themselves (absolute) and also relative to another: to God, *ipsum esse subsistens*, in the first place, and, because of this original reception from God and openness to him, to others. The gift-ness of the substance indicates the peculiar unity and distinction of an "absolute" being given to itself while being "relative" to others without collapsing the distinctions, that is, without making the affections of the substances secondary to the latter or losing substance to the multiplicity of the affections given to it. Since the relegation of substance to the category of relation is perhaps the most common reduction in this area, we need to clarify the nature of that reduction and the reasons why gift preserves substance's self-standingness without letting go of the constitutive relation to God and the other.

Among modern thinkers, Hegel is the keenest in presenting the deficiencies of understanding substance in terms of relation. We need not rehearse here the long historical process of the treatise on substance from Aristotle to Hegel. It suffices to recall two crucial points. First, by the time Hegel approached the philosophical arena, substance had been reduced to its passive meaning, that is to say, to a principle of unity that allows the identity of a being to weather non-essential changes successfully. In this view, the Aristotelian *ousia* is interpreted simply as *hupokeimenon*, the underlying thing.[123] Substance was no longer seen as the principle of intelligibility and that which accounts for the singular's being-at-work-staying-itself (*entelecheia*). Second, substance was subsumed under a category of relation

---

intellective and volitional faculties are seen as accidents. This distinction of substance and its corresponding definition of accidents as "that to which it belongs to be in something else" (Aquinas, *IV Sent.*, d. 12, q. 1, a. 1, ql. 1, ad. 2) are also crucial for the characterization of the divine persons as subsisting relations and the dependence of the world on God in terms of relation. Furthermore, this distinction enables Aquinas to elucidate the reasonableness of the eucharistic transubstantiation. For Aquinas, accidents are to substance what act is to potency. Aquinas, *De pot. Dei*, q. 7, a. 4; *ST*, I, q. 3, a. 6; *ST*, I, q. 77, a. 1. Although it could strike modern ears as nonsensical, Thomas indicates that grace and charity are accidents. This helps us to see that, for him, accidents do not represent the "least" and substance the "more" on the scale of being. In a sense, accidents bring the substance to perfection of expression either naturally (as when he claims that gender is an accident of the individual) or supernaturally (as it is with grace). The relation between substance and accidents is complex in Aquinas. Substance is material cause (it *receives* the accidents as act), final cause (it is the *end* of all the accidents), and, on a few other occasions, the active principle: accidents flow from it—although he does not specify what he means. See Wippel, *Metaphysical Thought*, 197–294.

123. For Aristotle, see, e.g., *Metaph.* 1029a20–28.

that was no longer understood as the orientation of one thing towards another but rather as something deduced from human knowledge.[124]

As Hegel saw it, in its inseparable relation with accidents, substance was the perplexing combination of determinacy and indeterminacy, of completeness and a perennial need to be fully determined by others.[125] According to this view, the substance-*substratum* (*hupokeimenon*) would be characterized by what it is not: the substratum is that which is not accidental; it is not its qualities. Negatively understood, for Hegel, the *substratum* is unable to account for those qualities that are perceived as necessary for the substance "to be itself." As Rotenstreich acutely remarks, for Hegel this way of conceiving the necessary link between the *substratum* and its qualities unfortunately lacks necessity.[126] Consequently, for Hegel, substance is not able to account for the unity of the singular (as Aristotle thought it did) precisely because unity, which for Hegel ultimately means identity, is possible only if the relation between terms is necessary. For this reason, Hegel contends for the need to dispense with representational thinking of the correlation between substratum and attributes and to acknowledge that accidents are "interior" to the substance. Rather than as a fixed, neutral, unchangeable center, for Hegel substance needs to be seen in terms of self-relation, that is, of a living, self-reflecting totality. For Hegel, substance is too fragile to bear the desired unity. Substance is indeed "the final unity of essence and being. . . . Substance, as this unity of being and reflection, is essentially the reflective movement (*Scheinen*) and positedness of itself."[127] For Hegel, substance properly understood is "being" insofar as it exists in and through itself and therefore includes all differences within itself. Nevertheless, since for Hegel substance is still too burdened by its necessary dialectic relation to its counterpart (accidents), it cannot be responsible for the total self-identification and *absolute* integration that characterizes absolute spirit. Hence, substance necessarily leads to its sublation in the Subject.

Hegel's reflection does attempt to include in ontology the role of subjective consciousness—a laudable effort—and views substance within the effort to understand unity. The point is indeed to overcome unilateral accounts of substance and to maintain the inner relation of accidents and substance. Unity, except in God, is always a complex unity. Yet an impoverished perception of form—deprived of its causal capacity and denied as a unifying

---

124. Aristotle, *Cat.* 6a35; Aristotle, *Metaph.* 1020b26–1021b11. See Kant, *Critique of Pure Reason*, A70/B95, A80/B106 for the deduction of the categories and A82/B224 for his account of substance in terms of relation of inherence.

125. Hegel, WL, 541–53.

126. Rotenstreich, *Substance to Subject*, 8.

127. Hegel, WL, 555.

principle—along with a dialectics of negativity and its logic of contradiction lead Hegel to give too little weight, if any, to the created *esse*. Substance, for Hegel, is insurmountably related to accidents: they bring determination to an undefined, empty center precisely because, for Hegel, being is an empty concept that must deny itself to affirm itself. His failure to begin with the concrete singular—despite his claims to the contrary—prevents him from seeing that the singular is totally given to itself and that the "promise" of being with which the *Science of Logic* begins is the enduring of the communion in which the singular already inchoately participates. As we saw, *esse*'s negativity—to give itself to what it is not and the "noughting" that remains present in the finite—is made possible by a self-subsistent *esse* that is the perfection of all perfections. Bereft of created *esse*, the category of relation will do to substance what Chronos did to his children, or, less tragically, the category of relation will remain the eternal opposite of an undetermined center—in which case Hegel's critique would find no adequate response. The gift of the created singular, instead, conceives substantial unity, not as a totality that includes the differences within itself, but as an inexhaustible wholeness that is itself in letting be what is given.

To account for the singular's perseity as given to itself but relative to others requires rethinking the meaning of "*per*"-seity. To be for oneself, at this ontological level, means that the concrete singular is given to enjoy its own being. This delightful fruition proper to be-ing has its highest expression in human awareness and freedom (angels, being bodiless, do not have the same mediating role). Yet subhuman creatures too are for themselves; they also, so to speak, take delight in their own being by be-ing what they are (*entelecheia*). Since the concrete singular is given to itself, its perseity is not a self-enclosed reality; it is not complete in itself. Positively stated, being gift, the singular belongs to another. Its being-gift (in the active sense of gift) entails therefore a destination that is not simply coextensive with the created "itself." Precisely because it is created *ex nihilo*, the singular cannot adequately represent the whole. Therefore, that the gift is for itself—in the active sense of gift—indicates that the concrete singular is intended to become itself in its going forward towards its *telos*, which is also its own origin (*en-tele-cheia*). To become itself therefore is not the Hegelian movement from absolute indeterminacy (*Sein*), through essence (*Wesen*), to determinacy (*Idee, Geist*). Rather, as the reflection on originary experience illustrated, it is the becoming ever more aware of the inexhaustible gratuity and wholeness of singular beings in their ever-new relation to the source. The "becoming itself," no matter how it may set the existence of the singular at risk, takes place within the form of gift: that is to say, the *agapic-erotic* and *noetic* entrusting of oneself to others.

Being for oneself, in the active return of oneself to the ultimate source, indicates the type of subsistence proper to the substance. To speak of the singular's destiny, in fact, does bring up the issue of the role of the presence of its own destiny within every moment of the singular's existence. At the same time, it also raises the question regarding the historical end of the singular, its death. The historicity of being is neither its absolute self-constitution, as the existentialists claim, nor the preservation of an inner kernel in the midst of changes, as some essentialists or neoscholastics contend. Subsistence involves both aspects (historicity and permanence) *together,* and united, the two retrieve the meaning they lost when separated: the ongoing, limited confirmation of the gift in its advancing return to the source along with all that is. Within this view, death looks like the absolute end of the singular's existence if the present loses its sourcing origin (past), which, with the gift of the present, gives the promise of what is yet to be given (future). Authentic existence is not a Heideggerian being-thrown whose ultimate possibility is death. If the singular is given to itself and for itself *ex nihilo,* then it does not lie within itself either to set its own final limit or to claim to comprehend the mystery of death. Because the original *nihil* is *oukontic* and as such is the expression of an *agapic* and *erotic* love whose final form is *koinonia,* the "nihil" that lies ahead (biological death) can only be *meontic,* relative. Subsistence (*hupokeimenon*) is rooted in the gift's incapacity to be called back. As Claude Bruaire says, rather than grounding subsistence in a "theomorphic delirium" of thinking that the concrete singular does not owe its existence to anyone and hence believes its present to be eternal, temporal subsistence indicates that historical time, as we examined earlier, lives from and in eternity. The gift could not endure if it were not given to itself. At the same time, as Bruaire writes, "the substance's subsistence does not liberate from the anguish before death nor from the groundless suffering of the other's death."[128] The gift (both the receptive and active sense) reveals the distinction between the chronological end of existence and its *telos*. From the point of view of the substance, death is final and cannot claim otherwise. Yet, since the gift of the substance rests in an *oukontic* creation, one cannot claim its "finality" (death) to be its *telos*. The presence of eternity in the temporal gift leaves the issue dramatically open. Like its origin, the substance's *telos* must be given to it. Here the second level of the singular gift's perseity emerges: it is for itself inasmuch as it is for this *telos*.

The foregoing elucidation of the unity of the singular substance as being in-itself and for-itself (perseity) discloses another dimension that

---

128. Bruaire, *EE*, 69. The following reflections are in dialogue with Bruaire's ontodology. See López, *Spirit's Gift*.

surfaced earlier in our anthropological account: since the substance is not the origin of itself, nor does it become itself by itself, its singularity always includes the other. In other words, since the source is transcendent and immanent, singular beings, analogically to God, exist only within a communion of beings. Creation is one single act in which God gives being to the whole world and to each concrete singular the capacity to give being. The gift of *esse*, bestowed wholly by God, is received in the form of a universal community of concrete singulars that participate in the giving and the receiving of being. In this regard, the community of beings that God creates has priority (ontologically and logically speaking). If the world is given to itself by God, it is not the case that concrete singulars exist first independently and then come together in order to live more fully. They all receive *esse* through their different forms and, by receiving the same being, at a deep level they are one without confusion of identities. Perseity is also being-with others. Communing in *esse* allows each concrete singular to be since it thus enters the reality of giving and receiving within which it fulfills its own *telos*.

The primacy of the ontological relation (to God and, in light of this, to others) that appears here as a fundamental part of the perseity of the concrete singular would undercut the integrity of the substance only if by "integrity" we meant independence, however "created." This perception of autonomous perseity is still under the spell of Hegel's account of substance and its interior relations. A different way to approach the singular's constitutive relation to God and to others, a relation required by our perception of the singular's gift-ness, is, as Bruaire and Schmitz suggest, to retrieve the category of the spirit (which is not immediately the Latin *spiritus*—opposed to nature—at whose root is the Greek *eidos*, nor is it the German *Geist*). The category of spirit allows us to see both that real dependence on another, although constitutive of the self, does not undercut the perseity of the singular. Modernity's dualistic account of our encounter with truth in terms of objectivity and subjectivity has accustomed us to think of singularity as insularity and, consequently, of relations between "insular" beings as either intrinsic or extrinsic to the self. To comprehend the singular's perseity requires seeing its relation to what is not itself in terms of indwelling, as we have indicated thus far. To speak of relations of indwelling is to indicate primordially the way of relation proper to the spirit. Spiritual relations, such as God's relation to the world, and the knowing and loving proper to the human being, are, as Schmitz notes, non-transitive, non-invasive.[129] They enter to form part of another without effecting a substantial change in the concrete singular. The Father's creation of the world in the Son and perfec-

129. Schmitz, "Created Receptivity," 106.

tion of it in the Spirit are examples of an action that does not effect a change. The Father, in speaking the Word, pronounces the world and, with the Son and the Spirit, loves it into existence. Yet this creative donation that is not a change establishes an ontological, spiritual relationship with every concrete singular without which the singular could not exist. Concrete singulars are also familiar with an intransitive, reciprocal dependence, which, though imperfect, is also ontological. To take, for example, the masters we have been given throughout our lives: their communication of their worldview has deeply formed our own worldview and our very selves, and yet this dependence, rather than alienating us, has helped us see things for what they are. The same goes for those in whose love for us we dwell. The interiority of the singular, in this sense, is not that of containing objects that are extrinsic to it, like books stacked in a box. Its internality is inhabited by others with whom the singular is constitutively related. Interiority should not be pitched against an idea of exteriority that is foreign to it. Interiority has to do with a relation of indwelling: the giver in the gift/receiver and the latter in the former.

Here the objection could arise that this presentation of "spiritual relations" has left the ontological level behind and moved on to the vague seas of spirituality. This would be true if "spirit" referred simply to a disincarnate existence that was far removed from the world.[130] If, instead, as Bruaire suggests, we retrieve the Greek terms that are translated by "spirit," *pneuma* and *nous*, it becomes possible to see that ontology and "spirit" are of a piece. Just as *pneuma* refers to the inspiration and expiration of the spirit, *nous* describes the acquisition of knowledge, which is not exempt from the dual movement of reflection into and expansion outside itself in the actual expression (word). For Bruaire, the noetic concept of the spirit entails a fragile, but nonetheless real, equilibrium in which the two indispensable pneumatological instances counter-flow. Both *nous* and *pneuma* follow the same rhythm, one with regard to life, and the other with regard to the mind. This rhythm proper to the spirit—of systole and diastole, reflection and expression, gift of self and conversion to itself—is an ontological one: there is no being, Bruaire says, without its spirit because it is the spirit that provides the uniting reflection of the singular. Spirit is "being in its subsistence, in

130. Bruaire himself poignantly describes that "for our culture, 'spirit,' in fact, unless residually and laughably, is no longer used: one distinguishes the spirit from the letter, but 'meaning' or 'sense' are more accurate terms; one who knows 'how to use the words' in the salons is said to be 'a great spirit' . . . But the thing is clear: 'spirit' does not designate anything, nothing of whatever is, nothing real, objective, observable and verifiable. This is indeed modernity's obliged agreement: having become irretrievable (*introuvable*), vague and obsolete, the spirit does not have being" (Bruaire, "L'être de l'esprit," 34).

its defeat of the erasing of the phenomena, precisely because it includes the uniting power" that holds together the secret and the phenomenon.[131] The ontological movement of reception and return of the gift, of perseity and *adseity*, as it is expressed in the asymmetrical relation between *esse*/essence and substance/accidents, is the movement proper to the spirit. Therefore, the singular's perseity and its constitutive relation to God and others are "spiritual" in that they are part of the complete form of the gift-character of the unity of being—spirit, in fact, in the sense explained here, secures the gift-character of the unity of being without effecting either a substantial change or a dissemination of origins, as Derrida would contend.

We saw what it means for the substance, including the human being, to be itself (perseity) and to be open, that is, being for and with another in reaching towards its own *telos* (adseity) and hence becoming itself. Analogically to the human being, one can find a perseity and adseity in every concrete singular. Since it is only with the human being that nature becomes aware of itself and can bring itself to act, the "for itself" of the subhuman substance is of a different kind.[132] Subhuman beings are also themselves inasmuch as they are given to themselves. They are subjects of their own being and hence enjoy *being* at their own level. Within the communionality just indicated, finite, subhuman beings also need the human subject in order to become themselves, and they need this belonging to the human realm essentially.[133] Their arrival in the human being's interior space without permission—as the spontaneity of human knowledge constantly witnesses—is not simply a superfluous addition to *what* they are. G. Berkeley's idealistic remarks go too far in making the subject the measure of what the human being knows through his senses, but he rightly intuits that the completion of the subhuman takes place in the human.[134] In light of the foregoing we

---

131. Bruaire, *EE*. See López, *Spirit's Gift*, 101–6.

132. Yet this also means that, in a certain sense, anticipations at the subhuman level of what is reason and freedom in the human level have to be present. This also enables us to extend the use of "spirit" outlined here to the subhuman, although it is adequate only to the higher beings (man, angels, God). At the subhuman level, "interiority" suffices.

133. This, of course, requires that we do not see created beings as objects to be used by the human person for a specific purpose—be it knowing God or preserving a nation from starvation. Created, subhuman beings are more than *data* or energy, neutrally available at our disposal. This does not mean that the opposite extreme of the technocratic misuse of nature (as seen in many of the ecological movements) is without flaw. What is needed, rather, is an ecological perception that integrates creatureliness and hence secures the identity of the cosmos in its relation with the transcendent origin. See, e.g., John Paul II, *Evangelium vitae*, no. 83 (AAS 87 [1995], 495–96).

134. Berkeley, *Three Dialogues*.

could see that it is only in the human being that the cosmos is united to its ultimate source and therefore is able to be itself. Furthermore, as Balthasar states, the cosmos's relation to the human subject "is even more indispensable, because it offers the object the chance to complete itself in a superior world, which obviously constitutes its *raison d'être*."[135] While naïve realism is admirable in its defense of the integrity of the singular, it does tend to reduce the unity between the human being and the cosmos in favor of a feeble affirmation that the cosmos might be just as well without him. "Missing from this picture of the world," Balthasar writes, "is the mysterious way in which subject and object expand within each other, thus helping each other in a common discovery of truth. . . . Once we realize that the appearance, the object's emergence in the space made ready by the subject, is something original, primary, and indispensable for the object itself, the appearance takes on its full ontological weight."[136]

The opposite side of this relation also needs to be affirmed: the human being needs the unfolding of the singular beings that occurs in him in order to become himself. "The subject's subjectivity," Balthasar continues, "is not a finished product that is already always latently present and merely awaits the arrival of the object to come into appearance."[137] The becoming aware of himself, as we saw in the first chapter, is coincident with pronouncing to the cosmos the original ideal that the cosmos itself awakens in human consciousness from within—that is to say, through the encounter with the cosmos and history that always precedes and claims the human person.

The relation between subhuman and human beings indicates that the unity of the gift is greater than the gift itself. It is not the case, as Mauss reads it, for example, that the gift puts in place a logic of excessive abundance that ultimately aims at interrupting the giving, but, more mysteriously, it is the case that superabundance belongs to the logic of gift.[138] To be in another fulfills the gift without closing or dissolving it. This ontological dimension is reflected later at the epistemological and affective levels of the human being. The asymmetrical indwelling of singular gifts discloses the richness of what it means to be—where being is understood in terms of life—precisely in the apparent poverty of letting the other be in oneself and allowing one's own fullness to be reached through being in the other. The human singular's enjoyment of the richness of his own being requires the reception of the other

---

135. Balthasar, *TL*, 1:63.
136. Ibid., 1:65.
137. Ibid., 1:67. See D. C. Schindler, *Dramatic Structure*.
138. Mauss, "Essai sur le don," 145–279.

and the acknowledgment that its belonging to the higher degrees of being, ultimately God, allows the concrete singular to be fully itself.

7. Gift's Bodily Perseity

Having dealt with substance and with the category of relation in the previous section, this chapter concludes with a few brief remarks on what gift discloses about the categories of quantity and quality.[139] If, as Bruaire indicates, the quantitative determinations are important for an ontology of gift, it is because "they express the substantial unity."[140] Quantity—the most proximate category to substance, though not identifiable with it—is not the "divisibility into constituent parts, each or every one of which is by nature some one individual thing."[141] Quantity expresses the gift-character of the unity of the singular according to the following three aspects.

First, the concrete singularity of a finite being is not that of the absolute. The finite being is singular without being universal—contrary to Hegel—because it is given to itself as a particular gift of being; it is a bodily gift. It is the body that prevents the human singular from thinking that his perseity is an expression of the universal. The body, as noted earlier, witnesses to the ontological difference between God and the human being not simply because God is bodiless, but, more importantly, because it is through his corporeal existence that the finite singular's gift-of-self takes place. The singular's inability to become a universal, rather than attenuating the image of the original giver, is expressive of the similarity between God and the singular. The bodily gift of self, carrying the memory of its having been given to itself through birth, is itself in giving itself. This gift of self, in a way that we cannot pursue here, extends from the mysterious encounter with the world, as outlined previously, to the intimacy of conjugal union between a man and a woman. The body expresses, within a *maior dissimilitudo*, the similarity and dissimilarity to God through the gift-of-self.[142] The body, therefore, is

---

139. Aristotle, *Metaph.* 1.983b10, 4.1003b5–10.

140. Bruaire, *EE*, 69.

141. Aristotle, *Metaph.* 5.1020a1–3. Aquinas anticipates the Cartesian error when he says that "it must be borne in mind that of all the accidents quantity is closest to substance. Hence some men think that quantities, such as line, number, surface, and body are substances. For next to substance only quantity can be divided into distinctive parts" (Aquinas, *In Metaph.* 5.983). Kant's second antinomy presupposes that the parts of the whole are conceived as being in act (*Critique of Pure Reason*, A434/B462).

142. D. L. Schindler, "Embodied Person." See also Aquinas, *ST*, I, q. 76, a. 3. As John Paul II's work has clarified, in its dual unity of male and female the body expresses at its own level the ontological dimension of the gift.

not a simple receptacle for a form—and hence indifferent to it—or a tool for the form to take up and use, but rather its expression.[143] The human being's access to and communication of *logos* and love is intrinsically somatic.

Second, the body indicates the impossibility of identifying one's own being with the form (*eidos*). In what could seem a second poverty, the gift of being is the positing of a particular individual whose ontological structure includes a somatic trace of the origin. Thus, the condition of possibility for there to be individuals, for many "ones," is that the gift of being be given to an embodied singular, and in the case of a human being, to an embodied freedom. The impossibility of incarnating the whole *eidos* is, for the concrete singular, its way to enjoy and participate in its specific form.

Third, the body indicates further the impossibility of identifying one's own Entity (*ousia*) with one's own *telos*. The body reveals that the end of oneself, though including the body, does not coincide with oneself or with what one can achieve. This disclosure, rather than revealing a cognitive or volitional weakness, indicates positively that one has been assigned a personal destiny that unfolds in history as one becomes oneself. The body entrusts the singular to a temporal existence, that is, to a participation, in the singular's own way, in the time proper to eternity. This is why one cannot anticipate one's own destiny. One can only receive it and wait for it to flourish, as the seed loses itself in the earth, and only after its death does its mystery yield the height, strength, texture, color, perfume, and fruitfulness that were unknown to the seed. Because one's destiny is given to oneself through the body, it is not possible, as we said, to reach that destiny without it or to let go of it once the destiny arrives. The threefold "poverty" that the body enfleshes (not being God, not being identical to the *eidos*, not being one's own destiny) is, at the same time, the openness to the reception and enjoyment of being in oneself and with others (perseity). These in fact are not denials of the singular but the affirmation of its unspeakable *haecceitas* in its unrepeatable historical relation to itself, others, and God.

---

143. This regards any bodily creature if the soul is to be understood with Aristotle as "an actuality of the first kind of a natural organized body" (Aristotle, *De Anima* 412b4–5). For Descartes, as is known, quantity has the same form of being as substance. He moves from considering extension in itself to thinking that extension has a separate existence. Yet to be able to conceive of something separately does not mean that the thing is able to exist separately. The identification of the body with *res extensa* could seem to be a mathematical truth; nevertheless, a mathematical object is always an *ens rationis* that exists only as an object of thought. What Descartes cannot admit is that extension can be an accident that can nonetheless be really distinguished from the corporeal substance. See Descartes, *Principia philosophiae*, 2.9. The reference to Descartes's *Principia* is taken from Millán Puelles, *Léxico filosófico*, 65–74.

The capacity to be well-disposed to act or to be acted upon, to love and to know—which capacity is Aristotle's second sense of *quality*—is also expressive of the gift-ness of the singular and its task of becoming itself.[144] We would like here to indicate a twofold dimension of this capacity—understanding capacity both as ability and as power—and so it applies primarily to the intellectual beings. First, as Bruaire says, the spiritual, dynamic character of the gift (*energeia*) expresses itself in the "conversion and manifestation, in the reflection and in the expression, in the independence and in action."[145] This circular movement of return to the source, which always presupposes the perpendicular movement of creation and the horizontal movement of history, is what, in fact, defines knowing and loving. Just as wisdom consists in having become one with what gives itself to be known without losing itself in the process, so love is the unity with the beloved to which one is drawn without either absorbing the beloved into oneself or denying oneself in the beloved. The human singular is given to himself and has to gather himself. Yet the retreat into himself is ordered from the beginning to a response, and he never overcomes the fact of having been given to himself. The gift of the singular withdraws into himself only to give himself in an unlimited openness. Just as silence and meditation precede the spoken word and communication, so the gift of self is the affirmation of oneself and the other. The gift of the singular is both things: reception of oneself and of the other into oneself, and gratuitous affirmation of the other. The reflection in this sense is for the sake of the expression, and this leads the singular further into the inexhaustible mystery of the Word. This spiritual movement of reflection teaches us, as we saw in the previous chapter regarding originary experience, not only that the gift and the *logos* form one unity (sign), but that this unity consists in a continuously becoming aware of the inexhaustible totality of the whole, an awareness that makes the gift of the self grow truer because it is a living (*lebendig*) relation with oneself, others, and God.

Second, the action of the human being, created *ex nihilo*, is a grateful response, although it will always be infinitely less than what was received, even if he were to give his own existence in return. The gratuity of the singular will never match the gift received. This utter disproportion remains present at every moment of the singular's existence. In a different sense from what Derrida expresses, one receives much from a source he will never manage to discover. The gift of the present contains the wealth of the past, of a tradition that gives itself to the singular and whose origins are never fully

---

144. Aristotle, *Cat.* 8b25–9a9; Aristotle, *Metaph.* 5.1020a7–32; Aquinas, *In Metaph.* 5.16.996–1000. For Aquinas, in fact, knowing and willing are qualitative accidents of the soul. See Aquinas, *ST*, I, q. 77, a. 1, ad 5.

145. Bruaire, *EE*, 71.

fathomed. That these sources remain unknown is neither a diminishment nor a denial of the gift, but rather a simple and astonishing sign of the superabundant nature of the gift. The richness of the singular also reveals his poverty. He has received everything, and, being given to participate in the perfection of all perfections, he wishes to reciprocate to the giver. The gift of the first act, as Aquinas tirelessly repeats, is for the sake of its operation: given in order to give.[146]

---

146. Aristotle, *De Anima* 2.1; Aquinas, *SCG* 1.45.6; *SCG* 3.113.1; *ST*, I, q. 105, a. 5; *ST*, I–II, q. 3, a. 2.

III. Reception and Reciprocity

THE RESPONSE OF WONDER before God's communication of *esse* deepens when we become aware that God gives the human person, along with the capacity to stand on his own, the capacity to act out of his own being (*autexousia*).[1] When God gives, he gives because he wants to share his giving. In fact, it would not be a real giving if God did not allow the concrete singular being to participate in his capacity to give, in his own freedom. The divine creating act goes so far that Aquinas claims that the human person is the cause of himself.[2] Gregory of Nyssa, speaking of human growth in virtue, dares perhaps even further when he famously writes that "we are in some manner our own parents, giving birth to ourselves as we will, by our decisions."[3] This capacity to act, despite its limitations and shortcomings, reveals the extent of the original gift of being. The present chapter intends to deepen how the "second act," the human being's capacity to operate, brings forth what is already present in the first act: the gift-ness of being. Rather than addressing a specific type of operation that thinks or wills something in particular, we will consider the operation that consists in the gift of self, that is, the reception of the gift of oneself and the reciprocation of the gift to the original giver. This "act," however, is not simply one among others. The reception and reciprocation

---

1. Persons, as Aquinas writes, are those rational substances "quae habent dominium sui actus, et non solum aguntur, sicut alia, sed per se agunt: actiones autem in singularibus sunt" (Aquinas, *ST*, I, q. 29, a. 1). See also Aquinas, *SCG* 1.3; *In Metaph.* 1.1.3 (no. 58); *In Nic. Eth.* 1.1.1.

2. "Liberum est, quod sui causa est" (Aquinas, *ST*, I, q. 83, a. 1).

3. Gregory of Nyssa, *Life of Moses*, 2.3.55–56 (PG 44:327). It is useful to recall the context: "All things subject to change and to becoming never remain constant, but continually pass from one state to another, for better or worse.... Now, human life is always subject to change; it needs to be born ever anew.... But here birth does not come about by a foreign intervention, as is the case with bodily beings ... ; it is the result of a free choice. Thus we are in a certain way our own parents, creating ourselves as we will, by our decisions" (ibid.).

of the gift is the form of every act and, as we shall see, includes the unity of freedom, reason, and will. Every volition, intellectual endeavor, and human activity is a different expression of the reception of the gift of oneself and the reciprocation (or not) to the original giver. The form of action is gift in this twofold sense: the content of action is a specific communication of love, and "gift" is the form of the action inasmuch as gift gathers into a unity all the elements that form a human action (the human person, with his enfleshed capacity to reason, to will, to desire, to be free, to intend; the world and historical circumstances; and God). Since the form of action is gift, then special attention needs to be paid to freedom. It is important, however, not to lose sight of the unity of human action as we present the meaning of reciprocation and reception.

Freedom is indeed a marvelous thing.[4] It tends to be considered abstractly, however—that is, detached from the singular's gift of being, from the concrete exercise of freedom that involves the entire human person as engaged with historical circumstances, from the world, and from God. The recollection that human action exercises an *esse* that has been given to the human person serves to combat this tendency to abstraction. The act of self-possession and self-determination to action is the self-possession of a gift. In this regard, to determine oneself through one's own action is, at its core, to receive and to reciprocate the gift. True human action is cast within the form of gift and serves the singular's growth as a person.

To see in what sense action expresses or obscures the gift-ness of *esse*, in what sense the singular's action is a reception and a reciprocation of the gift, it is important to clarify what it means to say that God gives his giving, that is, that he causes the human being to be free. An adequate perception of causality (section 1) enables us to see that God posits a person with the capacity and the task to respond to the call contained in the gift of being (section 2). Since human freedom exists only within the dialogue with God, the person's exercise of giving is one of receiving and responding to the original giver (sections 3–4). Finally, this larger horizon enables us to glimpse the abyss opened up by the rejection of the gift (section 5).

---

4. Literature offers us a beautiful example through Miguel de Cervantes: "Freedom, Sancho, is one of the most precious gifts heaven gave to men; the treasures under the earth and beneath the sea cannot compare to it; for freedom, as well as for honor, one can and should risk one's life, while captivity, on the other hand, is the greatest evil that can befall men" (Cervantes, *Don Quixote*, 2:832).

1. Giving Freedom

Originary experience allowed us to encounter the peculiar evidence of being's gift-ness and to seek its ontological structure. The examination of what it means for a concrete singular to be gift led us to the mystery of its dual unity of *esse* and essence, its openness to all of being, and its enjoying its own being and being-with others. Along with the question regarding the *whatness* of the concrete singular, originary experience poses a second question, inseparable from the first: *why* is it? The "what" brings the question of "why" because in being gift, the concrete singular does not belong to itself. It is precisely this belonging to a foreign origin, rooted in the singular's coming from nothingness, that permits the question regarding the why of its existence to surface in man. Aristotle explains that when we ask "why one thing belongs to something else," we are in fact seeking the cause (*aition*) that can account for the surprising existence of the concrete singular's movement.[5] The ontology of gift proposed here brings this "belonging to something else" to a deeper level, wherein the gift belongs to the ultimate giver in order to be itself. To ask, why is it? is to inquire into the relation maintained between the concrete singular and the divine source (*arche*). "Change," in this regard, is an expression of the relation with the source. In order to ponder the nature of this relation, we must start out from the source that begins and elicits (*arche*) it. In other words, our inquiry seeks to see how and to what purpose the source is cause (*arche, aition*) of the concrete singular gift.[6] To express synthetically what lies ahead, we can say that the source gives itself (*bonum; esse*), reveals itself (*aletheia*) without deception (*emeth*), pronounces itself (*logos*) to and through the concrete singular, and calls the singular to respond.[7]

We have already considered creation as a type of giving. With the ontological gift-ness of the singular in mind, we can thus briefly revisit the classic conception of fourfold causality and so suggest in what sense the account of gift and its transcendent origin retrieves causality from its current oblivion, and in what sense we can say that causality is also thereby purified.

---

5. Aristotle, *Metaph.* 7.1041a10–12; Aristotle, *An. post.*, chs. 1–2.

6. "Causality" has a long history and does not rank high in today's dominant scientific and technological worldview. This is not the place to offer a full account of how causality has been rejected. It suffices for our purposes to show the relation between donation and causality and how they shed light on each other. For the fate of causality, see Schmitz, *Recovery of Wonder*; Bieler, "Causality and Freedom"; Wallace, *Modeling of Nature*; Jonas, *Phenomenon of Life*; Burtt, *Metaphysical Foundations*; Schmitz, *Creation*, 97–130.

7. This is also how Balthasar structures the *Epilogue*, his own synthesis of his trilogy.

More than human making, causality, as the sourcing of *esse*, refers back to the transcendent God who gives creatures a limited participation in his own *esse* (efficient cause). Prompted by his own goodness (*agape*), the original giver separates himself from the gift by making the latter non-subsistent. God communicates his own *esse* to the receiver as non-subsistent. This creative outpouring is unlike any human activity that communicates a form to what is open to receiving it. Efficient causality, when referred to God's relation to the world, posits the gift as other by letting it participate in a limited and non-univocal way in the multiplicity of created singulars.[8] The separation from the source through the outflowing of the source's own *esse* reaches its furthest point in the material perseity of the singular. God, who is pure spirit, although, as Aquinas says, he is not directly the material cause of the creation, creates primal matter. God does not denigrate matter or view it as the degraded counterpart to what is pure and deserving of the name "being."[9] Rather than setting it aside in gnostic fashion, God considers matter a place where he can express himself. As we indicated with the human body, the concrete singular is also a sign in its very corporeality. Not only does God effect the actual communication of *esse* to what is other than him; ultimately he is also the formal cause, that is, "the form or pattern of what it is for something to be." God is the formal cause not because the singular maintains a univocal relation to God, but rather because the singular imitates God's essence at its own level.[10] This is why, from the point of view of the substance, the form of the singular seems to be absolutely necessary and eternal. Thus, God as giver is not only transcendent of the gift (efficient cause); he is also present in the gift. He creates a singular that is similar to himself (formal causality). This original giving of himself, as we said, is not an egocentric one. God gives being, communicates his *esse* as non-subsistent, so that the human person, and to its own degree the world, can enjoy God's light. Human beings are made to walk erect and to be able to speak so that they can encounter the paternal giver and respond to his overtures. The end of concrete singulars is to be radiant with God's light. God does not want to make the creature subservient to his own glory, but rather to let it participate in his own light and to see from within this light the gift-ness of being. God is that "for the sake of which" every singular is (final cause). God, in giving himself, wants his creatures to want him freely.

8. As we saw in the previous chapter, God is not a genus, and *esse commune* cannot be confused with *ipsum esse subsistens*. In addition to the works of Fabro and Geiger cited earlier, for participation and causality in Aquinas, albeit a less equally balanced view, see Te Velde, *Participation and Substantiality*.

9. Aquinas, *ST*, I, q. 44, a. 2; *SCG* 1.17.138.

10. Aquinas, *SCG* 1.50.426.

He does not draw them to him as a magnet draws pieces of iron; he bestows freedom on the concrete singular so that the participation in his life can be truly the singular's. *Arche* and *aition* are not, as we generally consider them since Galileo, an extrinsic push whose source remains behind after inflicting a force to change the direction of an object or bring it to a halt. On this restrictive view, cause is responsible only for topographical movement and is ultimately irrelevant in a cosmos mathematically conceived. Divine efficient causality is not a "push" or a sort of "big bang," after which the giver returns to Olympus. Sourcing and guiding are instead the communication of *esse* as other than the giver, *esse* that moves toward a return to the original giver.[11]

If the singular's gift-ness allows us to begin unfolding the meaning of fourfold causality, causality reinforces the alterity of God and the purpose of his giving of self. By freely giving himself, God also reveals himself. He wants to be known and seen by the concrete singular. God thus lets himself be seen through his "presence" in the present and in giving man the capacity to embrace him. God reveals himself (*aletheia*) without deception (*emeth*): without losing his transcendence, God lets himself be known and remains faithful in his communication of the gift of being. To see in what sense causality emphasizes the radical otherness of God, which is revealed through what it causes to be, we can take up again and deepen the distinction between our account of gift and causality and Heidegger's elucidation of *Ereignis* and its own interpretation of causality. This will enable us to see that the *esse* communicated freely by the God of love and desire contains the original essence of presencing and that there can be gift only when gift is cast within this metaphysical framework.[12] If we see the source's originating and eliciting of the concrete singular—the fourfold causality as just outlined—from the point of view of the singular itself and its historical existence, the singular's gift-ness is revealed as event-full (*Ereignis*). Because concrete singulars belong to the Good in being completely given to themselves, in contrast to Heidegger we understand "event" as the historical existing and unfolding of the gift-ness of the concrete singular in its asymmetrical, gifted reciprocity of *esse* and essence.

---

11. Language of "force," again, betrays an anthropology that conceives the human person as an isolated monad. Instead, the threefold axiom of causality—agency (*omne agens agit inquantum est actu*), similitude (*omne agens agit sibi simile*), and finality (*omne agens agit propter finem*)—has its ultimate ground in God's triune *esse*.

12. This is contrary to the argument proposed by Caputo that "gift" will not get the hearing it deserves if, extracted from a phenomenological horizon of donation (Heidegger, Marion) or from aporetic postmodern thought (Derrida), it is cast within a "classical metaphysics of causality" (Caputo, "Commentary on Ken Schmitz," 258).

III. RECEPTION AND RECIPROCITY   105

It may seem surprising to say that Heidegger's philosophy was not concerned primarily with "being," in either its ontological or its phenomenological meaning. Rather, it emerged that the *Sache des Denkens* (the proper object of thought), according to Heidegger, is what enables manifestation (*parousia*) or presence (*Anwesen*) to be given at all.[13] This, which according to Heidegger is philosophy's "fundamental question" (*Grundfrage*), can be posed adequately only by way of a leap out of metaphysics.[14] The metaphysical question about the eventful form of being triggered by the ontological difference is, according to Heidegger, nothing but a "guiding question" that leads to the need to spring over to that which "is."[15] To approach being first from the point of view of *Da-sein* (which means openness, and not "being-there" or "human existence"), and then as the "givenness" of entities (the phenomenological approach), prepares the ground for language to speak about what occasions the reciprocal belonging of *Da-sein* and what appears: *Ereignis*. Although *Ereignis* is normally translated with "event," for Heidegger "event" refers neither to a sheer historical occurrence of varying significance, nor to the act according to which a mysterious One would "give" being.[16] The dual unity of *esse* and essence in the concrete singular as described above is here hypostatized in a reciprocity (*Gegenschwung*) according to which givenness needs that to which it gives (*das Brauchen*) and the latter belongs to the former (*das Zugehören*).[17] In its appearing, one

---

13. "Das Sein ist nicht mehr das eigens zu Denkende" (Heidegger, *Zur Sache des Denkens*, GA 14, §44.6–7). "But Hegel also, as little as Husserl, as little as all metaphysics," comments Heidegger, "does not ask about Being as Being, that is, does not raise the question how there can be presence as such. There is presence only when opening is dominant" (Heidegger, *OTB*, 70).

14. See, e.g, GA 65, §117. Heidegger dedicates GA 4, §§115–67 to defining the meaning of *Sprung*. For *Ereignis* see GA 65 and 71. Also see GA 9 (*Wegmarken*, ed. Friedrich-Wilhelm von Hermann); English translation: Heidegger, *Pathmarks*. Also see GA 11 (*Identität und Differenz*); English translation: Heidegger, *Identity and Difference*. Although disagreeing with him on certain points, I am indebted to Thomas Sheehan's work on Heidegger's concept of *Ereignis*. See Sheehan, "*Kehre* and *Ereignis*"; Sheehan, "Paradigm Shift," 183–202. See also Richardson, *Heidegger*; Schürmann, *From Principles to Anarchy*; D. C. Schindler, "'Wie kommt der Mensch.'"

15. For an example of Heidegger's emphasis on thinking outside the ontological difference, in addition to GA 11, see GA 65, §258.

16. "What the name *Ereignis* names can no longer be represented by means of the current meaning of the word; for in that meaning 'event of appropriation (*Ereignis*)' is understood in the sense of occurrence and happening—not in terms of Appropriating (*Ereignung*) as the extending and sending which opens and preserves" (Heidegger, *OTB*, 20).

17. "Dieser Gegenschwung des Brauchens und Zugehörens macht das Seyn als Ereignis aus, und die Schwingung dieses Gegenschwunges in die Einfachheit des Wissens zu heben und in seiner Wahrheit zu gründen, ist das Erste, was uns denkerisch obliegt"

observes that what gives itself claims *Da-sein*, which is open to being, and, simultaneously, that *Da-sein*'s opening takes place only inasmuch as what gives itself appears. Thus, event for Heidegger is the movement (*kinesis*) of opening itself up and belonging, a reciprocal expropriation. In contrast to the account of event presented here, nothing else is required.[18] *Ereignis*, as T. Sheehan explains, is not what accounts for what is—it is not the ultimate ground, cause, or source of what is. For us, "what is" is the concrete singular, the world, and God. For Heidegger, instead, *Ereignis* is "what is."[19]

Is there anything that originates this mutual, symmetrical belonging? If *Ereignis* is what is, then there seems to be no need for a cause behind the event itself. "What gives" (*es gibt*) is not something outside of the event but part of the constitution of event. The reciprocal belonging of appearing and *Da-sein* is not grounded in having been posited by another, but rather in the "withdrawing" of *Da-sein*. According to Heidegger, withdrawing allows one to account for *Ereignis*'s whylessness without falling back into onto-theology. "But suppose," asks Heidegger, "that be-ing itself were the self-withdrawing and would hold sway as refusal?"[20] Withdrawal (*Entzug*) as gift is "what is peculiar to *Ereignis*."[21] Still, one might ask, why this withdrawal? Heidegger's "forgotten mystery of *Da-sein*," according to T. Sheehan, is man's finitude.[22] The giving and reception proper to the event is not due to a cause behind *Ereignis*, but to man's finitude itself. If *Da-sein*'s finitude accounts for *Ereignis*, not as the extrinsic cause but from within *Ereignis* itself, then finitude is no longer a dialogical partner of the infinite, as our anthropological reflection suggested. For Heidegger, finitude no longer corresponds to an absolute that is able to render its existence intelligible.

(Heidegger, *GA* 65, §133). "Being belongs with thinking to an identity whose active essence stems from that letting belong together which we call *Ereignis*" (Heidegger, *Identity and Difference*, 39).

18. This mutual belonging has led to the inaccurate English translation of *Ereignis* as "event of appropriation." Relying on *GA* 71, Sheehan explains that *Ereignis* does not come from *er-eigens* but *er-äugen*, which means "bringing something out into view" or "to appear by having been opened up." In this sense *Ereignis* would mean "the opening of the open on the basis of a concealment." See Sheehan, *Paradigm Shift*, 196–98. Stambaugh concurs with this reading; see her translation of *Identity and Difference*, 14.

19. "The deity enters into philosophy through the perdurance of which we think at first as the approach to the active nature of the difference between Being and beings" (Heidegger, *Identity and Difference*, 71).

20. "Wie aber wenn das Seyn selbst das Sichentziehende wäre und als die Verweigerung weste?" (Heidegger, *GA* 65, §129, §246). See also *GA* 65, §168. Heidegger's understanding of time presented earlier is built on this ontology.

21. Heidegger, *OTB*, 22. For Heidegger, as we saw, this withdrawal is what causes history to be.

22. Sheehan, *Paradigm Shift*, 198–99.

Without confusing the asymmetrical relationship between *esse* and *essentia* in the concrete singular (as disclosed by originary experience) and Heidegger's idea of the reciprocity between what gives itself and that which is claimed in this opening, a relation between the two accounts does emerge. The structure of the event, in fact, not only requires that the form of being be an interplay of ground and manifestation; it also requires, at the same time, someone to whom it happens. Nevertheless, it is still difficult to see how finitude can indeed be understood fully only within immanence, as Heidegger says. The question of why the concrete finite singular should be understood as withdrawal, and this negative phenomenon as that which gives, remains unanswered in Heidegger. His thought appears unable to justify the inexhaustible wonder before the fact of being, of having been gratuitously invited to be. Heidegger's understanding of *Ereignis* can indeed leave space for man's destiny, responsibility, and perhaps even admiration before existence, but it cannot account for the wonder of being. As understood by Heidegger, *Ereignis* traps man in a solitude so radical that it seems to make any discourse on the "gods" simply rhetorical.[23]

With this view of *Ereignis*, it is not surprising that Heidegger does not have much room in his thought for a causal relation between God and the world.[24] In contrast to a transcendent God whose *agape* invites man to share both in his own being and in the giving itself, "causality" can only objectivize beings. This reductive sense of causality views the concrete singular instrumentally or, as Marion indicates, it gives singulars over to "the *ego*

---

23. Perhaps Heidegger's conclusion is an echo of his radical decision to think apart from and thus against God. Heidegger himself expressed his position on religion very clearly: "The past two years in which I struggled for a fundamental clarification of my philosophical position and put aside all specialized academic tasks have led to conclusions I would not be able to hold and teach freely, were I bound to a position outside of philosophy. Epistemological insights extending to a theory of historical knowledge have made the system of Catholicism problematic and unacceptable to me, but not Christianity and metaphysics—these, though, in a new sense" (Heidegger, "Letter to Fr. Engelbert Krebs (1919)," in *Supplements*, 69–70, at 69). It is important to see that the radical opposition of Heidegger's philosophy to his own faith transformed his thought into a radically secularized reading of Christianity, which, although attractive, cannot be adopted by theological reflection without bringing about its own end. This is why Hans Jonas commented: "My theological friends, my Christian friends—don't you see what you are dealing with? Don't you sense, if not see, the profoundly pagan character of Heidegger's thought? Rightly pagan, as it is philosophy . . . ; but more pagan than others from your point of view, not in spite but because of its, also, speaking of call and self-revealing and even of the shepherd. . . . [For Heidegger] revelation is immanent in the world, nay, it belongs to its nature; i.e., that the world is divine. Quite consistently do the gods appear again in Heidegger's philosophy. But where the gods are, God cannot be" (Jonas, "Heidegger and Theology," in *Phenomenon of Life*, 248).

24. See Caputo, *Heidegger and Aquinas*; Schürmann, *From Principles to Anarchy*.

of a consciousness that intends them as a *noema*."[25] The finitization of the concrete singular's ontological horizon proposed by Heidegger, however, jeopardizes any use of the term "revelation"—a term that, as with much of his complex vocabulary, Heidegger borrows from a relinquished Christian tradition and empties of its original meaning. Let us examine now what he says about the nature of causality.

Heidegger claims that causality does not see the givenness of the singular; it does not perceive the primal mystery of all thinking: "*Es gibt Seyn.* It gives being. The 'gives' names the essence of Being that is giving, granting its truth. The self-giving into the open, along with the open region itself, is Being itself."[26] A metaphysics of causality, according to Heidegger, slips out of the event of being and replaces the thinking of being (in the subjective and objective senses of the genitive) with *techne*. "By and by," he writes to Jean Beaufret, "philosophy becomes a technique for explaining from highest causes. One no longer thinks; one occupies oneself with 'philosophy.'"[27] For Heidegger, the questions concerning causality and the essence of technology are inseparable: they reduce donation and being to an instrumental relation. Causality is, in this view, an expression of technology's making. Hence, it is mainly interpreted by Heidegger as a reductive efficient causality.

Technology, according to Heidegger, although the last philosophical epoch and the fruit of metaphysics, in its essence is already present in post-Socratic thought (Plato and Aristotle). The historical movement of being unfolds further and further not towards a panoptic Hegelian view of being but to presencing and eventful clearing.[28] For Heidegger, technology is the most dangerous fruit because it could either represent the beginning of thinking being adequately, hence away from metaphysics, or, as Schürmann puts it, it could be the final "*epoche*, the withholding or oblivion of presencing, its obfuscation by the principles."[29]

Heidegger, however, does not discount the discourse on causality as do many contemporary technocratic sciences (as well as some philosophies). Causality has dominated Western thought for centuries, not because the philosophers who took up the task of thinking were unfit, but because, according to Heidegger, causality (metaphysical thinking) was a way in which being gave itself to be known while also hiding itself. In fidelity to Heraclitus,

25. Marion, *Being Given*, 32.
26. Heidegger, "Letter on Humanism," 238.
27. Ibid., 221.
28. It is not by chance that for Heidegger, Hegel's work is the epitome of onto-theological thinking. See Heidegger, *Identity and Difference*.
29. Schürmann, *From Principles to Anarchy*, 35; Heidegger, "Concerning Technology."

Heidegger remarks that being's self-revealing loves self-concealing. He goes on to say, however, that only a philosophical reflection that resists the spell of onto-theology, and so does not lose sight of the radical temporality and finitude of thought, is able to perceive the ambiguity of causality and technology and thus avoid objectifying the transcendent God (for him the "godly God" is not that of Christianity, which subsequently has no place in philosophy). Only such a philosophy can see that causality, as Heidegger's reading of Aristotle's definition of movement indicates, has to do with revelation by way of ordering. Onto-theology, according to Heidegger, loses donation and appeals instead to a pendular relation between cause and effect. Let us see first in what sense "source" is an originating order. This perception of "source" naturally leads to the revelatory dimension of its ordering.

Heidegger notes that, according to Aristotle, the Greek polysemic term *aition* (cause; Latin *causa*) is very closely related to *arche* (origin, source; Latin *origo, principium*). "Nature (*physis*)," famously writes Aristotle, is "a certain source and cause of being moved and of coming to rest in that to which it belongs primarily."[30] According to Heidegger, "causality is only a derivative way of being an origin"; it is that which makes a thing "stable," that is, "to stand on its own," and which is responsible for its "enduring."[31] The relation that *aition* maintains with *arche* (the permanent source that is responsible for what it permits to be) suggests to Heidegger that *arche* has two inseparable connotations in Aristotle: to be the responsible principle of the beginning of something (either a natural being or an artifact); and to control or to rule that which has been originated.[32] To depict the source in causal terms, to search for principles in the form of causes, requires reading principle (*arche*) as *both* inception and domination.[33] For Heidegger, this "giving rise to" and "permanent governing" extends both to human manufacturing (*techne* and *poiesis*) and to *physis* itself (which is *poiesis* in its

---

30. Aristotle, *Physics* 2.192b22–24.

31. Heidegger, "On the Essence," 188.

32. As Schmitz notes, for Aristotle *arche* has these connotations: point of departure, to be the initial part (foundation), to be the guiding principle, and to be that from which something is knowable (Aristotle, *Metaph.* 5.1012b34–1013a17). See Schmitz, *TB*, 42.

33. Commenting on Aristotle's *Physics* 192b13–15, Heidegger writes, "Here in place of αἴτιον and αιτία we find explicitly the word ἀρχή. The Greeks ordinarily hear two meanings in this word. On the one hand ἀρχή means that from which something has its origin and beginning; on the other hand it means that which, *as* this origin and beginning, likewise keeps rein *over*, i.e., restrains and therefore dominates, something else that emerges from it. Ἀρχή means, at one and the same time, beginning and control.... We can translate ἀρχή as originating ordering, as ordering origin. The unity of these two is *essential*" (Heidegger, "On the Essence," 189).

highest sense).³⁴ Heidegger insists that *physis* is the originating origin and "ordering power" that accounts for and governs *kinesis* (movement).³⁵ The originating order governs through power that for which it is responsible.³⁶

While Heidegger rightly reminds us that *kinesis* is not primarily change of place but a mode of being, he proposes understanding the *arche* that is responsible for movement by disengaging it from causal representations.³⁷ He points out that for the Greeks, movement—which is what causality wishes to account for—appears in light of "rest," which for them is not idleness or lack of movement but rather a way of being that is best characterized as *entelecheia*. "The movedness of a movement," Heidegger writes, "consists above all in the fact that the movement of a moving being gathers itself into its end, *telos*, and as so gathered within its end, 'has' itself: *en telei echei, entelecheia*, having-itself-in-its-end."³⁸ In light of this, Heidegger translates Aristotle's epochal definition of movement as follows: "the having-itself-in-its-end of what is appropriate (*dynamis*, potency) as something appropriate (i.e., in its appropriateness) is clearly (the essence of) movedness."³⁹ Change or movement, as Heidegger reinterprets the Stagirite's definition, is not simply the acquisition or loss of a given form by a potency; it is coming into presence. Heidegger thus offers an understanding of causality as "revelation," as an unfolding (*aletheia*) of being that remains enclosed within historical finitude.

Heidegger gives an example: a silversmith is able to turn a piece of silver into a sacrificial chalice, he says, because what is appropriate to the silver appears in the rest (*entelecheia*) of what is appropriate. He explicates the fourfold causality: "The chalice is indebted to, that is, owes thanks to, the silver for that of which it consists [material causality].... [It] is at the same time indebted to the aspect (*eidos*) of chaliceness [formal causality]." Also "responsible for the sacrificial vessel . . . is that which in advance confines

---

34. Heidegger, "Concerning Technology," 317.

35. Heidegger, "On the Essence," 207.

36. In this reading of origin in terms of "power," Heidegger's thought comes close to the nominalist understanding of God in terms of will rather than the *agapic* being we are pondering here. Despite their irreconcilable differences, both Hegel's account of the absolute spirit's self-determination through the negative force of the spirit and Heidegger's interpretation of sourcing in terms of power and domination presuppose negativity at the fundamental core of the ground of being. With this decision they both illustrate that a reflection on being as gift cannot be circumscribed to the reflection on second act. This decision, however, prevents their reflection from grounding an understanding of being in terms of gift.

37. Schürmann, *From Principles to Anarchy*, 100.

38. Heidegger, "On the Essence," 217.

39. Ibid., 218.

the chalice . . . as sacrificial vessel," that is, to its *telos* (final causality), and, ultimately, "the silversmith [who] considers carefully and gathers together the three aforementioned ways of being responsible and indebted."⁴⁰ Yet, for Heidegger, the four causes are not responsible simply for the transformation of an undetermined piece of silver into a sacrificial chalice. They account for the "lying before and lying ready [which characterize] the presencing of something that is present."⁴¹ Causality and technology are not simply means to an end or the production of something out of something else; they are a way of revealing. The disclosure that takes place through causal thinking and leads to technological thought is a coming to presence. Technological thinking reveals by ordering what is at hand and considering it as energy in reserve. This "way in which the actual reveals itself as standing in reserve" (*Gestell*) is the new depth that technology discloses of the classical Western thought of causality. Just as the "it" of "it gives being" indicates a giving and not a transcendent God that gives, so "revelation" is a reciprocal belonging of what gives itself to be thought and the one who is claimed in that disclosure, *Da-sein*. The essence of technology is *Ge-stell*, challenging, "a way of revealing that challenges forth."⁴²

Heidegger's treatment of causality and technology aims to ground the "epochal" shift being takes in his thought: from *esse* to *aletheia*. His account of *aletheia*, however, makes his reflection incompatible with the ontological reflection on gift we are examining here. For Heidegger, what is primordial is not *esse* (either as self-subsisting or as created *esse*) but the disclosure in the coming to light of what loves to conceal itself (*aletheia*). Heideggerian being is not *actualitas* or *actus essendi*. "It is," as Caputo writes, criticizing Cornelio Fabro's failure to grasp Heidegger's understanding of *aletheia*, "the quiet splendor and simple radiance of what shows itself, which is wholly removed from all the categories of causality and actuality."⁴³ Caputo points out

40. Heidegger indicates that the silversmith cannot be considered the *causa efficiens* since in Aristotle this term is absent. Instead he writes that "the silversmith is co-responsible as that from which the sacred vessel's being brought forth and subsistence take and retain their first departure" (Heidegger, "Concerning Technology," 315).

41. Ibid., 316. The understanding of *Gestell* can be approximated to *Ereignis*, although the latter is considered to be free of the danger presented by *Gestell*.

42. Ibid., 335. He continues: "'Enframing,' (*Ge-stell*) as a destining of revealing, is indeed the essence of technology, but never in the sense of genus and *essentia*. If we pay heed to this, something astounding strikes us: it is technology itself that makes the demand on us to think in another way what is usually understood by 'essence'" (ibid.).

43. Caputo also notes that "the very discourse of St. Thomas about Being in terms of *actus* and *actualitas*, far from extricating him from the oblivion of Being, thrusts him into it all the more deeply" (Caputo, *Heidegger and Aquinas*, 225). According to Caputo, the works of Aquinas and Heidegger are similar precisely in what remains unsaid in

that for a metaphysics of *esse* within the Thomistic tradition, *esse* is a mode of revealing. Yet he also contends that the Thomistic understanding of *esse* does not have anything to do with Heidegger's *Sein*, or, more importantly, *Ereignis*. *Esse* does not contain the original essence of presencing. In this view, the perfection of all perfections is, so to speak, too full to leave any room for the play of concealment and unconcealment.

At this juncture we can list three elements that show the divergence of our account of gift and being from that of Heidegger. The first concerns the sense of fullness that being possesses. The Thomistic conception of *esse*, as we discussed in our account of the gift-ness of being, as pure act, is a complete principle that is open. *Esse*'s perfection is not a Parmenidean fullness—nor is the category of open principle a euphemism for indeterminacy. *Ipsum esse subsistens*, also for Aquinas—although as mentioned he does not take full advantage of it—is the triune God. Second, the inevitable turn to causality secures presencing and revealing precisely because the giver remains both other from and immanent in the gift. Concealment and unconcealment speak of a "hidden harmony," that is, God's gift and design.[44] Presence is a relational category—in the twofold ontological and anthropological sense of relation—that is incomprehensible without the reality of person. Detached from a transcendent God, rather than revealing we have a finite play of mirrors. Third, a unilaterally horizontal and hence finite concept of history neglects the fact that God's giving and the revealing of himself is not only *aletheia*; it is also *emeth*.[45] God lets himself be seen without deceit, which means that he remains faithful to the promise of more contained in the gift of being. Within the ontology of gift, *aletheia* refers to the revelation of one in another that leaves their respective integrities unmarred. Heidegger's *aletheia* and *Ereignis* are built upon an anthropology that does not contemplate the mystery of birth. Being's gift-ness, as elucidated here, allows us to see the mystery of being and presence in a deeper and more comprehensive way. Philosophical thinking, too, must be permitted to reach its ultimate giver, without whom there would be no donation to begin with. It is only in this way that an ontological understanding of event and truth that does not forget being may be carried out.[46]

Aquinas: his mystical experience. See ibid., 246–87.

44. "Hidden harmony is better than manifest" (Heraclitus, *Fragments*, no. 47).

45. This radical finitude is perhaps at the root of Heidegger's misunderstanding of the classical fourfold causality, which is perceived through an efficient causality that is technologically interpreted.

46. Marion introduces his understanding of givenness by indicating the limits of the phenomenologies preceding him: "Heidegger and Husserl thus proceed in the same way and to the same point. Both in fact have recourse to givenness and espouse its

If *esse commune*, as we saw, is not the origin of the forms of singular beings but simply makes them be by giving itself to them, and if the essences have their own priority over the *esse* that they limit, then the ultimate responsibility for the inexhaustible wholeness of the singular is to be ascribed to God. The wonder that sets the philosopher on the way to thinking (*Erfahrung*) makes him ask *why* there are things. Unable to account for the giftness of the concrete singular, Heidegger forgets the original question, "Why being?" Originary experience is a permanent, ever-deepening reminder that the relation between the singular that gives itself to be seen (through the singular being as such) and the one to whom the call is addressed is possible and real because of the absolute, free gift of God who pours himself outside of himself by creating what he is not. Originary experience guides us to contemplate being all the way to the end and to acknowledge that the non-necessity of *esse commune* presupposes the absolute, loving freedom of God without which the singular would not be. At the same time, only if finite forms are an analogical expression of God can their integrity (and hence the *logoi* of the gift) be preserved, and only in this way can real, non-technocratic thinking (a thinking that is not reduced to a form of making) actually take place. This is why *esse*'s universal quasi-unity does not absorb essence within it, as does the "new humanism" that Heidegger bemoans. If gift reveals the giving proper to "causality," "causality" reinforces the alterity of God and the purpose of his giving of self.[47]

Only if the divine source can create freely (out of nothing) and remain distinct from, while caring for, the creature, can there be an unconcealment that is the iconic presence of the source rather than a mirror held up to the beholder as in Heidegger. Revelation, in fact, requires a transcendent alterity that cannot be found in Heidegger's horizon. Deprived of the ontological difference between God and the world, the distinction among beings dries out into either a random succession of becomings (Heraclitus)

---

function as ultimate principle—by which they attest it and, at the same time, their respective geniuses. But one of them [Husserl], in ending up at objectness, lets givenness escape, while the other [Heidegger], by assigning beingness to the *Ereignis*, abandons it" (Marion, *Being Given*, 38). Marion rightly indicates that Heidegger abandons donation (*Gegebenheit*) in *Ereignis*. Yet, differently from our account and perhaps due to an excessively technological understanding of causality that privileges efficient causality and productivity, Marion proposes to understand gift by means of an ulterior phenomenological reduction: "so much reduction, so much givenness." For the French philosopher, hypostasized givenness is the only way to free donation from the logic of economical exchange of gifts, of which causality is yet another example. Marion, *Reduction and Givenness*. See also Marion, *Being Given*, 71–118. For an interesting review of Marion's work, see Hart, *Counter-Experiences*.

47. See Balthasar, *GL*, 5:420–50, 624–27.

or the pantheistic identity that Heidegger always rejected. When, instead, the ultimate source is acknowledged as a gratuitous giver and not an arbitrary power, the historicity of philosophical enquiry, as was the case with movement, is perceived in its true essence: as an expression of the eternal precisely in its historicity and in its movedness.[48]

Fourfold causality is about revelation (*aletheia*, *emeth*) because it is the communication of *esse*, which is a similitude of the divine goodness.[49] The content of this revelation therefore can only be the inexhaustible wholeness of the ultimate source in its ever-surprising gift of itself to the singular, which because of its constitutive relation with the source and with others, is also an irreducible part of the revelation of the gift of be-*ing*. What is at stake in "gifted causation" is the participation of singular beings in divine being (life) through created *esse*.[50] If *ipsum esse subsistens* were not also the dual union of *agape* and *eros*, *aletheia* would exhaust itself in its self-revelation (as in Hegel's absolute spirit). Furthermore, movement, as we see in the growth of a tree, the building of a dwelling place where life will be shared, or the maturing of the person, would not be the unfolding (*entelecheia*) of a potency (receptive sense of gift) inasmuch as it is a power (*dynamis*, active sense of gift). The reciprocal relation between causality and ontology illuminates movement for what it is: the active unfolding of what is given to be. Movement is permanently new, received actuality.

The communication of *esse* that causes singular beings to be themselves in their dependence on the *agapic* source frees the freedom of the gift; that is, it asks the singular to respond. The singular giver gives himself, reveals himself and says himself. To be responsible for (cause) the gift of the singular to himself entails allowing the singular to see the gift and to be free in responding. The gift would not be gratuitous if it did not permit the receiver to participate in the giving of himself (as we saw in the last chapter) and to others. In addition, the gift would not be real if it did not offer what is most precious about giving: allowing the receiver to have the capacity to love, that is, to welcome, thank, and suffer, and to ask for the paternal giver

---

48. It is important to note that God's absolute creative freedom does not require seeing God as *causa sui*. The coextensiveness of nature and freedom in God therefore needs to be thought not so much in the direction of freedom as self-determination but in the direction opened up by being understood as love. Only in this latter can we avoid the voluntaristic reduction of God's being and the idealistic interpretation of God as the cause of himself, while leaving the door open to an account of the coextensiveness of nature and freedom as eternal self-donation.

49. Aquinas, *De ver.*, q. 22, a. 2, ad 2.

50. Rooted in the axiom of similarity, the revelatory capacity of being, understood as gift-sign, requires the axiom of agency.

in order that the receiver can belong gratuitously to the giver, and so that the receiver may recognize him as that totality that makes everything be.

2. Ordering Freedom

The concrete singular's operation expresses the gift-ness proper to the singular in that the singular receives the faithful (*emeth*) self-disclosure (*aletheia*) of being and reciprocates this disclosure gratuitously (or attempts to obscure it) through whatever the singular does. Since absolute being's revelation rests on its truth and its free gift of self, the singular is called to respond to it with his own word and free action. The context within which freedom, along with reason and desire, emerges and participates in human action is indispensable for showing in what sense the gift-ness of being is also expressed through the singular's operation.

Building on our reflection on originary experience and the ontology of the gift, we can now plumb the threefold depth of the personal and ontological horizon of freedom. At the center of human freedom is God, who is the permanent, *agapic*, and yearning source of all that is, and whose *logos* reaches the singular through the multiplicity of beings. The family represents the second layer of freedom. The family is the place within which one's own given freedom is awakened to itself by the web of filial and nuptial relationships through which one learns the wealth of the gift of being and the promise it contains. Bearing in mind what we said about constitutive relations and indwelling in terms of the spiritual nature of the singular, we can say that the family is the personal and ontological place in which the concrete singular is introduced to the constitutive dialogue with the original giver. The third aspect to take into account is one's own nature, which links enfleshed freedom with its foreign origin and which, through reason's grasp of the truth and desire's inclination to the good, immerses freedom in the historical movement towards its own fulfillment. It is this larger context that shows the participation of the concrete singular in the unity with all that is (God, others, and the world), which participation is respectful of the gift character of being. Abstracted from these three aspects, however, the gift of freedom, despite its pride of place in the West since the Enlightenment, can only be denied or misunderstood. Let us look briefly at what this looks like.

Detached from the singular's God-given nature, the singular's being is easily supposed as identical with his freedom and its exercise. In this case, the singular's nature would appear self-made.[51] If "nature" is not gift and

---

51. Sartre, *Being and Nothingness*. Feuerbach and Pelagius, deeply influenced by Stoicism, offer different accounts of such a trust in freedom. Forschner, *Die stoische*

the source and cause of movement and rest but rather is viewed empirically, freedom is explained away as a biological epiphenomenon or neurological activity.[52] Removed from the historical, human context in which it originates—the communion (*societas*) first represented by the family and whose ultimate ground is the triune God—freedom could be understood as freedom from coercion, as Hobbes famously contended.[53] When freedom is abstracted from the encounter with nature and other singular beings, it is hard to perceive that the gift-form of the singular's unity calls, by means of beauty, the singular to receive the gift, and that the gift's intrinsic goodness contains a promise of more that can flourish only if both beauty and goodness are received in poverty. When isolated from the appealing beauty and goodness of the concrete singular gift, freedom is reduced to a choice of objects that are necessarily neutral if the person is to be free. In fact, if the goodness or badness of beings attracts or coerces human freedom, then one cannot be free.[54] The neutrality of finite singulars is advocated further by those who wish to carry out a scientific exploration in which endless progress is the only criterion.

The defense of freedom from coercion arrives sooner or later at the claim that to be free requires the singular's capacity to determine both the ends and the means with which he is to pursue what he has freely resolved to do. Partly due to Kant's influence, we still tend to think that we are free only if we determine both what we want (end) and how to obtain it.[55] If one claims that freedom's autonomy determines its *telos*, although one may disavow absolute power and reject its historical consequences, can one

---

Ethik; Scheffczyk, *Die Heilsverwirklichung*; Feuerbach, *Essence of Christianity*; Augustinus Aurelius, *De gestis Pelagii ad Aurelium liber unus* 18.42 (PL 44:3045).

52. See, among others, Eccles, *Evolution of the Brain*; Bergson, *Essai sur les données*. For a critique of the biologist position, see Jonas, *Organismus und Freiheit*.

53. Hobbes, *Leviathan*.

54. William of Ockham, *Quodlibetal Questions*. For a critique of this position, see Pinckaers, *Sources of Christian Ethics*.

55. Kant, *Critique of Practical Reason*; Kant, *Metaphysics of Morals*, A6. Rousseau wrote that "freedom is obedience to a law that the human being has given to himself" (Rousseau, "Of the Social Contract," 427). See Ratzinger, *Principles of Catholic Theology*, 1 and 8. It is true that one can choose the means for reaching an end. Yet, if ends are chosen or determined by human freedom, how is it that one discovers oneself always already desiring the good and the true? As Augustine writes in his usual transparent and cogent style: "Quid enim fortius desiderat anima quam veritatem?" (Augustine, *In Ioa.* 26.5 [PL 35:1609]). It is the knowledge of the end that grounds freedom, not vice versa. Aristotle, *Nic. Eth.* 1112b11–16, 26–29.

really avoid the conclusion that human free existence is either absurdity or solitude, whose predominant feeling can only be anguish?[56]

All these reductions seem to have a common thread: they conceive of human freedom unilaterally as self-determination and account for it in terms of in-dependence.[57] Rather than setting out from the positivity of being given, they take their bearings from an abstract negativity, that is, a negation blind to the positing of difference as an act of love that affirms the other as irreducible. Abstract negativity, symptomatic of an ignorance of the order of love that constitutes our own bodiliness, yields an apparently positive anthropology in which the human person is exalted to a place he had to grow into through relation with the source, but which was not given to him from the beginning. This purportedly positive anthropology, however, as our elucidations of Derrida and Heidegger illustrated, ends up denying the unity proper to the concrete singular's being and affirms instead a finite, tragic human existence. Since anthropology and ontology always have theological presuppositions, we also note that this idea of freedom, as Bruaire remarks, implies the assertion that absolute freedom is an absolute empty negativity, that is to say, "a model of God which poses that which he presupposes, but which is condemned by this native sterility to being effectively able to posit nothing."[58] The circularity between theology and anthropology can be expressed thus: we think that God is an absolute whose fullness precedes any relation because we wish to be the origin of our own being. At the same time, this theomorphic anthropology requires a theology that sees relation and receptivity as detrimental to the absolute. Detaching human freedom from the truth of God's gift of self leads finite freedom to attempt to produce the absolute knowledge it so intensely desires but cannot give itself; as history witnesses again and again, this attempt leads to the destruction of human existence.[59] Only within the context of an *agapic*, infinite freedom and of the cosmos as God created it can we account for the miracle of a finite freedom that is invited to participate in being's giving.[60]

---

56. See Marx and Engels, *Werke*, 3 and 33; Nietzsche, *Will to Power*; Heidegger, *Being and Time*; Beckett, *Waiting for Godot*; Kierkegaard, *Concept of Anxiety*.

57. This reduction becomes programmatic in Rawls's conception of liberalism. Rawls, *Political Liberalism*, 437–90; Murray, *We Hold These Truths*.

58. Bruaire, *Pour la métaphysique*, 135.

59. Bruaire, *L'affirmation de Dieu*, 165; Bruaire, *Le droit de Dieu*, 84.

60. See, e.g., Augustine, *De libero arbitrio libri tres* (PL 32) and *De spiritu et littera liber unus* (PL 44). It goes without saying that the preceding brief remarks do not suffice to fully show how each of the different works falls short, a task that does not concern us here. They simply propose a direction in which to reexamine each one of them.

The claim that finite freedom becomes comprehensible only within the horizon of infinite freedom cannot be taken lightly or hastily dismissed. Even positions radically opposed to ours, such as those of Sartre and Nietzsche, still hint at the great mystery of human freedom. Both were puzzled before this paradox: how can the divine mystery create something that is not identical with himself?[61] In their own way their negative responses also indicate the reality of human freedom, though without illuminating it. In contrast to the case of human reason, freedom seems to be "in competition with" the realm of the divine. However limited and fragile, human freedom tastes of eternity. Human freedom stands on its own; it is *autexousion*, being-from-its-own-being, and *autokratos*, self-governing, as Gregory of Nyssa writes.[62] At the same time, since this self-possession is given by God, the freedom always belongs to someone, a person, whose *esse* is permanently given to itself. This paradox does not only apply to the relationship between the concrete singular and the primordial giver. The mystery of human freedom, in its reciprocal asymmetry of being given to itself and existing only within a divine freedom, is reflected in the dual unity of self-possession and being always in communion with others. To locate freedom within the dialogue between the paternal, loving source and the concrete singular living in history opens the possibility of describing freedom and action in terms of reception and reciprocation of the gift.[63]

To receive the gift constitutes the perfection of the singular. At the level of both first and second act, the gift is not itself until it is received. Just as there is no revelation without a listener who welcomes and lets himself be changed by it, or as a child is not really fathered without the one who makes a place for him in himself and accompanies the child as he pursues his own destiny, so the gift of being is not complete until it is received. It is not just a case of finding completion in another; to look more deeply, receiving,

61. As is known, Sartre wondered how we can be free if God is absolute (Sartre, *Les mains sales*). In *Thus Spoke Zarathustra* Nietzsche wrote: "But let me reveal my heart to you entirely, my friends: *if* there were gods, how could I endure not to be a god! Hence there are no gods. Though I drew this conclusion, now it draws me" (Nietzsche, *Portable Nietzsche*, 198).

62. Quoted in Balthasar, *TD*, 2:214.

63. Balthasar clarifies that the justification of the mystery of human freedom, which regards the fact that personal, incommunicable singularity is coincident with absolute communication, can only be offered if the infinite is a triune mystery. Analogically to the divine persons whose incommunicability is coincident with the total communication of one to the other, the human person's freedom is self-possession inasmuch as it is relation with the divine source and the other singular beings—and the latter only with a gradation assigned to each singular freedom by divine freedom. With this Balthasar brings in the Fathers' Trinitarian reflection on human freedom. See, e.g., Gregory of Nyssa, *Quod non sint tres dii* (PG 45:111–31).

far from being a defeat, is the expression of the singular's power to affirm. To receive is to say "yes," to accept being an "absolute" origin (*autexousia, autokratos*) that is primordially relative to another because the singular is given to himself. The coexistence of these two poles means that we are born predisposed to being in all its transcendental dimensions: beauty, goodness, truth, unity. Because it is given to itself, our own nature tends to being. Yet this predisposition does not yield its corresponding action automatically or without mediation. To receive oneself entails freely accepting oneself from another—that is, taking oneself from (*accipere*) the others through whom one receives one's own being: those with whom one shares existence, and God, the ultimate giver of being. Because what is accepted is a gift, its reception finds gratitude to be its first form. It is this primordial gratitude that enables the self to be responsible for its own actions.

The acceptance of the singular gift regards first of all one's own bodiliness, since the body is the closest sign of the gift and the memory of God. The body is not designed by the receiver (though he can alter it); it is received, and as such it is a lasting reminder of the giving source and the *telos*. The reception of oneself includes further the lived communion with others, the spiritual and constitutive relations with them, and all that happens to the singular throughout his historical existence and through which he becomes himself. Just as we are called to take delight in having been born to parents not of our choosing, at a time we do not determine, and for a destiny that is unique to us, to exist and act is true, and thus creative, when it is a reception of being—even underneath ugly forms. Reception of oneself is neither stoic passivity nor Kantian duty. Nor is it resignation. To confuse reception with resignation is, once again, to dream of being what originary experience reveals to be a lie: to be the origin of oneself. When one's own action is not receptive of oneself in gratitude to God, one loses oneself in nostalgic acts, resentful at not being one's own origin. Consequently, only barren acts come forth from this denial, which, despite temporary appearances to the contrary, reject the light of being rather than communicate it. Reception of the gift of self, instead, is an arduous, ongoing task whose mature expressions are work, prayer, and play; rather than entertainment, this last is the enjoyment of being given to be with and for others. Accepting oneself is therefore filial thanks-giving to the loving source for the gift of one's own being, an action that cannot take place unless in it one gives oneself over to the other. To receive the gift of oneself is revealed to be the fundamental form of reciprocation.

Before moving on to consider what reciprocation is and how it invites further giving, the question arises as to why it belongs to the nature of freedom. Because one is given to oneself from nothing, there is of course a sense in which the gift cannot be reciprocated. The singular gift is totally given to itself and will not be called back. As Claudel strikingly puts it in his play *The Tidings Brought to Mary*: "For thou canst not give back to a father what he has given thee, when thou wouldst."[64] Reciprocation is not the same as the return of the gift.[65] In addition to the priority of the original giver's gift, the incapacity to "return" the gift indicates that reciprocation has to do first and foremost with oneself. Only a giving of self is an adequate response to a love that gives itself. What seems to be a necessarily incomplete return is, in reality, a response of the whole person to the *agapic* source. Gifts in which the self does not give itself are not love. They are transactions.

Rather than setting out from the fruitless dialectic of freedom and necessity, we can turn to the previous account of *eros* and *agape* to explain why reciprocity is intrinsic to the nature of gift; why, in other words, reciprocation expresses anthropologically the gift-ness of *esse*. The difference between the giver and the gift not only frees the receiver into his own freedom, it also allows the receiver to perceive that the giver both affirms (*agape*) him in giving both him to himself and any particular gift, and communicates desire (*eros*) for the receiver. The affirmation of the other (*agape*) for what he is (*logos*) is indeed gratuitous, but the latency of the giver in the gift announces the giver's desire for the receiver. If desire (*eros*) were foreign to gratuity (*agape*), philosophical reflection would be right to embrace pantheism or nihilism. What is true for discrete human acts of giving and receiving is also true for the singular's existence as a whole. That God gives the singular to himself, besides showing that divine omnipotence is not a matter of worldly power but of love (*agape, eros*), reveals something very mysterious about God himself, something ultimately ungraspable: the giver wants to be received by the receiver. In this regard the singular's desire (*eros*) to give himself in love (*agape*) to the original giver is always already an expression of grateful obedience to the giver. My action (*agere*) is always a being-carried and being-called forth by another. The difference between the primordial giver and the receiver in the gift gives freedom *and* elicits in

---

64. Claudel, *Tidings Brought to Mary*, 48. This non-reciprocity extends to teachers, friends, known and unknown people, and generations without which the singular would not be himself.

65. The term "reciprocate" expresses more adequately than "return" the response awaited from the receiver. It lacks the latter's utilitarian connotations and cannot be subsumed in a Hegelian dialectic of contradiction since it indicates that the return cannot be the identical repetition of the singular's self. If the singular being-gift is not an undetermined lack with the promise of fulfillment, nor an Arian fullness that knows no intrinsic relations, then the singular is given to himself; he is free, and he must become what he is given to be by reciprocating the original donation. The reciprocation of the gift thus also represents the constitution of the person.

the receiver the desire to respond to the original gratuity that constitutes him and all that is. Severing the *agapic* from the *erotic* dimension of the gift reduces ethics to an extrinsic addition to ontology and makes reciprocation yet another unfulfillable Kantian moral imperative.

The difference between the ultimate giver and the gift invites the receiver's response to the giver and the gift for three other related reasons. First, the difference that separates giver and gift represents the giver's truth, that is, his faithful (*emeth*) self-disclosure (*aletheia*). In this regard, the truth of the giver is an ongoing letting himself be seen by the concrete singular, to whom is given the capacity to see. When the mystery allows himself to be seen by the singular, which can never exhaust or fully comprehend the mystery, this permits the concrete singular to discover who he is in this relation of seeing and being seen by the mystery. The gift elicits the desire to know the giver, speak to him, and, without losing oneself, to become like him. Second, the faithful self-revelation of the giver is also the promise of a greater donation. That *esse commune* is not *ipsum esse subsistens* also indicates the decision to allow the singular to participate in being in ever-new ways. Contrary to Heidegger's humanism, originary experience reveals that the gift of human existence is not projected towards death. This would be looking backwards to an absolute nothingness. It is projected forward, towards the ongoing source of one's own being. Finally, the promise of the permanence of the gift includes the singular's own fruitfulness. The communion through which freedom is awakened to itself will grow through the singular's entrusting himself to the whole. These three reasons reveal further the paradox of the gift—expressed earlier in the internal relation of *eros* and *agape*. To reciprocate is beneficial for the receiver; it makes the desired unity with the giver possible inasmuch as the receiver lets his center be gratuitously (*agape*) found in the giver.

Because the original gift is a communication of love (dual unity of *eros* and *agape*) that bestows and promises ever-new communion (*koinonia*), the singular is both free *and* desirous to reciprocate the gift. The singular is for himself, can dispose of himself—even to the point of destroying himself—but he only collaborates in the constitution of himself because he responds to the one that gives him being. Therefore, freedom as the ontological and personal reception and reciprocation of the gift permits an understanding of itself as capacity for relationship.[66] A *free* human *action*, in whatever form it takes, is the lived relationship with the source. As originary experience reveals, just as human reason is the capacity to be aware of the whole, so "human freedom," says Giussani, "is that level of nature at which human

---

66. Ratzinger, "Truth and Freedom."

nature becomes capable of relationship with the infinite, capable of saying 'Thou' to this ineffable, incomprehensible, unimaginable presence without which nothing is comprehensible because nothing brings itself into being."[67] Rather than accounting for freedom in negative terms as in-dependence, or reducing it to a concatenation of choices, the ontological understanding of gift suggests that freedom and the gift of self (reciprocity) are coincident with human religiosity. Let us turn now to this question of reciprocity.

3. Reciprocity as Recognition

The suggestion that religiosity and freedom are coextensive does not cast religiosity as a species of freedom. The singular's freedom does not relate to religiosity as it does, for example, to freedom of speech or to the right to vote or have dignified employment. Nor does this statement identify freedom with following a specific religion. It presumes a different horizon, that of the very nature of the human being and what he is most fundamentally. Religiosity is not, then, limited to the exercise of freedom understood as choice, or to a freedom detached from the self-presentation of the truth (*aletheia-emeth*). Our present task is to reflect, with the help of L. Giussani, on the nature of freedom as the singular's receiving and giving. Just as freedom is bound up with the paradoxical relation of dependence on the giver—paradoxical because the singular cannot be apart from the paternal source and yet is other than him—so "freedom comes through religiosity," which is nothing but "the lived awareness of the relationship with God."[68]

We mentioned that the ontological difference between the giver and the receiver latent in the gift/receiver announces the desire that originates the acceptance and reciprocation of the gift. This means that the concrete singular's original seeking is attracted to someone, the giver, who is already in the singular himself. This seeking therefore is originated by an anterior resting on someone who is more than just an "object" of desire, that is, the giver. As the beginning of the dynamic of human freedom, the original needs or desires (which are different from biological needs) reveal that the human being, given to himself, is always moving towards the totality that attracts without compelling him.[69] The original needs constitute more than a limited chronological beginning. They accompany the human being throughout all of his existence in that they move him to desire the whole;

---

67. Giussani, *IPO*, 114; Giussani, *GTSM*, 164–65.

68. Giussani, *RS*, 92.

69. Biological needs, however, in a non-metaphorical sense, express at the somatic level the singular's constitution of the gift.

they order the singular towards the whole. The person desires to contemplate and to be transparent to the complete truth, to be seized by and to radiate all beauty, to taste and to communicate all goodness, to receive and to offer radical justice, to enjoy and to share full happiness. This desired totality, obviously, is not quantitative; a transcendent person is at the origin of the singular being's gift-ness. This is why desires come to a state of rest (*entelecheia*) when they enjoy the being that attracts them. Human beings, says Giussani, discover through their experience, that is, their being in action, that they are free when a desire is satisfied. "The phenomenon that makes me say 'I am free' is satisfaction. The phenomenon that defines freedom is the total satisfaction of myself, the answer to my thirst."[70] Satisfaction for Giussani is not a psychological category, implying pleasure or the appeasement of a whim. It is an ontological one: "Instead of satisfaction we can use a more metaphysical word: perfection. Freedom is perfection. In Latin *perficere* (to fulfill) means precisely *satisfaction*: a satisfied desire is a fulfilled desire, perfect."[71]

Linking freedom with satisfaction and conceiving this as the universal end the singular constitutively desires, Giussani offers a synthetic view of freedom that embraces both its beginning and its end. The beginning is not the singular's; it belongs to God. This is why human desires have a measure that is greater than the finite itself—it is universal—and why they move the human being only when the person is reached by the sign (gift-*logos*). The fulfillment, we just mentioned, has to do with the end. For Giussani, however, *telos* has the twofold meaning of eschatological fulfillment and the partial, historical ends that, because they participate in the final end, also "satisfy" human desires to a certain degree. *Telos* is thus both God, the mystery whose exuberance allows everything to participate in being, and, in relation to God/the mystery, singular beings. It is important here to note that "satisfaction" or the perfection of the concrete singular gift is never self-referential; it is not a resting in oneself at the expense of others. The singular's freedom is fulfilled when it rests in the one who draws it to him. In this sense, the singular's desires are not first restless and then find rest in some thing; the singular seeks what is already within him. The paradox of satisfaction consists precisely in this: that one rests in oneself only when one dwells in another whom one has welcomed. This belonging of the giver and the receiver also has a social dimension. As Origen beautifully writes, final satisfaction will take place once all those who are awaited arrive.[72] Giussani

---

70. Giussani, *USD*, 19.
71. Giussani, *PLW*, 1:60–64, at 63.
72. Origen, "Homily 7 on Leviticus, no. 2," cited in de Lubac, *Catholicism*, 397–402.

thus defines freedom as "the total fulfillment of oneself. Freedom is the possibility, the capacity, the responsibility to fulfill oneself, that is to say, to reach one's destiny. Freedom is comparison with (*paragone*) destiny."[73]

The singular's "comparison" with destiny is not a mere possibility that can be actualized at will, but the singular's primary responsibility. The human being does not owe his existence to himself and thus is responsible for seeking fulfillment. If a person wants to be true to the gift of himself, he must discover the divine one with whom he can be himself. This is the ontological imperative that the gift opens up in the existence of the singular when the singular is given to himself, that is, is made free. It is imperative because what is at stake is the truth of the singular himself. Freedom therefore comes into play not as a decision to take on or relinquish the task of "comparison"—a choice that the Greeks called *hubris*—but as the verification of the relationship between a singular and the *telos*. "Comparison" is not a dialectical interplay between the concrete singular and God or any other gift. Rather, the comparison between the concrete singular and God is an encounter in which the singular's discovery of God is always simultaneous with his going ever deeper into and outside of himself.

Giussani's perception of freedom discloses a startlingly positive sense of human nature within a dramatic account of the structure of being. To say that freedom is comparison with its destiny presupposes that the gift of being is irrevocably given to itself and placed face to face, so to speak, with its origin—which constitutes its inner core, to recall the fundamental evidence of originary experience ("I am you who make me").[74] In creating, God gives the human being a "heart" with which he wishes to be confronted.[75] Since, as we saw, Giussani's definition of "heart" is ontological and not emotivist or psychological, the comparison is not between what the human being feels about things or thinks of himself and of God, but between who and what they are. That the gift is totally given means that God has given the human person a reference with which he can verify the truth of what the mystery of being claims to be. It can seem scandalous, but if creation is the positing of someone and not the production of something, the human being can only be placed in relation with the original giver as other from the giver, that is, as free. God gives the person a heart (original needs) with which he can recognize the truth of whatever is and, above all, of God himself. The mystery of freedom rests on the incomprehensible fact that God created a

---

73. Giussani, *RS*, 88. Translation modified.
74. Giussani, *RS*, 105.
75. As explained earlier, "heart" is the unity of original needs that is coincident with originary experience.

singular to whom is given the capacity to belong to and to rest in God. A biblical reference can clarify further what this comparison means.

The evangelist Luke tells us that "Mary kept all these things, pondering (*sumballousa*) them in her heart" (Luke 2:19). The Greek verb *ballo* means "to meet," "to compare." With this verb, the evangelist tells us that Mary was comparing (*ballo*) what God has done through her with (*sun*) the prophecies that God had made throughout the history of Israel. As in other instances, a historical event proved the truth of a prophecy and distinguished false from authentic prophecies. Mary, in receiving the word, also accepted the task of verifying whether the unforeseeable presence of her son fulfilled the divine prophecies. To "ponder," in this case, meant to meet face to face with (*sumballo*) God in order to converse with him. For Mary, the content of this dialogue was the comparison of the unimaginable claim to divinity of the child with what God had done and revealed himself to be, and with what he promised through the history of Israel. Along with the promises made by God in history, we could say, God also gives every human being a fundamental "prophecy" when he gives man to himself: his own nature, whose fulfillment lies in the relation with the mystery that seeks to be received and reciprocated in freedom. It is the heart, no matter how confused and lost it may become, that has the capacity to recognize what is. Original needs, we explained, are and remain infallible. The mystery of being wants to be encountered by the human being. He gives man to himself so that he can stand face to face with him and converse. The reception of the gift demands this dialogical comparison with destiny, since the fact of not being one's own origin makes it impossible to receive oneself anywhere other than in this dialogue with the source, which includes all of the cosmos.

This "comparison," however, is not simply a mechanism of controls and checks. "Con-frontation" leads to a further step of recognition. It is at this moment that we can see with greater clarity the inseparable relationship between the exercise of freedom and the truth of being. As reception and reciprocation, gift of self brings together freedom, reason, and desire. "Freedom is need for total satisfaction. Because of this, freedom is adequacy to Being, that is, adhesion to Being. If Being, God, is everything, freedom is recognizing that God is everything. The Mystery wanted to be recognized by our freedom, he wanted to generate its own recognition."[76] To recognize one's own destiny is not simply to identify God as the origin of all that is given to be. God is not simply one object among others. The recognition of the "godly God" is not the result of the singular's decision or moral integrity. It is re-cognition, that is, knowing in being known. It is novelty within memory.

---

76. Giussani, *USD*, 19.

More than the simple recall of having met or been known by someone, it is, rather, accepting to see oneself through the memory of the one who gave one to oneself. In this regard, the divine desire to be recognized not only allows the singular to know of the existence of the giver and of himself, the receiver, along with the cosmos; it also allows the singular to possess and enjoy the one who, giving himself, wants to be in the singular that he is not and, received by the singular, makes him his own and thus allows the singular to be himself, to be a person who grows ever more in the life and communion of love that God is. Freedom's recognition that God is everything, then, permits God to form part of oneself. It is an affective knowledge—a knowledge in love, or *sapida scientia*, as mentioned earlier—in which the singular lets the one who gives himself to be known dwell in the singular himself. The human being is given to himself and is free in order that his destiny may be his own. With this, we see that to recognize the primordial giver is to give oneself over to the one who gives himself first in positing the singular and then in seeking a relationship with him. To recognize is to reciprocate, that is, to receive and to give of oneself. Giving and receiving is, at its core, the dramatic interplay of recognizing that God is everything and in that recognition letting the cosmos be, that is, allowing its form to reach a fuller expression. Awareness of oneself and other concrete singular gifts is the lived realization of the unity and difference between what is and the ultimate giver.

For Giussani, recognition is not a static, ahistorical appropriation. It is a personal relation that unfolds in history. Thus, freedom as "capacity to reach one's own destiny" is always becoming, tending towards the infinite, and the closer it gets, the freer the singular becomes.[77] At the same time, and precisely because of its historical condition, "freedom will take place, it is not yet; freedom will take place when man will be happy. If freedom is desire for happiness, the event of freedom will be fulfilled when the desire of happiness will be fulfilled."[78] This does not make history deceitful or freedom illusory, quite the contrary. Historical circumstances and creatures as such "are the way in which the infinite becomes present to man and awakens in him the thirst for him."[79] The free recognition of the giver is the gradual adhesion to the divine mystery as he gives himself to be known and loved. It is this dialogue of mutual giving and receiving between God and the human being that allows the singular to become himself, to be one with the divine source and yet remain himself. This also means that, from the

---

77. Aquinas, *De ver.*, q. 24, a. 4.
78. Giussani, *PLW*, 1:64.
79. Ibid., 1:67.

point of view of freedom, giving (reception and reciprocity) is a dynamic action that consists in following. If giving were just an exchange, detached from love and truth, it would only serve to affirm the giver or the receiver. This, however, as experience shows, is always insufficient. In every action something is affirmed as the meaning of the whole. This, as we shall shortly see, does not undermine the integrity of the act. Chopping wood remains chopping wood, but as an action, its form comes from the singular's affirmation of the meaning of the whole. At the same time, this affirmation of the meaning of the whole, God, gives the act of chopping wood its complete form and integrity. Since the recognition of the gift opens the singular up to the totality of the origin, it is the gradual becoming of oneself in relation with the mystery of being. At the same time, since the origin is other and giver of gifts, the fulfillment takes a form whose measure and actualization are not determined by the singular. It is always new and specific to each while also common to all.

It is within this context that Giussani elaborates on the meaning of choice. For Giussani, it bears repeating, "choice" does not belong to the essence of freedom. The nature of freedom is total satisfaction—being oneself with the giver and with others in an ever-deepening, reciprocal letting the other be within oneself. In fact, once this perfection is finally given, there will be no more possibility of choosing. To place choice within this larger horizon is contrary to modernity's tendency to think that choice—purportedly a self-originated, autonomous movement of the soul—defines freedom itself. For the concrete singular, particular, historical choices are instead the response of the person to the original giver, through which the person determines him or herself. The option is the answer given to *and* with the one to whom one is responding. Again, the choice of a particular method or the decision to carry out a specific action is always the affirmation of something as the meaning of the whole. Every human choice of a particular, however tacit, is *eo ipso* the affirmation of a universal. We affirm whatever ultimate we hold most dear in whatever we do. This is why for Giussani the *cognitio finis*, being itself as it gives itself to be known and enjoyed, and the capacity to govern oneself (will) are indispensable for there to be a free choice.[80] The paradox of freedom and free moral action resides precisely in this: the more the *telos* is permitted to determine the human action, the freer one becomes, that is, the more the person becomes him or herself. Human freedom, as religiosity, coincides with the lived awareness of the dependence of everything and everyone on the paternal giver. Freedom as religiosity reveals human

---

80. Ibid., 1:72–79. *Cognitio finis* is also considered by Aquinas to be a fundamental principle of human freedom (*ST*, I-II, q. 6, a. 1).

life as an arduous path, which, as Bernanos's impassioned critique of mediocrity makes abundantly clear, very few are willing to walk.[81] Yet it is only in this receiving of oneself and reciprocation of the original donation that the singular grows in the truth of himself. "True freedom," says Giussani, "is man's capacity to adhere to being: not only of deciding, approving being, but of adhering to being. In this way a connubiality, a profound nuptiality (*sposalizio*), is born. This nuptiality is the conception of the relationship between the self and all that surrounds it, between the self and the whole universe: it is a universal spousal image."[82]

4. Human Action and the Gift of Self

We mentioned at the beginning of this chapter that gift is the form of action in that it gathers the different elements that constitute human action into a dynamic unity. Acting, at its core, is the reception and the reciprocation of the gift of being. One may still wonder, however, whether the foregoing non-technocratic account of the reciprocation of the gift of self—acceptance of oneself and the recognition of God's ever-greaterness—does not in fact dissolve time into static presence, mistake action for ethereal contemplation of the whole, or instrumentalize the singular. Answering these objections requires us to approach the other sense in which gift is the form of action indicated earlier: the content of a human action is a specific communication of love. Love, so Aquinas says, "has the nature of the first gift and through it all gifts are given."[83] Without losing sight of our main concern—to show in what sense human action expresses the singular's gift-ness—let us consider in what sense gift is the form of action by pondering the singular's relation to others, work, and prayer.

A human action exercises the gift of *esse* when it follows the latter's outflowing from God and it returns to him. In every human activity, action, reciprocation of the gift, is the giving of one's own being. Human action is called to let the memory of being's gift-ness give form to it. This memory includes, on the one hand, awareness that the self is given to itself within a communion of being to which it also belongs. In this sense, reciprocating the gift of one's own *esse* occurs by giving oneself to the other singulars participating in this communion. On the other hand, the memory of being's gift-ness carries the singular further to the source of all that is. Since concrete singulars are a sign (gift-*logos*) of the original giver, giving oneself to

---

81. Bernanos, *Diary*. See also Balthasar, *Bernanos*, 340–68.
82. Giussani, *GTSM*, 167.
83. Aquinas, *ST*, I, q. 38, a. 2.

them acknowledges their own sacramentality and treats them accordingly. Expressing the order of God's gratuitous communication of *esse* therefore means that, when one gives to others, one is reciprocating God's gift, which is always prior to the giving of the concrete singular. Giving a gift to another person, or taking care of creation, is always a response to the source's ever-surprising gratuity for the singular other. It is only in this response to the divine source that there is a complete and gratuitous affirmation of the singular other for his own sake.

This circularity, which secures the unity of and difference between the giver, the gift, and the receiver indicated earlier, can be seen in many different instances. Giving to others, as in the giving of a present, could simply be a token to affirm the goodness of the life of the other, or of existence itself. This goodness, however, is preserved from banality only because the goodness of existence is rooted in the goodness of the original giver. Giving to others could also be the attempt to respond to a need. Feeding the hungry, forgiving a wrong, educating, or dying in another's place are human actions that seek to help the other bring the gift of existence to its proper fullness. The response to the other's needs is not egotistic philanthropy, however, when the root of this action is recognized to be, on the one hand, the reciprocation to the original giver for the gift of oneself and the other, and, on the other hand, the lived awareness of the relation of all things with the mystery of being. Human actions have the form of gift and are a communication of love if, in responding to the other's needs, the actor affirms the whole. In other words, the gift of self that attempts to meet the other's needs and to transfigure the world so that it can be itself more truly is a gift if it attempts to collaborate with the actual living out of the recognition of and the confrontation with the mystery of being—in and with the world. What one does for the other is a true, free action to the degree that it is transparent to the original, giving source and that it helps to recognize the mystery of being and its relation with all things.

Giving to others also must pattern itself after the proper measure of gift: totality. The total communication of one's own *esse* calls for a reciprocation of all of oneself. That is to say, in response to the gift of *esse* that posits a person, only the gift of one's own self expresses this gift-ness of being. The concrete examples we saw above are instances of giving because in each, to a certain extent, one gives one's self. To understand the totality that the reciprocation of the gift requires, it is perhaps more helpful to turn to the archetype of this totality, the "vow." When a man and a woman exchange vows at the liturgical ceremony of their wedding, or when a person offers all of himself or herself to God through vows of poverty, chastity, and obedience or the sacrament of ordination, in that single act they give all of themselves.

Giving oneself in each of these three cases is an affirmation, a welcoming of a gift received: the gift of one's own being, and the gift of one's own place in the *logos* of love. Because it is a giving of all of oneself within a prior, and permanent, being given to oneself, the giving of self is a response and does not rest on one's own capacity to utter an affirmation and sustain it throughout one's life. One chooses to have been chosen. It is true that a vow takes place only later in the singular's existence, yet it gathers up all the preceding and ensuing life in the unity with God, giver of all gifts. Every other human giving of oneself to others is an expression of this totality, either because it leads to it—and thus somehow participates in it—or because it is a fruit of it. Here again we see how human action reflects at its own limited level the primordial giving of being. Just as God's creative act gives everything at once and has in itself its fulfillment from all eternity, although this fulfillment is made manifest only at the appropriate time, so the grateful human giving of oneself to another expresses its unifying totality at the moment of the vow and unfolds itself in history through gradual, limited, and authentic attempts to give oneself to others. The graduality and approximation of grateful giving and receiving, rather than failures, represent the way in which the total gift of the limited singular unfolds itself in history. In light of the nature of the vow—which is also expressed in Christian martyrdom—we can see, on the one hand, that every human action, since it affirms the mystery of being and the other singular within it, is a total, albeit historical, gift of oneself, *and*, on the other hand, that the gift of self is only given through the whole life of the singular (and hence comprises the singular's entire historical existence). The complete gift of oneself in one single gesture is the affirmation of the mystery of being as the meaning of the singular. If deprived of this totalizing dimension—the gift of all of oneself to the original giver, given to, with, and through the other singular—every human gesture would remain meaningless, gift-less.

We call friendship the reciprocity gratuitously generated by the gift of self to another. To accept and shelter the gift makes love reciprocal. As Giussani writes, "The human self, made in the image and likeness of God, originally reflects the mystery of the one and triune Being precisely through the dynamism of freedom whose law will therefore be love, and the dynamism in which this love plays itself out can only be friendship."[84] Friendship shows in a beautiful way that what is at stake in giving is the constitution, in the enjoyment of the other's company, of the singular as person. Obviously, since friendship belongs to the gift of being (*esse commune* and human communion), we do not make it happen, nor do we plan out its significance

---

84. Giussani, *USD*, 20.

and endurance. Friendship is a gift within the gift of the communion of being. For this reason, friendship disappears like dew at dawn if it is considered an end in itself in which the friend is merely a replica of oneself or an instrument for obtaining one's goals.[85] The friend, as with the original giver and the singular, remains irreducible to oneself and is to be loved for his own sake. Certainly, at the center of this friendship is the enjoyment of the other's presence and the betterment of the world through work that, as expression of the gift, attempts to meet the other's needs, as well as to recognize the loving, giving source. However, the nature of the gift requires that the good shared in friendship, in and through all that is shared, be the ultimate giver.[86] Friendship, precisely because it is a shared life, is a living memory of the totality of the divine, *agapic* source and so must respect the order and the *telos* that this memory unfolds. In this sense the reciprocity of friendship, rather than formal equality, reflects the openness of the gift; at the beginning—a friendship's origin lies deep within God—at its center, and at its goal. It grows, therefore, when it obeys the truth of being. More precisely: the heart of friendship is obedience to the complete truth of being's gift-ness. This approach to the gift of self by way of vow and friendship opens up the other two dimensions of gift as the form of human act: work and prayer.

Human work, be it the building of a house, caring for the ill, defending the law, or preparing a meal, is at its core an act of love, that is, love is work's proper content. Obviously, this does not mean that one's action is empty or an excuse to show affection for someone. It means rather that the transfiguration of the world that takes place through work is a gathering of the world into a unity by love and, through each specific work, the communication of this *agapic-erotic* unity. Given the fragmentation of the world we live in, if we wish to perceive the nature of work it is crucial to recall the sense of home laid out earlier: the place generated by love, through the vows that one is given to pronounce, in order to allow those who are called to live in it to participate, dwell, and be educated in the truth of love. The home is therefore the place in which one deepens and rediscovers his own constitutive childlikeness precisely because the house is the memory of the

---

85. It suffices here to mention that Epicurus was the first to determine friendship as being born from the usefulness that one derives from the other. See his Vatican Saying no. 23 in Epicurus, *Essential Epicurus*. The Stoics, as is known, opposed this view. See, e.g., Cicero, *De senectute*; Seneca, *Seneca's Letters to Lucilius*, 48:2.

86. This comment of Augustine is very much to the point: "But those whose mutual love has the possession of God Himself for its object, will truly love one another; and, therefore, even for the very purpose of loving one another, they love God. There is no such love as this in all men; for few have this motive for their love one to another, that God may be all in all (1 Cor 15:28)" (Augustine, *In Ioa.* 83.3 [PL 35:1846]).

gift of one's own call to be. It is also a school of charity since, at home, one's permanent entrusting of one's self to the other—the giving of the gift—is renewed and experienced ever more deeply as love. It is thus that one is brought ever more deeply into the mystery of being.

Technological thinking tries to convince us that what happens at home and what one does at work are two separate things. Instead, given that they are both expressions of love, what one does at work flows from the love one is given to live at home, and what one does at work enlarges and deepens the concrete form of love one is given to live at home or in the monastery. Just as the child reminds the parents of the fruitfulness of their love and gives their love a radically new depth, so work is a sign of the fruit of the love one is given to live and enlarges that love through the transfiguration of reality that work accomplishes. Certainly, there is an asymmetrical reciprocity between the home or monastery and work that gives the home a certain priority since one's own place in being has a grounding dimension that work does not. The home enables the "worker" to remember that, although work contributes to his fulfillment, his task does not begin with him and does not have him as its goal. In other words, the task is at the service of something greater than himself, namely the love that gave him a home or monastery in the first place.

Without the attitude of wonder before the gift of being, work tends to be reduced to technological making, that is, to a form of production in which the person is never taken fully into account. If, instead, one keeps the full extent of the gift-ness of being in view, work recuperates the integrity of the person. Work thus conceived is not simply an expression of an individual's mastery over nature, that is, a demonstration of the extent of his power, but is an expression of the entire person, in both the utter poverty and wealth of the gift of his being. If wonder permits seeing the singular being for what it is—not a mass of data to be manipulated or processed, but a whole that cannot be severed from its relation with the source and that seeks its fulfillment in another—then work entails the transfiguration in the world of what is, that is, it allows the concrete singular to find its partial fulfillment in its relation with the source.

Because the concrete singular being is given to itself in order to be, and yet, at the same time—since it is not complete in itself—it reaches its fulfillment only in relation with others, the change that human work is called to bring about in the world is a participation in a deeper change that was neither begun nor will be completed by man alone. That beings are, that they exist in a communion of beings, and that each of them can neither become itself nor bear fruit without the others, means that human work is a participation in a far deeper working. The one who wonders and is aware of his poverty knows that the *logos* of the concrete singular is a participation in the divine *logos*, that is, in God's design. Wonder enables us to see that the world follows a hidden harmony, a divine design in which the human being is called to participate. In this regard, what the human being is called to "make"—through the infinite variety of human activity, from curing a cancer to washing dishes—participates in the fulfillment of the design that one can never master. The problem in technological making is not the legitimate need to be engaged with the world in order to collaborate in the revelation of what the world is. It is the failure to recognize that, on the one hand, this making (work) reveals a light that is not one's own but the divine mystery's and, on the other hand, that what one "produces" reflects one's finite glory only inasmuch as it reflects the mystery's glory. As we mentioned, technological making in its oblivion of God increases boredom and homelessness under the guise of novelty.

Seen as a true human action, work reveals the person's relationship with the mystery. The person works by giving form to everything (himself, those who live with him, his specific work) while remaining mindful that everything belongs to God. As Giussani's definition of originary experience indicated, the person collaborates in transfiguring reality (land, nature, and history) according to a plan that is suggested to him through the singular itself but that is not his (it is God's). Only as a participation in this love and its *logos*, which nourishes and educates the human person within a dwelling place, can man actually work (otherwise, he simply produces) in the awareness that his work, from the most banal to the most sublime, is always a tiny step inside the mystery that calls man to collaborate in the construction of the cosmos.[87]

How does a person recognize his specific task in carrying out the design that has been taking place since the beginning of the world, the fulfillment of which is accomplished by the Person in whom everything consists? Through work, the person is asked to take possession (within the poverty of not being the origin of oneself) of what God has created and to let gift emerge. Each particular way of taking possession of reality is also the expression of the person's most fundamental needs: beauty, justice, truth, freedom, and love. Note, however, that these needs are different expressions of the way love holds sway over the person by surprising him through its concrete, singular existence. Love itself elicits in some the expression of beauty through the various forms of art and constructive ordering; in others, it suggests the pursuit of justice so that peoples and persons can be affirmed for what they are and not reduced to disposable quantities; in others, love

---

87. See Giussani, *IPO*, 51–95.

generates the concern to express its *logos* (truth) through speech, reflection, writing, or more importantly, through education; finally, in others, it instills the patience to serve other beings through whatever they are given to do. Being in the world, the human person is surprised by the singular otherness of beings and is given to enjoy it and to contemplate it, that is, to let it be. At the same time, being in the world, man discovers the call to collaborate in the betterment of the world, to work, that is, to let it shine with the light that comes from the source of all that is.

Let us now approach the third instance through which we can see that gift is the form of action: prayer.[88] Recognition of the source and participation in the giving and receiving in which human life consists disclose too that, as Giussani says, "God desires that there exist one who asks Him to be, one who may say so entirely, so sincerely that He is everything, that he may ask Him to receive what He has already given: to participate in being.... That being becomes everything in him, in whatever he does."[89] True freedom flourishes in prayer, a prayer that asks to receive again what one has already been given. Rather than multiplying gifts or balancing presents with other presents, when the giving is transparent to the source, acceptance and reciprocation of the gift takes the form of prayer. Prayer is the apex of the reception of the gift and the singular's most important gift of self. The one who knows himself to be gift can ask, that is, put himself in the hands of another in order to receive being. To ask is to give oneself over to another. While it is the singular's action, it has a communal form—not only because it is the recognition of the unity with the mystery of being, but because within one's prayer the cosmos is gathered in unity.[90]

This prayer, since it is the echo of the gift of being as expressed through the singular's affective awareness of the whole, is always both gratitude and entreaty. It expresses the gladness of being given to be with the other and the desire for that communion to remain and grow—even when grief seems to be the only motive for prayer. In fact, to ask for what has already been given is not to seek "more of the same." It is to ask to remain in the relation with the giver, and that God, the infinite other, might ensure that this relation that confirms the gift of being be always the same but ever new. It is the ardent request for the source.[91] This coincidence of sameness and newness

---

88. We will return to the theme of prayer in the following pages. Our interest here is simply to indicate in what sense prayer reveals love to be the full form of human action.

89. Giussani, *USD*, 20–21.

90. Every human act of prayer finds its final form in the liturgy. The liturgical dimension is not an extrinsic addition to the irreplaceable prayer of the singular. Giussani, *Morality*; Guardini, *Spirit of the Liturgy*; Ratzinger, *Spirit of the Liturgy*.

91. In this way Giussani retrieves the New Testament understanding of freedom as

proper to the absolute gift is also what makes the relation with the mystery of being always the same and ever new. Precisely because of this reason, for Giussani, friendship exists not only between human beings. It is first and foremost with God: "friendship is a reciprocity of the gift, of love, because, for a created being, as the human being is, the supreme form of loving God is to accept to be made by him, accepting to be, accepting the being that is not ours, the being that is given."[92]

Freedom comes through religiosity because the latter is the lived awareness of the relationship with God, in which God, the mystery of being, gives singulars to themselves and makes them free so that they may find their being and their perfection with him. Religiosity protects freedom because it enables human freedom to resist being reduced, truncated, or manipulated by others. Only dependence on the ultimate giver and *telos*, the acceptance to live the dramatic and never-manipulable friendship with the loving source, sets freedom free to receive and reciprocate, to remain in the relation with the giving source that has given the singular the task of recognizing him.

5. Orphans, at Last

Hegel famously writes that "this idea [of Divine Love] sinks into mere edification, and even insipidity, if it lacks the seriousness, the suffering, the patience, and the labor of the negative."[93] While we will revisit later the category of negativity, we turn now to the possibility that always accompanies the risk of giving. The rejection of the gift, we know all too well, is not just a possibility. Although the gift of the singular is not itself until it is received and reciprocated, sometimes the incompleteness or imperfection of the singular himself—as with an inherited or acquired physical deficiency—can make the idea of "receiving" the "gift" of being seem an expression of risible naïveté. As human beings, we are used to giving and receiving gifts. Not only discrete presents, but, more importantly, gifts such as education, friendship, trust, power, our word, and even our very lives. Quite often they are rejected, disregarded, misunderstood, betrayed. Unfortunately, we are also familiar with the use of other people for ideological motives, the result

---

eleutheria, according to which the free person is not the slave but the one who inherits the house, remains in it, and thus is called friend (Gal 5). See Ratzinger, "Freiheit und Bindung," 48.

92. Giussani, *USD*, 55. See Giussani, "*Tu*," for further reflections on friendship—a theme that occupies a prominent place in Giussani's thought.

93. Hegel, *PS*, 19.

of which extends to the suffering of the innocent and even genocide—which is an expression of sheer madness. While pondering the extremes of moral and physical evil, however, we also need to acknowledge that the failure to reciprocate the gift is not something that simply befalls us. Again and again the rejection of the gift finds in us a more or less conscious collaborator.[94]

In the face of these events, we must ask: if the structure of being is gift and the human person has been given to participate in the original giving while being predisposed to the good, whence this rejection? What is this denial? What place does non-reciprocity occupy within the texture of gift? Does the reality of the rejection of gift undermine the overarching claim of this book, namely, that gift allows us to perceive unity and difference in such a way that the inexhaustible wholeness of each (the divine source and the singular), as well as their relationship, is fully respected? Does evil prove that gift, and hence metaphysics, is hopelessly romantic? To answer these questions, rather than looking at different single instances of gift-giving, we can turn to the essence of the original rejection of the gift to discover what is at stake.

Confronted with the mystery of evil, it is tempting to offer a system that explains evil away epistemologically. Once knowledge of reality becomes adequate, so Spinoza believed, evil will be revealed as an illusion, "an inadequate cognition."[95] Nevertheless, "if evil does not exist," we could ask with Augustine, "why are we afraid of it or try to avoid it?"; where does this illusion originate?[96] Hegel's solution is that any account of the reality of evil has first to excise any purported gratuitousness from its origin or redemption. To him, it is only the spirit's dialectic movement of absolute self-determination that proves the necessity and sublation of evil. Precisely because the absolute spirit denies itself in order to affirm itself, evil comes to the absolute from within itself; it is not extrinsic to it. For Hegel, evil with all its ugliness is ultimately a transitional and necessary passage through the particular so that substance can become a subject. Evil and pain show the extent of the separation and negation that the absolute spirit goes through before it is able to integrate each element within an all-encompassing unity.

---

94. In the following we will not deal with the meaning of suffering, which is to not share in the good, to be cut off from it, or to deprive oneself of it. "Man suffers on account of evil" (John Paul II, *Salvifici doloris*, no. 7 [AAS 76 (1984), 206–7]). In his beautiful lecture on evil, Paul Ricoeur seems to separate evil from suffering in order to give the latter its due weight, an attempt that, as X. Tilliette contends, is unjustifiable. See Ricoeur, *Le mal*; Tilliette and Riconda, *Del male*; Hauerwas, *Suffering Presence*.

95. Spinoza, *Ethics*, part 4, preface, definitions 1 and 2, propositions 8 and 64 with corollary.

96. Augustine, *Confessions* 7.5 (PL 32:736–37).

Evil requires the separation and at the same time is the ground for its own sublation. For Hegel, rather than destroying unity, evil reinforces it. Still, when faced with the suffering of the innocent, or with a cry like Lear's at the death of Cordelia, it is difficult not to concur with Desmond's objection: "Can dialectics take us beyond this Never? Can the universal of logic or world-history ever unharden the irrevocability of Lear's savage, reiterated Never?"[97] We can rightly wonder whether it is not in fact the case that even the most banal instances of evil reveal Hegel's misguided identification of the ethical with the logical, the anthropological with the theological. If God creates the singular from nothingness and gives him to himself, the separation from the source that evil (the rejection of the gift) represents should not be either denied or integrated within a totality at the expense of difference.

To understand what the denial of the reception and reciprocation of the gift means for the understanding of unity and difference presented here, we must return to the meaning of the singular's limitedness and then to the nature of the task given to the singular with his own being. The nature of the singular and his freedom are in fact the conditions of possibility for the rejection of the gift.[98]

In light of the existence of evil, it is common to think that to be finite or limited is to be "less," as if it were a defect not to be God. If this were the case, non-reciprocity would be a necessary outcome of the singular's limitedness. However, it is only a theological presupposition of absolute self-determination that perceives being other than God as "less." This theological presupposition values identity and equality as the necessary terms of being and "a priori" views inequality as a lack that is not to be borne. Accordingly, the reciprocation of the gift, as many gnostic systems defended throughout history, would be nothing but a return to the pleroma after an inexplicable fall.[99]

While it is the case that finite beings are not God, the difference from their source and their consequent limitedness do not demand an interpretation in terms of deficiency.[100] If causality is the communication of being,

---

97. The passage of Shakespeare that Desmond refers to is the following: "And my poor fool is hanged! No, no, no, life? / Why should a dog, a horse, a rat, have life, / And thou no breath at all? Thou'lt come no more, / Never, never, never, never, never." *King Lear*, 5, 3, 307–10; quoted in the remarkable fourth chapter of Desmond, *Beyond Hegel and Dialectic*, 189–250, at 235. For Hegel see, PS, 383–409.

98. It is thus unjustified to reduce evil to the exercise of freedom, as Kant proposes (Kant, *Religion*). For a cogent critique of Kant's position, see Milbank, *Being Reconciled*, 1–25.

99. See Irenaeus, *Haer.* (PG 7a–b), and Jonas, *Gnostic Religion*.

100. It is Christian revelation that introduces the perception of the infinite, not of limit, as perfection. For the Greeks, the limit (represented by the sphere) is what is

the singular's dissimilarity from the God that is love (*agape* and *eros*) comes from its being a non-subsistent *esse*, which, as *esse*, remains simple and complete. The created singular images God inasmuch as it is given to be, and it images him in a limited way—as emerged in the earlier discussion of the body. In light of the gift, therefore, the singular's ontological determination is a negation of divisibility, that is, an affirmation of singularity. The singular is that which is permitted to be. If causal donation is communication of being, the concept of limit or finitude does not only underscore the point of separation. More deeply, it indicates the relation with the original source. It is precisely this relation that makes the difference between the singular and the source possible. In other words, the limitedness of the singular gift does not reveal the singular as that which is taken out from the unlimited (Anaximander), but rather as that whose luminosity is a participation in the light of the source. If the singular is given to itself without being God, limitedness can only be the ground of evil, not its expression or necessary outcome.

We need to press this point further. If limitedness is, as such, a certain participation in being, then the relations between singulars and between them and God are not dialectic but analogical. The cosmos is a harmonic unity in which one depends on the other. Singularity is expressive of organic unity, in which one is distinct and yet inseparable from the other. For the ontology of gift, what belongs to the other is not what has been taken away from oneself, as in the idealistic interpretation of determination. Rather, what belongs to oneself is "for all" in its being of oneself. Divine beauty would not be able to express itself in a finite world unless there were degrees of being because it would be unable to express the richness of the unity proper to being as other from itself.[101]

Since the gift is totally given to itself, the singular, as limited, can only have an imperfect participation in being. What "imperfection" means in light of the ontology of gift, however, could be described as tension towards perfection and fulfillment. This tension is not the attempt to become an independent individual but rather to be a singular in the unity with and adhesion to the source. Creatures, as discussed earlier, reciprocate the gift in seeking their perfection and fulfillment. This means, of course, that neither perfection nor fulfillment is given to them mechanically or automatically. They are to seek it through their own activity, which, like their own being, also reflects the movement from nothingness into being. In this way the limitedness of the singular precludes infallibility. Just as the singular's limitedness is not evil, so the possibility of fallibility and error is not yet perfect.

---

101. Aquinas, *SCG* 3.71 passim.

the presence of evil. Fallibility belongs to the singular's becoming, that is, to its historical movement towards the gratuitous source of all being. It is the existence of becoming that opens up the possibility of the rejection of the gift.[102] To "become" is indeed a sign of the singular's creation out of nothing. It is also the gradual reception of the promise of being fulfilled. The singular person's becoming himself, therefore, is the movement forward that consists in the recognition of the totality that God is, a movement that is also open to being carried away. If the singular detaches himself from the generating relationship with the *agapic* source, that is, when he does not recognize God's totality, creaturely freedom permits nothingness to irrupt in the cosmos through the singular's own action and reduces the cosmos to chaos. This is how the unity proper to the gift is broken; it is freedom, not finitude, that brings evil into the cosmos.

"The actualization of nothingness," wrote Bulgakov, "is a metaphysical plundering that is made possible by the benevolence of the Creator of everything who prefers the world in its freedom rather than a world that is simply an object of its omnipotence."[103] The irruption of nothingness does not hypostatize the *nihil* into some sort of quasi-being. Yet, since creatures are taken out of nothingness, there remains in them an inclination towards evil, which inclination in itself is not evil. That human action permits nothingness to irrupt in the place of gift does not mean that evil is equi-primordial with the good. What principle could ground the coexistence of good and evil? Furthermore, if good and evil were coextensive, how to explain the creature's inability to succumb completely to the tendency to metaphysical suicide, which is permanently lurking within its denial of God's totality? Satan, in fact, wishes man's death, not his own. God's *fiat* to creation, which is given to itself, cannot be undone. To let nothingness irrupt through one's own action means that the human being, who as gift is in himself good, produces a privation in the singular. Evil is distancing from the source. The classical interpretation of evil as a "non-being" does not consider evil an illusion, à la Spinoza. It does not mean that evil lacks the force to destroy, that is, to separate one from one's own self and from every other. Human history is a continuous witness to the force of this irruption of nothingness.

---

102. While every singular being tends towards its source in receiving and reciprocating the gift that it is, only the human singular has a history, and to this history the fate of the subhuman is tied. It is both because the human recapitulates in himself the subhuman and because the human cannot be adequately grasped without the spiritual creatures, the angels, that through man's action—the one who was meant to unite everything to God so that in and with God everything could be—the subhuman is subjected to evil.

103. Bulgakov, *La luce senza tramonto*, 297.

By bringing about "nothingness" and darkness with one's own action, freedom makes the claim to be everything for itself, and, as such, it pretends to be from itself. For the created singular to attempt to be all and to be from himself is the attempt to cease to be, to prevent being from revealing and communicating its goodness.[104]

The question of why human freedom tends towards evil rather than to the good is the search for a "deficient" cause, as Augustine famously puts it. Trying to find an "efficient" cause that separates the singular from that which most delights him is "like trying to hear silence or see darkness."[105] Evil is a parasite of being and can be comprehended only in relation to it. This is why S. Weil writes that "we experience good only by doing it. / We experience evil only by refusing to allow ourselves to do it, by repenting of it. When we do evil we do not know it, because evil flies from the light."[106]

Both the Jewish tradition and some fathers of the Church teach that the original sin, that is, the source and essence of every rejection of the gift, took place due to Adam and Eve's original naïveté and inexperience. Had Satan not intervened immediately after their creation, their familiarity with God would have shown the lie of the temptation and enabled them to understand that the prohibition against eating from the tree was to help them realize that everything was given to them as a gift. The movement from image to likeness, to recall Irenaeus's account, consisted exactly in the growth of the gift, the reception and reciprocation of the original love. Yet the infancy and hence the need of time for the gift to be received and reciprocated, that is, to recognize God's totality and within it the dominion of the created world, enabled Satan, in the guise of the serpent, to seduce Eve and then Adam with a lie. They did not pass a single night in Eden.[107] "Creatureliness," writes Bulgakov, "contains luciferism as a temptation to be overcome. Luciferism has its foundation not in an accident or caprice, but in the very character of creatureliness as the union of free self-determination and the natural given."[108] God, who knows how to risk and how to weave

---

104. Pseudo-Dionysius, *Divine Names*, 4.19ff. (PG 716C–736B); Maximus the Confessor, *Quaestiones ad Thalassium* (CCSG 7:22); Augustine, *Civ.* 11 (PL 41:315–48); Aquinas, *ST*, I, qq. 47–49; *SCG* 3.2–16, 71.

105. See Augustine, *Civ.* 12.7 (PL 41:355). "Nemo igitur quaerat efficientem causam malae voluntatis: non enim est efficiens, sed deficiens; quia nec illa affectio est, sed defectio. Deficere namque ab eo quod summe est, ad id quod minus est, hoc est incipere habere voluntatem malam" (ibid.).

106. Weil, *Simone Weil Reader*, 383.

107. In this regard, while Genesis offers some hints as to how to understand man's original sin, the sin of Lucifer—jealousy, according to the tradition of the Church—remains beyond our comprehension.

108. Bulgakov, *Bride of the Lamb*, 156.

finite freedom into the revelation of his own glory from within, allowed man to be tempted and so gave him the opportunity to rediscover a unity with him that cannot be broken.

What is the nature of this temptation? We cannot overlook that evil enters history by way of man's relationship with God and not because of the breakdown of a self-imposed law. Rather than a failure, evil is a denial of who God is and what beings are. Since the denial (that God is all in all) is the negation of what being reveals itself to be, the form of this denial is the lie. Because of its denial of God, evil cannot but be a lie that, as the rejection of being, expresses itself as jealousy. Satan projects onto God his own perception of being: that God is jealous of man. Based on this jealousy it cannot be true that God is a father who knows how to give what is needed and who remains faithful. He, so the lie would have it, cannot be trusted and withholds the gift. He will not fulfill the promise, and, because he is afraid of giving, the Father is no longer someone to be loved. The singular being convinces himself that he is better off as an orphan, influenced by the devil's insinuation that it is possible to determine oneself while bracketing the gift-character of one's own existence. Under this dark light, adulthood, or inherited divinity in the scriptural term, is perceived as orphanhood. Fatherlessness is the consequence of defining one's own identity with a false measure, one that forgets its having been given to itself. Original sin therefore is the rejection of God's measure for the creature. The "no" contained in the rejection of the gift is thus the denial that God is everything, that is, the rejection of God's fatherhood.

Looking more concretely at this self-engineered orphanhood can illuminate what follows when the singular does not reciprocate the gift, that is, when he falls short of being, or when, expressed theologically, he "sins." If freedom is the capacity to fulfill oneself in adhering to being, sin can only be "the opposite of freedom" because "the truth of every thing is its relation with the infinite."[109] In light of this, sin, rather than a simple (bad) choice, is the denial of freedom. "The sin," says Giussani, "is every human action and relation that does not recognize that God is everything, as *telos* and method."[110] Disobedience, which for many is the essence of original sin, shows its ultimate ground here: rather than breaking a particular law, disobedience is the lack of recognition of God's totality. Thus, non-reciprocity (evil) is any human action that in any aspect denies that God is everything. Instead of the reception and reciprocation of the gift, in the evil action

---

109. Giussani, *PLW*, 1:68.
110. Giussani, *USD*, 22.

one "places oneself against the evidence that God is everything."[111] Giussani indicates that the recognition of God's totality also acknowledges the *telos* of every human action. Whatever act of human freedom that does not recognize or contribute to the recognition of God is, to use the expression adopted earlier, an irruption of nothingness. This *telos*, as we saw, is not simply the intention that the singular attaches to his action or to reality, but rather the consistency of all that is. Hence, to affirm another *telos* is to deny what beings are and, to a certain extent, to prevent them from being. The recognition of God also determines the method according to which human action proceeds, because God, as its origin, directs its unfolding until the singular fully adheres to him. When human action takes the singular as its ultimate meaning, it corrupts what it touches, that is, it breaks apart its unity (*cor-rumpere*). It asserts that a finite singular created from nothingness provides the total meaning of being. Existentially speaking, the rejection of the gift is to use the creature to satisfy oneself rather than to turn (*con-vertere*) and walk with it towards its *telos*. The error in this case does not reside in attending to the attractiveness that every singular has—due to its being an icon of the divine mystery—but in preferring a singular that does not lead to one's own destiny.

It is important to realize that evil follows the inverse path (method and *telos*) of the gift and in this sense is an action that falls short of the gift-ness of being. The promise contained within the gift, which needs to be fulfilled in time, is cut short. Evil promises immediate fulfillment at the beginning—hence the evil's promise does not open up a history for the return of the gift to the source and thus leaves no room for personhood—and, at the end, the discovery of the meaninglessness of suffering.[112] Only a particular that has been detached from its source and *telos* claims to give everything at the beginning, and this claim turns out false every time. Non-reciprocity spoils the gift. When, instead, the singular's freedom affirms that God is everything, it can be itself and, through its action, can place the finite it embraces in relation to its source.

Schlier's remarkable exegetical work on the epistle to the Romans helps us understand that, according to St. Paul, this denial of God's Fatherhood, for both Greeks and Jews (and so for all mankind), is ingratitude. Unwilling to give glory to God, as is proper to the nature of the gift of being, the pagans do not give God thanks (Rom 1:21). Refusing to recognize that the existence of all that is comes from God, they cannot perceive the light of the singular or recognize it as a sign of the creator. They remove themselves from the

---

111. Ibid.
112. Giussani, *PLW*, 1:60–67.

original gift and so are incapable of seeing. Deprived of sight, their thoughts become futile, banal, nothing (*mataia*). The rejection of the gift makes the light of being appear as darkness. St. Paul indicates that only gratitude allows a vision of the sign for what it is, rather than as a tool or power in reserve to be put at the disposal of whatever artistic or technocratic end one chooses. Deprived of this gratitude, freedom tends to interpret the sign (*logos*-gift) wrongly. Each of the sins of the pagans is a form of guilty ingratitude towards the God who reveals himself through the sign. For St. Paul, the root of the sin of the Jews is the same, though in a different form. The privileges of election, circumcision, the Torah, the law, the temple, and all the gifts they received made the Jewish people believe that they could judge others. This, comments Schlier, shows both oblivion of the fact that life is a gift of God and the belief that one's own measures suffice for life: "It is the same sin: unwillingness to acknowledge that one's existence is indebted to God. It is the sin of the one who wants to thank only himself."[113] The rejection of the gift is this basic, pervasive ingratitude that is unfaithfulness both to one's creatureliness and to what God causes to happen in history. Ingratitude is the lack of memory of the God who has given finite freedom the possibility to be his, when it gratuitously welcomes him.[114]

The rejection of the gift, since it does not recognize the totality of God as the destiny and form of one's action, separates the singular from himself, others, and God. This separation eliminates otherness and transforms every singular into simple identity with itself, that is, no-thing. In affirming an attractiveness severed from its relation with the whole, the rejection of the gift seems a liberation and a novelty at first. Ironically, this novelty turns out to be a sheer repetition of oneself. Contrary to the logic of gift, the logic of evil is one of formal, empty identity. Evil, wrote S. Weil, is "never anything new, everything about it is *equivalent*. Never anything real, everything about it is imaginary."[115] The rejection of the gift condemns the singular to absolute monotony. In light of this, it is possible now to see that pride is not excessive love of self but rather hatred of self. "Opposed to this humility and altruism of divine love is the pride of satanical unlove, which is incorrectly called 'self-love,' for this is a contradiction in terms: Love cannot be monohypostatic, egocentric, self-directed."[116] Egotism's self-identity is one

---

113. Schlier, *Grundzüge einer paulinischen Theologie*, 53–65; Schlier, *Der Römerbrief: Kommentar*.

114. Giussani, *RVU*, 191–202. It is this ingratitude that corrupts the cosmos. Physical evil is always an echo of man's original (*arche*) ingratitude.

115. Weil, *Simone Weil Reader*, 381.

116. Bulgakov, *Bride of the Lamb*, 156.

of monotony: placing himself under the need to draw everything from himself, the created singular can only produce copies of his own nothingness.

The refusal of the gift of self and the giving specific to it inevitably leads to the perception of the other singular as hostile to oneself. The other is either envied—because he possesses something that the first does not have or cannot produce—or feared as a threat to insularity. This is why, in contrast to the communion within which the singular gift is given to itself and also called to generate, the rejection of the gift expresses itself as profound, unspeakable hate of the paternal giver, oneself, and others. Hate systematically seeks the denial of the other by ignoring it, *etiamsi Deus non daretur*; eliminating it, and so giving in to the illusion that death can expunge otherness and the memory of the gift; or assimilating the other to oneself through power. The distortion by way of power is perhaps the most emblematic expression of the rejection of the gift and includes the other two forms. Rather than affirm and let the other be itself, work is reduced to technocratic manipulation and speech to monologue.[117]

In giving the singular to himself and making him free, God gives the human person a participation in his power. Just as the causation of the singular gift confers on freedom its dual characteristics of *autexousia* and indebtedness, so power, as capacity to do (*poiesis, techne*), is both domination and service. The singular's reciprocation and further giving entails the capacity to transfigure and dominate the cosmos. Every human action, as the exercise of freedom, is endowed with a foretaste of divine power. In his beautiful and unfortunately little-known book, Guardini explains that power has an ontological character precisely because it is "an immediate expression of human existence."[118] The nature of power follows that of human freedom, and its truth resides in respecting freedom's task and also its

---

117. In his characteristic style Bernanos writes, "At the present moment I know of no system or party to which one could entrust a true idea with the least hope of finding it intact or even recognizable on the following day. I possess a small number of true ideas. They are dear to me, and I will not send them to the public Welfare Office—not to say to the public house—because the prostitution of ideas has become a State institution the whole world over. All the ideas one sends out into the world by themselves, with their little pigtails on their back and a little basket in their hands like Little Red Riding Hood, are raped at the next corner by some slogan in uniform." Bernanos, *La liberté*, 208. Quoted in Balthasar, *Bernanos*, 43.

118. Guardini, *Das Ende der Neuzeit*, 109. English translation: *Power and Responsibility: A Course of Action for the New Age*, in Guardini, *End of the Modern World*, 129. In what follows the first page number refers to the German edition and the second to the English version. Ratzinger follows Guardini's lead when he affirms that "the power that is found in being itself is stronger. Whoever is on its side has the upper hand. But the power of being is not one's own power; it is the power of the creator" (Ratzinger, *New Song*, 55).

giftedness. For this reason, he argues, power has to do first with the transfiguration of the world and therefore its possession. To give oneself—according to the meaning of work explained earlier—is both ownership of the world and lordship over it. Guardini clarifies further that power is also obedience and service because "the human being operates within God's creation and has the task to develop in the realm of finite freedom, in the form of history and culture, what God in his absolute freedom has created as nature."[119] Power is the energy given to the singular (active sense of gift), which, governed by the singular's awareness of the whole, collaborates in the world's acquisition of its full form. As an expression of the singular's freedom, Guardini explains, there is no necessary relation between power and the effect it causes. Non-necessary, however, does not mean arbitrary or random action. It means, more simply, that the nature of power is in keeping with the singular's freedom, not that power is a neutral capacity to be used indiscriminately for one purpose or another. Power, Guardini writes, reflects both the giftedness of the person and the fact that the developing of history and culture is meant to unfold God's plan, that is, to become itself in the recognition of the inexhaustible wholeness of God.[120] It is only when freedom lets power express its own ontology that power is able to transfigure and give without destroying the other.

Without demonizing any historical era, Guardini comments that a change is taking place in our own. In the preceding epochs, man's creativity had an "organic" character. That is, it integrated all man's faculties: his reason, instincts, and capacity to contemplate the nature of the singular. Before our present time, "the human being seizes power over what is given, intensifies its forms, heightens its effects, without however breaking its structure (in its essence and as a whole)."[121] Guardini writes, however, that a new understanding of science, as the rational and mathematical grasping of reality, and of *techne*, as the quintessence of the possibilities that science affords, gives power a new character. Synthesizing his rich reflections, we can say that for Guardini the new sense of technology separates what the person creates from his own self. Man's work is detached from his own bodiliness; it is done at a distance, and therefore what he does is increasingly less and less "personal." The human being no longer experiences (*Erlebnis*) his work. Power is no longer an organic transformation of the world, and thus it generates an increasingly non-human world. With "non-human" world, Guardini describes the fragmentation between knowing, acting, and lived experience

---

119. Guardini, *Das Ende der Neuzeit*, 113/134.
120. Ibid., 101–9/117–30.
121. Ibid., 130/153–54.

(*Erlebnis*) that comes with the rejection of the singular's gift-ness. Work and hence the person become objectified, and human action is conceived as the manipulation of a reality whose *logos* and destiny no longer determine and guide human operation.[122]

We could say further that the loss of organicity that the contemporary understanding of power effects is expressive of a freedom conceived as ingratitude. Refusing to be measured by God, the singular imposes his own measure upon himself and the world, and thus, instead of contributing to the affirmation of the unity that is proper to the gift, the human being breaks things apart. Not surprisingly, according to Guardini, among the dangers brought by the new perception of power are violence and the spiritual and biological manipulation of man by man. Violence is, in fact, the easy way to deal with an antagonistically perceived otherness because violence excludes both the person and his or her freedom.

Following Guardini's reflection, Giussani writes that "power, in our modern historical times, has turned itself against Transcendence. To ignore it is in fact to be opposed to it."[123] Thus understood, power's capacity to intervene in nature (including man's own) and history leads the human person to believe that, through power, the human being can deify himself. In response to God, power is a participation in his power; detached from him, it becomes his replacement. In this regard power is no longer the capacity to indicate the *telos* common to all and the ordering of things to obtain this goal, but rather the affirmation of the self over and against *any* other. Thus, it is not by chance that, when power is turned inside out by the rejection of the gift, it systematically opposes freedom as it expresses its own religiosity. Just as religiosity alone allows freedom to be expressive of the gift-nature of the singular, so power can avoid using the other for its own purposes only if it affirms and defends the constitutive religiosity of freedom. If power, along with possession and domination, conceives of itself also as service and obedience, then it is able to transfigure the cosmos, that is to say, to allow it to unfold its own being within its constitutive relation with the *agapic* source. Otherwise, the power of one individual over another in an ever more perfectly bureaucratic society will continue to govern the fate of people, all the while maintaining the illusion that they are free and responsible and are

---

122. Ibid., 126–44/149–69. Guardini is careful with the terminology he uses and preempts the facile accusation of demonizing contemporary technology by indicating that no one epoch can serve to measure the other ones. The protagonist of every historical epoch is the human being who, having rejected the gift, is always in need of redemption. This, however, is not said to flatten his critique of modern technology but to correct its ideological reading.

123. Giussani, *IPO*, 10.

living a tranquil existence of peace and respect. In reality they experience subjection to rules and to a consensus whose content is determined by an unknown aristocracy.

The rejection of the gift and its consequent loss of unity cannot be undone by the human freedom that brought it about in the first place. The singular gift is not its own source. Surprisingly, however, evil does have a twofold positive outcome, as indicated by Giussani. Sin does not start out as the contemplation of the singular's own creatureliness, but perhaps in an even deeper way sin also helps the singular to recognize his own nothingness. On the other hand, sin introduces in the singular "the distant perception of the supreme adequacy of the offering of a help to his own existential being."[124] Without the first effect, which is neither a denial of creatureliness nor the exaltation of a pessimistic anthropology disguised as gift, human freedom would seek to perpetuate the nothingness that seeks to separate whatever exists from its source. Perceiving, instead, the need for a gratuitous recapitulation of the original gift, the human person does not remain lost in fragmentation and can recognize help when it comes to him.

---

124. Giussani, *RVU*, 224.

IV. The Son's Gift of Self

THE MYSTERY OF THE unity of being finds its archetypal expression in the eventful form of Jesus Christ. His person renders in flesh and in history the nature of the one God as an ineffable communion of love that radically responds to man's rejection. Translating his divine filiation into human existence, Christ's gift of himself to the utmost redeems humankind; that is, he corrects man's distorted perception of himself, God, and the world and offers to man the possibility of sharing divine life.[1] Thus, the Logos's kenotic descent, lived out as a constant, loving obedience to the Father in the Spirit, also reveals to us what it means to be human.[2] Christ's love for us therefore is simultaneously human and divine. His love for humankind, Giussani writes, is "unexpectedly and incomprehensibly human (even though it is incomprehensible it immediately feels human)."[3] Jesus Christ, however, does not simply reiterate that being is gift, but rather confirms the intuition of originary experience by fulfilling it superabundantly. He confirms the positivity of being by unfolding the eternal depths of the nature of the gift. Two methodological principles guide our reflection in this area.

First, the unity of the person of Christ. Just as the foregoing ontological and anthropological exploration of the unity of being in terms of gift was based on the integral mode of being, so here our christological reflection is born from and leads to the person of Christ. The event of Christ reveals the mystery of being through the unity of his person. Christ's two natures are *he himself* in his divinity and again in his humanity. As Maximus often illustrates, "according to both the natures from which and in which and of

---

1. Basil the Great, *On the Holy Spirit*, ch. 9, p. 23 (PG 32:109).

2. Vatican Council II, *Gaudium et spes*, no. 22 (DS 4322). For a critique of P. Schoonenberg's Christology, which accuses the councils of the Church of depersonalizing the humanity of Christ, see Bordoni, *Gesù di Nazaret*; Sesboüé, *Jésus-Christ*; Schoonenberg, *The Christ*.

3. Giussani, *PLW*, 3:19. Translation modified.

which he was the hypostasis, Christ made himself known as the one who willed and worked our salvation by nature."[4] Jesus Christ is "the one and the same (*allos dè kaì allos*)" Son of the Father who, as incarnate, is constituted by "this (human) and that (divine) nature."[5] If we do not begin with the unity of the person, our christological reflection, instead of clarifying the meaning of gift and the unity of being, will fall prey to an abstract interpretation of the mode of the union of the two natures in terms of an "exchange" of gifts. The Incarnation of the Logos and the Paschal Mystery are not just two instances of generous acts. As the christological controversies exhibit, to lose sight of the fact that the two natures achieve existential fullness only in the second person of the Logos is to reify the divine and human natures. It is better to follow the Third Council of Constantinople (DS 553–59) and, as Ratzinger reads it, to conceive of the relation between the two natures—already specified by Chalcedon (DS 301–2)—as "mutual indwelling."[6] This permits us to avoid the danger of a preconceived philosophy—even one that thinks of being as gift—absorbing theology into itself. By contemplating the person of the Pierced One, we see that, while preserving the irreducibility of the gift, the Logos's kenosis is a gift of self that can bring the singular to perfect unity with himself. This gratuitous redemption does not mean that the person of Christ makes unity automatic. Rather, by assuming a human nature, the person of the Logos "accustoms man to receive God, and God to dwell in man."[7] He thus shows man, from within his experience, that gift is the unity of being and that unity is the permanence of the gift.

The event of the person of Christ leads to the second methodological principle: his human experience of his divine filiation. This principle allows us to ponder what Christ discloses of the divine and the human, of the unity of being as gift, and also what he reveals of the relation between the two, in a way that is both in accord with the revealed data and organic with our present condition. His human experience of divine filiation permits a view of the novelty that Christ brings with himself. We see that Jesus Christ is not just the fully realized human being. He is the fully realized human being who, by means of the union with the divine nature in the *prosopon* of the Logos, is uniquely equipped to make all of the others, too, into fully realized human beings—that is, able to adhere to the *agapic* source while remaining distinct from it. As such, Jesus Christ cannot but be infinitely above us, even

---

4. Maximus the Confessor, *Opuscula theologica et polemica* 6 (PG 91:68D). English translation in Maximus the Confessor, *Cosmic Mystery*, 176.

5. Gregory of Nazianzus, "Letter 101," in *On God and Christ*, 155–66 (PG 37:180A).

6. Ratzinger, *Behold the Pierced One*, 38.

7. Irenaeus, *Haer.* 3.20.2 (PG 7a:944).

as man, and, at the same time, also able to communicate this transcendent divinity to us as our human destiny. His singularity shows further the unity and distinction with the Trinitarian dimension. Christ's human existence is the fleshing out of the never-ending mystery of the Son, the one who exists in the "form of God" insofar as he receives existence in the form of God from the Father through being begotten. As man, however, the Incarnate Son of the Father experiences his divinity in the "form of a servant" (Phil 2:5–11). His human experience of his divine sonship enables us to discover the gift-ness of being and to perceive the type of gift of self that constitutes the God of love (1 John 4:8 and 16).

To begin our examination, we start out from the circularity of theology and philosophy that has guided our reflection all along. Thus, we will delineate in what sense Christ confirms and fulfills the ontological exploration of being as gift presented earlier (section 1). This, while shedding light on the continuity and discontinuity between theological and philosophical reflection, will enable us to perceive the full form of Christ (section 2) and then, in view of this, to ponder his own experience of divine filiation (section 3), the nature of the gift of himself (section 4), and the gratuity of his gift (section 5).

1. On the Way of Being

Drawing on the work of Balthasar, this section attempts to give an account of what it means to say that philosophy is fulfilled in Christology, a fulfillment that preserves the integrity of both disciplines. This account will enable us to see in what sense the Incarnate Logos, in whom and for whom the human being is created, restores human nature and makes it possible for man to undertake his task, that is, to bring the whole, fragmented cosmos back into union with the Father. The two disciplines have an intrinsic, asymmetrical relation: philosophy is called to transcend itself into theology, and theology's speculative measure is the ontological difference.[8] The Chalcedonian dogma regarding the hypostatic union can help us see how Jesus Christ reveals himself "on the way of being," as Ulrich would say. Since there is

---

8. Ulrich, *Homo abyssus*, p. 81, fn. 145. He continues: "Die aus der Nichtsubsistenz, d.h. der Überwesenhaftigkeit des Seins, konzipierte Nicht-Andersheit Gottes offenbart sich darin, dass der Logos in der Inkarnation die Menschennatur nicht von 'oben her' ergreift, sondern in der Restlosigkeit der im Hl. Geist geschehenden Hingabe gleichsam aus der Menschenerde—als Menschensohn 'under Bruder'—von uns 'herkommt'" (ibid.).

nothing outside being except non-being, Christ's revelation can occur only by way of being if he is to be understood and welcomed.⁹

Christ is the gift of God become man. In him we have both the presence of the paternal giver in the gift—to the extent that whoever sees him sees the Father (his mission is to represent God's Fatherhood)—and the separation between the giver and the gift (Christ's prayer is the clearest expression of his self-awareness of being the Son of God).¹⁰ According to the first element, Christ is not simply a sign; he is the sacrament of the Father's love. He himself is the Father's love. With respect to the second element, Christ reveals himself to be other than the Father while being one with him. If we look at the ontology presupposed by the unity of the two natures in the incarnate person of the Logos (DS 302), we see that the relation between God's being and the world's eludes the terms set by univocity or equivocity. Univocity, as we indicated above, yields a pantheistic vision of the whole wherein the finite other is absorbed. Equivocity cannot distinguish what of the cause remains in the caused. Univocity does not permit a distinction between the giver (God) and the gift, since under these terms divine freedom is not sufficiently powerful to create another that the giver is not (efficient causality is unable to establish a real detachment between God and the concrete singular). God as giver simply repeats himself in the gift. With equivocity, we lose the unity between the divine giver and the gift because the giver is too complete to give himself without losing himself. Only an analogical understanding of donation respects the difference in unity stated by the Council of Chalcedon.

Nevertheless, even within analogy, as Balthasar insists, finite and infinite being do not stand opposed to each other as if they were two instances of a common genus—in our case this genus would be "gift." God is and remains other than finite beings. Every philosophical and theological reflection on being-as-gift therefore remains apophatic, that is, it must convey the mysterious light of God's ever-greaterness.¹¹ God is an enlightening

---

9. Ibid., 42, 56, 317, 412.
10. Bieler, *Befreiung der Freiheit*, 299.
11. Dionysius's apophatic theology cogently clarifies that any approach to God that claims to define him with any name has already missed him. "No unity or trinity, no number or oneness, no fruitfulness, indeed, nothing that is or is known can proclaim that hiddenness beyond every mind and reason of the transcendent Godhead which transcends every being. There is no name for it nor expression. We cannot follow it into the inaccessible dwelling place so far above us and we cannot even call it by the name of goodness.... But the real truth of these matters is in fact far beyond us. That is why their preference is for the way up through negations, since this stands the soul outside everything which is correlative with its own finite nature" (*Divine Names*, PG 3:981A–B). This apophatic emphasis, faithful to both Scripture and human reasoning,

mystery, and he remains such even when Christ reveals his name. That God is ever greater means that the proportion maintained by analogy between God and finite beings respects that God is creator and bestows his being on the creature. Hence, analogical clarifications set out from the position that the creature owes its entire being to God (*analogia atributionis*). Based on the analogy of attribution between God and the creature, Balthasar explains, there is primarily an *analogia proportionalitatis*, that is, a proportion between the way God is God and the way the finite creature is a singular being, and not a direct proportion between God and the finite creature.[12] As we indicated earlier, the similarity and distinction between God and finite beings entails seeing that whereas God's *esse*, the perfection of all perfections, is his *essentia*, the created *esse* is *aliquid simplex et completum sed non subsistens* (simple and complete, but not subsistent).

The hypostatic union presents us with the greatest of miracles: God has crossed over the abyss (*xorismos*) separating him from the singular being and, in a way known to him alone, without ceasing to be himself has become what he was not.[13] Is there a way to ponder the coherence between the hypostatic union and the ontology of gift we have been pursuing here? In his *De unione* Aquinas treats the way in which the hypostatic union of the two natures in Christ is also the form of the unity of the two different ways of being. He explains that Christ has one *esse* "simply speaking" (*simpliciter*) and a double *esse* "in a certain respect" (*secundum quid*). Due to the unity of the eternal hypostasis, Christ's *esse* is one simply speaking, and, thanks to the two distinct natures—which are one in the hypostasis—his *esse* is twofold. Aquinas thus says that Christ is also *aliud esse* not inasmuch as he is eternal but inasmuch as he has become man *temporaliter*. This "other being" is neither accidental (this would mean that the hypostatic union would not be real but only moral) nor primary (it is the hypostasis of the Logos, not of the man); it is a secondary *esse* that occurs within the principal one. In the Incarnation, the Word not only creates and assumes an individual human nature but also undergoes "substantification by means of a human nature" (*substantificatur per naturam humanam*), as if he were receiving hypostatic

---

can be retrieved both in the Greek and the Latin Fathers all the way up to Aquinas—despite the rationalistic reductions of his rich thought during the theology of the manuals.

12. See, e.g., Aquinas, *I Sent.*, d. 19, q. 5, a. 2, ad 1; *In Nic. Eth.* 1.7.95; *De ver.*, q. 2, a. 11.

13. In this way, God reveals not only what God can do for man (soteriology), but what the nature of the divine gift is (theology) and, in relation to God, that the singular gift is given to itself (ontology, anthropology) and called to participate in divine life (eschatology).

IV. THE SON'S GIFT OF SELF

being within the limits of and from human nature, without, however, ceasing to be the eternal Son of God.[14]

Pursuing this thread further suggests that Christ follows the path of being because at the Incarnation he recapitulates the way *esse* (*esse commune*) comes into being at the moment of creation as always already poured out into essences. The Incarnation of the Logos follows being's "event" of becoming a finite singular. Created *esse*, as we saw, does not have a hypostatic existence of its own. It exists only as already given to the essence that limits it, while the essence exists only because *esse* is always already given to it. The act of creation is the simultaneity of *esse* (which preserves its real unity in a non-hypostatic way) being in essences and essences existing as a result of *esse*. As we saw, this is the event (not a movement) of be-*ing* in which the two poles exist always for and with each other. As Balthasar writes, "The fact that being pours itself out into the plurality of creatures as both actual (*simplex et completum*) and non-subsistent and that it cannot be apprehended (let alone solidified in a concept) except in this outpouring, reveals it to be the pure and free expression of the divine *bonitas* (goodness) and freedom."[15] Expressing all of his divine nature within the limits of human nature, the Incarnate Son recapitulates the gift of creation in which *ipsum esse* (*simplex et completum*) *subsistens* limits itself, so to speak, in finite beings. The Word undergoes substantification by means of a human nature, without changing his divine nature in any respect.

The Incarnate Logos, in humbling himself, accepts the state of being all of himself within the limits of a human nature that he creates and assumes simultaneously—an event that cannot be understood without the Father's sending and the Spirit's adumbration. "The Holy Spirit," writes Bieler, "is the one who both guarantees the difference between the divine and human natures and bridges over it"—just as he is simultaneously the one in whom the Father and Son are united and kept apart.[16] Therefore we can say that the hypostatic union recapitulates creation not only because divine *esse* limits itself in finite being, but also because in the person of the Logos, finite being is given to reach its *telos*. Human nature is enhypostasized in the Logos, that is, it acquires its existential fullness in the person of the Logos.[17] The hypostatic union allows us to realize that the creative act, in which the di-

---

14. Aquinas, *De unione Verbi incarnati*, q. un., a. 4, c. In a. 1, ad 10, Aquinas states more succinctly: "Esse est et personae subsistentis, et naturae in qua persona subsistit; quasi secundum illam naturam esse habens. Esse igitur personae Verbi incarnati est unum ex parte personae subsistentis, non autem ex parte naturae."

15. Balthasar, *TL*, 2:182.

16. Bieler, *Befreiung der Freiheit*, 305.

17. Balthasar, *Cosmic Liturgy*, 230–33.

vine *esse* posits what it is not (*non-subsistens*), is the presupposition of the enfleshment of the Logos. At the same time, since the non-subsistence of created being is a participation in the fullness of being (*ipsum esse*)—created being is divine *esse* as participated, and thus in virtue of divine *esse*'s being given to created being, the latter images the divine in its being given away to essences—the Incarnation is the grounds of creation. In the wonderful union of the two natures in the person of the Logos, therefore, the non-subsistence of *esse* seems to be "sheer poverty," yet "this poverty (as such!) *is* the plenitude of God's self-giving in essences."[18]

It is within this framework that it is possible to understand the benefit of saying with Balthasar that Christ is the *analogia entis* in person.[19] The "imaging" of the divine being by the finite being as disclosed through Christ's human experience of his divine filiation reveals that *finite* being's dual unity (of *esse* and essence, of *esse* and *ens*) is good. It is a "gift" and neither the result of a fall (equivocity) or the self-constitution of the absolute (univocity). In becoming flesh, his divinity is not transformed or mixed with a human nature (as in Apollinarius). He forms a true unity: human nature cannot be separated or divided from Christ's divine nature (as Nestorius's twofold *prosopon* theory stipulates). In preserving the human nature in himself, Christ's mission confirms the positivity of finite being (man, and *esse commune*) because it shows that finite being is relation with God (and others), that is, it is created to share, through the Spirit, in the Son's knowledge and love of the Father. Given that Christ's hypostatic union is not a static event but rather exists only in the progressive event of the Incarnation, Cross, death, resurrection, and return to the Father, we can say with Balthasar that Christ is the analogy of being in person because in him, as true God and true man, God and man come into their own in a dramatic dialogue initiated by God. Finite being, as we see in man, is created in order to freely adhere to (obey) God's total gift of self. More simply, Christ is the *analogia entis* in person because his life shows the truth of God and the truth of man.[20] Christ, writes Balthasar, "represents God to the world—but

18. Balthasar, *TL*, 2:183. Emphasis added.

19. See Balthasar, *TD*, 3:149–259, especially 220–29; Balthasar, *TL*, 2:81–87, 171–317 (especially 311–16); Balthasar, *Theology of History*.

20. It is worth citing this long passage from Balthasar: "Jesus experiences his human consciousness entirely in terms of mission. The Father has commissioned him, in the Holy Spirit, to reveal God's nature and his disposition toward man. There is nothing one-sided about this revelation (as people like to think today); it is not simply that God takes the part of sinners and the needy: in his sense-mediated human nature, Jesus is to reveal all God's other attributes as well, that is, God's anger (for instance, over the sinful desecration of his place of worship); God's weariness at having to endure for so long these people who are so lacking in understanding; God's grief and tears at Jerusalem's

in the mode of the Son who regards the Father as 'greater' and to whom he eternally owes all that he is—and he represents the world to God, by being, as man (or rather, as the God-man), 'humble, lowly, modest, docile (*tapeinos*) of heart' (Matt 11:29)."[21]

We can press this point further: the hypostatic union recapitulates the structure of created being in its dual unity not only because Christ follows the way of being—if it were just this, the Logos would lose his transcendence and his mission would remain meaningless. More importantly, it is also because being is created in Christ and for him. It is here that philosophy must let itself transcend into theology in order to discover therein its ultimate ground. The hymn of Colossians contains much to be examined in this area (Col 1:15–20). For the present purpose (illustrating that the hypostatic union, in showing the ultimate positivity of the concrete singular, grounds and fulfills the gift-ness of the unity of being), however, it suffices to approach the crucial question of the difference and relation between begetting and creating. The origin and *telos* of the ontological difference between God and the world is ultimately located in the theological difference.

The Christian understanding of creation *ex nihilo* grounds the radical difference between God and the world, and so between the form of donation that we know as creation and the form of donation that is revealed as begetting. To recall the terms of the earlier chapter, we could say that "from nothing" means, first, that God, absolute gift in himself, cannot be understood in relation to his creature. The causal relation, understood in light of gift, between God and the world that is established by God's creative act includes an insurmountable distance: God is not the world and no concept can encapsulate him. Second, creation *ex nihilo* indicates that there is no preexisting matter that God can use to bring the cosmos into existence—not even Leibniz's *praetentio ad existendum*.[22] Lastly, since nothing is presupposed, creation can only be the free, irrevocable, and gratuitous fruit of God's absolute affirmation of himself. Yet here is exactly where the

---

refusal to respond to his invitation. We can even say that, in the cry of dereliction on the Cross, Jesus reveals how God is forsaken by sinners. Jesus' whole existence, including the aspect that the Greeks found so difficult, his *pathe*, is in the service of his proclamation of God. But he does this in a fully human conscious subject who simultaneously brings to light the full truth of man, and—since he primarily reveals the truth of God— the truth of man as God sees him" (Balthasar, *TD*, 3:224–25).

21. Ibid., 3:230. N. Healy writes of Christ: "The eschatological enactment of the God-world relationship both reveals and accomplishes the original embedding of the goodness of the world in its otherness within the trinitarian life springing from the Father's self-outpouring" (Healy, *Eschatology*, 118).

22. Aquinas, *ST*, I, q. 44, a. 1, ad 3. Leibniz's quote "omne possibile exigit existere" is from "De rerum origination radicali," in Leibniz, *Die philosophischen Schriften*, 302.

similarity is to be found. Precisely because no-thing precedes creation, finite being is a gift that is nothing but *"datio totius esse."* It is the gift of all of being, as Aquinas would say.[23] God gives *esse* and gives it to itself. Once again, the gift and the receiver coincide. The gift of creation is real because it posits another free being that God is not. Yet, and here lies the difficulty, if everything is given, how can there be a communication of being that is unlike the Son's? How is it possible to preserve the identity of being given (of the Son and creation) *and* the difference between the two?

Scripture helps us understand the difference and similarity between the begetting of the Son and the creating of the cosmos by placing the ontological difference between God and the world within the theological difference between the Father, Son, and the Holy Spirit. Whereas the Father gives the Son to have life in himself, that is, gives him the principle of life itself, to man, in contrast, the Father gives life, not its principle. In philosophical terms, the Father gives the Son subsistent being, whereas finite being is complete and simple but not subsistent. In light of the Trinitarian difference we can say that whereas in begetting there is a donation that is also a *communicatio sui*, creation is a donation that is not a communication of the divine self, although it is a true communication of the divine *esse* (as non-subsistent). "This birth of the Son from the Father," writes Aquinas, "is the origin of every begetting of another, for it alone perfectly takes on the nature of the begetter. Every other birth is imperfect, for in them the offspring receives a part of the begetter's substance or a likeness of it. All subsequent births, consequently, must have their origin in a certain imitation of the principal birth."[24]

How to express this difference more precisely? C. Bruaire writes that begetting indicates "identity in the absolute [theological] difference, a difference that reserves the inaugural priority of the absolute ontological initiative with respect to the reddition of the gift [the Son] to the gift [the Father]." In contrast to begetting, creating "signifies difference in the identity of being given, the alterity of the gift when the giving does not give itself there, and hence limits itself."[25] Created being, perfect, simple, but not subsistent, does not have the personal identity of the Son; it does not have life in itself. Begetting is a giving of being in which identity has priority over difference. This latter, theological difference is such that, as the early Fathers teach, the divine hypostases are not three different species of one common genus.

---

23. Aquinas, *SCG* 3.68; Aquinas, *ST*, I, q. 45, a. 1 and a. 4, ad 3; Ulrich, *Der Mensch als Anfang*, 84–85.

24. Aquinas, *In Boethium de Trinitate*, prol.

25. Bruaire, *EE*, 138.

They are radically other from each other. Unity, in this sense, differentiates. Creating is a giving in which the ontological difference has priority over the similarity that is the act of donation—the donation that we call begetting and that which we call creating. In light of this, it is perhaps now possible to say that the difference between creating and begetting resides in the fact that "creation is the gift of the being [*esse*] of the intradivine Expression [Word], creation is being available thanks to the real difference between the Reddition to the Principle [reddition that is the Son] and the Confirmation of Self [that is the Holy Spirit], in the rhythm of the absolute Spirit. This is the only adequate expression of the theological expression: creation *in* the Word."[26] The Trinitarian difference between Father, Son, *and* Holy Spirit is the grounds for the possibility of a finite gift to be itself. This means that the concrete singular gift is confirmed in the gift of *esse* by the Holy Spirit—sent by both the Father and the Son—so that the concrete singular can be itself in the Son and thus remain in relation with the Father through the Holy Spirit. The limitation of the absolute gift in the radical, complete, but not subsistent gift of creation can be stated positively as follows: the giving and receiving of creation (the dual unity of *esse* and essence, *esse commune* and *ens*) is oriented, beginning with the human being, to the rebirth made possible through the Incarnation of the Logos. Had God given the principle of life to what we call "finite" being, creation would not have been real. It would have been, once again, a pantheistic epiphenomenon of a monadic divinity. Instead, the distinction between the unity of being given in creation and that in the begetting of the Son enables man (and the world) to be himself. Yet the "himself" is not "for-himself" only; it is a for-himself that is always already open, that is, seeking his own fulfillment: the gratuitous response to the triune God in the Incarnate Logos.

Being created in the Son allows a fuller account of the classic doctrine of *imago Dei*.[27] The human being is a creature who is capable of receiving God and is always already turned towards him—so much so that, as Aquinas indicates, in every knowing and loving the human being implicitly knows and loves God.[28] The image of God in man is thus what grounds the possibility of the fulfillment of that mystery, according to which before all ages God planned "to mingle, without change on his part, with human nature by true hypostatic union."[29] Hence, for the Fathers, the *imago Dei* is both the

---

26. Ibid., 140.

27. See, e.g., Augustine, *Confessions* 10.18.27 (PL 32:791); Augustine, *Trin.* 10.8.11 (PL 42:979).

28. Aquinas, *De ver.*, q. 22, a. 2, ad 1; *ST*, I, q. 4, a. 6, ad 2.

29. Maximus, *Quaestiones ad Thalassium* (CCSG 7:137).

presupposition of the Incarnation of the Logos and the expression of man's stature and destiny: to be sons in the Son. Made in the image of God, the human being has the task to unify everything with God by acknowledging the meaning of being as gift, a task that is fulfilled first and foremost by Jesus Christ, who is both the icon of the Father's love and the true face of man. Just as the hypostatic union needs to be seen within the fullness of Christ's eventful form, so man's being-gift needs to be considered in his historical existence and specific task, which, to speak with Maximus the Confessor, is that of uniting all of the cosmos with God. Christ's human experience of his divine filiation enables man to fulfill his task of affirming being as gift—that is, of recognizing in wonder that God is all in all, that everything is given to exist in this recognition, and that through this contemplation he cooperates in the uniting of the world with God. In Jesus Christ, we see that the task given to the human being is that of mediating and bringing into unity the extremes: God's triune being and finite creatureliness.[30]

We can turn briefly to Maximus's *Difficulty* 41 to describe more concretely the nature of man's task to affirm being's gift-ness as revealed by and supra-fulfilled in Christ. In this *Difficulty* Maximus explains how Christ "institutes the natures afresh" and returns to the human being his primordial task: the union of all creation, through man, with God.[31] Borrowing the perception of cosmic being from Gregory of Nyssa, Maximus speaks of five divisions of being: uncreated nature (God) and created nature; created nature can be either intelligible or sensible; sensible nature is further divided into heaven and earth; earth is divided into paradise and the inhabited world; and man's being is divided into male and female.[32] Had man remained with the unmoved God, that is, the God who always is and does not come from nothingness, the human being would have united "the created nature with the uncreated through love (oh the wonder of God's love for us human beings!), showing them to be one and the same through the possession of grace, the whole creation wholly interpenetrated by God, and become completely whatever God is, save at the level of being, and receiving to itself the whole of God himself, and acquiring as a kind of prize for

---

30. Maximus, *Ambiguum* 41 (PG 91:1305B). English translation in Louth, *Maximus the Confessor*, 155-62.

31. The human being "proceeds harmoniously to each of the extremities in the things that are, from what is close at hand to what is remote, from what is worse to what is better, lifting up to God and fully accomplishing union. For this reason the human person was introduced last among beings, as a kind of natural bond mediating between the universal poles through their proper parts and leading into unity in itself those things that are naturally set apart from one another by a great interval" (PG 91:1305C).

32. Maximus, PG 91:1305A-B.

its ascent to God the most unique God himself, as the end of the movement of everything that moves towards it, and the firm and unmoved rest of everything."[33] The event of Christ's Incarnation restores human nature, and through his virginal birth Christ overcomes the division between male and female.[34] The division between paradise and the inhabited world is bridged when Christ forgives the sinner from the Cross and, after the resurrection, comes to be with the apostles.[35] At the ascension, Christ unites heaven and earth and shows that all sensible nature is one in the Logos.[36] Finally, since he is present before the Father with his human nature, he unites the uncreated being with the created.[37] "Thus he divinely recapitulates the universe in himself, showing that the whole creation exists as one, like another human being, completed by the gathering together of its parts."[38] The Incarnate Logos, in restoring unity to the fragmented parts by holding everything together in himself without confusion, completes the mission the Father assigned to him: to be the icon of his infinite mercy. Allowing humankind to participate in this ever-greater love, the triune God renews the nature of the singular gift. We can now turn our attention to the person of Christ in order to see how he reveals the gift-ness and unity of being through his human experience of divine filiation.

2. Approaching the Figure of Christ

Scripture offers us access to the mystery of Christ's human experience of his divine filiation. While not all of Origen's scriptural exegesis can stand the review of contemporary historical-critical and "history of the form" methodologies, it does teach us a precious lesson on how to approach the complete figure of Christ, which is essential to keep in view when facing this question of his human experience. The Word (Logos) is a multifaceted reality: the preexistent Logos eternally begotten by the Father; the man born from Mary who is present in the Scriptures; and the one who, through the Spirit, dwells in the Church.[39] The flesh of Christ embraces his body, Scrip-

---

33. Maximus, PG 91:1308C.
34. Maximus, PG 91:1309A.
35. Maximus, PG 91:1309B.
36. Maximus, PG 91:1309C.
37. Maximus, PG 91:1309D.
38. Maximus, PG 91:1312B.
39. "Just as this spoken word cannot according to its own nature be touched or seen, but when written in a book and, so to speak, become bodily, then indeed is seen and touched, so too is it with the fleshless and bodiless WORD of God; according to

ture, and the Church herself. To present the figure of Christ we must, on the one hand, be mindful of the three aspects of its historical plausibility and persuasiveness as indicated by Origen—the event-character of the person of Christ, the Trinitarian, and the ecclesiological—and, on the other hand, specify the very nature of revelation of which Scripture is a fundamental element.

First, at times, particularly at the beginning of the christological controversies, reflection on the figure of Christ was governed by the question of the mode of the union; at other times an account of Christ's sacrifice of himself on the Cross and its coherence with the triune mystery held sway over the course of discussion. While historical moments and cultural circumstances tend to emphasize one aspect over the other, it is important not to lose sight of the fact that, as Ratzinger explains, the more "static" Christology of the Incarnation can never be severed from the more "dynamic" Christology of the Cross and vice versa.[40] Thus, the full form of Christ is an event that encompasses all of Christ's existence, and not just one moment (the Incarnation) or the other (the Paschal Mystery).[41] The kenosis of Christ, as Bulgakov radically defends, encompasses both his *evacuatio*, his humble taking the form of a servant upon himself, and his continuous kenosis throughout his earthly existence.[42] Christ's kenotic gift of self includes his preexistence, Incarnation, historical existence, sacrificial death on the Cross, and descent into hell. The event of the Incarnation is not concluded, however, until the crucified-risen Lord breathes the Holy Spirit upon the apostles (John 20:21–23) and, seated at the right hand of the Father, sends with the Father their own Spirit—that same Spirit who, already playing a mediating role in the event of the hypostatic union, guided Christ throughout his historical existence. Only when Christ sends the Holy Spirit is Christ fully mediator between God and man (1 Tim 2:5).[43]

---

its divinity it is neither seen, nor written, but when it becomes flesh, it is seen and written. Therefore, since it has become flesh, there is a book of its generation." Quoted in Balthasar, *Origen*, 87–88.

40. Ratzinger, *Introduction to Christianity*, 228–43.

41. See, among others, Bordoni, *Gesù di Nazaret*; Welte, *Auf der Spur*; Barth, *Church Dogmatics*; Bieler, *Befreiung der Freiheit*, 291–311. For an account of the validity of "event" for a theological and christological reflection, see López, "Eternal Happening"; López, "Reasonableness of an Event."

42. Bulgakov, *Lamb of God*.

43. Aquinas indicates that Christ is mediator between God and man because, *as man*, he is able to unite human beings to God and to communicate to them adoptive divine filiation through the Spirit of the Father, his own Spirit. See Aquinas, *ST*, III, q. 26, a. 2.

Second, as indicated in Aquinas's insistence on the inseparability of the divine processions from the missions, the form of Christ cannot be severed from his relation with the Father and the Holy Spirit.[44] The descent of the Son is rooted in his "movement" from and back to the Father. The Son's "return" to the Father is always a return "forward," that is, a fruitful, overabundant response that is the breathing of the Spirit. The Father's sourcing of the Son bestows upon the Logos the capacity to give with himself the Holy Spirit. Christ's *exitus* from the Father therefore is always already a fruitful return to him, made possible by the fact that the Logos occupies the middle position in God. The spatial axes used so far (the vertical-horizontal of Jesus's mission; the circular of exit and return to the Father) are a graphic translation of what is constitutive of Christ's personhood: his relation with and for the Father in the Spirit and his relation with and for men. These relations constitute his very person.

The third aspect of the event of Christ is the inseparability of Christ from the Marian Church. Jesus Christ is the "head of the body, the Church" (Col 1:18), who is also his bride (Eph 5:22–33; Rev 21:9–10). Christianity, despite all its gnostic misinterpretations, is a religion of the flesh. Christ took flesh from Mary so that he could ascend to the Father with his glorified body, in which the wounds remain. Furthermore, there is already a foretaste of what is yet to come: Christ constituted the flesh as a sacrament of his presence—first the Eucharist, and in light of it, the Church herself. As his body, the Church is also made a communion of persons rooted in the communion that God is. Within this communion the believer becomes himself, acquires a new understanding (faith) and capacity to love (charity), and reads the Scriptures within the Church, whose light guides the believer ever more deeply into the mystery of the person of Christ.

The unity of these three dimensions—the event-character of the person of Christ, the Trinitarian, and the ecclesiological—emerges from the fact that Christ reveals the triune God and his relation with the world to be a *nuptial* mystery. Christ is the personified covenant between God and man. He is the perfect "yes" of God to humankind and man's perfect "yes" to God (2 Cor 1:19). "Nuptiality" here means the analogy of love proposed by John Paul II according to which God is the unique, radical gift of self to himself, first and foremost, and so to man. For John Paul II, God's gift of himself to man in Christ and the Spirit is both paternal and nuptial. Whereas the paternal dimension of the one divine love indicates its creating and redeeming aspects, nuptiality emphasizes the aspects of unity, difference, and

---

44. Aquinas, *ST*, I, q. 43, a. 2.

fruitfulness.⁴⁵ Christ obtains for us the gift of sonship, which remains the primordial way in which human beings, created in the Logos, participate in divine love. At the same time, God's redeeming love for the human being seeks the response of the bride, the Church, to whom he also entrusts his own mission.

The nuptial dimension of triune love also offers a compelling concept of revelation. Nuptiality, in fact, allows us to affirm the role played in the very act of revealing by the one to whom the revelation is addressed without eliminating the priority of the one who reveals himself. Furthermore, the nuptial understanding of revelation retains what is true in historical-critical exegesis without adopting the presuppositions that seem to freeze this exegetical approach in a pendular movement between the historical Jesus and the kerygma.⁴⁶ To alternate between the Jesus who lived and acted in Israel two thousand years ago and the Christ announced by the Church (the kerygmatic Christ) does not do justice to the relationship between the Church and Christ. Undoubtedly, God's revelation is a historical event that takes place through human flesh. The Father desired that the Word say itself through human flesh. This, however, is more than an interplay between speaking and hearing. The Incarnate Logos says himself through and with human words. Christ did not leave a single written word because he wanted to privilege the interaction of God's freedom with man's as revealed in himself, the true *analogia entis*. Precisely because God's relation with the world is a nuptial mystery, the event of revelation does not take place until it is heard, that is, received. The Church does announce the kerygma, and its proclamation is always both human and divine, though the sacramentality of the Church is always relative to Christ's perfect, full sacramentality. It is the crucified-risen Lord who proclaims the good news in the Spirit; but he does it in and through the Church. If history were a succession of self-enclosed moments, or if the resurrection were an a-historical event, or if Christ were simply an event of the past and not sacramentally present in the Church—leaving tradition a dry reiteration of codified truths and interpretations of rites and texts—Scripture would in fact have to be read "against itself," as modern exegesis attempts, in order to grasp Jesus's real

---

45. The analogy of nuptial love indicates the radical character of divine grace. See John Paul II, *Theology of the Body*, 500–503. As his reflections on Ephesians 5 elucidate, the nuptial and redeeming aspects of love are inseparable: Christ redeems man "to present the Church to himself without spot or wrinkle" (Eph 5:25–27).

46. It is not our task here to offer an exploration of the concept of revelation or to rehearse the history of contemporary exegesis. For the former, see Balthasar, *GL* 1, and *TL* 2; Rahner and Ratzinger, *Offenbarung und Überlieferung*. See also López, "Divine Revelation." For an account of the history of christological exegesis, see Bordoni, *Gesù di Nazaret*, vol. 1; Dunn, *Jesus Remembered*.

message and personhood (kerygma). Against a positivistic understanding of time, the nuptial understanding of revelation permits Scripture—read in its christological unity, which the Church has received—to offer us access to the *semper maior* mystery of the person of Christ: his human experience of divine filiation, that is, his lived self-awareness of being "the Son," the "sent one" from the Father.[47] The human experience of Christ, therefore, is the living out in history of the words that we hear at his Baptism and Transfiguration, words addressed to him from all eternity by the Father: "This is my beloved Son with whom I am well pleased" (Matt 3:17); "listen to him" (Matt 17:1).

Jesus Christ knows himself to be the beloved Son of the Father, and the Father's predilection exhaustively defines both his being and his action. Every person is aware of the unbridgeable gap separating what he is and what he does, and every person, although familiar with what he is, is always at pains to discover who he is. As Augustine confessed with his disarming simplicity, one's most ardent desire is to know oneself and God. By contrast, Christ's self-awareness of being the beloved Son of the Father has no historical beginning, and his mission, as has been eloquently illuminated by others, is coextensive with his person.[48] He is asked to reveal God's Fatherhood through his entire being, life and death, that is, to receive the Father's love and reciprocate it to the end. This overabundant and inexhaustible gift of self to the end is both what he sees the Father "doing," which gift constitutes him as Son and which the Father asks him to communicate to man through obedience unto death on the Cross (Phil 2:5–8; Heb 2:10–17), and what he longs to do.[49]

Jesus's gift of self extends to the utmost. This entails, first of all, that he speaks his divine filiation in a human form and so embraces from within human existence the gift of the Father's love. He, the beloved Son of the Father, is to receive the Father's love as man, son of Mary. Going to the

---

47. Here the theological distinction is presupposed between "Son of man," used by Jesus of Nazareth to refer to himself; "Son of God," a term belonging also to mythological theology and common to Eastern religions and the Roman worldview, which also saw the emperor as "son of God"; and most specifically, "Son." This is the biblical name that best identifies Jesus's awareness of himself. See Ratzinger, *Jesus of Nazareth*, 321–45; Ratzinger, *Introduction to Christianity*, 216–38.

48. The perfect identity between Christ's actions and his being, the giving of himself and his very self, his existence and mission, undergirds the inseparability of the terms Jesus and Christ as confessed by the Church. See Ratzinger, *Introduction to Christianity*, 204–5. In a sense, the christological heresies are ultimately a refutation of this identity. Yet it is precisely this identity that allows Christ to be truly God and truly man. See Balthasar, *TD*, 3:149–259.

49. Balthasar, *TD*, 3:172.

"utmost" also means reciprocating the gift to the concrete singular on behalf of humankind, who hated the Father. Christ's reciprocation of the Father's love takes the form of kenosis, all the way to the Cross, because man's rejection of the gift needs to be redeemed; that is, he must be made new. The concrete singular was in unspeakable need of redemption, and only a gift of self to the reckless end could elicit from within finite freedom the "yes" for whose utterance man was created. Only the bottomless wealth of the divine gift can divest itself of the form of God and pronounce its richness in the form of poverty. We thus turn now to Christ's human experience of his divine filiation to consider his awareness of his mission as expressed in his prayer. The following section starts by examining Christ's reciprocation of the Father's love through obedience to the end.

3. "You Have Given Me Your Name" (John 17:12)

A helpful check against approaching the action of Jesus Christ as though it were a fait accompli from the beginning, and also against a possible confusion of the divine *esse* with his historical mission, is to recall that Jesus Christ lives out humanly, that is, historically, the knowledge of both his eternal identity as the beloved Son of God, and his mission to give himself in order to redeem humankind.[50] Christ's mission to reveal God's Fatherhood and so restore the truth of gift determines both the content that occupies his self-consciousness—to represent the redeeming love of the Father through the gift of himself—and the mode of his awareness of this concern. As truly human, Jesus embraces time as the way to be himself, and so his divine self-awareness is present through a human consciousness. By becoming incarnate, the Logos as man accepts that he will grow in the knowledge of his own divine sonship through the mediation of history and interpersonal relations. This does not mean that Jesus Christ develops a divine self-consciousness of being the Son of God. Rather, as Balthasar clarifies, deepening the work of H. Schell and S. Bulgakov, this growth means that "Jesus is aware of an element of the divine in his innermost, indivisible self-consciousness; it is intuitive because it is inseparable from

---

50. The present section benefits from different contemporary Christologies that see in the concept of mission "a portrayal of the person of Christ that neither preempts the action undertaken by him nor falls back into the kind of purely ahistorical, static 'essence' Christology that sees itself as a complete and rounded 'part one,' smoothly unfolding into a soteriological 'part two'" (Balthasar, *TD*, 3:149). In addition to the works of Balthasar, Ratzinger, Giussani, and Bordoni already cited, see Giussani, *At the Origin*; and Guardini, *Das Wesen des Christentums*.

the intuition of his mission-consciousness, but it is defined by this same mission-consciousness."[51] Because Christ's human awareness of his divine sonship is at the service of his mission, both are true: "Jesus advanced [in] wisdom and age and favor before God and man" (Luke 2:52), and "you know all things" (John 16:30). The growth in knowledge of his own divinity does not mean that Jesus does not see the Father. He does. His *Jubelruf* witnesses to it (Matt 11:25–27). If he did not know the Father he could not claim to be identical with God (John 10:30). It is difficult, however, to describe this vision of the Father. Aquinas presents it in terms of a "beatific vision" of the Father, a position adopted by the Congregation for the Doctrine of the Faith in 1920 in order to correct the modernist claim that Jesus had no permanent consciousness of his own divine identity.[52] Yet this characterization seems problematic for at least two reasons: first, the beatific vision is the knowledge proper to the saints in heaven and so is not apt for Jesus's historical existence; and second, the different types of knowledge Aquinas describes as Christ's (*scientia beata, scientia infusa, scientia acquisita vel experimentalis*) seem to be merely juxtaposed rather than describing one person's ways of knowing. Certainly, distinctions among the three types must be maintained. Nevertheless, an organic unity among the distinctions is maintained only if the guiding principle for Jesus's vision of the Father, and the modalities of this vision, is his mission. What the Incarnate Logos sees and reveals is determined, moment by moment, as a function of his mission.[53] A. von Speyr writes that Jesus "has the vision of the Father. He *can* fall back on this vision. Yet he has to be attentive to what can be done within the limits of human capacities.... Obviously, the Son does not have faith in the sense we do (he is God after all). Nevertheless, he has on earth a form of vision whose closest point of comparison is the faith that we have. It is a new form of adoration (for vision, too, is adoration) whose primary characteristic is that the Son looks at the Father together with human beings ... and furthermore, that he experiences the relation of man to the Father in his whole bodily being, so that, in the totality of his humanity, he makes himself the gauge, the measure, of the relationship between the human beings and the Father."[54] The paradox of the *theantropy* of Jesus Christ resides in that, as Bulgakov

---

51. Balthasar, *TD*, 3:166.

52. Aquinas, *ST*, III, qq. 9–13. This is perhaps why, as Balthasar notes, Aquinas concludes that while Christ could learn from things, he could not learn from men, because in this case he would be dependent on the uncertainty of secondhand information (Balthasar, *TD*, 3:174).

53. This is also in *Catechism of the Catholic Church*, nos. 472–73. See Sharkey, *International Theological Commission*, 305–16.

54. Von Speyr, *Kostet und seht*, 162ff.

illustrates, Jesus Christ's divine self-awareness is given to him through the human and his human self-awareness through the divine.[55]

The reality of the Son's kenosis and the nature of the gift of self are seen in the fact that his mission, which he receives from the Father through the Spirit, is also given through his encounter with people and different situations. For Jesus, every singular is seen for what it is: in its otherness, as other, it is also a sign of the Father. Following Nédoncelle's epistemology, Balthasar contends that, as is the case for every human being, Jesus Christ, too, "is awakened to I-consciousness through the instrumentality of a Thou."[56] This is why, according to Balthasar, Mariology and Christology are inseparable. Mary, he clarifies, does not impart to Jesus a knowledge of his own divine sonship from outside: this would be simple adoptionism. Rather, Mary, perfect embodiment of the "daughter of Zion," teaches the child "the religious tradition that looks to the fulfillment of Israel's hope." In this way, the child's inner initiation, "under the guidance of his eternal Father, takes place in harmony with his external, historical initiation."[57] As a true human being, Jesus Christ undergoes a historical learning process—though it is not a development into something different than what he is—by which he comes to know himself and his mission. As do other human beings, whose ideas emerge through historical circumstances and encounters, so also the Incarnate Logos receives through the mediation of historical encounters, at the time that the Father determines, what has been decided by God from all eternity. For example, when seeing the hunger of those who, having previously been fed, burst into Capernaum's synagogue to make him king, he announces the institution of the Eucharist—from which the Church's existence follows—as the permanence of his own bodiliness (John 6:22–71). The discovery that the hour has come, that "hour" whose arrival he refuses to know beforehand (Mark 13:32), is also communicated to him when the Greeks express desire to see him (John 12:20–28). Christ's mission preserves the reality of the gift of self (he gives himself as man while remaining the divine Son), and so he also learns and grows in knowledge like a human being. It reveals, too, that with respect to knowledge, donation aims instead at the growth of the person, that is, at the person's being himself in and with another. This way of knowing and acting, however, does not relegate Jesus Christ to a passive tool in the hands of the Father. As expressed through his prayer, his active obedience to the Father is simultaneously his reception of the Father's will through the Spirit, and his own giving of his life (John 10:18).

---

55. Bulgakov, *Lamb of God*, 242.
56. Balthasar, *TD*, 3:175.
57. Ibid., 3:176.

Jesus's prayer is the point that illuminates how his human awareness of his divine sonship reveals the unity of being (God, man, and the world). We are so accustomed to viewing prayer as a separate activity conducted occasionally on the side that it is difficult to see that prayer is instead the dramatic dialogue with God that lies at the heart of every moment. Obviously, this dialogue becomes explicit in certain moments dedicated to prayer, but human existence is itself this dialogue. As Ratzinger says, "Prayer is an act of being"; it is the very act that expresses the lived awareness of oneself in dialogue with the Source.[58] According to Scripture, Jesus Christ's prayer is the historical rendition of the eternal dialogue that constitutes God himself. Christ constantly retreats to pray, but all of his actions are also prayer: the calling of the twelve proceeds from his conversation with the Father (Luke 6:12–17); he is transfigured while praying (Luke 9:19); the raising of Lazarus is the fruit of Jesus's prayer to the Father (John 11:41–43); and Jesus's death on the Cross, along with the meaning he gives it at the Eucharist, is itself a prayer.[59]

In Jesus we discover that prayer is the exercise of reason and love *par excellence* and that it includes all of one's bodily existence. Since he is the beloved Son of the Father, his prayer is the purest expression of gift. It illuminates the meaning of the unity and distinction of the two natures in the person of the Logos because it highlights the existential fullness of finite reason, freedom, and bodiliness in the Logos as an indwelling and loving dialogue with the Father. We can now examine the nature of the gift of self as described by Jesus Christ himself, and then turn to the implications of prayer for understanding time as gift.

What is most characteristic of Jesus's prayer, as J. Jeremias has eloquently shown, is his unique filial relationship with God, whom he boldly calls Father, *Abba* (Mark 14:36; Luke 3:22).[60] The "content" of the gift is sonship, personal relation with the Father. While in the Old Testament the people of Israel knew that God was Father to them, and that Israel was his firstborn son, their dominant perception of God was not Father but Lord. Jesus Christ, deepening the tradition into which he was born, speaks of God as Father (Mark 13:32). Yet, startlingly, when he addresses God directly, he dares to say what cannot be found in any preceding rabbinic literature: "my Father."[61] The total dependence on God that Israel learned from its own

58. Ratzinger, *Feast of Faith*, 27.
59. Ratzinger, *Behold the Pierced One*, 11–46; Bieler, *Freiheit als Gabe*, 166–72.
60. Jeremias, *Prayers of Jesus*; Ratzinger, *Jesus of Nazareth*, 128–42.
61. This address appears thirteen times in Matthew and twenty-five times in John. Mark 8:38; Matt 11:27, 16:27; Luke 2:49, 22:29, 24:29. See "πατηρ," in *TDNT*, 5:945–1022.

history and that was taught by patriarchs, kings, judges, and prophets—this dependence that taught them that God provides and takes care of everything, from conception to death, is presented here to be grounded in God's gift of his very self. What else could "Father" mean if not him who communicates his own being to another? Jesus claims total access to the Father, to be the only one who knows the Father because the Father has given *everything* to him (Matt 11:25–27; John 3:35). This totality, of course, is not a "thing"—for example, a reified divine *esse*. It is the knowledge of God's name: Father (John 17:11). By giving the Son his name, the Father wishes to be addressed by him. The Father's gift of self to the Logos, who is eternally turned towards the Father and contemplates his face, is a permanent dialogue in which both persons stand, so to speak, facing each other in perfect knowledge of the other. This knowledge is perfect communion with the Father, the one whom man desires to see and whose face cannot be beheld without dying.[62] "No one has ever seen God; the only Son, who is in the bosom of the Father, he has made him known" (John 1:18). Through his prayer Jesus reveals to the apostles the very center of his life: the relation of absolute, non-creaturely dependence on the Father. In calling him Father, Jesus claims simultaneously that it is given to him, Jesus, to be like the Father, and that in being addressed as "Father," he remains another.

Scripture, particularly the Johannine corpus, reveals that it is through prayer that Jesus unfolds the awareness of his own sonship as a life that is an eternal, triune gift of self for, in, and with the other. The Father gives everything to the Son, his being and his mission. Explaining what he was sent to do, Jesus constantly indicates that he receives everything from the Father. The Father gives him the power to judge, although Jesus judges according to what he hears from the Father (John 5:22). The Father places everything in the Son's hands (John 3:35). The Father gives Jesus the words that he is to give to the apostles (John 3:34, 14:24), words that are nothing other than the expression of Jesus himself, who is God's Logos (John 1:1). From the Father he also receives his teaching (John 7:16), his works (John 5:36, 14:10), and authority on heaven and earth (Matt 28:18). In the gift of himself, the unpreceded origin remains always with the Son. What Jesus does is never accomplished on his own, apart from the Father, because his will is also his Father's (John 5:30).[63] What the Father gives is truly given; it is the Son's. This giving reveals that the Son's working, judging, speaking, etc., are deeds, judgments, and words that reveal who he is and, at the same

---

62. See the beautiful account in Gregory of Nyssa, *Life of Moses*.

63. See "*arrabon*," in *TDNT*, 1:475; "*didomi*," 2:166–73; "*korban*," 3:860–66. See also Brown, *New Dictionary*, 39–44.

time, are also of the Father. The relation of the giving and receiving of one in the other can be radical to this extent because it is the expression of an eternal communion. The Father gives Jesus his own glory (John 1:14) from the beginning (John 17:5) because of the love he has for him before the foundation of the world (John 17:24). The Father places everything in the Son's hands (John 3:35), giving him, first of all, to have life in himself (John 5:26). Jesus's eternal and permanent origin is the Father (John 17:8). The giving and reciprocation of the gift is an expression and a communication of love: the Father loves Christ without measure (Luke 3:22; John 10:17), and Christ loves the Father (John 14:31) within and above everything (Mark 12:30; Matt 6:30). The relation of giving and reciprocating is not extrinsic to either: since the hypostatic union permits the hypostasis of the Logos to be the existential fullness of both the divine and the human nature, Jesus can say that he is in the Father and the Father is in him (John 14:10–11, 10:38).

The ever-greater giving and receiving of the Father and the Son fleshed out by Christ does not collapse the one into the other because the unity of the gift is itself a third. Jesus Christ's proclamation of his total unity with the Father (John 10:30) implicitly contains the affirmation of the Consoler: "even as you, Father, are *in* me and I *in* thee" (John 17:21). The Father's being "in" the Son indicates both a distance and an identity that is represented by a third, the Holy Spirit (John 14:9). Because it is he in whom the Father and the Son are united, the Spirit of the Father is the one Christ gives to communicate the life he brings to human beings (John 3:34–35, 14:15–28, 16:6–11); it is he who will teach them to pray and call God "*Abba*" (Rom 8:15). This triune omnipotent love opens up the space for a finite other to be, and this concrete singular is so treasured by the Father that "he gave his only Son, that whoever believes in him should not perish but have eternal life" (John 3:16). Once he assumes flesh, every human event of Jesus's life spells out, without exhausting its mystery, the ever-greater love that the Father, Son, and Holy Spirit is.

Jesus's own prayer and the prayer he teaches others reveal the eternal and historical dimensions of the gift. His prayer opens up new dimensions of what we discussed earlier regarding the meaning of the present and time in terms of originary experience. When he teaches his disciples to pray, he insists that prayer should be ongoing (Luke 18:1) and hidden from others. Hiddenness, rather than privacy or isolation, seeks fundamentally to acknowledge the constitutive relation with the Father. One prays to the Father, asking him to give the gift of being that he has already communicated, but one's prayer cannot be diverted into an affirmation of oneself. Of course, rather than pitting hiddenness against liturgical prayer, the latter enables, sustains, and deepens the former, and the former (prayer in private) ensures the authenticity and personal expression of the latter. Continuity, praying at all times, shows that history is a constitutive part of the dialogue with the Father. Jesus insists too that one should pray with certainty that the Father will listen (Luke 11:1–11). Moreover, those who ask with faith should "believe *that you have received it*, and it *will be* yours" (Mark 11:24).[64] As one who knows himself to be the gift of God (John 4:10), Jesus is certain that the Father is faithful, that he has never ceased and never will cease to give. Contrary to the Evil One who deceived Adam and Eve, the Father is not a liar: to those who ask, it will be given, and to those who knock, the door will not remain closed. Jesus's certainty shows that his present is an eternal receiving himself from the Father (the eternal past, to use Schelling's words), a donation that knows no end (the eternal future).[65] The eternal *nunc* of the Logos therefore contains the certainty of *having received* everything, of being completely one with and yet other from the paternal giver, and being confirmed in being: the gift *will be given*. This is what he prays for and teaches his disciples: the Father will unfailingly send the Spirit to whomever asks with certainty (Luke 11:9–13). "More" will be given to those who pray. According to Scripture this "more" is not a quantitative reality; it is, once again, a relation with another, the Holy Spirit, who overabundantly confirms the original being given. So it is for man: the prayer is addressed to the Father in Christ through the Holy Spirit.

Jesus also unveils what it means to be the gift of the Father and the meaning of time and eternity through his discourses against worldly anxiety, when he invites his disciples not to permit themselves to be caught up in care for the future (Matt 13:22; Mark 4:19; Luke 21:34). Regard for the future must keep alive the memory of the Father's delight in man's created existence, and of the eschatological promise of eternal fulfillment made through the patriarchs, kings, and prophets of Israel. What Jesus Christ communicates by insisting on prayer with certainty and on letting go of anxiety for the future is precisely the reason why he does not wish to know when his hour will come. He knows that time confirms the Father's original donation. His prayer, in this sense, unfolds the meaning of time as something beyond the succession of discrete moments and days; it participates in the truth of eternity, that is, the perfect, non-extensive self-possession coincident with divine fullness. If eternity is a type of life, entirely present to itself inasmuch as it gives all of itself to itself, then God's "I am" is the present of the divine persons. This present can be characterized in terms of "presence" to each other in a "coming from" another, being "with" and "in" the

---

64. Ulrich, *Der Mensch als Anfang*, 72ff.
65. Schelling, *Ages of the World*.

other, and being "for" the other. Having its truth and archetype in eternity, the threefold dimension of time (past, present, and future) is then a "passage from one life [history] to the other [eternity]," as Plotinus suggests.[66]

If the Incarnation is being God as other (man) while being truly both God and man, and the fundamental act of the person is prayer, then to give is to pronounce oneself in and through another, without confusion or separation.[67] The coextensiveness of the transcendentals appears in their concrete form through Jesus's prayer: giving (*bonum*) himself to the Father is both revealing and pronouncing (*verum*) himself, that is, expressing the beauty (*pulchrum*) of the unity (*unum*) with the Father. The word gives itself to be known, and to let itself be known is its gift. The Enlightenment's severing of language, reason, meaning, and history from each other leaves us prone to the idea that truth and gift go their separate ways and meet only occasionally. It is true that, given the fallen condition, human speech is often ambiguous. What one says frequently conveys something other than what one means.[68] Nor can we underestimate how much the lie that man forges or submits to damages language itself, to the extent that certain words become unusable. Nevertheless, in the triune God, where everything is given, fragmentation is not possible. Since in God there is no ontological difference between *esse* and *essentia*, *bonum et verum convertuntur*. Jesus Christ is both the "beloved Son of the Father," the one who is the Gift of the Giver, and His Word, the one in whom the Father pronounces himself and everything else. The gift-Son, as Bonaventure says, is simultaneously the *expressio* of the Father.[69]

The "expression" is neither a reiteration of the paternal giver nor simply a word uttered into a void. It is only evil's denial of the gift, as we saw, that brings redundancy and monotonous self-identity. The Father *is* his speaking, and his begetting of the Logos is also the eternal dialogue with the beloved, eternal Son in the Spirit. The personal epistemology we saw earlier with regard to Christ's human awareness of his divine filiation is true, *mutatis mutandis*, for God. There would be no Logos in God if there were no possibility of dialogue. It is not a coincidence that both the Aristotelian

---

66. Plotinus, *Enneads* 3.7.11. Obviously Plotinus means the relation between time and eternity in a different sense. See López, "Restoration of Sonship."

67. Rahner also tries to elaborate a symbolic ontology to ground sacramental theology. Although there are interesting insights in his well-known work, it suffers from an inadequate christological foundation. See Rahner, "Theology of the Symbol."

68. It is interesting to note that, as the episode of the Tower of Babel illustrates (Gen 11:1–9), language acquires opacity due to man's hubris. When language does not serve its purpose, to praise God, it loses its transparency.

69. Bonaventure, *Collationes in Hexaemeron* 3.7.

Unmoved Mover and the Plotinian One dwell in silence and solitude. The God of Jesus Christ, instead, reveals himself to be a communion of persons in which there is nothing but absolute, ever-new communication. Response and reciprocation, as we saw, belong to the nature of the gift. This we also learn through Christ's prayer. Prayer in fact is a grateful *response* to the presence of another. The one who prays recognizes that he belongs to the one to whom he prays, and the one who asks abandons himself into the hands of the one who can take heed of his request. Prayer, as an expression of the dual unity of love (*eros-agape*), is the reciprocation to the paternal origin with all of oneself. Although the most liberating gift, as human experience shows, the gratuitous abandoning of oneself to another is also the most difficult gift. This recognition of belonging and "abandonment" into the hands of another is also in God, though without creaturely dependence and unmarred by sin. Donation generates a belonging, a joyful "being owned by" the giver and the need to respond to him. While we leave the first aspect for later, we turn now in more detail to Jesus's reciprocation of the gift of the Father's love, and consider in what sense it restores man's rejection of God's gift.

4. Making All Things New

At the center of the fallen human condition, Jesus Christ ardently desires to fulfill the Father's will: "to give his life for the ransom of many" (Mark 10:45), to eat the Passover with his disciples (Luke 22:15), and to die on the Cross so that those who receive him "may have life in abundance" (John 10:10). He wishes to communicate to those who welcome him "all that I have heard from my Father" and thus introduce them into the unspeakable gift that fulfills man's desire to see the face of God: friendship with God (John 15:15). For Jesus it is evident—in the sense of truth's offering meaning and inviting man's free reception outlined earlier—that the Father is everything, that he is at the center of all things, and that only in him is reality good and true. After the human rejection of the gift, the act of love in reciprocation of the Father's love takes the form of obedience unto death: "obedience defines Christ's behavior towards the Father: Christ recognizes, accepts, and adheres to the Father's design. When the Father's design entails his death, Christ recognizes that that is the path of his life. Obeying the Father, for the man Christ, is to follow the Father."[70] Jesus is not spared adherence to the Father's plan even when, as at the inner passion in Gethsemane, the Father's will seems incomprehensible. The desire (*eros*) to reciprocate the Father's love (*agape*)—that is, to welcome and to communicate the truth of God,

---

70. Giussani, *SPVVC*, 119 (Italian).

being, and man—becomes, in the face of sin, the embrace of the sacrifice of affirming the design to restore unity between God and the world. In Christ's obedience unto death on the Cross, we see that obedience is the affirmation of the truth of being, which is coincident with the handing over of oneself in utter love to him whose will it is to confirm and renew the gift. "The Son of the Father," writes Balthasar, "is a gift because of his kenotic obedience to the norm of the Father with whom he is one yet not identical—and this norm is mediated to him by the Spirit."[71] Jesus Christ's obedience unto death thus liberates freedom in allowing it to adhere to the mystery, and so renders it truly human from within. Let us look now at his redemptive obedience, the gift of his very self, which enables the Father to make all things new.

Christ's kenotic obedience encompasses the complete event of his enfleshment. Its first moment regards his descent: "although he was in the form of God, he did not count equality with God a thing to be grasped, but emptied himself and became man" (Phil 2:6). The Logos does not jealously cling to the form of God because his begetting is a love in which everything is continuously being given. In God there is no place for an anthropomorphic fear of not receiving the gift of one's own existence. Utter wealth—*ipsum esse*, which subsists in the total gift of self—and utter poverty—giving all and receiving all—are coincident in God. The Logos's not holding onto himself suggests then that something like gratuity and gratitude form part of God's love itself. The triune unity of the divine love is such that the person of the Logos can "take the form of a servant" and, without ceasing to be what he is from eternity, in a manner known to him alone (Cyril), can appear in the "likeness of man" (Phil 2:7). Christ's divine filial identity is revealed precisely *through* his kenosis. The "emptying" allows us therefore a glimpse of the ever-greater immensity and profundity of what it is for God to be gift.

The Son's kenosis does not stop at his taking flesh from Mary. It remains throughout his existence as his continuous obedience to the Father. Just as his birth from Mary images his eternal being begotten of the Father, his obedience to the Father translates into time his eternal being begotten of and relation with the Father. "He became obedient unto death, even death on a cross" (Phil 2:8). Christ's obedience, learned through suffering, is the human act of the person of the Logos that reveals his identity as a divine person inasmuch as he receives all of himself from and responds to the Father. Christ's "economic" obedience reveals that for him to be "for himself" (*autexousia*) is to be not only "one" with the Father (John 10:30) but more radically "for" him in the Spirit, and to be so gratuitously. In this sense, the humiliation of Jesus is not only undergone, it is embraced from within.

---

71. Balthasar, *Epilogue*, 76.

The kenosis of Christ comes to fruition in the resurrection, which, rather than a simple return to the Father, is a return with his own crucified, glorious body. He thus allows human beings to receive the Father's name and to "confess that Jesus Christ is the Lord, to the glory of God the Father" (Phil 2:11). Obedience, thanks to Jesus Christ's gift of self, can be embraced as the historical expression of love (*eros* and *agape*) because it is guided by the light of his glory, the glory the Father gave him from the beginning (John 17:24) and the glory he received after accomplishing his mission (John 17:4–5).

Jesus Christ's obedience to the Father entails opening to us God's love for man. To give the Father's love, in obedience to him through the Spirit, is to give himself for man—to place himself at man's service. While, as we saw, in rejecting the gift man embraces a logic of power detached from the nature of being, Christ's reciprocation of the Father's love shows that power unites, affirms, and transfigures when it is at the service of another. The Incarnate Logos presents himself as the one who serves (John 13:1–20). His service, however, is not that of a slave who simply does what the master tells him. It consists rather in speaking the truth that the Father has given him, the truth that the Father is. Christ serves because the prophetic announcement of the truth of God and the truth of man—a truth with which he identifies himself (John 14:6)—educates man. To serve, to give himself, is to educate, that is, to enable man to discover and live the relationship with the Father. To this end, Christ's service corrects the lie rooted in the heart of man. He has first to draw it out (John 8:39–41), not in order to condemn (John 3:17), but to allow his listener to respond. Having unearthed the lie, Jesus compels man to decide whether he "also wants to go away" from him (John 6:67) or, alternatively, wishes to let himself be washed (John 13:9). Christ's service, besides speaking and educating in the truth, is also the service of a king (John 18:36–37). He is king not only because everything, from nature to the devils, submits to him, or because his authority is uncontestable. He is a king primarily because he guides, waits, and accompanies, and does so like a shepherd, never leaving his flock untended (John 10:1–21). Furthermore, he is always ready to do what no shepherd would ever do for a lost sheep (Luke 15:3–7). His power, although apparently foolishness and weakness (1 Cor 1:18–25), is strong like no other. He is able to lay down his life and to take it up again (John 10:18). Note, however, that laying down his life is not simply an option he chooses; it is the center of his mission and expressive of his very personhood. In so doing he fleshes out before man's eyes what he has seen the Father doing from all eternity: he gives himself for the sake of the other. Christ's power, since it is at the service of man, gathers people into a unity of ineffable beauty (John 17). This is not in order to keep a tight rein on the few who respond to him, but rather to communicate through them the life he has been given (Mark 6:7) and, to some, his capacity to forgive or to retain man's rejection (John 20:22–23). Christ tirelessly reveals that the gift of himself is surrendering, handing himself over for the sake of the other. This is why he serves not only by preaching, educating his listeners to walk in the truth, and gathering people under the Father's love. He is the priest offered like a sacrificial Lamb to die upon the Cross, so that man can cross over to the other shore (1 Cor 5:7) and enter into the Father's house (John 14:2). He allows himself to be offered up, and he himself offers, in the Spirit, the body that was prepared for him (Heb 10:15). As the true gift of the Father, Christ allows himself to be given away without remainder and gives himself over without being afraid to drink the cup of wrath the Father will give him. Jesus Christ is the priest who, hanging upon the Cross, lets his side be pierced so that the sacraments may flourish in the care of Mary, the Church in person (John 19:34). Through them, his redemption is able to reach all. Christ's service is the expression of his own thankfulness to the Father, the communication of his joy. It discloses that he reciprocates the Father's love by permitting, through being handed over to those who were still his enemies (Rom 5:8), that the Father's love may be fruitful in them; his sacrifice begets the Church.

Jesus's gift of self, therefore, is an act of pure thankfulness (the delight that is *entelecheia*), or eucharist, and his work (*ergon*) is the expression of this thanksgiving. Jesus explicates the meaning of this word with his entire existence: to give thanks is to permit all of humankind to be in relationship with the Father. In this way, Jesus brings to light the full depth of the circularity between freedom and religiosity proper to the singular gift, which we pondered in the previous chapter. Thankfulness, however, is also sacrifice; not only because the former grounds the latter, but because both are an affirmation of the truth. To be thankful is to welcome and reciprocate the giver. To sacrifice oneself is to oppose the lie. After the rejection of the original gift, man shuns sacrifice, or perpetuates the lie of what he did in that rejection. With Christ's gift of self, one discovers that "sacrifice is not suspending the will for something, suspending love for someone or something; it does not mean to eliminate anything, but to rein in the will that is behaving against the nature of the thing."[72] Christ's sacrifice of himself thus shows that sacrifice is not against the truth of what things and people are; rather, it declines to allow the singular to be defined by what it is not. Christ's sacrificial act of thanksgiving does not only show that sacrifice is to affirm what things are, however; since God's gift of being to man was for the sake of man, that man might respond—just as the Father's gift to the Son is

---

72. Giussani, *PLW*, 3:78.

both himself and the begetting of the Son so that the Son may be one with him in the Spirit—so the sacrifice of thanksgiving is to "recognize a presence. The person, instead of affirming himself, affirms another."[73] The truest sacrifice is to forget oneself in the affirmation of another, to cause this other to live through the gift of one's own life (John 15:13). The affirmation of the other, so we see in Christ's sacrificial gift of self, is to defend the truth of the person, his relation with the Father. It is thus to acknowledge that only in receiving oneself from the Father does one exist; hence, it is to acknowledge, to recognize the Father, who for all eternity has always already given himself to the Son, to whom and in whom he has given all that has been created.

Jesus Christ's obedient love for the Father is coincident with his passionate communication to all of the Father's reckless love. In light of God's love, we see that to give is not simply to transfer an object from oneself to a different owner. To give is to give oneself, and to give oneself as a self means sharing all of oneself with another. Here we see that the immanence and transcendence of the giver in the gift, which elicit the receiver's desire to reciprocate the gift, are a sharing of the giver's existence with the receiver so that the latter can be himself in responding to the giver. That Christ shares himself with those who had originally rejected friendship with God means, first of all, that he forgives. Christ's kenotic obedience to the Father is a sharing of his life with men, calling them back to an unsuspected friendship with him. To share one's own life with someone who has rejected the Father as giver is to for-give him. During his earthly existence Jesus showed that to forgive seventy times seven (Matt 18:21–23) is simply to allow one's betrayer to be part of one's life, to allow him back into one's sphere—even more, to entrust him again with one's work (John 21:15–19). When Christ forgives he not only renews God's love, he entrusts the forgiven one with a responsibility. To forgive restores to power the energy sapped from it by man's hate. Power, reborn through Christ's forgiveness, is first of all a response to the Father's mercy. Within this response, power appears in its truth, that is, the communication of the Father's mercy that alone transfigures the ravages left by the rejection of the gift.

Although Scripture portrays Jesus explicitly forgiving sins only twice—in the account of the paralytic man (Mark 2:1–12) and in that of the sinful woman who anointed him at the Pharisee's house (Luke 7:36–50)—he speaks repeatedly about the need to forgive sins. The most common way for Jesus to extend the Father's mercy is, as N. Perrin elucidates, to eat with sinners. Sharing a meal, in fact, means to share life and, above all, God's

---

73. Ibid., 79.

blessing, and so the love of God—Christ himself (Mark 2:15; Luke 15:2).[74] Christ shares meals with sinners like Zaccheus, invites many to accept God's forgiveness, and allows some to remain with him, to share his life and his mission. He also calls public sinners to be his disciples (Matthew, Mary Magdalene). In sharing life with them, he gradually introduces them into divine sonship, the relation with the Father. Sinners who were heretofore cast out from society and salvation are offered *gratis* the possibility to live out a relationship with God the Father. Unlike John the Baptist's call for conversion, Jesus's redemption is given for free. Neither poverty, nor age, nor gender, nor social status could merit it or exclude it. All are invited to enter into relation with the Father gratuitously. This, of course, does not mean that evil and sin do not mean anything. If that were the case, love would also be meaningless. Rather, this radical gift alone respects justice because it renews what was originally given to the person and hence "belongs" to him. Once the Father's mercy has been welcomed, a new, far more radical conversion begins: one enters into the disposition, the mind of Christ, that is, lives in him and like him, without having anything at one's exclusive disposal—an availability that, as the Immaculate Conception shows, is the only way to be oneself.[75]

Christ's forgiveness was gained for us through his obedience unto the Cross. We just saw how his kenotic gift of self is his reciprocation of the Father's love through his service and work for others. Now we must see how his reciprocation of the Father's love entails accepting to drink the cup of wrath and to obey unto death on the Cross. This path is an arduous gift in which he, as man, lets himself be exposed to temptation. Before dying on the Cross, to carry out humanly the Father's will, he suffers an inner passion at Gethsemane. These two circumstances—temptation and inner suffering—are most indicative of his human freedom and its fulfillment in the obedient relation with the Father. Christ is tempted several times by the devil in the desert (Mark 1:13; Luke 4:1–2), recapitulating in himself the temptations of the people of Israel. Each time he affirms God's logic over and against worldly logic: God is more important than bread; God will give a sign to show his faithfulness, and it will not be worldly power; God, and not the Liar, is the true God. Christ is also tempted when others try to convince him, as Peter did, to do the Father's will in some way other than going to Jerusalem to die; when they insist, as his relatives did, that he is someone else; and when they demand that he come down from the Cross to prove his own divinity. By permitting himself to be tempted, Jesus shows

---

74. Jeremias, *Eucharistic Words of Jesus*; Perrin, *Kingdom of God*.
75. Jeremias, *New Testament Theology*, 85–121.

that, as Balthasar writes, "God does not only oppose the enemy of the divine from an external or superior standpoint, but also does the unthinkable: he exposes himself to Satan's fascination in order to burst the dazzling bubble from within."[76] Unlike the Hebrew people, however, Christ does not succumb. In this capacity to bear temptations without giving in, Jesus's humanity reveals that his being one with the divine nature does not weaken or eliminate freedom; rather, this unity liberates freedom to embrace the good for which it was originally given to itself.

The most controversial passage regarding Christ's freedom, as is well known, is that in which Jesus appears to resist the hour, which has been patiently anticipated until this point: "*Abba*, Father, all things are possible to thee; remove this cup from me; yet not what I will, but what thou wilt" (Mark 14:36; John 12:27ff.; Heb 5:7–8). In his dispute with Monotheletism—a heresy whose origin can be traced to Sergius of Constantinople's *Psephos*—Maximus the Confessor clarifies that this mysterious entreaty manifests a real human freedom reciprocating the Father's will, rather than a change of mind. Otherwise Christ would not really be the true gift of God as man, and the real nature of God would be revealed to be power and solitary unity. In numerous opuscula and more specifically in his *Disputatio cum Pyrrhus*, Maximus explains with his unique clarity and profundity that Christ's anguish is genuinely human, sinless passion and not a sign of wavering. That Christ reciprocates the Father's will with human freedom means that Christ desires our salvation as God *and* as man.

In Maximus's account, the Monothelites rightly claimed that Christ was a divine person made man, and that hence he could not humanly will independently of his divinity. Yet, because Pyrrhus and the Monothelites presupposed that finite human freedom in its fallen state ineluctably resists God's will, the integrity of Jesus's mission seemed to demand that he either lacked human freedom or, if not, that its proximity to the Godhead rendered this human freedom de facto inoperative. Maximus says in response that, regardless of how the difficulty is explained, it cannot be denied that the Markan passage indicates two freedoms in Christ. They pertain therefore to his natures, not to his person. Maximus then shows that the freedom that asks for the chalice to pass cannot be divine. If that were the case, there would be an internal contradiction in God—which would be tantamount to saying that God is not God. The request has to be of the human nature. It is important to understand that his human freedom was a complete one, and that since his human nature has its existential fullness in the *prosopon* of the Logos of the divine nature, Christ enjoys the fullness of freedom.

---

76. Balthasar, *Does Jesus Know Us?*, 26.

It is important here to recall Maximus's positive perception of the created world. Even fallen nature preserves its *logos*, its proper nature, although it no longer acts in the way (*tropos*) that accords with its nature. Since human beings are created in the image of God, human freedom (*autexousia*, that is, one's self-determination, or authority over oneself) reflects God's being, which is love itself. As such, human freedom is the capacity to turn towards God, from whom one receives "being, being-good, and being always."[77] The fullness of freedom is to say "yes" to the Father, to be with him who is the supreme good. "If anyone were to say," writes Maximus, "that something natural had resisted God [who is the supreme good], this would rather be a charge against God than against nature, for introducing war naturally to the realm of being and raising up insurrection against himself and strife among all that exists."[78]

The human being, for Maximus, naturally possesses the impulse towards what is good. Yet he experiences the goodness of any singular through deliberation and research. Fallen human nature, with its natural will, operates in a way (*tropos*) that does not correspond to its proper nature (*logos*). Choosing the good (*gnomic* will in Maximus) is a way of using freedom, not its definition.[79] Christ, Maximus contends, did not have a gnomic will. To understand Maximus's delicate and profound understanding, we need to see that *gnomie*, rather than deliberation or choice, means more accurately, as A. Walker clarifies, the pattern of willing into which a person settles.[80] Normally, this habit arises through inquiry, deliberation, and choice. It indicates the person's capacity to move towards God or to reject him. Had Adam and Eve accepted that the cosmos was given to them as a gift and not claimed it for themselves by grasping the forbidden fruit, there would be no need for inquiring, assessing, and choosing. That Christ did not have a gnomic will means, for Maximus, that his moral integrity, although truly human, did not follow the same path as ours. In the union with the divine nature it adhered to God's will from the beginning. If he had to deliberate about action as we do, the hypostatic union would be a moral, not an ontological, union. It can be tempting to interpret this adhesion to the Godhead to mean that Christ merely acted a part to edify us, or that he did not really suffer (Nestorianism). But when Christ embraces the form of a servant he embraces all that

---

77. Maximus, *Ambiguum* 42 (PG 91:1325B).

78. Maximus, *Opusculum* 7 (PG 91:80A). English translation in Louth, *Maximus the Confessor*, 185.

79. Maximus, *Disputation with Pyrrhus* (PG 91:308C). English translation in Maximus the Confessor, *Disputation with Pyrrhus*, trans. Farrell.

80. My understanding of Maximus's account is indebted to Adrian Walker's unpublished work. See also, among many others, Louth, *Maximus the Confessor*, 61.

is to come—not to preempt his way of the Cross, but to ensure that every choice is an expression of his desire to give himself for us. His a priori obedience to the Father, as A. Walker clarifies, "enables him to live each action he performs in time as something genuinely new that he receives from the Father."[81] Christ's natural freedom recognizes and embraces God's totality, humanly. In asking for the chalice to be taken away, then, Christ shows us his true humanity. The more divinized human freedom is, the more human it is. But if his request is not an expression of fear of death, what is it?

Christ did have fear, yet this "passion" was not the sinful one that results from the fear of death. For Maximus, as for the other Fathers, in addition to the passion of being created—the passive sense of gift that defines the creature—one distinguishes among the passions that pertain to human nature as such: those that are not sinful, and those that are.[82] There are, according to Maximus, two types of fear: one according to nature and another against it. The first is born from the capacity of every creature that comes from nothingness to tend to preserve its own given being. The other, against nature, is an irrational fear that is the fruit of sinful death.[83] The desire to hold onto being is a good passion, which Christ embraced passionlessly, as St. Cyril would say.[84] The fear of death, perceived as the annihilation of one's own being, is an irrational, sinful passion that a human nature united to the divine nature of the hypostasis of the Logos cannot have. "Since he was entirely God with the humanity, and he himself entirely man with the divinity, he, as man, in himself and through himself submitted his human will to God the Father, offering himself to us as an authentic and sublime model to imitate, so that we, looking at him like the author of our salvation, may submit our will to God freely, so that we may only will what he wants."[85]

Christ's experience of human (sinless) passion is the same as every human being's. He is truly affected by something else. On the other hand, in a different way from us, "Christ enters into this being determined by another as an expression of his human loving obedience."[86] He does not simply "accept" or "undergo" the passions. He embraces them from within as a sign of the Father's love for man and the way to renew human nature. Everything

---

81. Adrian Walker, "The *Gestalt* of Christ in Maximus the Confessor," 14, pro manuscripto.

82. Maximus, *On the Utility of the Passions* (CCSG 7:47–49); see Maximus, *Cosmic Mystery*, 97–98.

83. Maximus, *Disputation with Pyrrhus* (PG 91:297D–299A).

84. "Patiebatur autem impassibiliter." Cyril, *Scholia de incarnatione Unigeniti* 35 (PG 75:1409D).

85. Maximus, *Disputation with Pyrrhus* (PG 91:308A).

86. Walker, "*Gestalt* of Christ," 15.

IV. THE SON'S GIFT OF SELF   181

Christ does or says is thus an expression of his human and divine love for humankind, of his obedient gratitude for the love of the Father that begets him from all eternity. In this way, as Maximus is fond of repeating, Christ came to "institute natures afresh," not to change their *logos*.[87] Christ's vicarious representation does not mean that he simply gives himself up to death for us, that is, *instead* of us. He does not render superfluous our own embrace of the Father's love. Rather, Jesus "comes to experience the nature of sin from the inside, the center of the Passion lies not only in his perfect death (Anselm, K. Rahner), but equally in his experience of mortal anguish and of being forsaken by God."[88] To experience sin from within (2 Cor 5:18) is to suffer what the sinner deserves for having chosen an autonomy that rejects indebtedness: separation from God. Yet, since the separation from the giver that Christ experiences on the Cross (Mark 15:34) is an experience of the Incarnate Logos, as Balthasar explains, it reaches a dimension that no other human being can attain.[89]

The Paschal Mystery, which is also the prayer of Jesus, represents the summit of his superabundant response to man's rejection of the gift of being.[90] The Paschal Mystery, seen in its synchronic unity of institution of the Eucharist (Holy Thursday), death on the Cross (Good Friday), and resurrection (Easter Sunday), fleshes out for us the totality, gratuity, and fruitfulness of Christ's kenotic and redemptive obedience. The eucharistic sacrifice of Christ is that of his own body (Luke 22:19), which means that his person is the very gift of God (John 4:10), offered once and for all (Heb 7:26–28, 9:25–28; Eph 5:2) to make us part of his own body (Eph 5:30). Christ's sacrifice, as expressed in the Eucharist, confirms and fulfills superabundantly our ontological and anthropological explorations of the gift of self. It suffices to mention three aspects here.

The first is that Christ's kenotic gift of self restores unity with God. The redemption of the gift allows man to see that unity with God is possible and

---

87. Many of Maximus's *Ambigua* express this central concept. See, e.g., *Ambiguum* 42 (PG 91:1316A–1349A).

88. Balthasar, *Does Jesus Know Us?*, 32–33.

89. The ultimate root for Christ's obedience, once again, is the triune mystery of God. Certainly, one cannot talk about "obedience" in the Godhead as if there were three different wills in God. Maximus cogently clarifies that will belongs to nature, not to person. Since God is triune, however, the one divine will is enjoyed by each person differently: as given by the Father, as received by the Son, and as had with the others by the Holy Spirit. In this regard, the eternal, divine being-for another is what roots the historical obedience of Jesus and what human obedience, the gratuitous return of the gift, is called to become.

90. Besides Ratzinger's texts already cited, for the sacrificial aspect of the gift as presented in Hebrews, see Vanhoye, *Our Priest Is Christ*; Vanhoye, *Structure and Message*.

that it generates a whole that is greater than its parts. St. Paul's discourse on the different gifts, according to which God calls some to be apostles, others pastors, others prophets, etc., shows the church in Corinth that the unity of participating in the same Eucharist and in the same life of the Spirit precedes particular gifts or individuals and is distinct from their total number. The body of Christ is not just the sum of its members, just as our bodies are not the result of different parts being welded together. The priority of the unity indicates that the Eucharist effects the promised indwelling of the triune God in the believer and of the latter in God. It also reveals that being in Christ means enjoying his same relation with the Father and their same glory. In this way, those who partake of this sacrificial gift become a sacramental sign of the one to whom they belong (Matt 10:40).

At the same time, the second aspect emerges: the unity is not monadic; it is a communion. The unity of the body does not absorb and annihilate its members. On the contrary, belonging to the body allows each member to participate in the life that Christ brought in abundance. The communion that Christ brings enables the person to discover and be himself at the service of the other. Just as his being is from and for the Father and this relation is the ground of his pro-existence, so those who belong to him are themselves in being radically at the service of the other. The communion that Christ generates does not "equalize" its members. They are made one (Gal 3:28), but each has a unique place within this communion, the generating source of which is always the Father. As a gift of the Father, in Christ, through the Spirit, this communion has the Father at its center and lives out a historical unity by virtue of those who are called to represent Christ, the beloved Son of the Father. The historical father, again, does not hold this central position as an affirmation of himself, but as total relativity to God and to the members of his Church. In this regard, like Christ, he helps them to be and to grow ever more human in their relation with the triune God. Within this communion each finds his place, and within it, too, it is given to each to enjoy and live the totality of the gift of the Father's love.

The third aspect I wish to highlight is that Christ's eucharistic gift of self reveals that offering is the truth of prayer and so of human affection and reason. Offering, as the liturgical celebration of the Eucharist shows, consists of two moments: It is first of all a memory (*anamnesis*) of God's gift of self. Christ brings the eternal gift of the Father into the present. In asking his disciples to repeat his gesture, he asks them to participate in the memory that constitutes his very person. At the same time, the *epiclesis* implores the descent of the Holy Spirit, that he might transfigure the species of bread and wine into the body and blood of Christ. The memory of God's gift bears the entreaty to the Spirit of the beloved Son of the Father. In this sense the

Eucharist shows Christ's offering: his gift of self so that the Father can send the Holy Spirit. This dual unity of *anamnesis* and *epiclesis* is the heart of human prayer because to pray, to offer, is to go to the depth of oneself as a singular, to remember one's original giver and ask him to come. This asking, as with participation in the Eucharist, is not self-serving. Christ's offer of himself is for the sake of all. Those who partake of his body allow themselves to be taken, broken open, and given away, as he did at the Cross and in every liturgical celebration of the Eucharist. In so doing, they experience the beautiful paradox of being scattered, like seeds sown on a field, while also being themselves in bearing fruit in others.

The blood of Christ is shed from the Cross, just as his body is pierced there. Christ's gift of self embraces death in its ugliest form. His gift of self, of humbling himself to the end on the Cross, makes all things new because it unites heaven and earth, and all peoples to himself. As Balthasar indicates, the sacrificial aspect of the Eucharist, manifested at the Cross and eternalized and universalized by the resurrection, "presupposes that Jesus has taken our sins and defects on himself, in his Passion, so that we can be given what is his [divine life], not as something alien, but as what—beyond all imagining—is our very own, leading us from alienation to authentic personal being."[91] It is in this sense that his death is the culmination of his love—not only in that he dies out of love "for many," but also in that his death is an expression of his love that alone can regenerate what was lost. Jesus is, as explained earlier, more human than we are human because, as man, he can make all of us truly human, that is, children of God, from within human nature. In this way he allows the Father's mercy to regenerate and reunite at a deeper level what man's original rejection closed off *(felix culpa)*. The resurrection confirms that Christ's gift of self, contrary to how it seemed at the time, was not for nothing. To lose oneself to the end for the sake of others is the narrow path to finding oneself in the Father's bosom.

Christ is the ultimate "self-expenditure of God."[92] God's gift of self gives rise to the response that contains the giver and the gift (united without confusion, separation, or division): sacrificial thanksgiving (Luke 23:46). To conclude our reflection on Christ's sacrificial offering of himself and how it effects the gifted unity of man and the world with God, we will now develop more fully these two aspects: the infinite gratuitousness of Christ's gift of self, and the desire to reciprocate elicited in those who receive him. Just as Christ ardently desired to give himself freely for man, so those who

---

91. Balthasar, *TD*, 3:232.
92. Ratzinger, *Introduction to Christianity*, 261.

welcome his Spirit breathed from the Cross and see the uniqueness of his gift of self also desire to return the gift *gratis*.

5. Gratuity's Owning

The Logos's kenotic and redeeming obedience reveals the "radical" nature of the gift precisely in the *gratuity* of his gift of self to the end: becoming one like us so that he can give himself totally to God for each. Man knows from within his own experience something of this gratuity. Existence itself implies the original goodness that calls him out of nothingness. The human being is born, is loved into existence, and does not determine the length of his days. Created in the image of God who is Love himself, man also knows from experience that there is nothing truer to the nature of what is than to affirm and be affirmed without calculation or ideology. What every human person desires most is to be loved by and to love gratuitously the one who knows who he is and what he has done. A gratuitous action, therefore, affirms man's being because he is and as he is. It is only by being so loved and affirmed that one can truly grow as a person. Yet, as we saw, since there is nothing more interior to man than God himself, to affirm (to love) the human being for his own sake means to affirm him in his lived relationship with God. Only within these parameters can the human being affirm being for its own sake, without bending it to preconceived ideas. The human being does reject God, however, and so does attempt to bend being and history to his own predetermined and partisan interests and to his own contrived images. This is why Jesus Christ's gift of self appears as both utterly fitting and radically other. Fitting because "gratuity," as Giussani says, "is the supreme interest of the human being."[93] His gratuitous gift of self is also radically other from our common experience because the human being cannot on his own invent the utmost affirmation of another's good, an affirmation that is able to regenerate from within the rejection that it encounters. The human being betrays and cannot be merciful.

What is gratuitous about Christ's gift? To address this question, which also touches on the reasonableness of the Incarnation, we return to our grounding perspective: the person of Christ and what he says about himself. As Athanasius beautifully suggests, we must look first to God, rather than to man's sinfulness, if we are to grasp this gratuity: "It was impossible that God should leave man to be carried off by corruption, because it would be unfitting and unworthy of Himself."[94] This "impossibility" does not imply terms

---

93. Giussani, "Quella prima carezza."
94. Athanasius, *On the Incarnation*, 32 (PG 25b:105–7).

IV. THE SON'S GIFT OF SELF

of logical necessity or coercion—as if the sins of the human being could call God's being into question. Rather, God maintains his own glory. God, as the earlier reflection on causality indicated, does not desire the human being to be subservient to his divine glory. The opposite is true: God wishes to give man his own glory. "Contrary to other ideologies," writes A. Orbe, "God seeks to divinely glorify the human being in everything. God wants to pour himself into man, that he be clarified with God's own clarity."[95] The glory that God seeks is that the human being live (*gloria Dei vivens homo*), that he participate in God's own divine life. This is why the man who lives is the man who sees God (*vita autem hominis visio Dei*).[96] What is gratuitous is that God wishes to bestow his glory upon the human being even though the human being does not initially welcome it. Jesus, to the scandal of many, loves men as the sinners they are. He wishes them to see the Father's glory while they are still enemies of God, that is, while they hate the light. Thus, gratuity has to do with the restoration of that gifted *unity* between God, man, and the cosmos. God's mercy does not return man and the cosmos to a prelapsarian state. It brings them forward and deeper into the event of love in which the giving of oneself is sheer joy and ever-new unity. God loves gratuitously because he wants to give *anew* from within the human being the possibility of participating in his divine life, even while the human being is still a sinner. Gratuity is in this sense "unity without boundaries," which God gives through Christ's sacrificial offering of himself.[97]

The gratuitous nature of Christ's gift allows us to see that the unity renewed by Christ's gratuitous love is not a pantheistic absorption into a monadic God. It is the sharing of oneself with the other in order that the other might be in relation with the source. Gratuity in this sense is Christ's gift of himself for the good of man and the cosmos, a good that he himself is. Jesus's prayer and offering of himself are, in this regard, the culmination of gratuity: the affirmation of the other that freely binds all things to the Father in the Spirit: "all things hold together in him" (Col 1:17).

Jesus's human experience of divine sonship reveals that the gratuity of his gift of self, in reestablishing a unity between God and the human being, is also a way of "owning" the other—of being for, with, and in the other— a way that is best described with the term "virginity."[98] Christ's donation

---

95. Orbe, "*Gloria Dei vivens homo*," 263.

96. Irenaeus, *Haer*. 4.20.7 (PG 7a:1037).

97. Giussani, *AVS*, 201.

98. I prefer to use the term "virginity" rather than "celibacy" because it seems that the former term permits the novelty of this form of love to emerge more adequately than does "celibacy"—normally understood dialectically, and hence negatively, as the "state of being unmarried" (*Oxford English Dictionary*). The understanding of virginity

generates a *belonging* that virginally affirms the other in his relation with the triune God. If it did not generate a belonging to him and a desire to reciprocate his gift of self on the Cross, it would not be a true gift. At the same time, if the belonging were not virginal it would not have the form of a gift. It would be mere "possession." The hypostatic union of the Incarnate Logos reveals that the total human and divine gift for the sake of the other frees the other, not by abandoning man to isolation, but by redeeming him in the acknowledgment of his relation with the paternal source and thus establishing a unity that permits him to "be." As Giussani explains, in reference to the relationship between unity and virginity: "Virginity is the miracle of unity, because it is only the love that is aware of Christ's presence that makes it possible to perceive that everything forms part of a unity and that every relationship is in function of the other."[99] This "miracle of unity" is constantly taken up by Giussani, whose understanding of virginity we follow here, as "possession with detachment within it."[100] Virginity is thus both the way Christ loves and man's response to Christ's merciful love. Let us look at this more closely.

In our contemporary culture, virginity is easily misunderstood by friends and foes alike as a marginal form of loving. It either does not make sense at all that man, created to be fruitful and multiply, does not beget children, or, granting that it is in some way reasonable to make this sacrifice, it remains difficult to see virginity as anything more than a form of love reserved for a few who, after all, have abandoned the world. If, rather than pitting the two states of life against each other, we recognize that virginity is the way that Christ loved, then both states can be understood as participating differently in Christ's form of love. Virginity indicates the possession of the other and the world that is born from gratuity. The person called to live virginally has the task of recognizing God's inexhaustible wholeness by witnessing to the totality of Christ's love. The unity of marriage, whose task is the begetting and education of children, finds its ultimate roots in Christ's virginal form of love and is called to participate in it sacramentally to a certain extent, inasmuch as the spouses learn to "love each other in Jesus Christ" and for him, in whose love their own is rooted. Realizing that marriage has its roots in Christ's sacrifice of himself for the Church on the Cross, and, hence, that marriage is the memory of what took place on the Cross, we can express the circularity of marriage and virginity with John Paul II: "In

---

as presented here follows the work of Giussani. See, for example, Giussani, *PLW*; *TT*; and *SPVVC*.

99. Giussani, *VNC*, 257.

100. Giussani, *AVS*, 454–55.

virginity or celibacy, the human being is awaiting, also in a bodily way, the eschatological marriage of Christ with the Church, giving himself or herself completely to the Church in the hope that Christ may give Himself to the Church in the full truth of eternal life.... By virtue of this witness, virginity or celibacy keeps alive in the Church a consciousness of the mystery of marriage and defends it from any reduction and impoverishment."[101]

To avoid confusing what Giussani means by "possession" with the idea of people and other beings as "property" at one's disposal—an error that reduces detachment to a denial of ownership and makes virginity incomprehensible—one cannot lose sight of the inseparable relation between knowing and loving. For Giussani, as we indicated, to know is not to acquire information in order to manipulate reality. Rather, to know, to discover the meaning (*logos*) of something, is "to discover the link that something has with everything else." This meaning, however, is not created by the human but rather acknowledged: "God is precisely that unitary meaning which nature's objective and organic structure calls human conscience to recognize."[102] To say that "meaning" is acknowledged implies seeing that God is the totalizing meaning of everything (Col 3:11), and that this happens only when one embraces this mystery or, to speak with St. Paul, when one lets oneself be known. Originary experience reveals, contrary to modernity, the affirmation of truth as an act that encompasses the entire human person: reason and affection, body and freedom. With this understanding of knowing in mind, Giussani writes that "virginity is extreme rationality in action. Virginity, according to the Christian mentality, is to look at every reality ... without breaking the nexus that this reality has with the totality of meaning, with the cosmos, which means the order of meaning's totality." To be sure, to claim that virginity is the apex of reason and charity does not mean that it is simply a human reality, a way of loving that people can choose or not. Virginity, Giussani says, is the "word most pregnant with eternity."[103] Virginity is lived, enfleshed eternity and as such can only be given. Since Christ is the one in whom all things hold together, the word in which every being finds its ultimate form, virginity is "not to break the nexus between what you have in your hands (a stone or a person) and Christ."[104] This is when we can call people and beings truly "ours."

It may be useful to show how virginity informed Christ's love when he communicated the Father's mercy. This will also clarify the dynamic unity

---

101. John Paul II, *Familiaris consortio*, no. 15 (AAS 74 [1982], 97).
102. Giussani, *ROE*, 99.
103. Giussani, *SPVVC*, 510.
104. Ibid., 515.

that gift generates, in which the other is "respected" (viewed in its relation to the Father) and not absorbed into a monadic unity. "The greatest miracle, which left a deep imprint on the disciples every day," writes Giussani, "was not the healing of crippled legs, the cleansing of diseased skin, or the restoration of sight to the blind. The greatest miracle of all was that truly human gaze which revealed man to himself and which was impossible to evade."[105] What is specific about Jesus's gaze is his capacity to grasp man's heart. He unveils that the heart is "a complex of needs and 'evidences,' which casts man in the comparison with all that is."[106] He also discloses that this complex of needs and evidences, the heart, is comprehensible only in the intrinsic and concrete dynamic of this relation with God. For example, when Christ looks on Mary, from whom he took his flesh, he does not only see in her the one who welcomed him in faith and who thus represents the new Eve; he knows that his Father gave her to him (John 17:11–24) and that, from now on, "she belongs to the name of God in such a special way that whoever would praise him cannot leave her out of account" if he wishes to praise God's name rightly.[107] The seeming rejections of Mary (Luke 11:27–28; John 2:4, 19:26) are not only her participation in Christ's kenosis but also seek to make room for her, as other, to be, a space of love in which those whom Christ makes his own in the Father's love are called to embrace the world. Christ's relation with Mary is never unconscious of her origin and mission. He knows, in a way that Mary herself cannot fathom, that his mother is called to be given along with him from the Cross to the world. The Samaritan woman (John 4:1–42) finds herself known by him whom she has never met, and at the same time she is offered the possibility of "worshipping the Father in Spirit and in truth" (John 4:23). His knowledge of her does not leave her isolated in her own misery but binds her to the Father. The woman caught in adultery realizes after Jesus forgives her that she belongs to him more deeply than to the one from whose arms she was taken. Jesus does not treat her according to common expectations, but rather according to the design of the Father. He has come to reveal the Father's mercy, to save man. He thus knows her more deeply and purely than anyone else does. He knows that his judgment will be understood only after he has fulfilled his mission. Yet for the woman caught in adultery, it is within that love that she feels free, totally herself in being totally his. The same is true for Matthew when he finds himself taken from the place where he collected (due and undue) taxes.

---

105. Giussani, *At the Origin*, 53.
106. Giussani, *RS*, 7. Translation modified.
107. Ratzinger and Balthasar, *Mary*, 63.

We mentioned that through this way of looking at people, Christ's gift of self generates a gratuitous belonging in the other not because he refers the other to himself, but because, in him, he enables the other to live in relationship with the Father. Christ communicates the mercy of the Father by allowing the men and women he meets to experience the unity of their historical existence with the ultimate, paternal source for whom they are made. Instead of trying to possess the gift of life and existence, Christ's virginal sacrifice of himself makes it possible for human beings to maintain the constitutive relation that binds everything and everyone together with God. The unity of the gift, therefore, is never simply between the gift and the giver; it exists in a third.

What this means for the human being is that true love for another, that is, love according to what the other is and not what one might receive from that relation, reaches its apex when the lover looks with the eyes of faith, which see the divine triune love from which the beloved continuously emerges and for which he is made. At the same time, this gaze of faith must acknowledge that hope for the loved one's eternal existence rests not on one's own endeavors, but upon the beloved's remaining in the place ascribed by divine love. Virginity, in this regard, is the affirmation of everyone and everything within a memory that allows triune love, the source and destiny of all, to give concrete form to everything and so to reveal itself. This "informing," to which the virgin gives his grateful and complete assent, allows reality and human existence to remain and grow in the relation of love between the Father and the Son in the Holy Spirit. Virginity, then, is not simply the fruit of man's magnanimous effort to love truly. It is the eschatological anticipation of the living form of love that God is. As such, it is a grace given to a few, as it was freely given to Mary, so that everyone might discover love's true affirmation of being.

Virginity, requiring the recognition of human destiny as God and union with him, also entails a continual sacrifice. As the response to Christ's crucified love, virginity carries the Cross within it. The desire (*eros*) to love (*agape*) as Christ loves reveals its gratuity in the ready embrace of the same sacrifice that Christ makes, which is welcomed for the same reason that brought him to give himself to the end: so that communion with God may take place. Virginity is the sacrificial, complete gift of self. Sacrifice, as we saw, is to affirm the singular's true nature.[108] Sacrifice, Giussani writes, is "not to believe in idols."[109] What is idolatry, in fact, if not the substitution of the divine image with one that the human being has made for himself? In

---

108. Giussani, *PLW*, 3:78.
109. Giussani, *SPVVC*, 500.

this sense, the sacrifice of virginity consists in affirming the truth of what being is, first and foremost. It is in this sense pervasive and inevitable, but thanks to Christ's gift of himself it becomes the doorway to possessing the divine life he brings.[110] Christ, in fact, gives all of himself for humankind so that, through the Spirit, men and women can reach the one for whom they are created. "Vocation's supreme form, that is, of the task in the world (the place one occupies in the world and the task in the world)," writes Giussani, "the greatest form of each, just as Christ's death on the Cross was for man, is the total gift of self to God for man. The total gift of self to God for man is called virginity. The Cross upon which Christ dies is virginity. Virginity is that way in which everything is sacrificed, all the objects of man's thirst and desire are sacrificed (in the way just explained, not in the sense of 'denied'), and therefore everything is possessed, and hence realized as relation with the eternal, and thus risen (resurrected)."[111] In this regard, Christ's bodily gift of self reveals that giving all of oneself, as an act of gratuitous love for the other's sake, is the greatest delight and sacrifice. It is the greatest delight because the apex of love is to give one's own life for another (John 15:13). It is a sacrifice because to accept the giftedness of one's own being and the relation with God is to deny the lie. This sacrifice is not a denial of the body, a gnostic flight from the flesh. It is rather the affirmation of what bodily existence is, that is, received life that finds its fulfillment in the gift of itself to another. The virgin's fruitfulness is a participation in Christ's fruitfulness. Christ's bodily sacrifice of himself on the Cross introduced into history a limitless fecundity that is not deterred by death. The sacrifice of one's own bodiliness, therefore, points in the direction of that eschatological unity with the pierced and risen Lamb through whom the Father, the unpreceded giver, confirms the original gift of being.

---

110. John Paul II, *Salvifici doloris* (AAS 76 [1984], 201–50).
111. Giussani, "*Tu*," 259.

V. The Unpreceded Giver

THE ULTIMATE, ETERNAL ORIGIN of the gift, God the Father, offers the path for understanding the meaning of gift and the unity it posits: eternal communion. Mindful that the Father always remains an ever-greater mystery and that even the eyes of faith cannot bear his eternal light ("You cannot bear it now," John 16:12; "It has not appeared as yet what we will be," 1 John 3:2), this chapter sets out to consider divine fatherhood by reflecting on the meaning of begetting, the constitutive personal property of the first hypostasis of the Trinity. In what sense is the Father the permanent origin of the divine triune communion, and what does it mean that without him this communion cannot be? The Father *is* his giving, and this giving is his begetting of the Son, and with and through the Son, his spiration of the Holy Spirit. The Father, as gift and giver, is "the source and origin of all of the divinity" (DS 490).[1]

Revelation invites us to approach the mystery of the Father through what later philosophy would call the transcendental properties of being. It is the Father who accounts for divine union: he can thus be considered, in a certain sense, the "absolute person," from whom all divinity comes (section 1). To be "father" means to reveal oneself, to let one's own beauty shine through another (section 2). The Father's allowing another to participate fully in his own glory is coincident with his pouring out of himself to the end in another, in order that this other might exist. To better perceive the Father's goodness in and through the primordial gift of self, the role of difference within God must be addressed; we will approach this by way of Hegel's conception of negativity, which, though also stemming from scriptural revelation, ultimately offers its most radical alternative (section 3). Since the beauty of the Father is the outpouring of himself in another

---

1. The Council of Toledo VI states that "Patrem ingenitum increatum, fontem et originem totius deitatis" (DS 490). See also Tertullian, *Adversus Praxean liber* 8.5–7; Gregory of Nazianzus, *Or.* 2.38 (PG 35:445) and 30.7 (PG 36:112–13); Augustine, *Trin.* 4.20.29 (PL 42:908–9); Councils of Toledo XI (DS 525) and XVI (DS 568). See also Congar, "Le Père"; De Villamonte, "El Padre"; Ladaria, "Dios Padre."

without losing himself, his personhood can be understood only along with the constitutive relations with the Son and the Holy Spirit, each of whose procession "retroactively affects the origin . . . without neutralizing the order of origination."[2] Divine truth is thus an unfathomable relation of love. These constitutive relations, seen from the point of view of the eternal gift that they are, will help us clarify further the meaning of person (section 4). Since its ultimate ground is the Father who reveals, gives, and is himself in eternal relation with the other two hypostases, divine unity is always a communion of persons (section 5).[3]

A brief methodological point: the light of God's deeds cannot illuminate its ever-greater source if we sever the divine economy (God's action in history) from the theology (God in himself), or collapse one into the other. Describing the shift brought about by Scotus and Ockham, Marie-Joseph Le Guillou claims that "if the freedom of the divine economy does not manifest the truth of the essential and personal being of God, his mystery is not one of *paternity*, but rather the enigma and the scandal of *arbitrary omnipotence*."[4] A nominalistic epistemology (with its univocal conception of God) permits no intrinsic relation between the intradivine order and God's creative, pure, and unlimited freedom. The consequences are well known: creation no longer bears an *imago trinitatis*, and the economy does not offer an adequate expression of who he is.[5]

This conception of God, which lies at the origin of the Protestant reformation, surfaces again in various forms of contemporary nihilism and

---

2. Balthasar, *TL*, 2:147.

3. Given that the three persons are the one God, both statements are true: on the one hand, each of the persons reflects the glory, truth, goodness, and unity of the divine *esse*, and, on the other hand, a transcendental can be appropriated to the Father (see Bonaventure, *Breviloquium* 1.6). At the same time, we cannot appropriate a transcendental to a hypostasis without seeing that it can also be predicated of the others: unity is expressed in the Son and consummated in the Holy Spirit—the one in whom the Father and the Son are united. The Holy Spirit is the Spirit of truth, a truth that the Son is because he eternally receives it from the Father. The Holy Spirit is love (*amor*) and gift (*donum*) and hence goodness, a goodness that he receives from the Father and the Son. It is important to note that this approach to the mystery of the Father does not project philosophical categories onto theological speech. While theological reflection on the mystery of the Father sheds light on the philosophy of being and the latter helps the former, we cannot ascribe to philosophy the capacity to account for God's divine fatherhood.

4. Le Guillou, *Le mystère du Père*, 128. Emphasis added.

5. One of Balthasar's greatest contributions to contemporary Trinitarian reflection is the deepening of the scholastic axiom that whatever is and takes place in the economy has its roots in theology. See Balthasar, *TD*, 5.247–65. Here Balthasar also seeks to correct Luther's theology of contradiction. See his *TL*, 2:317–61.

makes it even more difficult to approach the mystery of the Father. While much needs to be said to justify this claim, it suffices here to indicate that Le Guillou's "scandal" is one "of divine omnipotence" only because it is first and foremost the scandal of a human, finite freedom that appears incapable of reciprocating God's love. Finite freedom, scandalized by its own sinfulness, denies the possibility of genuinely receiving and reciprocating the gift of itself and of God's action in history. Granting God's totality and glory but overcome by its own weakness, the singular's freedom considers it impossible even for divine grace to eradicate evil and to make of man a new creature. Yet a finite freedom that turns in on itself in solipsism, radically unable to receive God, can only regard him in turn as an arbitrary, alogical power. Rather than "wishing to keep to oneself the nothingness that God desired in the woman's lap," as Paul Claudel writes in the *Satin Slipper*, and thus "preferring [nothingness] to that which is, resting content with one's essential difference," it more befits the nature of man and the action of God to accept that God created a real, finite freedom, which "belongs to us only that we may enhance by our admission of [our nothingness] the being of Him Who is."[6] This admission surpasses complacency, for to recognize that God is all in all (Eph 4:6; 1 Cor 15:28), and to desire to give him everything, means conceding his ability to change man and thus to provide a means to allow man to know and discourse with him in a real way.[7] The omnipotent power of God, which is revealed through the Paschal Mystery, is not the arbitrary freedom of an unknowable God. This would impose on God the image of a human power that rejects its own state of indebtedness. It is rather the love of a provident, merciful Father who asks and allows his beloved Son to go

---

6. Claudel, *Satin Slipper*, 196. Through the dialogue between Doña Prouheze and Don Camillo, Claudel wishes to address the difference between Islam and Catholicism. It is worth recalling here that Duns Scotus's philosophy, in addition to being influenced by Henry of Ghent, was also influenced by the work of Alfarabi and Avicenna—particularly the latter's concept of essence and *esse*. This suggests that a concept of God as undetermined, arbitrary will underlies the oblivion that engulfed Trinitarian reflection after the Protestant Reformation.

7. Offering reasons for his own conversion and showing the respective greatness of Protestantism and Catholicism as well as where they differ, Bouyer, following Gilson, poignantly states: "What, in fact, is the essential characteristic of Ockham's thought, and of nominalism in general, but a radical empiricism, reducing all being to what is perceived, which empties out, with the idea of substance, all possibility of real relations between beings, as well as the stable subsistence of any of them, and ends by denying to the real any intelligibility, conceiving God himself only as a Protean figure impossible to apprehend? In these circumstances, a grace which produces a real change in us, while remaining purely the grace of God, becomes inconceivable. If some change is effected in us, then it comes from us, and to suppose it could come also and primarily from God amounts to confusing God with the creature" (Bouyer, *Spirit and Forms*, 153).

even to the "folly of the Cross" (1 Cor 1:18) so that, through the Holy Spirit, man may see the Father as he is, that is, may behold him with the Son from the Son's eternal place in the Father's love.

1. Unpreceded Origin: The Father as Absolute Person

Christ's human experience of his divine filiation reveals that *within* the divine origin itself there is an unbegotten and personal principle, a Father, who is the source and origin of the entirety of the Godhead. Who this source is, what it means to be a source, and why there is a source within the Godhead are perhaps the most pressing questions if we accept that God, rather than being an "object" of thought, is an absolute subject. These questions require avoiding the temptation to read the Greek understanding of the first principle back into the Father of Jesus Christ, which would mean losing the Christian novelty and would reintroduce the sense of causality we corrected earlier. We thus need to indicate in what sense we can understand the divine, paternal origin to be an "absolute person," that is, in what sense the Father is the person from whom the divinity originates, from whom it is eternally given.

Human reason can readily accept a concept of "absolute person" that views whatever comes forth from this absolute person as external to and other than that person. St. Athanasius's critique of Arius's anthropomorphic methodology draws on Scripture to teach that fatherhood is instead a perfection proper and internal to God himself. It does not depend on the Father's being the creator of the world.[8] Thus, the Father's giving in the generation of the Son is not similar to the giving through which the human being is created. Since the Son participates fully in the essence of the Father, he is neither a creature nor the result of an emanation of the Father's goodness, as the neoplatonic tradition inclines to understand it.[9] What is begotten remains in God; it is equally God (*homoousion*). Only reason strengthened by faith can begin to perceive what it means to generate from within oneself and not from without, actively and not passively, eternally and not historically—to be a father without having been the son of a previous father.[10] This unique Father generates someone, the Logos, who will never become a father himself. What is begotten, although God (*homoousion*), is not identical

---

8. Athanasius, *C. Ar.* 1.21–23 (PG 26:56–60). See Anatolios, *Athanasius*; Widdicombe, *Fatherhood of God*.

9. Athanasius, *C. Ar.* 1.22 (PG 26:57–59).

10. Athanasius, *C. Ar.* 1.26–27 (PG 26:65–69).

with the paternal origin; it is another. We have never encountered such a father or such a son.

The paradoxical coexistence of identity of substance and personal difference that Athanasius presents prevents us from falling into the anthropological extreme of Eunomius, in which unbegottenness defines both God's essence and the proper meaning of divine hypostasis.[11] Both Eunomius and Arius, precisely in their flawed accounts of the Trinitarian mystery, illuminate a crucial point regarding the meaning of "origin." It is true that "origin" and "principle" indicate one "whence another proceeds," another who is equal to and yet different from that origin and principle.[12] Nevertheless, to speak of the first hypostasis as origin, principle, or source does not necessarily bring us to the personal God revealed in Scripture. The Christian novelty does not simply indicate that the Logos is God and hence "internal" to him. It also claims that both the source and the one proceeding therefrom are persons and that person "signifies what is most perfect in all nature."[13]

According to Scripture, what it means to be origin is found in what it means to be Father, and not vice versa. To understand "origin" beginning with the divine *paternity* revealed through Jesus Christ, then, helps us see that gift aims at the constitution and being of the person, not substance. It also clarifies why, as we claimed earlier, divine giving is not a causality that binds the source and the singular within the realm of entity. The Eastern and Western theological traditions concur in this: the Father is the unbegotten origin and principle of the other two persons. It is possible in this sense to think of the Father as an "absolute person," the origin from whom the other two proceed. Yet, since the terms "un-generated," "source," and "principle," when referred to the Father, are relational terms, they cannot be fully understood without reference to what is thereby principled, begotten,

---

11. The interplay between identity and difference in the Godhead, the earnest defense of divine simplicity, and a conception of "order" and "hierarchy" that (too burdened by Greek philosophy) understands hierarchy only in terms of inequality and subordination are some of the factors that led Eunomius to understand the unbegottenness of the Father as the main property of God's *being*. See Basile de Césarée, *Contre Eunome* (PG 29b:497–773); Basil the Great, *On the Holy Spirit*; Gregory of Nyssa, *Quod non sint tres dii* (PG 45:111–31). Augustine also explains that the term "un-generated," or "unbegotten," simply means "not a son," and hence is a relational and not a substantial term. See Augustine, *Trin.* 5.7–8 (PL 42:916). Aquinas, agreeing with Augustine, states that "'unbegotten' imports the negation of passive generation" (Aquinas, *ST*, I, q. 33, a. 4, ad 1). Bonaventure, clarifying the ontological implication of this terminological precision, indicates that "unbegotten" is precisely the reason why the Father is the fontal plenitude of the Godhead: "Innascibilitas in Patre ponit fontalem plenitudinem" (Bonaventure, *Breviloquium*, 1.3.7).

12. Aquinas, *ST*, I, q. 33, a. 1.

13. Aquinas, *ST*, I, q. 29, a. 3.

or commonly spirated.¹⁴ The "absolute" person is always already a "relative" one. While the approximation between "origin" or "source" and "fatherhood" allows us to think of the Father as an "absolute person," we cannot forget that "origin," by itself, does not constitute a person: only relation does this. The circularity between source and fatherhood resists any unilateral resolution of the following polarity: On the one hand, the Father is an absolute person and so can be understood as the one from whom the other two proceed—otherwise, as the following will illustrate, God would not be the Trinitarian communion of love revealed in Jesus Christ. On the other hand, the Father is always a relative person: there is no time at which the Father did not have a Son, and no moment at which the two were not one in the Spirit.

2. The Father's Unfathomable Light

In the attempt to describe the paternal, unbegotten, and giving origin, without claiming to define who he is, we can benefit from Scripture's explanation of God as spirit (John 4:24). Being spirit, God is not "for" himself; he is himself in being always "for" another. This, which is true for each of the hypostases, is primordially so for the Father, who cannot but speak, reveal himself, and disclose his beauty. From all eternity, the Father "shows the Son all that he is doing" (John 5:20); only the Son is allowed to see him (Luke 10:22; Matt 11:27; John 1:18). The Father's act of begetting is the eternal radiation of all his glory to the Son (John 1:14, 17:5, 24). It is not that the Father allows the Son to see his glory or to be transfigured by it, as is man's hope for himself (1 John 3:1–3). Rather, the Father gives the Son equal share in the fullness of glory. The unceasing contemplation of the Father and the hearing of his voice is, as Origen says, what it means to be the only-begotten, to be *homoousios* with the Father.¹⁵ He is the Father's Logos who, while pronouncing all that the Father is, is not simply a reiteration of the Father. He is someone else. Begetting, therefore, has to do first of all with a "revealing" and a "letting-know" that is coincident with letting the other be other than

---

14. The Father is *persona absoluta* but not in the sense of Moltmann, who claims that if the Father were dependent upon the Son and the Holy Spirit, he could not be their origin. See Moltmann, *Trinity and the Kingdom*, 162–65.

15. "*The* God, therefore, is the true God. The others are gods formed according to him as images of the prototype. But again, the archetypal image of the many images is *the* Word with *the* God, who was 'in the beginning.' By being 'with *the* God' he always continues to be 'God.' But he would not have this if he were not with God, and he would not remain God if he did not continue in unceasing contemplation of the depth (*báthous*) of the Father" (Origen, *Commentary on the Gospel*, 99).

the origin, while at the same time being one with it. In this sense, man's wonder before his own existence and that of the cosmos is only a pale echo of the Logos's radical wonder before the Father's revelation of himself to him. When the Incarnate Logos, who claims to be identical to the Father (John 10:30), proclaims the Father's greatness (John 14:28), he is not only saying that the Father is "greater" because he is the origin of the Son.[16] He is also communicating in history his eternal amazement at his own being generated.[17] The Father's self-disclosure, his revelation to the Son, who is God because he remains in the bosom of the Father, is what allows the Son to bring the glory of the Father to each man who welcomes him, reaching him even where man considered himself beyond finding.[18]

In his book on the Holy Spirit, S. Bulgakov adopts the category of "revelation" in order to ponder the meaning of God and, more specifically, of fatherhood. "Revelation of the noumenon in phenomena," he tells us, "presupposes a subject, a predicate, and the copula between them. It presupposes that which is revealed, that which reveals, and a certain unity or identity of the two: a mystery and its revelation."[19] For the Russian theologian, the Father reveals himself in the two hypostases: in and to the Son and the Holy Spirit (John 5:26). The Father's revealed being-for and being-open-to another means that the source is life in himself and the giver of all life.

The term "revelation" shows further that begetting is not the gushing forth of the persons from a neutral divine substance. "Revelation," in fact, requires the awareness and freedom of the hypostases. If the term "spirit" translates both nous (mind, *logos*) and pneuma (life), then we cannot disassociate word and love, logos and life.[20] In this sense, the source of the

16. Gregory of Nazianzus, Or. 30.7 (PG 36:112–13); Augustine, Trin. 4.20, 27 (PL 42:906–7); Athanasius, C. Ar. 1.20 (PG 26:53) and 3.6 (PG 26: 332–33).

17. Balthasar roots christological amazement within divine generation: "We can be sure that the human child Jesus was in amazement over everything: beginning with the existence of his living Mother, then passing on to his own existence, finally going from both to all the forms. But this amazement derives from the much deeper amazement of the eternal child who, in the absolute Spirit of Love, marvels at Love itself as it permeates and transcends all that is" (Balthasar, *Unless You Become*, 45).

18. John Paul II, *Redemptor hominis*, no. 9 (AAS, 71 [1979], 272–74); John Paul II, *Dives in misericordia*, no. 2 (AAS, 72 [1980], 1180–82).

19. Bulgakov, *Comforter*, 360. The "bihypostatic and dyadic revelation of the Father" he calls "Divine Sophia, the image of the Holy Trinity in its proper depths, the Divine world, Divine-humanity" (ibid., 366).

20. The term "spirit," as shown by Claude Bruaire, translates both *pneuma* and *nous*. According to the former (*pneuma*), spirit indicates the rhythm of unity and difference proper to the Trinitarian persons. The latter (*nous*) indicates the aspect of intelligibility that is identical and different in each of the persons (hence we cannot say that the Father knows himself in the Son and loves himself in the Holy Spirit, and hence that he

revelation is someone, a person, whose act of begetting is a personal one. Hence while it is true that the Father generates from his substance (DS 215), generation and common spiration are acts of the Father. The Father, as God, generates the Son from his substance.[21] But, since the divine processions are both personal and notional acts, the Father begets the Son as Father and not as substance (DS 804). With Bulgakov we can thus say that the Father, as Father, reveals all of himself to the Son and the Holy Spirit. There is not a divine substance that comes to fruitful expression in the Father and reveals itself in and to the other two hypostases.[22]

The Father's revelation of himself is free (2 Cor 3:17). However, unlike man, whose revelation of himself to another follows a decision to do so and is never complete, the Father's eternal, free allowing of the Son to see his face is an act that takes place beyond necessity and will (DS 71). In God there is no opposition between the two (DS 526). This paradox strikes us as an oxymoron because, in the aftermath of the idealist separation of logic from metaphysics, there is a general belief that logic is adequately expressed only in terms of formal logic, at whose basis lies a principle of non-contradiction that considers unity an empty principle that determines its content dialectically. If this interpretation of the law of non-contradiction has the last word here, what is necessary cannot be at the same time gratuitous. Neither is the unity of necessity and freedom served by dissolving the one into the other. Necessity and freedom are united without confusion in God because, as he has revealed, divine "logic" is one of absolute love (1 John 4:16). The Father

---

does not in himself have full knowledge or will). Each divine person, being one God, must reflect in his own way the aspect of gift and the aspect of reason. See Bruaire, *EE*, 20–27.

21. Interestingly, as Luis Ladaria notes, the council of Toledo XI (DS 526) describes the Father's substance with the term "womb": "Nec enim de nihilo, neque de aliqua alia substantia, sed de Patris *utero*, id est, de substantia eius idem Filius genitus vel natus est." See Ladaria, *El Dios vivo*, 303.

22. In contrast to the understanding of revelation presupposed here, the Russian theologian's account of begetting and processing in terms of revelation is pitted against the classic understanding of "production," "relations of origin." He considers all the hypostases equally eternal and holds that any speech in terms of production and causality necessarily leads to subordinationism or modalism by limiting the eternality of the persons. The only adequate way to present the mystery of the unity and difference in God without eliminating the hierarchy in the Godhead, so Bulgakov contends, is the mutual revelation of the hypostases. Yet for Bulgakov, revelation is also the way to preserve the primacy of the Father. See Bulgakov, *Comforter*, 377. While affirming the necessity of keeping "relation of origin" to elucidate the meaning of the divine hypostases, Aquinas, like Bulgakov, also points to the imprecision of using "causality" to indicate relations of origin in God. See Aquinas, *ST*, I, q. 33, a. 1, ad 1. Contrary to Aquinas, however, it seems that Bulgakov's understanding of causality is too determined by modern thought's reductive account.

is neither coerced into begetting, since in that case he would not be God, nor does he generate merely because he wishes to—in that case, the Son would be a creature. Scripture shows that the Father begets according to his nature (John 5:26), love, and that his begetting is an act of his love (John 3:35, 5:20, 10:17). These two things are thus simultaneously true and as such remain ultimately ungraspable: since God is supreme love, the Father cannot but beget, and this generation is the expression of love's *liberalitas*. The coextensiveness of necessity and will indicates that necessity is not mechanical self-diffusion and that freedom is not illogical arbitrariness.

The gift of fatherhood consists precisely in this eternal radiation of beauty. While the Father's abyssal glory remains a "luminous darkness" for man, a light that escapes man's comprehension, for the Son and the Holy Spirit it is nothing other than the ever-new communication of his divine life. The Father's bestowal of glory is his pouring out all of himself in the other two.

3. A Father Like No Other

The Father's personhood is characterized by the total gift of himself to the Son and to the Holy Spirit. In pondering the nature of this gift, however, we need to avoid thinking of the Father's constitutive gift in terms of a radicalized exchange of property. The Father's gift of self is not simply quantitatively different from the exchange of gifts between two human lovers, for example. Unlike the Father's gift, every finite gift is always a response to a prior gift. We are not familiar with a giving that takes place before a prior gift has been given to us. Man never has the initiative. The Father's gift, instead, is not prompted by anything and has no limit: his gift is "from himself" in an evergreater way that surpasses our understanding. When Origen writes of Abraham's sacrifice, "Behold God contending with men in magnificent liberality: Abraham offered God a mortal son who was not put to death; God delivered to death an immortal son for men," he is not only speaking of the greatness of the Father's gift.[23] He is also underscoring the fact that the Father's gift "from himself" is simultaneous with an equally ungraspable "for another." Being from himself, the Father's gift is a gift of himself to another person, and, because it posits another person who is equal to him, an immortal Son, the Father's love can also be communicated to finite creatures. Here again God's gift "for another" is different from man's. "Being for another" is, at the human level, marked through and through by the reality of creation *ex nihilo*. Whereas man's being for another is both an ineliminable dimension

---

23. Origen, *Homilies*, 144.

of his being and a historical undertaking, the Father's gift "from himself" is "for another" who, although begotten, has not at any time "come into being." Hence his gift of self already contains another, who is not the Father. Since God is not a body, this "containing" does not refer to a physical *ubi*. It is instead a reciprocal, personal abiding who is a third, who is identical to the Father and the Son. The gift of self of the Father, eternally from himself and for another, generates an "abiding," a communion.

Both the unity and the distance between the Father and the Son, which the Father's gift permanently generates and confirms through the gift of the Spirit, are infinite. This infinity makes it possible that, within the economy, the Father can *hand* his Son *over* (Rom 8:32) without losing his very self or destroying the gift. Why this sacrificial offering of the only-begotten Son for man has to do with real paternity and is not sheer folly shows in the fact that the offer of his own Son is only complete with the resurrection and the gift of the Spirit. The resurrection is the confirmation of life's inexhaustibility as gift of self, a confirmation that is coincident with the gift of the Holy Spirit, God's very presence. With the resurrection, man learns that the Father's gift of self aims at making another "be," eternally. The Father desires that man live, that is, that he participate in the Father's own life by which everything is made new. Yet, in our fallen condition, the Son had to die (Heb 9:15–19) for us to inherit the promise of eternal adopted sonship. Only in the light of the Father, which comes to us from the crucified-risen Lord and which transfigures man's heart through the Holy Spirit (Rom 5:5), can we see that what previously seemed to be painful, prolonged separation ("How long, O Lord? Will you forget me forever?" Ps 13:1–3, 79:5) and unbearable, cruel silence on Good Friday (Matt 27:46; Mark 15:34) is nothing but God's long-suffering patience, that is, the unfailing gift of self that knows how to find its way to man and to elicit his free, gratuitous response. This light also reveals that the Father's gift of self to the Son can leave space for an immeasurable separation between the two ("even death on a cross," Phil 2:8) and that such a distance witnesses to the unbreakable unity of the Father and the Son in the Spirit. Christ's forsakenness is not, then, a mythological divine struggle to be himself or to repair what man's original sin destroyed. The Paschal Mystery signals that the gift of self of the Father is a generation (and spiration) so profoundly fruitful that all the drama and beauty of the economy of salvation is unable to enclose it. Unlike man's gift, the Father's gift is coextensive with his very person: it is the total gift of self. The Father is his giving (DS 805), and, what is impossible for man, this giving does not represent the loss of himself (DS 528). Before we turn to the relation between the Father's giving and the Son's reception and reciprocation of this gift, we must first consider the extent of the Father's donation of self.

Starting in the sixteenth century, some Lutheran theologians began to describe the Father's gift of self with the term used by St. Paul for Christ's emptying of himself to save man: *kenosis*. This theology, however, becomes dominant only in the nineteenth and twentieth centuries, and, although it attempts to be faithful to what is revealed in the Scriptures (Phil 2:6–11; Mark 8:35), the influence of German idealism determines much of its form and content.[24] With different nuances, theologies of kenosis consider Christ's economic kenosis as based in the "Original-Kenosis" of the Father.[25] In "giving up what he possessed" and taking the form of the servant—this is in fact what kenosis means—the Son does what he sees the Father doing (John 5:19). As the Father gives all of himself to the Son (John 17:10), so the Son gives himself to the end for man. To examine whether the Father's divine goodness, the total communication of himself, can be understood as a *kenotic gift*, we must briefly refer to Hegel's understanding of the absolute spirit's absolute negativity. For Hegel, the annihilation he sees in the Son's historical kenosis (self-abasement) becomes the governing principle of spirit's self-constitution. In Hegel's system, God, the absolute spirit, is itself in its being an infinite becoming whose circular movement of self-reflection follows the rhythm of negation, negation of negation, affirmation of self. More than any other theology of kenosis, Hegel's system allows us to see that there are only two ways to think of the original gift: either the infinite is an absolute act that generates from itself and confirms (spirates) the original gift overabundantly, as Catholic Trinitarian doctrine has it, or, as Hegel contends, absolute spirit is an absolute circle of negativity whose ontological poverty makes God move from original, abstract universality to absolute, concrete subject. Hegel's negativity, because it is the exact opposite of what we intend by "gift," has much to contribute to our reflection on the Father's love (gift) and to the meaning of person. We cannot give a full account of Hegel's system here but will attempt simply to show how "negativity" sheds light on these two terms.[26]

---

24. The most comprehensive introduction to kenosis is P. Henry, "Kénose," in *Dictionnaire encyclopedique de la Bible: Supplément* (Paris: Laffont, 1987), 5.7–161. See Bulgakov, *Lamb of God*, 213–47.

25. The term is Balthasar's. See *TD*, 4:323. As is well known, Balthasar takes this from Bulgakov. Two major differences between these authors are relevant here: First, although Bulgakov's kenosis is of a piece with his sophiology, Balthasar thinks that he can follow the former without embracing the latter. Second, whereas for Bulgakov kenosis applies to each of the divine innertrinitarian relations, for Balthasar, there is no kenosis of the Holy Spirit. For a thorough presentation of Bulgakov's concept of kenosis, see Coda, *L'altro di Dio*. For Balthasar's kenosis of the Father, see Turek, *Towards a Theology*, 97–154.

26. Building on the Cappadocian distinction between the divine *ousia* and the three

Hegel understands the task of logic and hence of philosophy as "to show that this idea [absolute idea of philosophy, the Trinity] is what is true as such and that all categories of thought are this movement of determining."[27] In sublating theology, philosophy does not seek to unmake it but rather to show "the rational content of religion."[28] In this regard, while it is true that Christianity, consummate religion, *itself* requires moving beyond itself into philosophy to find its own fulfillment, philosophy only pronounces speculatively the absolute truth of all that has been affirmed and denied in history. The difference between them is that, as Albert Chapelle argues, philosophy shows that the rich identity of the absolute spirit is self-generated by the spirit's freedom.[29] Philosophy enables us to see that absolute spirit's final unity, laboriously pursued throughout the movement of its conceptual necessity (from Logic to Nature, and from Nature to Spirit), is in fact what it was already presupposed to be at the beginning.[30] It is because philosophy unfolds the rational content of what the absolute spirit has pronounced of himself in history that it must speak a different language, unlike that of revelation. Philosophy is thus able to see the unity in difference of the opposites because it negates and sublates the approximations of the discourse on history. Only speculative language (*Vernunft*), while being faithful to revelation, is able to pronounce absolute spirit (God); representational (*Verstand*) and dialectic thought are only the necessary steps toward absolute knowledge.[31] Hence the terms "Father," "Son," and "Holy Spirit" must be

---

hypostases, and on Aquinas's account of divine persons as subsisting relations, one task that remains is to ponder whether the meaning of "opposition" in the subsisting relations does not require some sense of the "negative" in order to preserve the integrity of the "positive."

27. Hegel, *VPR*, 3:290.

28. Ibid., 247. See also Hegel, *Encyclopedia*, §577.

29. Chapelle, *Hegel et la religion*, 3:127. See also Hegel, *Encyclopedia*, §554, §573.

30. Hegel, *Encyclopedia*, §18. This perception of the absolute spirit entails seeing that, as Spinoza understands substance (as self-determining totality), it is in fact a living, self-reflecting totality whose life consists precisely in the affirmation of itself brought forth by the negation of its own, original negation. It is the concept of "spirit," thanks to which Hegel emphasizes both the "living" and "revelatory" dimensions of the absolute substance. See Spinoza, *Ethics*, bk. 1, definitions 1, 3, 6–8. Hegel embraces this in *WL*, 376; Hegel, *Geschichte der Philosophie*, 104–5.

31. For Hegel, if thought, as understanding (*Verstand*), "sticks to fixity of characters and their distinctness from one another and treats every such limited abstract as having a subsistence and being of its own" (*Encyclopedia*, §80), in dialectic "these finite characterizations or formulae supersede themselves, and pass into their opposites" (*Encyclopedia*, §81). For Hegel, dialectic—which is not understood as "thesis, antithesis, synthesis"—is nothing other than an intermediary and necessary state, prior to but never excluded from speculative knowledge (*Vernunft*). "The speculative stage, or stage

replaced respectively by "universality" (*Allgemeinheit*), "particularity" (*Besonderheit*), and "singularity" (*Einzelheit*); the term "person" by "subject";[32] and the terms "procession," "begetting," and "relation of opposition" by the terms "kenosis" (*Entäusserung*), two-sided "self-determination," "alienation" (*Entfremdung*), and "sublation."

With this in mind, it is possible to understand in what sense Hegel's philosophy is guided by the light of the Cross. Hegel claims that since there is in God no distance between who he is and what he does—as there is in man, whose action never *fully* reveals who he is—then the economy fully reveals who God is. Thus the fact that God dies on the Cross on Good Friday means that death, and so negativity, is part of his being. Not to embrace this principle of negativity (with all its philosophical implications) would mean, for Hegel, a thorough misunderstanding of Christianity. A famous passage from the *Lessons on Religion* shows Hegel's conception of kenosis as spirit's necessary, free, and eternal denial of self: "'God himself is dead,' it says in a Lutheran hymn, expressing an awareness that the human, the finite, the fragile, the negative, are themselves a moment of the divine, that they are within God himself, that finitude, negativity, otherness are not outside of God and do not, as otherness, hinder unity with God. Otherness, the negative, is known to be a moment of the divine nature itself. This involves the highest idea of spirit. In this way what is external and negative is converted into the internal."[33] Hegel thus argues that absolute spirit has to be considered in light of this (speculative) Good Friday, which proves that negativity is internal to God himself.[34] The transition from the Father to the Son, according to Hegel, rather than a generation, is the (necessary and free) denial of the first in the second. That the Father begets means that he denies himself in the Son. This denial, by the sheer power of spirit's negativity, denies its own negation and so affirms itself in the (Holy) Spirit.[35] Since the passage from one moment to the next is one of separation and

---

of Positive Reason (*Positive-Vernünftige*), apprehends the unity of terms (propositions) in their opposition—the affirmative, which is involved in their disintegration and in their transition" (*Encyclopedia*, §82). See Hegel, *PS*, 9–49.

32. Hegel, *PS*, 19. See Schmitz, "Substance Is Not Enough."

33. Hegel, *VPR*, 3:326.

34. The term "God" tends to disappear in Hegel. It is replaced by "spirit." This is required by the self-effacing nature of the absolute spirit and by Hegel's perception of God as ultimately apersonal. "God," writes Hegel, "in his eternal universality is the one who distinguishes himself, determines himself, posits an other to himself, and likewise sublates the distinction, thereby remaining present to himself, and is spirit only through this process of being brought forth" (Hegel, *VPR*, 3:284–85). See Brito, *Hegel et la tâche*, 141–42.

35. Hegel, *PS*, 490.

contradiction, though logical and ontological, it causes infinite pain. Pain and evil come to absolute spirit from within itself.[36]

At the representational level it is true that "God is love" and that "God's death on the Cross is love."[37] It is also true that "as 'love' he is a person, and the relationship is such that the consciousness of the One is to be had only in the consciousness of the other."[38] Yet, while Hegel agrees that personality is the highest degree of being, the principle of negativity demands a move beyond "love" and "person" in order to think of them speculatively.[39] For Hegel, "love" requires *from itself* giving way to spirit, and "person" requires giving way to the different moments of absolute spirit's self-determination: "If one holds fast to personality as an unresolved moment one has evil. For the personality that does not sacrifice itself in the divine idea is evil."[40] It is kenosis, this sacrifice of self for the other, that posits both the need to reach the level of "person" (otherwise the denial/transition of one in the other would not be radical enough) *and* the denial of "person" (otherwise the sacrifice would be merely apparent, not real).

Hegel understands "person" in terms of the sacrifice of itself to the end, which can seem similar to the concept of gift presented here. However,

---

36. See, e.g., Hegel, *Encyclopedia*, §382, §472, §570. In the *Zusatz* to §382 we read: "The Other, the negative, contradiction, disunity therefore also belongs to the nature of spirit. In this disunity lies the possibility of pain. Pain has therefore not reached spirit from the outside as is supposed when it is asked in what manner pain entered into the world. Nor does evil, the negative of absolutely self-existent infinite spirit, any more than pain, reach spirit from the outside; on the contrary, evil is nothing else than spirit which puts its separate individuality before all else."

37. "Death is love itself; in it absolute love is envisaged (intuited).... Through death God has reconciled the world and reconciles himself eternally with himself. This coming back again is his return to himself, and through it he is spirit" (Hegel, *VPR*, 3:120).

38. Hegel continues, "This is spiritual unity in the form of feeling. In the relationship of friendship, of love, of the family, this identity of one with the other is also to be found. It is contrary to the understanding that I, who exist for myself and am therefore self-consciousness, should have my consciousness rather in another; but the reconciliation [of this conflict] is the abstract content—the substantial, universal ethical relationship as such" (Hegel, *VPR*, 3:193).

39. Divine Love needs to be considered speculatively because otherwise "this idea sinks into mere edification, and even insipidity, if it lacks the seriousness, the suffering, the patience, and the labor of the negative" (Hegel, *PS*, 19). For the significance of the passage from *Liebe* to *Geist* and the identification of the latter as *Begriff*, see Coda, *Il negativo*, 362-64.

40. "The understanding does not have any other category but this childlike relation (Father, Son, Holy Spirit) to indicate the movement of the Spirit. *Vernunft* can see that the universal needs to deny itself in the singular in order to become the absolute (particular) subject, the Spirit" (Hegel, *VPR*, 3:194). In addition to Chapelle, *Hegel et la religion*, 2:82-94, see also Splett, *Die Trinitätslehre G. W. F. Hegels*.

the two cannot be reconciled. For Hegel, "sacrifice" means that the "relation" between the Father and the Son is in reality a "contradiction."[41] In this view contradiction is not only a perfection, it is so by always being double-sided *and* sublated into a negative unity by means of the same negative force of spirit.[42] This negative unity is contradiction resolved by the sheer negative development of the spirit. Negativity is therefore a "relative" principle: the opposite other always forms part of the determination of oneself.[43] One-sidedness, which Hegel sees as the constant risk in thinking, is only overcome by understanding, first, that every determination is a negation (to be father is also not to be son, and to be a son is also not to be a father; one is thus internal to the other) and, second, that the unity posited at the end is what is presupposed in the beginning.[44]

What we called the original gift of the Father would be for Hegel nothing other than the process in which absolute spirit necessarily and freely denies itself and separates itself (*Entzweiung, Urtheil*) in the Son who is infinite particularity, "the realm of appearance." The latter, having become incarnate to guarantee man's certainty of the truth of the absolute, must deny itself on the Cross, and dies in order to sublate nature. The resurrection of Christ and the coming of the Holy Spirit represent the birth of the community that, without neglecting its content, internalizes and spiritualizes what was acquired throughout the history of Christianity. In this third moment, the Holy Spirit shows itself within the life of the community as defining itself in terms of the unity of the other two (Father and Son). Hence, "the

41. "The fundamental contradiction is that of the Absolute which limits itself (every determination is negation, as much as every negation is determination), and in this determination, in this self-limitation which is negation, it negates itself again, posits itself therefore concretely as itself in its opposite. . . . The Absolute is therefore only through this division—which is negation—this opposing duplication in which each of the terms is a determination, but such that it exists only in its relation to an other, to its other" (Hyppolite, *Logic and Existence*, 98–99).

42. The following Platonic insight is crucial for Hegel: "But it is not possible to combine two things well all by themselves, without a third; there has to be some bond between the two that unites them. Now the best bond is one that really and truly makes a unity of itself together with the things bonded by it, and this in the nature of things is best accomplished by proportion" (Plato, *Timaeus* 31c–32a).

43. Piero Coda, elucidating the "relative" sense of Hegelian negativity, along with Boehme's gnostic work and the work of Schelling and Fichte, attributes its origins to Hegel's reading of Plato. See Coda, *Il negativo*, 117. Plato states that "since we showed that the nature of *the different* is, chopped up among all beings in relation to each other, we dared to say that *that which is not* really is just this, namely, each part of the nature of the different that's set over against *that which is*" (Plato, *Sophist* 258e).

44. This is why, for example, Hegel manages to bring together Anselm's and Kant's ontological arguments proving God's existence (Hegel, *VPR*, 3:175) and to assert that man is *simul iustus et peccator* (Hegel, *VPR*, 3:198–211). See Hegel, *WL*, 68–172.

differentiation that the divine life goes through is not an external process but must be defined solely as internal, so that the first, the Father, is to be grasped just like the last, the Spirit. Thus the process is nothing but a play of self-maintenance, a play of self-confirmation."[45] The Holy Spirit is the spirit within absolute spirit that makes it be one, be itself, in all its richness. Yet, at the same time, it does not "add anything" to the Father, it is simply the "confirmation" (*Vergewisserung, Bewährung*) of the origin that denies itself in the Son and so affirms itself. The absolute is this infinite process of becoming in which no "pure act" needs to be reached because life itself has proven to be this eternal struggle. Hegel's understanding of negativity (the negative force of the spirit), therefore, sets out first from the Father's radical emptying of himself; second, the sacrifice of self establishes a total difference between the Father, Son, and Holy Spirit that includes within itself all of creation and history; and, finally, this separation is at the same time the circular, eternal movement of the spirit's return to itself, proving that what is, is the spirit's being spirit through a dynamic unity of difference and identity in which everything is included, preserved, and sublated. The radical kenosis of the spirit posits both its distinction and its unity.

As has been frequently noted, the relation in Hegel's system between God and the world, the economy and theology, is pantheistic. Yet at the same time, his system helps us see the necessity of thinking of the unity between God and the world as something that neither simply collapses the history of God into the history of the world, nor views the world as incapable of enriching (*bereichern*) a Godhead that has revealed itself in Christ as an unchanging, ever-new fullness. Understanding the Holy Spirit in terms of the confirmation of the spirit is a profound insight to be preserved along with the perception of the internal relation of the one to the other. Nevertheless, it also reveals that in Hegel's system the Father is speculatively irrelevant; there is no original gift.[46] Rather than fullness, the Father is a lack that has already passed into its opposite by denying itself. For Hegel, both aspects are true of the spirit: the beginning of absolute spirit's movement is a poverty that seeks its own fulfillment and, since infinity is eternal becoming, "poverty" is a permanent characteristic of absolute spirit.

In the Hegelian system, the Holy Spirit takes priority over the Father; what is posited by the Father (the Holy Spirit) is presupposed. Unfortunately, when the procession of the Holy Spirit is thought of not in terms of gift and person but rather in terms of a self-determining lack or of moments of the self-constitutive reflection, as we see in Hegel, it becomes impossible to account for the Father's total self-gift; any kenosis under these terms fails to

---

45. Hegel, *VPR*, 3:195.
46. Chapelle, *Hegel et la religion*, 2:105.

maintain the mysterious radicality of the Paschal Mystery or of the Father's eternal gift of himself to the Son. It is true that, as we saw earlier, there is a sense in which *eros* can be ascribed to God.[47] Can this be done, however, if the Father is not an absolute fullness that is always already given away, without having lost itself? In other words, if the Father is not this absolute fullness, are we not deifying man and annihilating God when we ascribe Hegelian "poverty" or "lack" to the absolute?

Christ's sacrificial gift of himself does reveal the seriousness with which God confronts man's betrayal. Yet contradiction (death) as the inner principle of absolute love depends on three false assumptions. First, the assumption and affirmation that there is no distance between what God does and what he is fails to take into account the fact that God, while truly revealing his face to man in Christ, is and remains ever greater (John 1:50, 5:20, 10:29, 14:28; 1 John 3:20).[48] Jesus Christ safeguards the invisibility and transcendence of the Father (Matt 11:27), and he does so by making him present as a Father who gives away his own Son for man's salvation (Rom 8:32). It is triune love that discloses what the Holy Spirit is and not, as Hegel seems to think, the other way around. In this regard, according to Scripture, the Holy Spirit confirms the original donation of the Father; it is not the negation of an original, self-denying lack.

Second, Hegel's sense of determination as negation seems to confuse being's being posited with its being limited (negated). Lacking an intuition of being itself (*ipsum esse*), it might seem reasonable that we can only understand being itself, God, by doing away with any degree of positivity, and so conceive of it (*esse, Sein*) as sheer indetermination that has always already passed over into its opposite (nothingness). In this case, the opposite would also be true: what one knows about the positivity of any finite being is precisely its being limited. It is not possible, however, either to grasp being itself (*ipsum esse*) or to deduce finite beings from it. Hegel seems to have identified *esse commune* with *ipsum esse subsistens*. The latter is the origin of the former, and it is only through the former that beings are and are understood—and this always partially, since, contrary to Hegel, a finite being cannot be grasped exhaustively through concepts. The identification of *esse commune* with *ipsum esse subsistens* seems to be rooted in the anthropological assumption treated earlier: the conception of finite freedom principally as bodiless in-dependence, with the emphasis on the negation. In that case, non-dependence cuts a poor figure next to the idea of the infinite. It is this weak understanding of creation that leads Hegel to dispense

---

47. Benedict XVI, *Deus caritas est*, no. 9 (AAS 100 [2008], 225).
48. Irenaeus, *Haer.* 4.2.33ff. (PG 7a:977).

with any significant logic of the human spirit and to concern himself rather with that of the absolute alone.

Third, and more fundamentally, Hegelian negativity is not sufficiently radical, however drastic its talk about infinite pain and the death of God may seem, and despite the fact that it does bring out the necessity of mutual belonging. "Otherness" requires not only that one and the other be both mutually intrinsic and different, which Hegel seems to sustain, but also that the other be irreducible to oneself. Only when these two poles are held together can there be a real other both in and outside God. The "sacrifice of self," in order to be true, requires that the giver preserve his own identity. Hegel would concur with Jesus that there is no greater love than to give one's life for another (John 15:13) and that only the "grain of wheat that dies bears much fruit" (John 12:24). Yet, Hegel does not accept that these claims are true because "who loses his life for my sake finds it" (Matt 10:39). The goodness of the Father is indeed the gift of self, a "poverty" that is also richness because the paternal origin has revealed itself as unfathomable generosity. The circularity of Hegel's system, as we shall see in the following section, seeks to establish a unity and difference in God. What his system does not account for is that the gift (*agape*) of the Father desires (*eros*) but does not claim to be reciprocated. The totality of the gift elicits and waits for a gratuitous response as absolute as the original donation. Contrary to Hegel, the confirmation and constitution of the Father by the Son and the Holy Spirit are possible only because from all eternity the Father is the permanent source of all divinity.

Hegel's inability to grasp that, while God truly reveals himself, he remains ever greater leads him to conclude from Christ's death on the Cross that death, nothingness, and negativity form the defining element of the life of God. This claim, however, is a philosophical maneuver that imposes a preconceived idea onto Christian revelation: human, sinful death is held up here as an analogate for innertrinitarian *difference*. This Hegelian contention, seemingly ontologizing the biological concept of death, claims that the concept of death is able to grasp the mystery of death. Thus, Hegel cannot apprehend the greater dissimilarity between human, sinful death and the divine "not," the difference between the Father, Son, and Holy Spirit.[49] Start-

---

49. Adrienne von Speyr's reflections are very much to the point: "We understand life as constant endeavor. But the poverty and need that are at the source of our striving are altogether foreign to eternal life. Life for us is an anxious affair, and we snatch what we can, whereas eternal life is free and open, all giving and receiving, accepting and granting, an undisturbed flow of riches; eternal life is love." She continues: "... In another sense both life and death are images of God. Of course, one cannot say that death, as an end, is in any sense in God, since his eternal life is unending. But if death is understood to mean the sacrifice of life, then the original image of that sacrifice is

ing out from the recognition that God remains ever greater, one could describe the gift of the Father as "kenotic." Yet this term should not introduce the idea of a suffering internal to God into our theological reflection.[50] This would treat pain and suffering as coincident with the theological difference, as Hegel proposes. Kenosis, as Balthasar indicates, has to do only with the relation of love between the Father and the Son. There is no kenosis of the Spirit. The kenosis of the Father and Son "is the precondition for the procession of God's absolute, non-kenotic Spirit of love."[51] To extend kenosis to the Spirit within absolute spirit is to lose the Father's (and being's) goodness, to reduce him to a speculatively irrelevant principle that does not know the power of the resurrection. A "kenosis" of the Holy Spirit could not avoid making the divine gift ultimately ineffectual. If the Holy Spirit is not the (non-kenotic) outflowing gift of life (*donum doni*), God's being has no real existence.[52] The Father's total, "kenotic" gift of self is a relation in which one person, while identical to the other it posits, is irreducible to this other. To understand the "irreducibility" of the one to the other, their circularity, the extent to which we can talk about reciprocity in God's gift of self, and thus how the gift of the Father is the begetting and spiration of the other two hypostases, we will next examine how the relations among them are established and preserved without losing the unity of the Godhead.

---

in God as the gift of life flowing between Father and Son in the Spirit. For the Father gives his whole life to the Son, the Son gives it back to the Father, and the Spirit is the outflowing gift of life. This 'living death' is the absolute opposite of the death of sin in which man ceases giving. . . . Sinful death and sacrificial death are as fire and water, opposites that have nothing in common. The death of sin is annihilated by the death of Christ on the Cross" (von Speyr, *Word Becomes Flesh*, 39, 42–43).

50. We could rightly ask whether the use of "kenosis" is legitimate, since it does seem more fitting to describe God's action in history rather than the movement of love proper to the divine persons. Unfortunately, we cannot offer an adequate discussion of this issue. While this critique could be the case, there are two elements highlighted in the term "kenosis" whose preservation is indispensable. The first one is the *radical* nature of gift that the term "kenosis" entails, the second is the attempt not to let go of the theological difference between the divine persons, and hence, of the role that the "negative" plays in God.

51. Balthasar, *TL*, 3:300.

52. The faulty understanding of the confirmation of the spirit is perhaps one of the reasons why Hegel, despite his claim to the contrary, has been regarded as one of the promoters of contemporary atheism. Only if the confirmation of the spirit means that the Holy Spirit is the one in whom the Father and the Son are united while remaining different can God be one absolute gift, can he be himself.

4. Hierarchical, Constitutive Order

Christian revelation speaks of an eternal source within the one God, a Father, who bestows all of his glory on and in another. This total gift of self is the affirmation of another who, identical with the Father, is an irreducible "other." Scripture uses the transcendental term "truth" to describe the constitutive relations that originate in the Father's original gift of self. Truth, here, is conceived in terms of the person as such, and it is in relation to the Incarnate Logos (and the relations that constitute the person as such) that every other form may be perceived.[53] When Jesus Christ promises his disciples that the Spirit of truth will come and guide them into the whole truth (John 16:13), he does not mean that the Spirit who proceeds from the Father (John 15:26) will bring knowledge that was not already contained in his own body (Col 1:19). The Spirit whom the Son will send (John 14:17) will witness to the truth that the Son is (John 1:14, 14:6), a truth the Son heard from the Father (John 8:40) and received from him. It is in his flesh that we can see the face of the Father, and, hence, it is in relation to the Incarnate Logos that we are given to perceive the meaning and form of everything that is. By inserting man into the Son's resurrected body (Rom 6:17), the Spirit of Christ allows man to "know the truth" (John 8:32); that is, he introduces man into the relation of love that binds the Father and the Son (John 14:23), the relation that is the ultimate ground of creation. To man's continuous astonishment, the Father has handed his Son over so that man may abide in his truth. Within that relation, man discovers that the Father is not a deceiver but a faithful giver, who desires that the other be and that he "walk in the light" (1 John 1:6).

That Christ reveals truth to be God's innertrinitarian *relation*, and that this relation is the absolute affirmation of the other person, invites us to realize that the Father, as Balthasar says, possesses the Godhead "insofar as he begets before thinking about it [*unvordenklich*]; he possesses it only as given away."[54] Precisely because the gift of the Father is eternal, both the co-eternality of the persons and the relation to an unbegotten origin are necessary for an adequate grasp of "person as subsisting relation."

First, with regard to the positing of the divine person, the Father's absolute gift of self is coincident with the begetting of the Son, and with the Son, the spiration of the Holy Spirit. The gift of the Father is absolutely

---

53. This understanding of truth proposed by *Dei verbum*, no. 2, moves away from an abstract, ahistorical comprehension of truth and, while guarding against a relativistic or anti-intellectualistic understanding of truth, retrieves truth's identity as "historical event." See de Lubac, *La révélation divine*, 39–43; John Paul II, *Fides et ratio*, no. 23 (AAS 91 [1999], 23).

54. Balthasar, *TL*, 2:135–36.

radical because it gives "what is most perfect in nature," that is, the Father posits another person.[55] In this sense, the Father has always already given the Son and Holy Spirit "to have dominion over their own actions; and which are not only made to act, like others; but which can act of themselves (*per se agunt*)."[56] The gift would not be absolute if the other did not share the same degree of being, that is, if the other did not enjoy, at the same level but differently, one *esse*, volition, and reason.[57] In fact, since the "gift" of the Father is himself, who is "spirit," the gift (*agape*) of absolute spirit is also one of the Word (*logos*), who himself "descends" (Phil 2:7–8), and of the Spirit of truth, who searches the depths of God (1 Cor 2:10) and blows where he wills (John 3:8). The gift of the absolute spirit means both *agape* and *logos*, inseparably. Since "gift" is coextensive with "spirit," the former always entails the unity of *agape* and *logos*. With his giving, the Father gives to the Son and the Holy Spirit to be equally God, which also means that their responses of love to the Father are not predetermined by the Father's gift of self, and that they are already given overabundantly. That each of the hypostases is endowed with "will" and "mind," therefore, cannot be interpreted to mean independent centers of consciousness and freedom. They are one with the Father. This is the greatness of the Father's gift and the truth of the inner-trinitarian relations: to allow the Son and Spirit to be equal to him and yet another (John 5:26).

Second, as Hegel intuits, what is posited has always been: the Son and Holy Spirit are *co-eternal* with the Father. Yet, contrary to Hegel, the "presupposition" does not entail a becoming in God precisely because the Father's gift of self is one of wealth (fullness) "emptying" itself without losing itself. The generation of the Son does not "posit" someone who did not exist beforehand. Similar to the Father's *being* his giving, the Son is always being begotten and has always already been begotten.[58]

55. Aquinas, *ST*, I, q. 29, a. 3.
56. Aquinas, *ST*, I, q. 29, a. 1.
57. Since the communication in the hypostases is absolute, we need to maintain two things: that there is only one will and one mind (and not three), and that this mind (*nous*) and will is enjoyed differently by each of the hypostases: as giving (Father), as received and reciprocated (Son), and as commonly shared (Holy Spirit). Without reducing person to a univocal concept that would be equally applicable to man and the Trinity, Scripture invites us to acknowledge a real "personhood" of the hypostases that does not fracture the unity.
58. The images of the "line" or the "circle" are often used to represent the ungraspable unity of self-possession and gift of self. Both representations fall short. Thinking of the Trinitarian processions in terms of a horizontal line respects the Trinitarian *taxis* (the begetting of the Son and co-spiration of the Holy Spirit), but does not include the eternal co-presence of the hypostases. Thinking of them as a "circle"—an image dearer to the Platonist tradition—indicates the co-eternality of the hypostases and their

According to the first aspect—the Father's gift posits the other two persons—faith acknowledges an unchangeable order in the Godhead, an order without which there is no real distinction in God and so no relation. To assert the contrary would empty Christian revelation of its most proper content: Christ is the one sent by the Father to do his will so that, through the Spirit of truth, man may enjoy the Father's love overabundantly. In light of the second aspect—the co-eternality of the persons—the hypostases proceeding from the Father receive and reciprocate the Father's original gift and thus "retroactively affect the origin itself without neutralizing the order of origination."[59] Let us ponder this second statement first.

In affirming the order of the processions, we can avoid any sort of subordinationism (which would place the Son and the Holy Spirit on the side of creation, or assign them a secondary place in the Godhead) by focusing on understanding the gift of the Father and the relation he originates between the persons. The Father's total, non-jealous gift of himself posits another who is *not* the Father. The giver, however, remains within the gift as the origin from which it proceeds. In God, then, gift is both identical to its source and different from it. Since it is given without return (*datio irredibilis*), it implies "free use or fruition (*liberum usum vel fruitionem*)" of itself.[60] This "not being the Father" is thus not a negation of the Father but a relation (a relative negation, as we mentioned earlier with respect to Hegel) that not only posits the Son and the Holy Spirit but also constitutes the Father as Father.

To affirm the monarchy of the Father over and against the other two hypostases, as if the Father were simply the "absolute person," would obscure the fact that without the Son and his eternal, overabundant response, the Father cannot be himself. St. Hilary's bold claim that "the Son perfects (*consummat*) the Father" allows us to see what Balthasar means when, deepening Aquinas's understanding of "constitutive" relations, he seeks to give a more "adequate picture of the real and abiding face-to-face encounter of the hypostases."[61] The "completion" of the Father does not indicate a lack. As the

---

necessary and eternal relations according to which one person always leads to the other two; nevertheless, it loses the specificity of the Father, who is the source and origin of all divinity. Since we are unable to overcome time in speaking about God, we have to retain both images while acknowledging that neither is fully satisfactory.

59. Balthasar, *TL*, 2:147.

60. Aquinas, *ST*, I, q. 38, a. 2 and a. 1, ad 3. While Aquinas is speaking here of "gift" as a personal name of the Holy Spirit, what he says about the nature of gift, given the identity of essence of the three hypostases, can be analogically applied to the Son. This, of course, requires seeing both God and the hypostases in terms of love, in line with Augustine, Richard of Saint Victor, and Bonaventure.

61. Hilary, *De Trinitate* 7.31. Quoted in Ladaria, *La Trinità*, 220. See also Balthasar,

resurrection of Christ and the presence of the Holy Spirit in history witness, absolute spirit has revealed itself to be overabundant fullness. Nor is the Son's "perfecting" of the Father a simple return of the gift, which would balance out the Father's original donation and so negate it. "Completion" indicating lack would entail finite rather than absolute spirit, and the idea of simple return still views the relation between the Father and the Son in terms of a formal, empty, self-negating dialectics. That the Son "perfects" the Father means, instead, not only that the former is internal to the latter but also that the Son, in receiving himself from the Father and reciprocating overabundantly, makes the Father be Father, so to speak. The Son's perfecting of the Father, which, following Bruaire, we can describe as the *reddition* of the gift, is not a simple reiteration of the Father's gift: the Son is *other*, and his gift brings with it the exuberance and gratuity proper to the Father's gift while remaining other. In fact, the Father, in giving all of himself, also gives the Son the capacity to give, and thus the Son's eternal response to the Father's eternal begetting is at the same time another, the Holy Spirit, who is posited by both.

If the Son is the *reddition* (reciprocation) of the gift, the Holy Spirit is the confirmation of the Father's gift. The third person thus discloses the gratuitous nature of divine *agape*. Because the Holy Spirit is given by the Father, with and through the Son, as the overabundant confirmation of the gift that God is, no other person proceeds from him, nor does he need to "empty" himself. Like the Son, the Holy Spirit is co-eternal with the Father. He is both posited and "presupposed" and so is the confirmation of the infinity and effectiveness of the Father's gift. In an analogical sense to the Son's "perfecting" of the Father, the Holy Spirit also "completes" the Son because it is the Holy Spirit who unites and distinguishes the source (Father) and its perfect expression (Son). The Spirit, *donum doni*, binds together the Father and the Son while preserving their difference. Although we cannot define the relation between the Father and the Holy Spirit in terms of sonship, we can say that, because it is the Spirit in whom Father and Son are united and distinguished, the Holy Spirit also "perfects" the Father and not only the Son. In this sense, as in Hegel's Trinitarian doctrine, the Holy Spirit, by confirming the gift, also contributes to the Father's being a person, but not because the Holy Spirit is another Son; the contribution is as Spirit. The Father is a person because he is his relation with the Son, yet it is only because this relation is confirmed by the Holy Spirit that there is a difference and a unity between the first two hypostases.[62] Because there is no kenosis

---

TL, 2:38.

62. This does not make the names of Father, Son, and Holy Spirit irrelevant.

of the Holy Spirit, that is to say, because the Spirit confirms and, while being posited, contributes to the constitution of the Father and of the Son, God can be in himself love eternally given away. It is because the hypostases are irreducible to each other and because, while identical, each is the one God in a uniquely different way, that in God to be begotten and to beget, to be commonly spirated and to spirate, have the same dignity and glory.

The preceding reflections, in dialogue with Hegel's understanding of negativity and with a real appreciation for the value of Hegel's speculative relevance here, sought to indicate a way to approach both the Father's absolute gift and the difference within God (and so relation); our reflections present us with a new sense of unity. At the same time, they open up a way in which the "relative negation" can be "positively" conceived. To state that the Son perfects the Father, in fact, opens the door to an understanding of *passive action*, not only, per Bonaventure, in the Son who receives the gift of himself from the Father, but also in the Father himself. While it is perhaps easier to grasp that the Son is himself precisely because he is eternally given to himself, it is more difficult to see how the Father, who does not come from any other person, could "receive" his being a person from the Son (and the Holy Spirit) without ceasing to be the beginning without beginning. We can only indicate here, through what the Father has disclosed of the divine gift in the Incarnate Logos and the Spirit, a direction for further reflection on the understanding of act as an open principle.

If it is true that, as Origen says, the Father "is not himself without suffering," but that he suffers in such a way that the Son's passion is not imposed on the Father (from the outside by man or from the inside by a Hegelian lack), nor is the Father's suffering identical with his Son's sufferings (it is the Father's Son who dies on the Cross, not the Father[63]); and if, as John Paul II says, the Father "feels compassion for man, as though sharing his pain,"

Without them, the relation between God and the world would appear as an emanation. See Ratzinger, *Jesus of Nazareth*, 139–42.

63. Origen writes, "He came down to earth out of compassion for the human race, feeling our sufferings even before he suffered on the cross and decided to assume our flesh. For if he had not suffered, he would not have come to live on the level of human life. First he suffered, then descended and became visible. What is this suffering which he suffered for us? It is the suffering of love. And also the Father himself, the God of all 'slow to anger and abounding in mercy' (cf. Ps 103:8) and compassionate, does he not in some way suffer? Don't you know when he directs human affairs he suffers human suffering? For 'the Lord your God bore your ways as a man bears his son' (cf. Deut 1:31). Therefore God bears our ways just as the Son of God bears our sufferings. The very Father is not without suffering. When he is prayed to, he has pity and compassion; he suffers something of love and puts himself in the place of those whom he, in view of the greatness of his nature, cannot be" ("Homily on Ez 6:6," in Balthasar, *Origen*, 122). See de Lubac, *History and Spirit*, 259–80; Ratzinger, "Paschal Mystery," 51–56.

that "inscrutable and indescribable fatherly 'pain' [which] will bring about above all the wonderful economy of redemptive love in Jesus Christ, so that through the *mysterium pietatis* love can reveal itself in the history of man as stronger than sin";[64] then the reciprocal, constitutive relation between the Father and the Son also requires a polarity within each that, however, does not impose onto God any human *pathos*. The Father would not be creator, provident, or rich in mercy if the generation of the Son did not also entail a perfection for the Father.

If, as revelation indicates, God's absolute being is an event of love, the "action" proper to the divine gift has both an active and passive sense in each of the hypostases. Now in God, who is pure act (*ipsum esse*), there is no distinction between nature and existence (*esse*) and hence "acting" (begetting) is not a "making" in which a "cause" (e.g., the Father) produces an "effect" (e.g., the Son). The Father is his giving. God's action, therefore, cannot be conceived in terms of "human" action. Man's giftedness always presupposes an ontological "passivity": he is created from nothing and any action of his is always a response to the preceding, constitutive communication of being.[65] Man, unlike God, is never identical with his form and is always able to receive other forms that affect his *esse* to various degrees. Hence, for finite beings created *ex nihilo*, "action" is inseparable from "passion." Finite beings are the mysterious dual unity of essence and *esse*. However, when we speak of "active" and "passive" action in God (giving, receiving, and the reciprocation of the gift), it is an attempt to elucidate the meaning of "action" in a being who knows no separation between nature and *esse*—God is *ipsum esse subsistens*—as is the case in man. The relation between "*actio*" and "*passio*" in God, therefore, is analogical to the one found in creation, that is, it is located within a greater dissimilarity. God's power has to be conceived in the manner of an "active power" that does not presuppose (in any of the hypostases) an ontological passivity. "Passive" *action* in this sense is not the reception of a form after the manner of created beings.[66] It must be thought in terms of *action* coincident with a love that desires the other to be and that "lets him be." As Balthasar indicates, following Bonaventure's insight,[67] the

---

64. John Paul II, *Dominum et vivificantem*, no. 39 (AAS, 78 [1986], 853).

65. Schmitz, *Creation*, 28–34.

66. It is in this sense that Aquinas's contention is right: "The power which we attribute to God is neither active properly speaking nor passive, seeing that the predicaments of action and passion are not in him, and his action is his very substance: but the power which is in him is designated by us after the manner of an active power" (Aquinas, *De pot. Dei*, q. 2, a. 1, ad 1).

67. "There is a passive generative potentiality in the Son predisposing him to be begotten" (Balthasar, *TD*, 5:85).

language of "wanting the other to be," the affirmation that "it is good for the other to be," and "letting the other be" seek to preserve the unity of active and passive action without reading into them any connotation of created activity and passivity. Action in God is identical and yet different in each hypostasis.

While Hegel's reflections on negativity fall short in their speculative reading of Good Friday, they nonetheless seem to point in the direction of acknowledging that the irreducibility of the divine persons requires an active and passive *action* (affirmation and letting-be) not only in the Son and the Holy Spirit, but also in the Father. If the circumincession of the persons is to be taken seriously, then the relation of fatherhood that defines the Father as such requires that there be in him a receptivity that would allow the necessary, constitutive reciprocity between the persons to be real, and not simply modal, ways of being God. When positivity is given its due priority over negativity, "determination as negation" turns out to be a non-jealous affirmation of the other (Son) who is one with the one (Father) who affirms in a third (Spirit).

Otherness requires both irreducibility and, at the same time, the interiority that welcomes the other within itself. The Father's act of begetting, as we saw, is an act of surrendering all of himself to the Son without losing himself. As Balthasar states, following von Speyr, contrary to the human generation in which no one is asked his permission to be begotten, the Son participates, so to speak, in his begetting by allowing himself to be begotten by the Father. To the Father's act of self-surrender, the Son responds with an equal offer of himself. "The Father's act of begetting," says Balthasar, "contains a gratitude to the Son for letting himself be begotten, just as the Son's willingness contains a gratitude to the Father for his wanting to beget him. So, even in the Father's 'active *actio*' there is a certain passivity, qualified by the 'passive *actio*' of Son and Spirit."[68] A non-creaturely gratitude, the root of human reception and reciprocation of the gift, is in the Father, as, for lack of a better term, a "response" to the Son's offer of himself in return.

In order to clarify the polarity of the Father's action (both passive and active), we have to avoid, on the one hand, thinking of the Father as an already constituted person who only gives himself at a second moment—this would be Arius's one-sided Trinitarian theology—and, on the other hand, conceiving the Father as a universal indetermination that seeks to particularize itself so that it can become a concrete and universal subject (Hegel)—this would make the Father a result of his own begetting. To speak of the "receptivity" (or passive *action*) required for the Father to be Father is not

---

68. Ibid., 87.

an attempt to bring Hegelian negativity in through the back door. Negativity is not coextensive with positivity; rather, it is the Father's plenitude to be always already given away without the loss of his own personhood.

Only the unchangeable hierarchy of the processions can secure the "positive" sense of "negativity" (which is perhaps better described as "difference" and "receptivity"), according to which the other's identity is not the negation of oneself, but rather that gift that is the positive affirmation and letting be of the other, whose gratuitous response is expected without being demanded or grasped. That the Son "perfects" the Father does not make the Father "son of the Son." Nor does the fact that the Holy Spirit confirms and witnesses to the unfathomable generosity of the Father's gift by uniting him to his Word and keeping both distinct make the Spirit father of the Father. It is true that, as Hegel's syllogistic system seems to indicate, each person necessarily leads to the other two. Yet a lack of order would imply a modalistic, alogical *agape*, that is, it would mean a conception of God as absolute, arbitrary power in which there is no real difference. If that were the case, it would be impossible to ascribe any real weight to the divine "not," the irreducibility of the persons within the identity of substance.

While some contemporary theological reflections claim that the polarity of active and passive action in God trumps the order, the absolute equality of the hypostases requires hierarchy in order not to collapse into an undetermined solipsism. The order of the processions in the theology cannot be altered without embracing an absolute that resembles more the Plotinian One than the triune God revealed in Jesus Christ. Without hierarchy, absolute equality means a formal, empty self identical to itself whose historical expression can only be a nihilistic, self-destructive logic. If the Father does not preserve his primacy, there is no true affirmation of the other, that is to say, no real freedom (in God or outside of God). Precisely because the Father gives all that he is to the Son, and with him to the Spirit, the Son and the Spirit can respond in gratitude, each in his own unfathomable way, to the Father. If the Father did not give all of himself, or were to give all of himself without distinguishing himself from what he begets—hence without the desire for an eternal and gratuitous response, which is both "awaited" without demand and already superabundantly fulfilled by the response of the other—there would be no real personal otherness. The Son would not enjoy the one unique divine mind and will and so would not be free to receive and to respond eternally to the Father's gift. Freedom would still be the exercise of arbitrary power and not the conscious response of love. When Christ states that only he who receives the inheritance of being a son of the Father may dwell in the Father's love, he is not fostering another political movement (John 15; Gal 5). He is revealing to man the ever-new richness of a continuous response to the Father's perennial gift of self, that is, to be sons in the Son through the gift of the Spirit. Order within the Trinity, therefore, implies ontological difference and inequality only when the underlying theory of participation is that of Greek, neoplatonic metaphysics (as in Eunomius). "Participation" does not entail inferiority, thanks to the simultaneity of both identity and self-gift, or of "wealth and poverty," to use the terms of Ferdinand Ulrich, from whom Balthasar draws much of his own reflection. The Trinitarian God revealed in Jesus Christ shows that difference is not only compatible with equality, but that in love difference and equality actually require each other. Only if we are able to see why it is good to be, even though we are not God, can we see that to be infinite gift without being the "beginning without beginning" does not diminish the divine glory.

When equality means the dissolution of hierarchy, divine love is reduced to (worldly) power in the earlier sense of the exercise of freedom without acknowledgment of origin, and thus to a self-affirmation that cannot conceive of itself beyond the horizon of death. The nothingness from which finite being is created is thus elevated to the ultimate hermeneutical ground that grants meaning to (or deprives meaning from) whatever exists. Without a Father who gives all of himself "before thinking about it" to allow the other to be, there can be no freedom. Once again, only preserving the irreducibility of the difference between the persons and the constitutiveness of their relations in their identity with the divine *esse* permits power to be understood as kenotic self-gift, in which the gratuitous affirmation of the other and the act of letting him be are coincident with the self-effacing affirmation of oneself (John 15:13–15). The distinction that the gift of the Father eternally generates sets the other two persons at such a distance that what in the economy appears as the "death of God" is eternally only life, joy, and unity. At the same time, this distinction establishes the living unity in which each one is himself within the total communication of self.

5. Eternal Communion

After examining the Father's communication of his own glory to the Son and the Holy Spirit through the absolute and gratuitous gift of himself, we turn now to consider the unity proper to the innertrinitarian relations as one of divine communion. God's unity is always already a unity of divine communion precisely because it has the Father, the beginning without beginning, as its permanent ground.⁶⁹ The Father always exists as having given himself away to the Son, and with the Son he gives himself over to the Spirit.

The Fourth Lateran Council points to the necessity of keeping our fragile, limited speech about the Godhead oriented to God's ever-greaterness (DS 806). No theological speech will ever be fully adequate for the impenetrable simplicity of the unity of the divine essence, or for the three hypostases who fully and eternally share the Godhead. Though we exist in time and cannot avoid speaking sequentially, God has no before or after: he is not a "unity" that at a second moment becomes fruitful in three hypostases, nor is he a "social gathering" of three divine persons, who unite in a (moral) decision to share completely their essence. God's unity is always already communion, and the divine communion of persons is always already the one God.

Trinitarian reflections also have a penchant for anthropomorphization. To privilege the faculties of reason and will for the unity of the divine processions is to privilege an image of God patterned after the Father. This account is helpful in distinguishing the processions while affirming the simple unity of God. It also remains limited, however: intellectual and volitional acts are not persons—as Augustine and Aquinas are fully aware. Furthermore, thinking and knowing always presuppose the encounter with another. To approach God by setting out from his image in man (*imago Dei*) and to locate this image primarily in the spiritual faculties of the human being always presupposes this personal encounter. While an account of divine unity in terms of a communion of persons makes room for the face-to-face encounter between the persons and permits us to speak of their gift of self to the other two and their delightful awareness of this gift, such an account cannot draw on bodily difference to ground theological difference and unity. Faith knows both that the Father, Son, and Holy Spirit exist in their relative opposition and that they are one God. Each is fully God, and each is never without the other two, with whom each fully shares the entire Godhead from all eternity. The paradoxical unity of these two facts—three hypostases, one God—should not cause us to devolve into ideological conversation and clichés. This type of thinking pits one approach against another and tends to disregard the vision of the whole that Christ offers the human person to embrace. Theological accounts of the divine unity need

---

69. Aquinas, *ST*, I, q. 39, a. 4, ad 4. In his response Aquinas quotes Augustine's *De doctrina Christiana* 5.5: "In Patre est unitas, in Filio aequalitas, in Spiritu Sancto unitatis aequalitatisque concordia."

to hold fast to the insurmountable paradox of the dual unity of the two elements, without attempting to resolve the tension between them.[70]

Both accounts (the *imago Dei* in the spiritual faculties, and the communion of persons) are relevant, and neither is simply the fruit of theologians' imaginations. Both are set into motion by the relation between God and man. In the present context, two important elements invite us to acknowledge that the one triune God is a communion of persons. The first regards the human person himself; the second, God's relation with mankind. When we ponder the mystery of the being of God, starting out from what in man is similar to him (the *imago Dei*, which constitutes man's greatness and dignity), we need to recall that the human person is created in Christ. He thus images God in a filial way; that is, as one whose being is constituted by the relation with the Father who always precedes us, calls us to be, and guides us to him through his two hands, the Son and the Holy Spirit. Rather than thinking of the *imago Dei* in terms of a fatherhood from which notional and volitional acts proceed, it is important to see that the human being is called to be son in the Son. Man's acts of knowing and willing are always a response to the giving, eternally faithful Father. The second element that suggests seeing God's unity in terms of communion comes from letting theological reflection take its bearings from divine revelation itself. Divine revelation

---

70. M. R. Barnes has called attention to the enormous and still active influence of Théodore de Régnon's faulty Trinitarian cliché: that the Greek model follows a *communio personarum* theology, whereas the Latin model upholds an essentialist one. The former, so the cliché goes, begins with the persons and is thus more faithful to Scripture, whereas the latter begins with the divine unity. Barnes indicates that while English-speaking followers of the French theologian (e.g., J. Mackey, J. O'Donnell, D. Brown, C. LaCugna) adopt his work without citing him—and hence take his analysis as an authentic account of early Trinitarian theology—French-speaking authors (e.g., H. Paissac, A. Malet, G. Lafont, Le Guillou) try to criticize him by showing how, in reality, the Cappadocian Fathers (and not only the Latin tradition) rely heavily on the doctrine of *homoousios* and hence are burdened with essentialism (thus their difficulty in arriving at the concept of person and their extreme apophaticism). The French also contend that Augustine's Trinitarian model is truly personal, since, as seen in his adoption of the psychological images, he privileges relation and hence person, whereas the Greek model of participatory causality (light from light, etc.) is essentialist. This cliché can also be found in Russian authors such as V. Lossky (in whom the influence of Eckhart cannot be underestimated) and perhaps, we may add, in Bulgakov (for whom Hegel seems to enjoy a great ascendency). Barnes demonstrates the complementarity of the two traditions by showing how Augustine not only describes the second hypostasis as Word (supporting the French critiques of de Régnon) but also as "power"—and hence as following the pattern of participatory causality of the Greek Fathers. This second aspect is not mentioned by the French-speaking theologians—an absence that shows to some extent the degree to which their reflection remains under the shadow of de Régnon's analysis. See Barnes, "De Régnon Reconsidered"; De Régnon, *Études de théologie positive*.

discloses a relation between God and man that is a covenant, a nuptial relation of sorts, in which God promises to be eternally faithful. While in the Old Testament, God's holiness, lordship, and rightfulness (with mercy) are preponderant, in the New Testament, God reveals himself as the loving, merciful Father who, in bringing about justice for human sin through the offering of his Incarnate Son on the Cross, unexpectedly fulfills the promise of unifying his creatures with himself by transforming them, through the Spirit, into sons in the Son, and by bringing them out of their broken human unity into the one communion that Scripture calls the Church, the bride of the Lamb. The God of Jesus Christ is essentially love. He is a Father who has given everything to his beloved Son with whom he is united in the Spirit. Christ's affirmation that, although the Father is greater (John 14:28), he is one with the Father (John 10:30) implicitly contains the third, the Consoler: "even as you, Father, are *in* me and I *in* thee" (John 17:21). The Father's being "in" the Son indicates both a distance and an identity that is represented by a third, the Holy Spirit (John 14:9). Scripture discloses for us a type of unity that is far richer than the monadic form of the Greek culture; it is a unity that brings to full light the intimations of unity that the Hebrew people experienced.[71] Christ reveals the highest expression of unity in the communion of reciprocal love of the three hypostases.

A further unfolding of Christ's relation with the Father and the Holy Spirit is that this communion is a *perichoretic* indwelling of one person in the other. The unity of the divine *esse* poses no threat to the three persons who dwell and are themselves in each other; rather, communion is reciprocal indwelling, and this reciprocal indwelling (*perichoresis*) is the highest possibility for union.[72] Synthesizing the works of Hilary of Poitiers and

71. It is also important not to pit Boethius's understanding of person too strongly against that of Richard of Saint Victor. In fact, although there are ambiguities in Boethius's understanding of "rational" substance (applied to God, angels, and man without sufficient distinction), we should not forget that human reason cannot be either separated from our bodily condition or thought of apart from the preexistence of language (which remains always anterior to man's knowledge and hence cannot be reduced to it). Just as there is no reasoning without its actual exercise (and hence without its intrinsic link with the whole of the logic of human existence that entails bodiliness, desire, reason, freedom, and relation with others), there is no actual exercise of reason prior to having been spoken to by another. On the other hand, while there are also limits in Richard's understanding of person (persons in God are not seen in their singular personhood; the relation between the economy and theology does not give form to the doctrinal reflection), there is no personal self-standing that is not rational and free if *amor* is understood adequately. At the same time, both concepts of "person" are incapable of arriving at the superabundance proper to the divine triune life. This deficiency does not, however, limit Trinitarian theology to radical apophatic thinking.

72. The Greek noun *perichoresis* (περιχώρεσις) is taken from the verbs *perichoreuo*

Augustine, John Damascene is the first to use the term *perichoresis* in a systematic way.[73] He adopts the term to explain the union without confusion of the divine and human natures in Christ and the mutual in-existence of the divine persons.[74] The term was also helpful for Trinitarian theology. According to Scripture, the personal relation of the Father, Son, and Holy Spirit is one of ecstatic love, according to which it is in the other that one is himself. With regard to God, therefore, the *perichoresis* of the hypostases points to both the dynamic aspect of love and the more static dimension of love.[75] According to the dynamic aspect of love, that is, God's very nature, *perichoresis* indicates the mutual, asymmetrical gift and com-penetration of the hypostases. The hypostases are themselves in the asymmetrical gift of all of self to the other. According to the more static dimension of love's ecstasy, *perichoresis* is the presence of one in the other, the indwelling of one in the other. God's personal, essential love is the eternal gift of one to the other and with the other, in which the one always already rests (is) in the other. Reading the unity of communion as *perichoretic*, the fathers of the Church avoided both a modalistic account of the Godhead, according to which donation would never be real since the hypostases would be only manifestations of the one God and never really other persons, and a tritheistic explanation, according to which the gift would not be the entire divine *esse* and so would be incomplete.[76]

Perichoresis refers then to the dynamic proper to essential love. It is not something that God "does"; it is what God *is*. Just as there is no distinction in God between *esse* and essence, so there is no distinction in God between his acting and his being (which is not the case, obviously, with God's action *ad extra*). The "dancing" of one around the other does not indicate therefore an external, spatial movement of preexistent dancers. Rather, it indicates the

---

(περι-χωρείω, to dance around) and *perichoreo* (περι-χωρέω, to walk around). It was probably first used by the philosopher Anaxagoras in order to express the co-presence and relation of the natural elements operated by the *nous*. Anaxagoras, *Fragments of Anaxagoras*, B59, fr. 12.

73. Hilary, *De Trinitate* 3.1—4.22-25 (PL 10:76-78, 90-95); Augustine, *Trin.* 6.10.12 and 9.5.8 (PL 42:932 and 965).

74. John Damascene, *De fide orthodoxa* 1.14 (PG 94:859-62).

75. These two senses (dynamic and static) are indicated in the Latin appropriation of *perichoresis* with two different words: *circuminsessio* (*circum* = around; *insidere* = to seat, to be above, inside) and *circumincessio* (*circum* = around; *incedere* = to go forward). The former emphasizes the unity of the essence and the latter begins with the persons. Bonaventure uses the latter. See, e.g., *Commentaria in quatuor libros Sententiarum*, bk. 1, d. 19, q. 4. Aquinas does not use the terms *circumincessio* and *circuminsessio*, but does deal with the topic. See, e.g., Aquinas, *ST*, I, a. 42, a. 5.

76. The Church adopted this explanation at the Council of Florence (DS 1330-1331).

internal, eventful, and spiritual relation in which each is constituted by the eternal relations of origin, in which being posited by the Father is coincident with participation in one's being given to oneself and with over-fulfilling reciprocation of the superabundant original gift. That God reveals his own being-love (*agape-eros*) to be a *perichoretic* communion (*koinonia*) confirms the nature of the gift of creation by exceeding it. The original, creative donation does not stop at the level of the substance, but aims at that of the person. God creates the world from nothingness because he wishes there to be another who, at this other's own level, receives, enjoys, and reciprocates his love. In the unforeseeable Incarnation, the Logos of love redeems the human being by obediently adhering to the Father's love mediated to him by the Spirit while bearing his divine wrath. In this way, Jesus Christ not only enables man freely to embrace the Father's merciful love, but he also permits us to see that the gift's ability to become another while remaining itself (the hypostatic union of the divine and human natures in his divine person) reveals the purpose of the original gift: personal indwelling. Jesus Christ's sharing with mankind the love of the Father, through the Spirit, reflects this ineffably beautiful mystery of being fully oneself by being one with the other. To be oneself (gift's perseity) is not only to be from another (abseity), for another (adseity), and with another. The original gift is received when one lets the other *be in* oneself and lets oneself *be in* the other. Such is the unspeakable gift, the communion whose eternal origin is the Father.

It is true that there are certain created analogies that point in the direction of this being in another. The spiritual images (i.e., the most perfect), in turn, might seem to offer an understanding of this reciprocal indwelling of the divine hypostases by way of an analogy to what is known being present in the knower, the beloved in the lover, friends in each other, or to the sacramental union of the spouses. All these, however, fall short of the reciprocal indwelling of the divine hypostases announced by Jesus Christ (Matt 11:27; John 6:56, 10:28ff., 14:10–11, 15:1–9, 17:21–22; 1 John 1:1–4). They fall short with regard both to the *esse* and to the action. For the concrete singular, just as being and action are not identical, so *esse* and essence do not coincide. The constitutive, spiritual-ontological relations just listed, while true, are those of a limited creature, and so are imperfect. The images are still valid, however, provided we see them from their christological center and for what they ultimately are: to be an image is to be a real though limited participation in God's being-love. *Perichoretic* divine unity is perfect communication of the entirety of being (gift)—the three persons are *homoousios*—coincident with perfect personhood. The spatial preposition "in" reveals the perfect and absolute love of God (1 John 4:8 and 16) that is itself in the threefold "letting the other be in oneself," an other in whom one is always already permitted to be. Three aspects of this preposition relate to our present context.

First, the dual unity of *eros* and *agape* reveals that the lover, who gives himself to the beloved, desires that the beloved welcome the lover into himself. Second, and at the same time, the lover desires to be like the beloved. Finally, since divine *perichoretic* union is not waiting to happen but is rather always taking place and has always already taken place, to be in another also indicates the fruition of being oneself in the other. The indwelling unfolds as a relation in which one enjoys being one with the other while remaining oneself in a third. If the second aspect of *perichoresis*—likeness of the hypostases—indicates the total unity in God according to which each of the divine persons is God, and the first—personal otherness—refers to the divine difference between the three hypostases, the third discloses the fruition that is possible only because the union is always already present in a third. This fruition is the union of knowledge, freedom, and love. It is not simply a case of knowing or loving the other, while also being known or loved by the other. Divine communion is rather a reciprocal, never-ending knowing and an ever-new sapiential loving and being loved by the other. Our own constitutive ontological difference leaves us in a constant search to discover the "content" of this *perichoretic* communion. But the idea of being able to take an eagle's-eye view of God's essence is just a temptation to hubris. God is always greater. His action in history, which fills man with ever-new wonder, opens onto a ground that is beyond our comprehension. He is a triune communion of love that creates from nothingness what it is not; that goes to the utmost to give itself in the Paschal Mystery; and that gives the redeemed ecclesial community a sacramental foretaste of final union with the Father in the Lamb, standing as though slain, through the Spirit.

While divine communion illumines what the human person is and what human society is called to be, and human relations of love thus allow us a limited view of divine love, keeping a grasp on God's eternal communion of persons—which has its beginning in the Father's absolute gift of self—means navigating a variety of pitfalls opened up by ecclesial and anthropological agendas and controversies. Communion does not eliminate the theological difference or the order (*taxis*) between the persons. The reciprocity of love has nothing to do with an androgynous anthropology that defines the person in terms of a freedom that is neither received from nor knows of an eternal being that is itself in the total gift of itself to another. Such an impoverished view of freedom continues to regard whatever one gives as the simple result of his own goodness and generosity. Faithfulness to Scripture instead requires maintaining this communional understanding of unity, in which one is distinctly oneself and at the same time eternally identical with another. It also requires us to acknowledge that, if it were not for the Father, the unpreceded giver, there would be no communion to begin with; there would be only a monadic, Parmenidean unity or a multiplicity of origins.[77]

In the attempt to underscore this understanding of divine unity in terms of *perichoretic* communion, it is sometimes argued that to ground divine unity in the processions of origin—as we are suggesting here—would undermine the very existence of communion. There is a fear that the Father's primordiality throws the "play of love" proper to the relation of the divine hypostases off balance. An "unpreceded giver" seems to preclude a truly reciprocal indwelling, and there could not be a real "dance" of one around the other and the other around the one. This view requires understanding the divine essence as an interpersonal "event" of love, in which each of the three divine persons has his own being from another. It also claims that communion, to be such, must ultimately be fatherless.[78] According to this view, to avoid any idea of sequence—for sequence can seem impossible if the persons are constituted by the relations of origin—it is important to acknowledge that the divine essence is always and only realized in the communion of persons. If love truly constitutes the divine essence, these authors conclude, then unity is nothing but the reciprocal indwelling of the persons.[79]

The previous reflections on fatherhood, truth, and how the origin in the Godhead is "affected" by the other co-eternal persons could in fact seem to lend credence to this idea that understanding the unity of the Godhead in terms of communion means eliminating the order of the processions, and so the place of the "beginning." But communion means more than the three hypostases sharing the divine substance. The divine tri-unity is one of communion only because the origin of the divinity is the Father, who possesses himself as always already given away. The Son and the Spirit receive the gift of the divine essence from the Father fully yet differently. Even though, as we saw, the Son and the Holy Spirit contribute in their own way to the "constitution" of the Father, it is the latter who generates communion with

---

77. This is what we see in the works of, e.g., Boff, *Trinity and Society*; Johnson, *She Who Is*. For a thorough presentation of the meaning of *perichoresis*, see Durand, *La périchorèse*; Rossetti, "La perichoresi."

78. See Greshake, *Der dreieine Gott*; Pannenberg, *Systematic Theology*, vol. 1.

79. A radical reading of this reciprocal understanding of *perichoresis* can be found in Moltmann, *Trinity and the Kingdom*. Thomas F. Torrance believes, contrary to Moltmann, that *perichoresis* undergirds the order of the processions. See his *Christian Doctrine of God*, 203-34. For Barth's use of *perichoresis* to think of God's three different ways of being in unity and distinction, see Barth, *Church Dogmatics*, 1:370-71.

the gift of self through which he reveals himself to the other two and is one with them. It is the Father who generates the divine communion expressed perfectly in the Logos and confirmed and witnessed to by the Holy Spirit. Without a principle that remains such, there is neither revelation, nor gift, nor personal difference, and hence no communion. The beginning without beginning is not a Plotinian One at a distant remove; he is rather one who has always already given himself over to the other without losing himself. The Father's allowing himself to be fully "of" another without losing himself bursts open our ideas of identity and communion while superabundantly confirming what originary experience discloses about the unity of being as gift.[80]

Perichoresis underscores that God's essence is love and that this love exists as an eternal communication that is always personal. As such, in the perfect communication of the entire divine substance, the reciprocity is always asymmetrical. Asymmetry affirms the total communication that takes place in God, without losing sight of the difference in the giving, receiving, and reciprocating. Each of the persons is for, in, and with the others in his own unique way. The Father is God as Father, that is, in his relation with the Son whom he generates from all eternity and to whom he also gives the capacity to give. The Son is God as Son; he loves, receives, and is himself in the Father. He is an eternal response of love that always includes the spirating, with the Father, of the third person. The Holy Spirit is God as spirit-gift. The Holy Spirit is in the Father and the Son as the one who expresses and witnesses the common love of the Father for the Son and the Son for the Father. It is the Holy Spirit who makes God *be* one.

Perichoresis also clarifies that "reciprocity" does not follow the logic of worldly power that, in attempting to form its own unprecedented origin, and not giving all of itself without losing itself, ends up perpetuating a self-destructive orphanhood. To speak about "reciprocity" in a *perichoretic* communion, in addition to highlighting how the relation with the other two persons constitutes each, emphasizes that the reciprocity in each case is one of perfect fruition. Rather than being an equalizer—in the anthropomorphic sense of the term—the *perichoretic* interiority of each of the persons in the others indicates that the gift is fully reciprocated and thus enjoyed by both giver and receiver in another. The total gift of self is always already a sheer enjoying of oneself with and in the other. The total gift of self of the Father to the Son and, with him and through him, to the Holy Spirit

---

80. Approaching the divine absolute act from the point of view of the reciprocal indwelling that is called *perichoresis* provides an ultimate ground for our previous reflection on open principle. It is here that we see what it means to be fully oneself in another without losing oneself to a logic of decentered selves or radical indeterminacy.

constitutes him as Father, who utterly enjoys being Father and origin of the Holy Spirit.[81] Abstracting from the personal names of the hypostases, we can say that one loves the good of the other and that this other loves another as he is loved by the one. This is why reciprocity, as the perfect expression of love, always requires a third.

If divine communion has its source in the Father and is expressed in the Son, then the Holy Spirit, the spirit within God's absolute spirit, witnesses to this communion's unspeakably beautiful nature without exhausting it. In the Father's revelation of himself, he seeks to give himself to another to such a degree that his gift of self is not only the begetting of the Son, but it is also the spiration of the Spirit. Because the Holy Spirit proceeds from the Father and the Son as love and gift, he can be distinguished from the Son, and, in turn, he reveals that the love of the Father for the Son and the Son's love for the Father do not collapse into a monad. The personhood of the proceeding hypostases is secured only if two persons originate from the Father. But, since the Holy Spirit also proceeds from the Father through the Son, the Spirit also witnesses to the unending fullness and inexhaustible gift of God. The Father's begetting and the Son's eucharistic return show their exuberance in the third hypostasis, who explores the bottomless depths of God. The filial and spiritual reciprocation of the Father's original, unpreceded gift shows that the communion begotten by God the Father is a unity in which there is a reciprocal, ineffable revelation (glory), communication (truth), and bestowal of one to the other (goodness). The Holy Spirit, as the person-love, brings to light, without himself being seen, the gratuitousness of God's gift.

---

81. Coda's latest book offers Rosmini, Bulgakov, and Chiara Lubich as proponents of three plausible accounts of this reciprocity. See Coda, *Dalla Trinità*, 86–93, 463–67, 563–67.

VI. Gift's Unifying Memory

Our attempt to understand the unity of being in terms of gift so far has brought to light the primal character of gift. Gift is a primal, a principle, inasmuch as it is a permanent source. The positivity of concrete singular beings suggested by originary experience rests on the permanent, personal principle of originating and ordering, a Father whose face we are invited to see in his beloved, Incarnate Son. Gift is also a primal because it indicates "first-ness." According to this second sense of "primal," being's primordial unity is an ever-new beginning. Each concrete singular being is created; it has a historical existence, which, at its own level, is a participation in God's eternity. Our previous reflection set us on the road to pondering the meaning of both the unity of gift and the sense of time and eternity proper to that unity. Yet it is only the specificity of the Holy Spirit, the person-gift, that overcomes the anthropomorphic temptation to reduce God's gift to a sterile, pendular give-and-take, or the eternity of the divine act to a momentary stillness. The dual relation of the Father's begetting and the Son's grateful response does not collapse into monadic identity because the divine gift is always already tripersonal. Just as the Father is the unpreceded, eternal origin of the divine unity, and this unity is expressed eternally by the Word, so the Holy Spirit, the one in whom the Father and the Son are united and love each other, is the person who shows God's unfathomable, eternal unity. Schelling's question—"Why is there being at all rather than nothing?"—receives its illuminating response in the mystery of God's gifted tripersonal unity.[1] The task of this chapter is to revisit the twofold connotation of the primal—the eternal, giving source—in light of the third hypostasis.

Reflection on the Holy Spirit enables the full form of the tripersonal gift-ness of God's unity to emerge, while, at the same time, it becomes possible to see how the divine unity is a fruitful and gratuitous communion of

---

1. Schelling, "Einleitung," 607–9; Schelling, *Philosophie der Offenbarung 1841/42*.

persons. The preceding chapters laid out the case for understanding this mystery of divine love in terms of gift. In God, too, the dynamic of gift requires a giver, a receiver, and a gift. Thus we can say that the Father is the unpreceded giver, the Son is himself in receiving himself from the Father and giving himself in return, and, as we shall now see, the Holy Spirit is the gift. At the same time, it has been a constant concern to steer clear of any unilateral identification of the Father with the giver, the Son with the receiver, and the Holy Spirit with the gift, which would obscure the theological difference and the ontological equality of the divine persons. Moreover, it would overlook the fact that giving and receiving are proper to each of the persons, though in differentiated ways. An additional element of the discussion has been the sense in which the divine gift is gratuitous in itself. Admittedly, to speak of gratuity in God is a difficult task. Yet if revelation permits thinking of God in terms of gift and also provides the statement that in God there is no distinction between *esse* and essence, then gratuity characterizes God's being before it describes his action *ad extra*. To frame our reflection on divine gratuity within the terms of a dialectics of freedom and necessity, or of reasonableness and arbitrariness, would doom us to insurmountable contradictions. God is beyond the polarity of freedom and necessity: divine gratuity unfolds itself, first of all, as a fruitful unity. God's gift-ness knows neither jealousy, nor rejection, nor unfaithfulness. The Father's gift begets the Son without envy and, with the Son, he gives further to the Holy Spirit. Both of them eternally receive and reciprocate the Father's gift of self. God's being is gratuity itself because in him there is no trace of evil, no grasping at the other, and no ingratitude for the gift of being.

This chapter sets out to ponder the role of the Holy Spirit as the unifying memory of God's gratuitous gift of self and begins by assembling the properties of the third hypostasis disclosed by Christ (sections 1–2). The Holy Spirit, *donum doni*, the person who witnesses to the unity and inexhaustible fruitfulness of God, thus opens up for us the first aspect of the gift-form of God's gratuitous unity (sections 3–4). Within the larger framework of God's threefold gift, the chapter concludes with an exploration of the gratuitousness of God's gift in terms of divine recognition, availability, and prayer (section 5).

1. God's Fruitful Gift

Every pneumatological reflection moves in two directions. On the one hand, it leads back to the Father through Christ, and on the other, it shows that the Holy Spirit fulfills his mission by presenting in history what he is from all eternity. Although it is discreet and implicit, the Holy Spirit has a clear personal presence in the economy, including a specific identity and role. This twofold direction reveals the glory of the Father, who, rich in mercy, allows Jesus Christ, the icon of his love, to enlighten, warm, ignite, expand, deepen, and unify our lives through his forerunner.[2] The Father, who is himself only in the gift of self to the Son, and in the gift with and through the Son to the Spirit, creates through the Son and completes his work through the Spirit, the divine person who has no name.[3] The Father extends his gift of self to us through "his two hands" and through them lifts us up so that we can respond to his call of love.[4] Just as Christ's mercy and obedience unto death are the fleshing out in history of the love that the Logos eternally receives from the Father, so the Holy Spirit's gift of divine communion expresses in history his divine personhood.[5] The Holy Spirit has the mission in history to communicate Christ, the beloved Son.[6] He thus not only brings Jesus Christ to every human being, but, since he is the "seeing eye," he enables man to see and embrace Christ from within God's mystery of love.[7]

The full form of Christ's existence cannot be severed from his union with the Father who sent him, or from his relation with the Holy Spirit. In the economy, the Holy Spirit precedes and accompanies Jesus, who gives him from the Cross and, in union with the Father, sends him after the

2. "Christ is conceived, the Spirit is the forerunner" (Gregory of Nazianzus, *Or.* 31.29 [PG 36:68-69]); also see Basil the Great, *On the Holy Spirit* 19 (PG 32:100-104).

3. "The Father creates through his will alone and does not need the Son, yet he chooses to work through the Son. Likewise the Son works as the Father's likeness, and needs no other cooperation, but chooses to have his work completed through the Spirit" (Basil the Great, *On the Holy Spirit* 16.38 [PG 32:136]).

4. Irenaeus, *Haer.* 4.7.4 (PG 7a:993); Irenaeus, *Haer.* 5.28.4 (PG 7b:1200).

5. It is thus that Christology and pneumatology recall each other and ground the circularity of ontology, anthropology, and Christology explored earlier. Their inseparable relation illustrates in what sense the *telos* of being and of man is a participation in the Father's glory.

6. It is Irenaeus who beautifully describes the Holy Spirit's mission as "*communicatio Christi*" (Irenaeus, *Haer.* 3.24.1 [PG 7a:966]).

7. The characterization of the Holy Spirit as the "seeing eye" is from Balthasar. "This Spirit is breath, not a full outline, and therefore he wishes only to breathe through us, not to present himself to us as an object; he does not wish to be seen but to be the seeing eye of grace in us, and he is little concerned about whether we pray *to* him, provided that we pray *with* him, 'Abba, Father,' provided that we consent to his unutterable groaning in the depths of our soul" (Balthasar, *ET*, 3:111). A further methodological clarification is in order. That the Holy Spirit rallies mankind to God does not mean that God's mystery is totally unveiled. If God is pure act, understood as triune gift of self, the mystery of God is never-ending. Furthermore, the revelation of God's unfathomable unity through the Holy Spirit, rather than exhausting, heightens the mysterious light of the Father. Scripture offers this law: the greater the revelation the greater the mystery.

ascension. The Virgin Mary conceives by the Holy Spirit (Luke 1:35), and thus, unlike the other prophets, Jesus has the fullness of the Holy Spirit from the beginning.[8] At his baptism, the Spirit descends upon and remains on Jesus (John 1:33; Matt 3:17). He leads Jesus to the desert to be tempted (Matt 4:1) and accompanies him throughout his human life (Luke 4:14). The Holy Spirit's presence in Jesus Christ's human existence can be perceived in both his actions and his very being. He operates miracles in the power of the Holy Spirit (Matt 12:28; Luke 11:20), offers the sacrifice of himself in the Holy Spirit (Heb 9:13), and, by means of the Holy Spirit, knows that he is not forsaken by the Father: "And yet I am not alone, because the Father is with me" (John 16:32). Like every action of God *ad extra*, the resurrection, too, is attributed to the Father (Acts 3:15), the Son (John 10:17), and the Holy Spirit (Rom 8:11).

Jesus Christ's being cannot be separated from or confused with the Holy Spirit's. The apostles perceive the ungraspable unity and difference between the three hypostases at the transfiguration, when they contemplate the Holy Spirit who manifests himself as glory in the bright cloud (Matt 17:5). Furthermore, the relation between Christ and the Father takes place in the Holy Spirit. Jesus addresses the Father in the Holy Spirit and rejoices in him when he speaks to the Father (Luke 10:21). It is important to note both elements: the Holy Spirit is the one in whom the Father and the Son are joined *and* this union is one of fruition, enjoyment. Jesus Christ, as John Paul II wrote, "rejoices at the fatherhood of God; he rejoices because it has been given to him to reveal this fatherhood; and he rejoices, finally, as at a particular outpouring of this divine fatherhood on the 'little ones.'"[9] Because Jesus "rejoices" in God's fatherhood through the Holy Spirit, we can say that the unity in difference that the Holy Spirit witnesses to and unfolds before us is one of sheer gladness, ecstatic joy.[10] It is precisely because of this unity with the Holy Spirit that Jesus Christ claims that whoever speaks against the Holy Spirit denies him and thus refuses his own salvation (Mark 3:28–29; Matt 12:31–32; Luke 12:10). Conversely, whoever receives the promised Consoler, whom Jesus, with the Father, sends after his return in glory (Acts 2; John 4:14), receives Christ and the Father who sends him (John 14:20). Christ came to give the Holy Spirit from the Cross (John 19:30), as symbolized by the water pouring forth from his pierced side (John 19:34) and as

---

8. With this we wish to correct any adoptionist reading of Jesus Christ's divinity. For the reception of the Holy Spirit at the baptism and the real growth of the Spirit in Christ, see Irenaeus, *Haer.* 3.16–18 (PG 7a:919–38). See also Ladaria, *El Dios vivo*, 58–113; Granados García, *Los misterios*, 231–70.

9. John Paul II, *Dominum et vivificantem*, no. 20 (AAS 78 [1986], 828).

10. Ibid., no. 21 (AAS 78 [1986], 829).

prophesied by Isaiah (Isa 55:10–11). After Jesus Christ breathed the Holy Spirit upon the apostles after his resurrection (John 20:19–23), those who welcome him are given to breathe with the same Spirit of God and to enjoy, in the Son, the very life of God.

The Holy Spirit's descent upon the apostles is final. Without leaving the Trinity, the Holy Spirit does not return to heaven, nor does his presence suffer any interruption throughout history (John 14:16). It is through the Holy Spirit that Jesus Christ, the beloved Son of the Father, remains with us until the end of the age (Matt 28:20). It is thanks to the ongoing presence of the Holy Spirit that we can definitively affirm that God extends his own communion to mankind. Through the Spirit of Christ, the Church, that is, redeemed humanity, can continue to grow in truth through history. When the Lord makes his long-awaited return from heaven, as Basil says, the Holy Spirit will distribute spiritual glory to those who recognized Jesus Christ, while it will be taken from those who rejected him.[11] Staying within this context of the revelation of the economy, we can now consider what is specific about the person of the Holy Spirit.

The Holy Spirit has the task of bringing Christ's redemptive gift of self to every person in history, which means he guides those who receive him to the whole truth (John 8:40, 4:6). The Spirit's gift would not be such if it were not transparent to its own *logos*. Redemption is the gift of being embraced by the truth. The embrace of truth is intrinsic, though it does not take place apart from the objective, present form of Christ's body, the Church. The Holy Spirit "will teach everything" and "remind" us of all that Jesus said and did (John 14:26). He thus "will bear witness" (John 15:26) and "guide into all truth" (John 16:13); that is, he will speak of the relation of the Father and the Son. The Holy Spirit is the Spirit of truth. He teaches the truth because he introduces us into the memory of the truth that Christ is, the truth he received from the Father. The Holy Spirit "reminds" us of the truth of this love—this love that is the truth—by showing it to us. He is memory because he is witness and witness because, being memory, he leads us onward to the fulfillment of the Father's original promise: to be sons in the Son, to enjoy and dwell in friendship with God.

To carry out his mission, the Holy Spirit must convince human beings of their sin. He, the Spirit of love, by placing man within the light of Christ's love, allows him to grasp his constitutive ingratitude. The Holy Spirit thus unfolds for man the link between his sins and Christ's crucifixion. Obviously, this task does not aim simply to punish, but rather to show human beings from within that in the Father's plan, mercy has the last word (John

---

11. Basil the Great, *On the Holy Spirit* 16.40 (PG 32:141–44).

16:7–11). It is by being with man that the Holy Spirit "con-vinces," wins man over, in order to lead him into the light of God. Through the Spirit of Jesus Christ, the human being discovers in wonder that the Father's response to rejection is a faithful and ever-new giving.

Just as the Father's gift of himself is the begetting of another who is both *homoousios* with and other than him, so the gift of the Holy Spirit is a complete, personal participation in the same life. The gift that the Holy Spirit is would not be real or complete if he did not fully participate in the Godhead, and specifically as a third person. Beyond what a pneumatological reflection limited to the Old Testament might reveal, in the life of Jesus Christ we see that the Holy Spirit is not an energy with which the Incarnate Son accomplishes his mission. He is consubstantial with the Father and the Son, as another person who belongs to both and as such can be sent by them.[12] Just as the Son gives him, so the Father sends him (John 14:16–26, 15:26). Gregory Nazianzen explains that the Holy Spirit, as a person, can not only say things (Acts 13:2), decree (Acts 13:2), be vexed (Isa 63:10), and be grieved if he is rejected (Eph 4:30);[13] he is also endowed with an absolute freedom: "you hear his blowing, but you do not know whence he comes and whither he goes" (John 3:8). The Holy Spirit is fully person. St. Basil clarifies further that the greatest proof that the Spirit is a divine person and so one with the Father and the Son "is that He is said to have the same relationship to God as the spirit within us has: 'no one comprehends the thoughts of God except the Spirit of God' (1 Cor 2:11)."[14]

2. *Donum Doni*

If "person" is the apex of being because it indicates a relation of love, how are we to understand the relation that constitutes the Holy Spirit as person? Although the Spirit is a person, and although Jesus addresses the Father through him, the Son does not address the Holy Spirit as he does the Father. The Holy Spirit is not the Son's "thou." Although he also proceeds from the Father (John 15:26), he is not named "son" as is the Logos. The Holy Spirit is other. Augustine helps illuminate how, following Scripture, the particular personhood of the third hypostasis is given with his very name. "Holy Spirit" designates what is common to each of the hypostases—sanctity and spirituality—and, by being hypostasized in a third, shows that what is common to God is common precisely as shared. His personal particularity is

---

12. Gregory of Nazianzus, *Or.* 31.10 (PG 36:144).
13. Gregory of Nazianzus, *Or.* 31.6 (PG 36:140).
14. Basil the Great, *On the Holy Spirit* 16.40 (PG 32:44).

what they have in common. What it means to be the person-communion, Augustine tells us, is elaborated through the other two characteristic names of the Holy Spirit: "love" (1 John 4:7–16) and "gift" (John 4:7–14). The circularity of love and gift indicated earlier finds in the person of the Holy Spirit, the love within absolute love, its clearest expression. The Holy Spirit witnesses to and recalls the truth because he is the person-love. God is indeed love in himself (1 John 4:16), and love is also from God: "God's love has been poured into our hearts through the Holy Spirit which has been given to us" (Rom 5:5).[15] "What then is love," Augustine asks, "except a certain life which couples or seeks to couple together some two things, namely, him that loves, and that which is loved?"[16] The Holy Spirit is "the absolute love (*summa caritas*) which joins together Father and Son, and joins us also from beneath."[17] The Spirit, as the person-love, binds the Father with the Son, and so generates abiding in God and in the economy, as Ratzinger notes.[18] The preposition "in," which we examined as revelatory of the *perichoretic* nature of divine communion, finds its personal expression in the Holy Spirit. To be the person who joins in himself the Father with the Son is to let each be himself by dwelling in the other. Bulgakov notes that both the "in" of John 17:21 ("as you, Father, are in me and I am in you") and the "with" of John 16:32 ("the Father is with me") refer to the Holy Spirit. These prepositions, Bulgakov writes, indicate that "the Father Who is in heaven abides with the Son (Who has descended to earth) in the Holy Spirit, Who has been sent by the Father to repose upon the Son; . . . this 'with,' this *met'emou*, which unites the two of them."[19] The Russian theologian applies the same logic to the *en mesoi* of Matt 18:20: "Where two or three are gathered together in my name, there am I *in the midst* of them."[20]

Augustine clarifies that just as the names "Father" and "Son" do not indicate either substance or accident but rather the persons' being-relative to each other, so the "love within absolute love" refers to the being-relative to the other hypostases rather than to the divine essence itself.[21] What is "relative" in the term "love," when appropriated to the third hypostasis,

15. Augustine, *Trin.* 15.19.37 (PL 42:1086).
16. Augustine, *Trin.* 8.10.14 (PL 42:960).
17. Augustine, *Trin.* 7.3.6 (PL 42:938).
18. Ratzinger, "Holy Spirit as *Communio*," 327–29.
19. Bulgakov, *Comforter*, 252.
20. Ibid. It bears repeating at this juncture that the unifying property of the Holy Spirit also needs to be acknowledged in the Son, albeit differently (see Athanasius, *C. Ar.* 3.24 [PG 26:373]; Basil the Great, *On the Holy Spirit* 45 [PG 32:149–52]), and, as indicated earlier, in the Father.
21. Augustine, *Trin.* 5.5.6 (PL 42:914).

Augustine tells us, emerges fully with the term "gift."[22] Gift, as we know, indicates a giver, a receiver, and something given.[23] Scripture witnesses on numerous occasions that the Holy Spirit is the "gift of God." Augustine contends that only because the Holy Spirit is gift in God from all eternity is he able to be given to humankind. The Holy Spirit, love from love, is the "gift" that calls for the presence both of the giver and of those in whom he is poured out.[24] The Holy Spirit as "gift" could suggest that the "relative" specific to the third person consists in being the "gift" the Father and the Son give each other, but this path quickly leads astray. Augustine clarifies that the Father gives but is not thereby "Father of the gift."[25] While the Father remains the principle from which the Spirit proceeds, the Spirit is not generated (*natus*) but given (*datus*), and thus is not Son, but Holy Spirit.[26] Although the Son gives, his giving the Holy Spirit is with the giving of the Father and not a giving to him—the Father and Son are one principle in the giving of the Holy Spirit. The Holy Spirit proceeds eternally from the Father and thus is not chronologically subsequent to the generation of the Son. Yet, it is also not possible to say "Son of the gift" because the Spirit does not fill the role of the Father in the generation of the Son.[27] To speak of the Holy Spirit in terms of gift, in accordance with the Trinitarian *taxis* in Scripture, requires the formulations "the giver of the gift" and the "gift of the giver."

If "gift" reveals the relational aspect of love (*caritas*) in the immanent Trinity, love in its turn discloses the meaning of gift because the Holy Spirit is called gift "on account of love" (*dilectionem*).[28] In light of love, gift does not indicate a mere "inclination" of the Father towards the Son, but, more radically, the person "in whom the other two are united."[29] He is thus a "certain

---

22. Augustine also knows that love speaks of a lover, a love, and a beloved. Yet, on the one hand, whereas it is easy to perceive the lover and the beloved as two persons, to speak of "love" as a third person could seem an unwarranted leap. On the other hand, the close relation of this imagery with human love, with all its existential fragility and lack of essential unity, discourages him from using it (Augustine, *Trin.* 8.10.14 [PL 42:960]).

23. Augustine, *Trin.* 15.19.35 (PL 42:1085).
24. Augustine, *Trin.* 15.19.36 (PL 42:1086).
25. Augustine, *Trin.* 5.12.13 (PL 42:919).
26. Augustine, *Trin.* 5.15.16 (PL 42:921).

27. Augustine, *Trin.* 15.17.27 (PL 42:1080). For the thesis that the generation of the Son takes place in the Holy Spirit, see Durrwell, *Jésus Fils de Dieu*; Durrwell, *Le Père*; and Weinandy, *Father's Spirit of Sonship*. For a balanced critique of this position, see Ladaria, *La Trinità*, 272-319.

28. Augustine, *Trin.* 15.18.32 (PL 42:1083).
29. Augustine, *Trin.* 6.5.7 (PL 42:928).

ineffable communion of the Father and the Son,"[30] a communion that "may fitly be called friendship."[31] He is the kiss of peace and unity of the Father and the Son, as St. Bernard writes.[32] Augustine's reflection helps bring to light that, according to Scripture, the unity proper to God is Trinitarian and not monadic. With the Holy Spirit, "the Person-Gift," the dyad of Father and Son comes full circle as Trinitarian *perichoretic* communion.[33] This "much richer" unity will secure, as we shall see below, true dialogue in God.[34]

God's *perichoretic* union is not a closed, sterile circle: it is eternally fruitful. Balthasar notes that in addition to manifesting the unitive aspect, the Holy Spirit also reveals the fruitfulness of the divine gift; he is both the bond of love in which the Father and the Son are united and the fruit of their love. Fruitfulness describes both the generation of another person and the fruition of being with him, a delight that is open to being given even to what the divine gift is not. God's gift is overabundantly fecund; it posits another with whom he shares all of the divine life in delight. Granting the many intimations that human love may offer for the fruitfulness of the gift, it remains true, however, that God's superabundant fruitfulness is unthinkable and unforeseeable for us, and that we only know this dimension of God's unity through divine revelation. Scripture presents the overabundant fruitfulness of God's eternal, triune gift on numerous occasions, incarnated by Christ's very existence. He unfolds it at the multiplication of bread (Matt 14:20) and the miraculous catch of fish (Luke 5:1–11); he speaks of it through the analogy of the vine (John 15:5), when he promises the hundredfold to those who follow him (Mark 10:30), when he insists on forgiving seventy times seven (Matt 18:21–23), and when he discloses the Father's reward to those who pray: the Holy Spirit (Luke 11:13). More importantly, this overabundant nature of the gift is revealed through Christ's eucharistic and sacrificial gift on the Cross, which is accomplished for everyone and which gives rise to the sacraments. As St. Paul says, the Father has given everything in giving us his Son (Rom 8:32), whose sacrificial gift of himself is complete, lacking nothing. It is the Holy Spirit through whom God's fruitfulness is communicated

---

30. Augustine, *Trin.* 5.11.12 (PL 42:919).

31. Augustine, *Trin.* 6.5.7 (PL 42:928).

32. "For [the bride] it is no mean or contemptible thing to be kissed by the kiss, because it is nothing less than the gift of the Holy Spirit. If, as is properly understood, the Father is he who kisses, the Son he who is kissed, then it cannot be wrong to see in the kiss the Holy Spirit, for he is the imperturbable peace of the Father and the Son, their unshakable bond, their undivided love, their indivisible unity" (Bernard of Clairvaux, *Song of Songs*, sermon 8, no. 2).

33. John Paul II, *Dominum et vivificantem*, no. 10 (AAS 78 [1986], 819).

34. Gregory of Nazianzus, *Or.* 31.15 (PG 36:149).

to us (Rom 5:5), he who hypostasizes the divine communion. Because of who he is in God, the Holy Spirit can sanctify the human being, making human beings become and grow as persons in communion with God.[35] That the Holy Spirit is the gift itself of the communion of the Father and the Son means, in its overabundant offering, that we are constituted as persons.

This superabundant fruit, therefore, does not point to a quantitative feature of divine gratuity. Certainly God translates his infinite triune love within world history also through the uncountable richness and overabundance of the created world and his actions in time. This "quantity," however, is a limited, historical expression of the infinite, never-ending otherness within God and the *perichoretic* relation of the divine persons. "Fruit" refers to God's being love, personal *summa caritas*. The Holy Spirit then is not "fruit" because he is the desired (and so optional and delayed) outcome of the reciprocal love of Father and Son. He is fruit because he eternally proceeds from their mutual love and because he is other than they are. Furthermore, as fruit, he is an expression of life and fullness that is called to be given further. In this regard, we can say with Balthasar that the Holy Spirit's personhood has two dimensions. The first, emphasized by the Latin tradition, considers the Holy Spirit as the one in whom the mutual relationship of Father and Son bears from all eternity its ineffable perfection. Yet, as hinted by Augustine and more fully developed by the Greek tradition, the Holy Spirit is also the ever-fruitful opening of God in himself and outside of himself. "What God has prepared for those who love, God has revealed to us through the Spirit. For the Spirit searches everything, even the depths of God" (1 Cor 2:10). Following Scripture, the Greek Fathers clarify that the Holy Spirit proceeds from the Father through the Son into God's infinity, and thus it can be given to him to communicate God's richness *ad extra*. It is he who reposes on Christ and leads him throughout his existence, and it is he whom the Son sends from the Cross and breathes into the apostles. These two aspects are inseparable: the Holy Spirit is sent out by both the Father and the Son as the confirmation of the Son's return to the Father (Latin aspect), and as the promise of the Father who will never leave mankind (Greek aspect). Balthasar writes that "this double personal aspect—reflection (of the Son to the Father) as love, and emanation (of the Father through the Son) as love—casts a light back onto the essential aspect in which God as Spirit is absolute, self-contained self-possession *and* absolute, poured-out totality of being: as love."[36] The God who is absolute, ever-greater gift is

---

35. Augustine, *Trin.* 15.18.32 (PL 42:1083). See also Basil the Great, *Epistola* 38, no. 4 (PG 32:329).

36. Balthasar, *ET*, 3:107 and 3:117–34; Balthasar, *TL*, 3. Balthasar offers an account of fecundity through the analogy of conception: see Balthasar, *ET*, 3:105–16. See also

one God not only because he is triune, and vice versa—triune because one God. He is also ever-greater tripersonal gift because his unity reveals itself to be overabundant fecundity. In this way, while preserving the hypostases' differences, the Spirit "unifies" God and reveals God to be superabundant, absolute act as gift (Father, Son, Holy Spirit).[37] Let us now examine why it is that because of the Holy Spirit, God is one, absolute, gratuitous gift, and that without him, *per absurdum*, the divine gift would collapse into monadic identity.

3. Divine Memory

Although man recognizes that he is responsible for evil, he also sees that evil is greater than he is, and so he is tempted to locate it somewhere outside of himself (as does Manicheism). The Greek gods had no end of strife, internal wars, and betrayal. Some natural religions grant equal status to good and evil, order and chaos. Some, partially influenced by the Judeo-Christian tradition, perceive God's radical otherness in a way that makes him responsible for evil in history—which, although not necessarily making God evil in himself, leaves the question open. Admittedly, finite human freedom is so determined by biological and historical circumstances that, at times, it seems difficult not to make God the ultimate ground of evil. Nevertheless, do these human limitations and the evil with which human beings are connivent necessarily imply a form of ingratitude in God? Does God really know in himself that irruption of nothingness so familiar to us? Is there a denial of the gift in God?

Looking at the simultaneity of the Father's remaining himself while giving himself totally away, and at the equivalent simultaneity of the Son's reception of himself as the Father's gift while being irreducible to that gift, there remains the question of whether we are neglecting a complete denial of the gift. Is it not the case that the Father's total generosity is undone by the equally absolute grateful reciprocity of the Son? If the Father gives all of himself and the Son reciprocates with the same divine totality, why would

---

Nichols, *Say It Is Pentecost*; J. R. Sachs, "Deus semper major"; Tossou, *Streben nach Vollendung*.

37. This is also why we may speak of each of the divine persons as fruit: "He in God whom we call 'Father,'" Balthasar writes, "is the 'fruit' of his self-giving to the One we call 'Son'; he exists as this self-giving, and the Son exists as receptivity, gratitude, and giving-in-return. Again, this giving-in-return does not close the two persons in on themselves but opens them to the fullness of the 'with' (the 'co-' of 'communion'), which is made absolute in the Spirit who is common to both. Only in this perspective does grace become intelligible" (Balthasar, *You Crown the Year*, 144).

the divine gift not cancel itself out? In other words, does the reception and fruitful reciprocation silence the gift? If the gift is given and received without indetermination or partiality, what is the nature of the enduring permanence of the gift itself—if there is such permanence? Given the totality of the gift, if God's gift were to apply only to the persons of the Father and the Son, could they remain distinct in their reciprocal giving themselves to each other? It seems that if God's gift were only in the persons of the Father and the Son, what we call gift would be nothing but ontological egotism. Without the third hypostasis, the balancing of God's gift in the twofold giving and receiving would mysteriously ground absolute ingratitude. If God were not tripersonal gift, it would be difficult to see why God is and why ingratitude and evil are not rooted in him.

What does the Holy Spirit disclose of the Father and the Son's giving and receiving that establishes God's gift and clears him of the charge of being the ultimate source of ingratitude? Richard of St. Victor can help us grasp what would be missing in God's gift if, *per absurdum*, there were not a Holy Spirit in God's spirit: the "excess" proper to love.[38] Positively stated, the Holy Spirit reveals that the Father and the Son's reciprocal being in each other (differently) is always already ecstatic towards the other because it is always already ecstatic towards a third. Because of this "excess," God is himself a tripersonal, one God, who selflessly takes delight in himself and thus knows himself. Certainly the term "excess" does not introduce a quantitative category. Rather, as Balthasar suggests, it indicates the way that absolute love (*summa caritas*) posits its own difference within itself. The meaning of "excess" becomes clearer when we draw out the economy's intimations of the divine processions. Scripture invites us to see that the Father, who sends "the Son of love" (Col 1:13) out of love for us (Rom 8:32) and who pours his love (Holy Spirit) into our hearts (Rom 5:5), can only eternally beget his Son and cause the Spirit to proceed out of love. In light of Christ's revelation of the God who is love, we understand both God, *ipsum esse subsistens*, and the processions of the Son and the Holy Spirit in terms of love.[39] Let

---

38. Richard of St. Victor, *De Trinitate* 3.7 (PL 196:919D). English translation in Richard of St. Victor, *Twelve Patriarchs*, 371–97. Much of the following reflection on Richard of St. Victor's Trinitarian theology is the fruit of conversation with Professor A. J. Walker. See, among others, Walker, "Personal Singularity."

39. Love, in this sense, is the ground of all divine wisdom and freedom. Balthasar claims that even though thinking about the first procession in terms of the human faculty of knowing and the second in terms of volition (as Augustine and Aquinas propose) or liberality (as Bonaventure indicates) aims at distinguishing the two, it is perhaps more accurate, i.e., less anthropomorphic, to contend that love posits its own difference in itself as excess. Human knowing and loving always presuppose the human substance created out of love, and both knowing and loving require another person in

us consider now the "necessity" of the third person for God to be *summa caritas* (absolute charity).[40]

Richard, following Gregory the Great, explains that *summa caritas* is composed of both *caritas vera* (true charity) and *caritas summa* (absolute charity).[41] Absolute love is the love of a lover (*diligens*) who tends towards another (*dilectus*), who must be equal to him (if love is to be *caritas summa*) and other from him (if love is to be *caritas vera*). If the beloved were not equal in being to the lover, if he were not *condignus*, we would be casting God in the position of one being among others, rather than approaching him as he is, as *supersubstantiale esse*. From another angle, to take the beloved as less in being than the lover would be stopping at God's relation to the world rather than asking about God himself. However, though the *condignus* is granted the same dignity as the lover, if the beloved were not also different from the divine lover, the divine lover would only love himself.[42] This act of love, in which the lover tends to the beloved, does not involve any historical initiative taken by the lover towards the beloved. *Summa caritas* is an eternal act.

In a further dimension, God, *summa caritas*, is not only his giving himself away; he takes delight in doing so. "Delight" refers, far from a passing emotion, to the coming together of loving and knowing. To take delight is to be lovingly aware of oneself and of the other as other from oneself. There is no true love without the awareness of who the other is, but there is no true awareness of the other if the one does not rejoice in loving the other, who remains other while being identical with the lover. To take delight, therefore, is not simply an action that remains in the subject who loves or in the one who is loved. Rather than closing off, delight reveals the union

---

order for there to be love and knowledge in the first place. See Balthasar, *TL*, 2:164–65. The negative connotation that "excess" seems to entail (useless, unreasonable abundance) dissipates when we see that "excess" means "fruitfulness." That said, however, the apparent "negative" connotation of "excess" also defends the reality that God is simply other than the singular. The Holy Spirit, excess of the divine gift, thus hypostasizes the intrinsic total communication of self as the gift of one towards the other that God is.

40. The question regarding the necessity of a third, a Holy Spirit within God in order for God to be God, would be rank human hubris if it grew out of the attempt to justify God's existence from oneself. Such an approach to the question of God's being inevitably reduces God to a finite being or to a being who could be the cause of himself. What we seek instead is to show, on the one hand, that there is no gift until there is a third person in God, and, on the other hand, only because there is a third in God, can God be said to be. The alternative to this position is to ascribe to nothingness a primordial status over being, which, as we saw in the third chapter, is contradicted by what human originary experience reveals of the ontological structure of concrete singulars.

41. Gregory the Great, *Homiliarum in Evangelia* 17.1 (PL 76:1138D).

42. Richard of St. Victor, *De Trinitate* 3.7 (PL 196:919D).

that binds lover and beloved. Delight therefore is the expression of shared communion. If there were no absolute, asymmetrical, reciprocal belonging, that is, if the one did not "exceed" towards the other, we could not speak of absolute delight.

Since *caritas* refers both to the communication of self and to the delight in the other and in being with the other, the beloved has to fully share both the being of the lover and the delight experienced in being loved by another. Otherwise, the beloved would not be *condignus*. "He who is loved," Richard writes, "wants another to be loved as he is loved."[43] In order to be loved as one is loved, that is, in order to be loved as "other" from the lover, the eternal presence of a third is needed. The necessity of a *condilectus*, one who is loved-with, is a radical one. The excess of the two towards a third is required not simply for the sake of a greater love between the lover and the beloved, but in order for this love to be at all. Let us consider this fact more carefully.

If there were only an (absolute) lover and an (absolute) beloved, who without a third could not share the joy of being loved by another, then it would not be clear whether the love of the one for the other and of the other (beloved) for the one (lover) is a gratuitous, pure gift, or a possessive gift. If one could not share the experience of being loved, of taking delight in being loved, then to love the other *completely* would mean either to give oneself to the other to the extent that one would no longer be oneself, or to keep the other all for oneself to the extent that the other would no longer be himself. The absence of the third would keep the relation of the giver and the gift, the lover and the beloved, in a sort of dual egotism. They would either cling to themselves or take turns in annihilating themselves, so to speak, for the sake of the other. Both clinging to oneself and renouncing oneself are expressions of egotism, which, counterintuitively, is a denial of oneself. Since both gratuity and jealousy are considered here in their ontological and not their axiological meanings, there is no question of the purity of intention with which the gift of self is given and received; it is rather a question of the very *nature* of the gift itself. Hence, if there were only two, then what we would have in reality would be two monads dialectically opposed to each other. In that case, one either univocally absorbs the other into oneself, or one equivocally maintains the difference. Only when there is a mutually loved third (*condilectus*) can the lover and the beloved simultaneously and eternally share the fact of being loved by each other without having to deny themselves.

---

43. Richard of St. Victor, *De Trinitate* 3.11 (PL 196:922C).

Let us note, however, that a basic presupposition undergirding the foregoing argument is that it is not the same to love oneself as to be loved by another. Certainly, as human experience witnesses, to love oneself requires another through whom and in whom one becomes aware of oneself and loves oneself. The child becomes aware of himself through the love of the parents, and the presence of the child makes the parents more aware of themselves, their unity, and the gratuitous fruit of their love. Yet, if to love oneself were the same as the experience of being loved by another, then there would be no "self." To say that loving oneself is not the same as being loved by another indicates that one always has to receive himself from the other. To love oneself, or, to use the language we have been using so far, for the receiver not to lose himself in the reception and reciprocation of the gift, there has to be another, different from the giver and the receiver, who shares in the delight of loving and of being loved. We all know that, for instance, when two human lovers do not wish to share what of their love can be shared, their love soon dwindles away. What can be shared can range from simply permitting their common life to be seen in public, to allowing their love to be fruitful. When conjugal intimacy bars fruitfulness a priori, it reveals itself to be an exercise more in solitude than in communion.[44]

What we have just said about human love is so because, *mutatis mutandis*, in *summa caritas* the difference and unity of the *diligens* and *dilectus* are preserved through a third, a *condilectus*.[45] In other words, selfhood exists inasmuch as it is doubly excessive: of each of the persons towards each of the others, and of the mutual self-excess of the lover and the beloved towards a jointly loved third. Father and Son are themselves by tending towards each other *and* by doing so both objectively and subjectively, that is, in terms of fruition. Fruition, thanks to the third, is the apex of both subjectivity *and* objectivity. It is the Holy Spirit who makes it possible for divine love never to be an exclusive self-affirmation (*singularis inveniatur*).[46] Hence, in God there is neither exclusive self-affirmation nor alternating self-denial because the presence of the third allows the delight of being loved by another to be shared by all.

If we think of the relation between the divine persons and the divine *esse*, we can see that the existence of the third secures both the unity and the distinction of the other two. Three persons are needed if we are not to make the divine *esse* into a fourth reality that is fruitful in various persons. The revelation of the third hypostasis prevents us from falling back into

---

44. See Grant, "Faith and the Multiversity," 619–21.
45. Richard of St. Victor, *De Trinitate* 3.15 (PL 196:925B–C).
46. Richard of St. Victor, *De Trinitate* 3.20 (PL 196:928A).

Arianism, that is, from identifying the divine essence with the person of the Father and considering the Son and Holy Spirit ultimately as creatures. How could the divine *esse*-person distinction be maintained without a third who hypostasizes the unity? If the distinction among persons depends on a distinction between persons and the divine *esse* (each enjoys the same divine *esse* differently), then, supposing a personal distinction of *diligens*, *dilectus*, and *condilectus* and an identity of divine *esse*, one of the persons must correspond to the undivided, simple divine *esse*. There is unity according to the essence and plurality according to the existence because in *summa caritas* there is an *amor debitus* (Holy Spirit), that is, a person whose "incommunicable existence" is a giving, an absolute reciprocation without any further return.[47] The Holy Spirit is a giver to whom nothing is to be restituted.[48] Precisely because the Holy Spirit "perfects" the divine love of Father and Son in showing its superabundant, excessive nature, difference in God is theological (i.e., between persons themselves) and not ontological (between persons and being).

That the Holy Spirit permits us to speak of a divine fruition in God's *summa caritas* helps us see further the gratuitous nature of the relation of gift that constitutes the divine persons. This is, in a sense, the ultimate, incomprehensible "miracle" or wonder of being: to take delight in the others—that is, to be lovingly aware and consciously loving of the being of the other persons and of the belonging of each to the others—is to let oneself be in the others, who are both identical to oneself and yet different because of the excessive nature of the divine gift. The Father gives all of himself, says all of himself in his Word, and his Word, as the Spirit witnesses, remains another. The gift gives all of itself and because of this total, simple, ever-greater communication of the self, is always already tri-hypostatic. Both are simultaneously and eternally true: On the one hand, whatever the Father is, the Son is; whatever the Father and the Son are, the Holy Spirit is. On the other hand, they are infinitely (personally) different in their loving relation.

---

47. Richard of St. Victor, *De Trinitate* 4.18-19 (PL 196:941C-943B).

48. Richard of St. Victor, *De Trinitate* 5.16 (PL 196:961B-962B). If the Son images the Father in that with him the Father gives further, excessively, to the Holy Spirit; if the Father has not given in every way until he gives with the Son; the Holy Spirit's lack of giving further to another person (a fourth!) does not make him "less" than the other two. His fruitfulness, before that of sanctifying the human being, is precisely to be the overabundant return of the gift that explores in absolute freedom the depths of God and thus makes God be eternal, ever-new, and gratuitous beginning. Just as the Son, as the image of the Father, is the only one that is *incarnabilis*, so only the Holy Spirit, as the one that confirms without return the generation of the Word, can be sent to communicate through his gifts the life of divine, loving communion that Christ incarnated.

The gratuitous relationality of the one to the other reveals too that, without altering the Trinitarian *taxis*, each person is lover, beloved, and *condilectus*. Speaking of the divine persons in these terms—or in terms of giver, receiver, and gift—allows us to say something that the personal names render difficult to see: the constitution of the persons is always already threefold. Of course, the limit imposed on us by the personal names of the three hypostases also reminds us that the nature of God's gift remains ultimately incomprehensible to us. We can still attempt to describe the mystery of the threefold constitution of the divine persons, preserving their names revealed in Scripture as follows: The Father's love for the Son is fruitful in a third, and, as clarified earlier, the Son and Holy Spirit's reception and reciprocation of the original gift constitute him as Father. The Son's response of love goes both towards the Father (because the Father is absolute love *per se*) and, with the Father, towards the Holy Spirit, with whom he is one with the Father. In fact, as Balthasar contends, following Bonaventure, the Son is image both as noun and as verb. As noun he is Word; he says and is all that the Father is and reveals to him. Yet as verb, the Son images the Father in that he "coexecutes the movement of groundlessly loving self-expression, and does so together with the ground that produces the Logos."[49] The Son's loving response is not only a conversion to the paternal origin from which he ongoingly comes; it is further giving to yet another. Therefore the Son's gift first follows the same direction as the Father's, that is, "outside" of himself towards another, the Holy Spirit. The second direction is towards the Father inasmuch as his very substance "subjectively" coincides completely with that of the Father. Thus, there is never a moment in which the Son's being "from" the Father does not have a "toward" the Holy Spirit, and a "toward" the Father in thankful response.[50] The Holy Spirit reminds them of what his person presupposes, coming from both, and coming from the Father through the Son. The Holy Spirit confirms the original love in bringing the Father's gift (the Son) to the light in total abnegation of himself. What the third hypostasis represents, therefore, is that God's gift "always wills to, indeed, must, give more, in excess of every 'proportionate' measure."[51] The Holy Spirit, to follow Balthasar's pneumatology, is himself the subjective fruit of the love of the Father and the Son because he is a person

---

49. Balthasar, *TL*, 3:152.

50. Ibid., 153.

51. Ibid., 163. Excessive, overabundant gift, as any name for the Holy Spirit, is applicable both to the Holy Spirit and to the other two hypostases.

consubstantial with the Father and the Son. He is also the objective bond of the love of the Father and the Son.[52]

4. Eternal Beginning

We can turn again to our account of the Holy Spirit in terms of the fruit of love in order to examine the permanence proper to the absolute communication of the gift of self of the three hypostases. If through the Holy Spirit we see that God's fruitful unity is an eternally delightful gift of self to himself in another, then eternity is not simply an automatic unfolding of the divine life. This unfolding as gift does not imply an original hesitation on the part of the Father before he gives himself away to the Son and, with the Son, to the Holy Spirit. Rather, if gift is the form of divine unity, God's unity serves as an exegesis of the permanence of his gift. God's life eternally expresses itself through the supreme novelty proper to its gratuitous unity. Let us see first in what sense the Holy Spirit reveals gift to be the form of God's unity, and then consider the eternity proper to the latter.

When the Father gives all of himself to the Son, the total, gratuitous response of the Son does not exhaust the paternal donation, because the Father breathes the Word that says him *anew*. The Son, although of the same substance of the Father, does not reiterate the Father. He is another. Just as there is no Word without the Father whom the Logos images, so there is no Word without the spiritual breath in which it is pronounced. The Word is never without its eventful positivity, so Bruaire contends, because the "eternal event of the advent of the Son" is uttered in and proffered through the Holy Spirit.[53] The Son's expression of the Father can be heard, so to speak,

---

52. Upon this interpretation of the Holy Spirit, Balthasar builds the other connotations of witness: the one who brings us into the whole truth, and the charismatic and pneumatological aspect of the Church. See Balthasar, *TL*, 3:251–411. We need to mention here, unfortunately without being able to develop it, that precisely because absolute love, tripersonal gift, posits its own difference within itself, "the procession *ab utroque, filioque*, is identically of the Father through the Son, in being of the Father for the Son, given that the Son is absolute offering of himself in return" (Bruaire, *EE*, 187). Balthasar explains further that because the Logos images, that is, co-executes the movement of groundlessly loving self-expression along with the Father, and hence the Logos comes from the Father and toward the Holy Spirit, "it becomes an idle debate whether we say that the Father produces the Spirit with the Son (*filioque*) or through the Son (*dia hyiou*), but it is also idle to attempt to define his joint action once again (restrictively) as a single 'principle of spiration'" (Balthasar, *TL*, 2:152–53). Of course, neither Balthasar nor Bruaire pretends that the controversy over the *filioque* is pointless. Rather, they state that it is not as insurmountable as it sometimes seems. See also Balthasar, *TL*, 3:207–18, and Congar, *Je crois*, 695–792.

53. Bruaire, *EE*, 185–86.

thanks to the gratuitous and silent act of gift of the Holy Spirit, the person without name. The discrete existence of God's seal differentiates the Father from the Son. The image of "breath" helps in three ways to lift out the Holy Spirit's role in witnessing to the form of God's being gift. First, breathing is an activity in which all of the air breathed needs to be taken in and let out, more so than in the case of taking in food or drink. It indicates both a constant and a complete dependence—the human person can go on without eating or drinking for a while, but not without breathing. Second, being a total dependence, breath is a synonym for life, which subsists as permanently given to itself, and which in order to be itself needs to receive itself and give itself away. Without the spirit, life ceases to exist. That the Father breathes the Word indicates both the type of unity between the unpreceded giver and the Logos, and that this unity is life itself. Finally, to breathe is a movement of inhaling and exhaling that unifies the organism in itself and with its environment. The Holy Spirit hypostasizes that movement of *exitus* and *reditus* and shows that the unity proper to God unfolds itself in a movement of donation and reciprocation. While in God there is no temporal before or after, there is procession, a coming out from oneself to be oneself in the other who is also identical to oneself. There is also a return to the source. The giving proper to the Holy Spirit (the subjective dimension of the gift, to speak with Balthasar) is "to be that act of being that makes God be."[54] The Father confirms the Son's reception and reciprocation of the gift with the further gift of the Holy Spirit, who, by hypostasizing God's unity, makes God's absolute act be because through him shines forth the fullness of its unity.[55] If the tripersonal movement of gift expresses God's unity, and without unity there is no being, it is the person of the Holy Spirit who fully accounts for God's *esse*.

Since the Father's gift and the Son's gift in response are absolute, what the Spirit can give is not something that either the paternal or the filial donation lacks. Just as the Son says all that the Father gives by being other from him, so the Holy Spirit says *anew* the divine *esse* that both the Father and the Son are. Being the pure memory of the love of the Father and the Son, the Holy Spirit is other from them precisely inasmuch as he represents their common love.[56] As memory, he continuously presupposes the original donation of the Father to the Son and, together with the Son, to the Holy Spirit. By being the eternal memory of the love from which he proceeds, the

---

54. Ibid.

55. Ibid., 152–57.

56. Augustine (and others) attributes "memory" to the person of the Father. See, e.g., *Trin.* 15.7 (PG 42:1065–67).

Holy Spirit sheds the light he receives and exposes, so to say, both the greatness of the paternal giving and the greatness of the Son of the Father's love. Thus, as memory, the Holy Spirit attests to the Son's gratuitous response to the Father's love while remaining anonymous. The Holy Spirit's anonymity, as Scripture describes it, is not simple self-concealment—an egotistic denial of self—but rather letting the Son and the Father be in each other.[57] The Holy Spirit's "secret" reveals the ecstatic superabundance of the gift.

As memory, the Holy Spirit's attestation of the love from which he proceeds refers back to the origin of his procession and forward to the divine eternal future. He refers to God's eternal, ever-fruitful "past" and to the unfailing, "future" donation. He "searches everything, even the depths of God" (1 Cor 2:10), and opens up towards God's ever-new eternal future. The Holy Spirit is memory because he witnesses *anew* to the past and attests the future *anew*. Human reasoning gropes unsuccessfully in this most beautiful and ungraspable terrain. Limping ahead one step at a time, one must speak of a before and an after where there is never any chronological succession. Nevertheless, since eternity is the fullness of man's historical time, rather than a denial of it, we can now see what our meditation on the Holy Spirit suggests for the understanding of eternity: the permanence of the divine gift, its eternity, is the novelty that is proper to the identity of the divine gift. By uniting the persons while maintaining their distinction, the Holy Spirit witnesses that each divine hypostasis is the same God while being utterly different from each other. The Holy Spirit reveals that there is absolute being (*summa caritas*) rather than nothing because God's gift *is his eternal, ever-fruitful beginning*.

That God is his eternal, ever-fruitful beginning does not mean that he represents the beginning of the world or the beginning of himself from an immemorial decision (Schelling). Nor is God the starting point of a history that will never take place. He is absolute act-love. There is no history in God, neither the beginning nor the end that characterize the concrete singular gift. God is not an undetermined ground that at a certain moment decides for his own existence. The divine *esse* is not an act of a divine freedom that, preceding his own nature, chooses his own divine essence among different patterns. That God is himself a tripersonal gift does not mean that he is the

---

57. "Divine fatherhood and sonship," says Rossetti, "exist only *Spiritu* (absolute ablative), that is, in total *perichoresis* and correlativity: The Holy Spirit is love personalized who proceeds as Witness and Glorification of the encounter of the Two. He does not identify himself with the love of the Father or with the love of the Son, he is rather reciprocal love. If active spiration is the *perichoresis* that is common to the Father and the Son; passive spiration is the Holy Spirit as intradivine personal *perichoresis* that *witnesses* (and here is where his activity resides) to the Father's paternally being in the Son and the Son's filial being in the Father" (Rossetti, "La perichoresi," 568).

cause of himself. He does not bring himself out from nothingness. Instead, God *is*, because he is nothing but eternal beginning, an unpreceded beginning that expresses itself *anew* in a Word in which he is, which exists only in the one who utters it, a reciprocal *indwelling* where the Holy Spirit fruitfully seals the unity of two who remain eternally other from each other. The third hypostasis, remembering the gratuitous donation, binds and opposes one to the other by letting the one be in the other. "Beginning," therefore, indicates that God's being is always the same and always new.

We usually think of novelty as a certain point at which something takes place that had never happened before. We esteem novelty as the arrival of what was not previously there or as the retrieval of what was lost. Instead, novelty in God pertains to this beautiful and ungraspable mystery: in their essential identity, the persons remain always different from each other. Divine novelty, that mystery we seek under the image of "eternal, ever-fruitful beginning," is the paradoxical unity of identity and difference. If evil, as we saw, is the sheer, ungrateful identity of the one seeking only itself, novelty instead reveals the positivity of the divine "not." That the Son, though *homoousios* with the Father, is not the Father and that the Holy Spirit, though *homoousios* with the Father and the Son, is neither the Father nor the Son, means that the ever-same God is ever-new. Evil, not God, lives a monotonous reiteration of the same. As ever-the-same and ever-new, God holds an eternity of surprises for himself. He is an ever-new fountain of life.[58]

If our acquaintance with time, our experience of being's positivity, and the revelation of God's being as absolute charity lead to our understanding of the triune God as an eternal, ever-fruitful beginning, God's *eternal* being also causes us to reconsider our perception of the meaning of "presence." The divine simultaneity of giving, receiving, and giving in excess is always "present" to itself. Yet, again, "present" is neither "this instant" nor the modern reduction of the person to monadic self-consciousness that results in consciousness as total, unmediated self-transparency. This idea of self-consciousness yields only infantilism as the mature form of the self. Contrary to every created singular that begins without having given its own permission, God is eternal beginning in the impenetrable tripersonal unity

---

58. "The Father who speaks and the Word who listens to the Father," writes Ulrich, "hold an eternity of surprises for each other, an eternally new, eternally youthful fountain of life: the personal *we-form* [*Wir-Gestalt*] of love's *unity* of life and death in Father *and* Son. This overflowing mutuality of the love of both we call 'Spirit'" (Ulrich, "Unity of Life," 102). To clarify what could be misleading in this passage it is important to know that, as he indicates, "life and death" is an image "that, like all images, is unequal to expressing the mystery" (ibid., 99). The unity is of wealth (the undiminished plenitude of the divine life) and poverty (the emptying-out of self). For an account of "surprise," see López, "Eternal Happening."

and distinction of the gift of self to itself. Although only the Father is unpreceded origin, God's beginning is triune. There is no moment at which the Father did not have a Son and in which their persons were not always already united and kept distinct by the Holy Spirit, the person-joy. In this sense, therefore, and unlike the concrete singular, the Son and the Holy Spirit take full part in God's eternal beginning. God alone is fully present to himself because he is ever-new beginning: constantly revealing and giving himself to himself in unpronounceable ways. It is always the same absolute gift that is always new.

The human being cannot bring himself into unity with himself and others. As we saw, rather than fulfilling the task for which he was created—to recognize God's ever-greater wholeness, being, and the world as gift—man rejected the original donation that constantly gives him to himself. The unity with himself, others, the world, and God that he now seeks has to be given to him. Certainly, "present" and "beginning" are limited, human categories that attempt to express what no human speech can utter. Nevertheless, in light of the triune God, time's "distention" and "recollection" (past, present, and future) are indeed an image of God's way of being: just as the Holy Spirit confirms that each divine person is himself with and in the other, so the human being is present to himself only through the twofold movement of receiving himself from the permanent source and returning to it by entrusting himself to others. The search for novelty reveals that attachment to the source, and not the ungrateful rejection of that source, offers the possibility finally for man to be himself while enjoying the ever-new confirmation of his own being. The permanence of the gift of God's being, the eternal and ever-fruitful beginning of divine unity, is the first aspect that the Holy Spirit reveals of the gratuity of the gift. We can now turn to look further into the novelty of God's gratuitous being.

5. The Gratuity of the Divine Gift

It can seem more apposite to speak of the gratuity of the gift when the issue at stake is God's relation with the world rather than God's own being. We would thus need to elucidate that God's gift is gratuitous because, in both the creation and the redemption of the world, there is nothing in the singular that coerces God's attention. It is always the divine initiative that wanted to create the world in and for Christ and to bring it into the Triune communion through the Father's two hands. God loves the world gratuitously, brings it into being, and goes to the utmost to educate man to his and the world's liberating truth: belonging to God and dwelling in God (John 14:2).

Important as this is, however, here we will focus more specifically on the sense in which gratuity pertains to God's own being. It could seem apt to consider God's original gratuity in terms of freedom from coercion, rather than in relation to evil and the truth of the gift as we attempted to do in the previous sections. While gratuity does have to do with the nature of freedom, there are two poles to avoid. First, an unreflected understanding of freedom and necessity cannot be transposed onto an absolute being that is its own eternal and ever-fruitful beginning. This refers back to our earlier comments that freedom is adherence to being, rather than the capacity to choose from among different possibilities, and that "reason" does not refer to the technological manipulation of data but to the capacity to contemplate in wonder being's inexhaustible wholeness: a grasping within being grasped. Second, any reflection on divine gratuity founders if it is framed within a dialectic of necessity and freedom. It is well known that the psychological model of the two processions in God defines the procession of the Son as by way of nature and that of the Holy Spirit as by way of will (*voluntas*) or liberality (*liberalitas*). Yet, as Balthasar rightly wonders, is it possible to circumscribe liberality to only one procession if God has revealed himself as love? Balthasar contends that if God is love, then both processions are simultaneously by nature and by liberality. Due to "a recapitulation of the nature-based processions in the divine freedom that goes to their very origin," there is neither "ontic priority of mere necessity over divine freedom" nor "arbitrary exercise of will; God is beyond the terms 'necessity' and 'freedom.'"[59] If, rather than asking whether the Father is free or constrained to give all of himself to the Son, and with and through him to the Holy Spirit, we recall that God is a spirit who exists always already as a triune gift, then the question regarding the gratuity of the gift *in God* opens up to four different aspects.

Our methodology remains the same as established earlier: reflection on the immanent Trinity takes its bearings from the economy. It is by looking at Christ's incarnation of charity, and at what the Church is given to experience through the Holy Spirit, that we can indicate some elements of God's ever-fruitful mystery. Undoubtedly, God's love for man is creative, redemptive, and nuptial. Yet these different aspects of divine love for man are God's communication of and a participation in his own love and thus offer to man a real entryway to this ever-greater, divine love. Leaving for later a reflection on the meaning of the unity in each man and of man with God that the Father's love regenerates, we can focus here on the purity proper to divine love, a purity of which God's redeeming act is the expression. Since

---

59. Balthasar, *TL*, 3:163.

the restoration of the concrete singular gift consists in bringing the human being closer to his own original divine likeness, it is possible to ground analogically in God what the love within absolute love, the Holy Spirit, permits redeemed human beings to taste.[60]

The first aspect of gratuity is the *unity* and *fecundity* proper to the gift, which was examined in the previous section. Paradoxically, it is the very necessity of the third hypostasis that secures divine gratuity. Divine unity is radically uncalled-for; it is utter gratuity, precisely because the unity of the divine origin is the Father's absolute gift of himself to the Son, the Son's reception of the gift and return to the Father that always includes the direction towards the Holy Spirit, and the Holy Spirit's unifying memory as the excessive fruit. Divine, tri-hypostatic unity is never a Fichtean self-identity but an eventful, eternal identity whose existence is gratuitous because the Holy Spirit proves the selflessness of the Father and Son's love. The gratuitous nature of the tri-hypostatic gift does not therefore reside in its capacity to be what it is or to determine itself to be something altogether different. The intratrinitarian processions viewed under the light of gift does not mean that the Father generates the Son because he so wills it, or that their spiration of the Holy Spirit could have happened otherwise—these still presuppose a concept of freedom as "choice." Gratuity in the God who is absolute love does not mean arbitrariness. Instead, the gift that constitutes the unity of the absolute spirit is utterly free precisely because it gives *and* because it receives and reciprocates the gift of itself completely, that is, according to the "ever-greaterness" unique to God's *Trinitas*. Gratuity is a personal unity not because it is undetermined or because it determines itself through some sort of historical process, but because it is always already hyper-determinate as tripersonal gift. Because of the relationship between gratuity and fecundity, the unity of the triune gift is to let oneself be in another as other, a triune letting-be that reveals itself as an ever-new and eternally delightful indwelling.

Second, if the nature of finite freedom is to recognize that God is everything, and if, as we saw, this recognition is also adherence to being, then in God, who remains *semper maior*, divine gratuity reveals something of the mystery of *recognition* of the other persons' wholeness, a knowing oneself in and through the other. The recognition of the three hypostases is the expression in each one of God's one will and one mind. "The recognition in God," says Giussani, "is given by the Son. . . . The mirror of the Father is the Son,

---

60. The present section offers therefore the ultimate ground of what was earlier elucidated as the nature of freedom and of reason (chs. 3 and 1). The aspects of gratuity indicated here are considered also in light of the numerous essays of Giussani on the meaning of Christian charity.

the infinite Word, and from within the infinite and mysterious perfection of this recognition—in which vibrates for us the infinite and mysterious beauty of being's Origin, that is of the Father (*Splendor Patris*)—the mysterious creative potency of the Holy Spirit proceeds."[61] Gratuitous freedom is pure, wonder-full recognition of each of the persons by the other two.

"Recognition" is the obverse side of the absolute spirit's self-revelation. In giving himself to the Son and the Holy Spirit, the Father reveals himself; he lets himself be known. The Father is always already revealed to the Son; he communicates to him all that he is, and the Son hears and receives all. This revelation is always already given with and through the Son to the Holy Spirit, who freely explores the depths of God and lets the Word of God be breathed forth. In this regard, to "recognize" does not consist in "looking at" another "individual." It is to know the other person and oneself in being known by the other as other. This knowing oneself in and through the other hypostases is perfect *perichoretic* indwelling without approximation or lacuna. The three persons' absolute knowledge is inexhaustible in that it contemplates the whole of the other person in his ineffable inseparability from the other two persons. If the recognition of true human lovers is the unity in which each consents to be defined by the other in their reciprocal and prior being given to each other, how much more is this true for God who is *summa caritas*?

God is not an eternal past. Although everything has always already been given, the revelation of the three persons is not coincident with an "already known." Since what is given by each divine person is the whole of the divine being, knowledge of each person is both an eternally already having known *and* the always-new, inexhaustible recognition of each other. As the role of the Holy Spirit makes clear, each divine person remains distinct from the other two in a perfect unity with them and is thus the one God anew. To recognize is a grasping of the other within a being-grasped. In God, this "grasping" takes the form of selfless gift, in which one "exceedingly" inclines towards the other two. It is thus a threefold affirmation of each other, an expression of love. This circularity of knowing and loving directs us back to the mystery that the persons are themselves only in their relations with each other. From the point of view of donation, "knowing" is the subsisting of that relation of giving, receiving, and confirming everything, even as everything has always been given, received, and confirmed.

The recognition proper to the divine persons, as Jesus discloses it, is a grateful wonder at the eternal, ever-new donation of one to the other. Balthasar writes that "when Jesus says to the Father 'all that is thine is mine,

---

61. Giussani, *USD*, 19–20.

and mine is thine' (John 10:17) we see that in each of the persons are things that are peculiar to them. But, even that which is the foundation of the Persons as such is common to all of them, and they know this communion in the Holy Spirit."[62] To recognize the other, in God, is therefore absolute "freedom": to acknowledge the other is to receive all that he gives, his very self, and to give in return. It is thus being with the other and in the other. Thanks to the Holy Spirit, the free recognition of the divine hypostases is gratuitous; it is the knowing of a revelation that is an eternal and unfathomable giving of the one to the other two. Rooted in this giving, divine knowing is the purely free and eternal allowing oneself to be known and welcomed by the other. In a way mysterious to us, in giving himself over to the Son the Father does not impose himself on the Son; that is, he reveals himself without claiming a return. The true gift of self gives itself without remainder, without any claim to a response. At the same time, since, as we saw earlier, there is also a sense in which divine *agape* includes a yearning (*eros*), the absence of a "claim" does not mean the giver's indifference to the other's response but that he does not impose his own expectations. The divine unity of *eros* and *agape* is eternal because, on the one hand, there is no before or after—everything is always already given and gratuitously reciprocated—and, on the other hand, what is given is all of God's overabundant and ever-fruitful love. Balthasar says in this regard that the Son, in awe at the gift of the Father, always already responds to the Father, with the same yet personally different overabundance of the original gift. So it is with the Holy Spirit, who, by being the person-gift, "surprises" with his absolute freedom the original dual gift that he binds together. There is nothing mechanical or "acquired" in the persons' eternal recognition of each other in God. It is all both already given and eternally new.[63] Gratuitous recognition is tripersonal transparency to the original flow of the gift in its excessive nature.[64]

62. Balthasar, *TD*, 5:89–90. Here Balthasar cites von Speyr, *Farewell Discourses*, 328–29.

63. Man's dramatic relation with God, as exemplified in the history of the main figures of the Old Testament, and then intensified with Jesus's claim to divinity, is hence rooted in this ineffably free threefold donation of God's being.

64. As von Speyr writes: "Thanks is the first declaration of this love which has come to be. The Father wishes to beget the Son and expects him to be as he wants him to be. And in coming forth, the Son perfectly fulfills the Father's expectation from the outset, so that the Father feels bound to him in gratitude from that first moment. . . . And yet at that moment when he is before the Father it is as though the Son has exceeded the Father's boldest expectations. For he is not a lifeless replica but a living Thou. . . . And the Spirit so fulfills and overfills the expectations of the Father and the Son that they see more in him than they looked for: In him they experience a totally unsuspected proof of their love. So they are bound to him in gratitude, just as he is to them" (von Speyr, *World of Prayer*, 29–32).

The third characteristic of gratuity is *availability*. Eternal gratitude, the ever-present form of divine *agape*, implies a dynamic, ever-new being for the other. It is not an idle possibility that needs to be actualized but a readiness that is always already communicated anew. Since the divine giving is also the eternal positing of the divine persons, a Trinitarian life of communion, the divine giving is coincident with a never-ending readiness of one for the other. If, as Aquinas explains, the divine missions of the Son and the Holy Spirit are an expression in history of their eternal processions, their being sent indicates a prior holding of themselves at the disposal of the other divine persons. God is an absolute, ever-fruitful love that expresses the same will and the same mind in three persons. The grateful readiness for the other takes place according to the specific properties of each divine person.[65] This divine availability does not mean, of course, that we can consider the three divine hypostases as three separate selves that agree on a specific action or way of being. It rather highlights the mystery that to the Father's eternal giving of himself there corresponds an eternal, grateful response of the Son, a "reciprocity" that overflows in the Holy Spirit's gratitude. This lack of jealousy makes it possible for the Logos to empty himself and take the form of a servant (Phil 2:7). It is the opposite of Spinoza's static divine substance: the divine interplay of gift is a divine *life* in which the one subsists with and for the others according to what is specific to each divine person.

Christ's human experience of his divine filiation sheds light here, too, as a confirmation of our human existence in explicating "availability" as the coincidence of freedom and obedience. The two together show that the availability to receive and reciprocate the gift represents the fulfillment of one's own being (*esse*). The existence of the concrete singular gift follows a divine plan, not one designed by the human being. The human person, as concrete singular, receiving the gift of being that constitutes him, seeks in love the fulfillment of the promise contained in the gift that unfolds itself according to God's plan. As recounted in Scripture, the greatness of a human being—as in, for example, Abraham or Mary—resides precisely in the utter readiness for God; that is, his or her availability to receive what God gives, when he gives it and as he gives it, without worrying too much about what and how God is going to give the following day. Availability is the gratuitous response to God's love. It is a response that seeks without demanding what God gives. God, however, does not obey an outside plan, nor is there in

---

65. With regard to God's action in history, we can say that since the Son, as image, is the expression of the Father, he is the only one who can be incarnated. Since the Holy Spirit is bond and fruit, it is he who can gather humankind into the body of Christ so that human beings may experience from within the love of the Father, who will not stand man's rejection.

him any movement from a free offering to an obedient reception. Rather, in God, "availability" is eternal readiness for God's own ineffable glory. This readiness, the willingness for all of what the other, principally the Father, might want, does not mean that God has his own history to construct or that the triune God is the perfect symphony of three distinct wills. God *is* his own glory. Yet, at the same time, since the glory is the radiance of the Father that freely reflects itself in the Son and shines further in the Holy Spirit, it exists only as this threefold self-communication. God exists as the ever-new affirmation of his own triune glory. This divine "yes" to himself— the eternal, triune affirmation of himself, which is also the ultimate ground for anthropological availability—is such an overabundant affirmation that it is itself the root of the creation and redemption of the world.[66] The eternal presence of the Holy Spirit confirms that the triune God lives in an exuberant "yes" to himself that is always already given. Thus, the divine triune "yes" is not the choice of one option among many, but the sheer enjoyment of being in, for, and from the other. Divine availability for his own glory does indicate a personal difference in God. Yet "detachment" in God, as we saw with respect to Christ's virginal way of loving, is not an expression of distance but of absolute "proximity": what the Father is, the Son is, and what they are, the Holy Spirit is. Availability for his own glory is the utter and never-ending fruition of his own *perichoretic* communion.

The last characteristic of gratuity, the one that mysteriously binds the other three together, is *prayer*. Gratuitous donation is also prayer because prayer is the total, ever-new abandonment of oneself to the other. As with the other characteristics of gratuity—unity and fecundity, recognition, and availability—so here access to the meaning of prayer is offered by divine revelation itself. It is helpful to revisit the place of prayer in Christ's existence: Christ encourages his followers to pray constantly to the Father just as he does (Luke 11:1–11, 18:1–8); he spends nights in prayer (Luke 6:12); and he intercedes for man with the Father (John 17). He also prays for himself at Gethsemane (Mark 14:32–42) and at Golgotha (Mark 15:34). He teaches his disciples to pray to his Father, extending his sonship to them (Matt 6:9–15), and sends the Holy Spirit so that those who welcome him may pray in the Spirit of the Father to the Father who is rich in mercy (Rom 8:15, 26–27).

---

66. "The Father's love which goes out toward the Son, is the basis of all the effects of love that God imparts to creatures; so too the Holy Spirit, who is the love of the Father for the Son, is also his love for the creature, since he imparts his perfection to it. So the procession of love can be regarded in two ways: insofar as it goes out to an eternal Beloved (and thus it is an eternal procession), and insofar as it is love for a created beloved . . . , and so it is termed a temporal procession, since, because of the new effect, the creature acquires a new relation to God" (Aquinas, *I Sent.*, d. 14, q. 1, a. 1, sol.).

We should not circumscribe Christ's prayer to the historical perimeters of the Incarnation. Scripture, in fact, indicates that Christ's intercession for humankind does not cease after the ascension. If Christ is the high priest (Heb 10:21) who enters into the Father's presence on our behalf (Heb 9:24), his prayer to the Father (John 17:20–24) is said eternally. Thanks to his mediation, the Holy Spirit is sent. For the Holy Spirit to allow us to see the icon of the Father's love means also to allow us to pray. We can thus speak anew to God and address him as Father. "God the Father has sent the Spirit of his Son into our hearts, crying: 'Abba, Father!'" (Gal 4:6). The Holy Spirit, never separated from the prayer of the Son, allows the human being to pray and, in time, to become prayer, an ever-grateful entrusting of oneself to God that continually longs for an intensification of what one has already received.

Christ's desire (*thelo*) that those whom the Father has given him should be with him where he is, that they may behold the glory the Father gave him before the foundation of the world (John 17:24), is an expression of God's own asking. The God who reveals himself in Christ is not only a God who listens. He is a God who asks. God, through the archangel Gabriel, asks the Virgin Mary to receive him (Luke 1:28–38). Once he takes on flesh, Jesus Christ asks man to believe in him (Luke 18:8; John 14:1–11). As the prayer of the second hypostasis, Christ's offering of himself is not simply a "human act" pertaining to his human nature. The circularity between the *imago Dei* in the human being and the person of the Logos, for whom and in whom the human being is created, points to the mystery that there is prayer in God. Of course, divine prayer is devoid of the creaturely, fearful supplication that characterizes human entreaty. Had he been a mere man, Christ would never have dared to address God as "Abba." If God takes a risk in asking man to believe in him because he wishes to be gratuitously welcomed rather than simply obeyed, it is because prayer is not foreign to him. The donation of love that defines God's being, as Jesus Christ's historical existence suggests, is an ongoing dialogue.[67]

That there is prayer in God—or rather, since in him there are no accidents, that God is prayer—does not mean that in him three different volitions are morally united. God, who is a communion of persons, has only one will and one mind (*nous*). Yet, since he is a tri-hypostatic spirit (*pneuma*), each of the persons enjoys the one will and one mind according to what is

---

67. The human being, as Bruaire says, knows of a speech about God (theology, philosophy) and for God (apologetics). He also knows of a speech to God (human prayer). Yet all are possible because God, as pure, threefold act, is nothing but an eternal conversation. Bruaire, *L'affirmation de Dieu*, 229–52. Bulgakov also speaks beautifully about this in *Comforter*, 371–77. The present account of prayer is also partly indebted to Bulgakov's study.

proper to each. Christ's priestly prayer gives a glimpse into the unfathomable content of prayer in God himself. "If you then, who are evil, know how to give good gifts to your children, how much more will the heavenly Father give the Holy Spirit to those who ask him!" (John 11:23). Teaching his disciples how to pray, Christ insists that the Father, in his unending goodness, will send the Holy Spirit, the giver of all gifts. Recalling that the Holy Spirit is the person-love, in whom the Father and the Son are united and who is himself the overabundant fruit of that love, we see that prayer asks precisely for love, a love that is also truth and light. The Holy Spirit will come and, by indwelling man's heart, will allow him to experience (see and taste) the Father's love. Jesus's priestly prayer to the Father spells this out further for us. At the heart of his prayer is the recognition that the Father has put all things at his disposal and that whatever is the Father's is also the Son's, and vice versa (John 17:10). In this unity, which we now know is hypostasized in the Holy Spirit, the Father gives everything to the Son: the divine nature and the whole world. The recognition of this unity is the expression of the gratitude proper to the divine love. This love that Christ gives to those whom the Father has called enables the disciples to see in him the Father's face. Christ has kept them in the Father's name and he wishes the Father to let them abide in it (John 17:11). Love grants knowledge. It enables those who indwell it to believe in God and in his love, that is, to recognize it as everything and to entrust themselves to it without fear. To pray for love is to pray for the bestowal of love and to be brought into knowing (John 17:25). When Christ prays to the Father for their love to be communicated to his disciples, he asks him to extend the divine unity to those who, weakened by sin, have rejected him. The content of prayer is to communicate love and to grow in the unity proper to it: "that they may be perfectly one (*teteleiomenoi*)" (John 17:23). Christ's priestly prayer, asking for the Spirit to be sent to those who believe in him and who will come to believe in him after his ascension, seeks for the divine glory to be communicated to them. Christ came to manifest the Father's name (John 17:6–26) in order to extend his glory to humankind (John 17:23).

Since God exists only and always as a tri-hypostatic gift, the giving and receiving proper to his divine nature cannot but be coincident with, for lack of a better word, asking for and speaking in gratitude that infinite love that is eternally given. Since God reveals himself as gift in the person of the Holy Spirit, it is possible to make both statements: love gives ever-more love and also asks for this ever-more love. God's triune entreaty, to whose boundlessness the Holy Spirit attests, has nothing to do with our fear of death or with our not being the origin of ourselves. God's gift is free of both ingratitude and origin in another. In recognition of the totality of the Father's gift, and at his disposal as we saw, the divine overabundant gratitude always "asks" more of itself. This asking, again, is not due to a lack in the giving or to concealed plans or secrets, but to the ever-greaterness proper to the Father's total gift of self, which is revealed to us through his two hands. If Christ asks that those who believe in him might behold (*theorosin*) the glory that the Father has given him since the beginning, it is because eternal life is this threefold, incomprehensible, and delightful beholding of the other as other (person) and as identical (*esse*) to oneself. As self-offering and sharing of oneself, prayer in God, if it is permitted to use this seemingly inappropriate term for God's dialogue, points to the unique, loving relation with the other as other. Divine triune being is unfathomable, gratuitous life because the permanence of the gift unfolds as dialogue, as an ever-greater entrusting of one to the other.

The Father sent the Son and with him he sends the Spirit so that he may hear his own divine, triune gratitude resonate in a human voice. He went to the utmost to enable men and women to dwell in a unity, where everything is shared without loss or denigration, in a dwelling place where the human being is purely available for God's eternal glory. The one triune God, being ever the same and ever new, extends to the human being his own fruitfulness and wipes away the lie brought about by finite ingratitude.

VII. The Unexpected Gift

WE HAVE APPROACHED THE circularity of being and gift by saying that whereas gift indicates the unity of being, unity points to the permanence of the gift. The inseparability of the gifted unity of being from the question of time arose through the examination of the gratuity of the gift: the entryway to the meaning of being's time and eternity. Pondering God's own gratuity revealed that the tri-hypostatic being is one precisely because God is eternal, ever-fruitful beginning. Eternity is the tri-hypostatic gift that is simple, perfect, self-subsistent, and ever-fruitful beginning. We also arrived at the relation between being and time that is proper to the concrete singular by way of the gratuity that constitutes it as finite gift. Pondering both the mystery of birth and the singular's specific gift-ness, which is reflected in the ontological difference between *esse* and essence, led us to the dynamic nature of the present and the relation between being and time. The concrete singular discovers the present as its being permanently given to itself, tending towards the reception of the future gift of being with all the richness of its own past.

Their similarities notwithstanding, the permanence of God's being-gift is different from that of the concrete singular. The unity of the latter is gratuitous not because it is its own beginning, but because the permanence of its own being is given to it. The being that constitutes the creature is simple and complete, but non-subsistent. Creaturely gift is indeed totally given to itself. Yet, unlike the Logos, creaturely gift is given without return precisely in its being finite. The concrete singular's finitude, rather than a failed infinity, is an ongoing participation in God's eternal beginning. We also saw a further difference. Whereas in God there is no degree of rejection of the gift, and the reception of the gift is absolute and eternal, the human concrete singular knows an original rejection of the gift and sees in death a seeming barrier to a future donation. He is thus called to receive and reciprocate the gift of his own being within an original ingratitude, an original fall. Although the "original" ingratitude does not annihilate the singular's created positivity, it does, however, affect the singular's reception and reciprocation of the gift at the level of both first and second act. Through his ingratitude, the concrete singular regularly stifles the reception and reciprocation of the gift. The twofold difference between the triune God and the concrete singular makes it impossible for the latter to confirm the gift of his own being. Not being his own origin, he must be confirmed by his source. Man's rejection of the original gift cast him and all the cosmos into an ontological and axiological fragmentation, and the original unity is beyond his grasp to recover. The confirmation of the gift of being that secures the unity of the concrete singular must, then, overcome rejection from within. The present chapter is therefore dedicated to the study of the unity of the concrete singular, that is, of the participation of his temporal being in eternity.

The constantly desired unity of the singular being—understood always within the communion of beings in which he comes to be and remains in existence—with the eternal God must be gratuitous, on both ontological and soteriological grounds. Gratuity does not only lead us to the meaning of time; it also illuminates time as the dynamic proper to gratuitousness. It is true that the concrete singular gift is given fully to himself and that his being contains the promise of a further donation. Yet this further giving cannot be deduced from the singular's being, nor can it be imposed on the original giver. If the singular could claim to dwell independently in being, if he could determine from himself the confirmation of the gift of his own being, based on having irrevocably been given to be, this claim of unity would actually bring about the disappearance of his own self. Since gift is the form of unity, the concrete singular cannot be himself if he does not gratuitously receive and reciprocate the gift of being. The concrete singular is thus called to wait for the gratuitous renewal of the gift of being. As indicated, it is also the case that the original rejection of the finite gift introduced death into history and elicited in the concrete singular the realization of the need to receive the confirmation of the gift, should it be given. Nevertheless, just as its ontological precariousness cannot be willed away, so the restoration of unity is not effected by longing for it. The concrete singular cannot eliminate his own ingratitude. The enduring unity with itself, the world, and God that the concrete singular gift awaits, without having a claim to it, is given *gratis*, if it is to be at all.

It is not only the historical and ontological condition of the concrete singular that requires the gratuity of the singular's redemption, his permanent participation in the eternal, divine life. God's own gifted unity also demands it. On the one hand, the offering of the transfiguring and divine love in and through Jesus Christ, who sends the Holy Spirit along with the Father, is the unforeseeable, unmerited, and surprising denial of man's claim to be everything for himself. It is a radically uncalled-for gift. On the other hand, the offering of this unexpected gift is the fruit of the Father's eternally faithful giving. The confirmation is gratuitous precisely because it is both unwarranted gift and faithful, divine giving. God's faithfulness, being its own eternal, ever-new beginning, surprises the concrete singular with its own unfathomable, ever-fruitful spontaneity and rejects the singular's ungrateful response. God deals mercifully with the concrete singular. He gives anew; he for-gives.

Before we explore the meaning of this unexpected gift, the final unity of being and time in eternity, a semantic clarification is in order. The theological term "mercy" is often reduced through frequent usage to the simple, ontological perpetuation of final existence beyond the singular's death or to a forgiveness that is owed to the concrete singular who repents. Mercy, instead, is a radical novelty, whose novel character resides in its unexpected capacity to fulfill what was originally given. The fact that Jesus Christ's existence has made mercy visible to us does not mean that it ceases to be a mystery. On the contrary, Jesus Christ's deeds reveal mercy's apophatic nature. Giussani, who, like John Paul II, speaks extensively and with a unique profundity on the meaning of mercy, writes that "mercy is the victory over the spirit's death, over man's denial. The vastness of this word, the borders to which it draws us, cannot be thought by us."[1] On his own the concrete singular can neither conceive nor enact the "gift" we refer to with the term "mercy." Mercy is neither a human idea nor a personal capacity. Just as virginity is not a form of love that the singular draws from his own resources, so mercy is not a form of love and time at the disposal of the human being. If the original creative donation is a totally uncalled-for gift, so the gift's renewal (mercy)—inasmuch as it is the restoration of unity and hence a new relation with oneself, God, and the world—is a rebirth that takes place only on the path that leads to the resurrection through the narrow door of the Cross (John 3:1–21). Giussani indicates that the term "mercy" is identical to mystery; it is a synonym for God.[2] In this regard, he contends that "mercy is not a human word. Inasmuch as it communicates itself to man's experience, mercy is identical to the Mystery from which everything comes,

---

1. Giussani, *La libertà di Dio*, 40. To emphasize the apophatic nature of this term, Giussani rhetorically suggests removing it from human vocabulary. See, e.g., Giussani, *Avvenimento di libertà*, 55.

2. To illuminate the relationship between the ontological and theological reflection on gift and the concept of mercy, we will refer to the works of John Paul II and Giussani, though without claiming to give an exhaustive presentation of what either author means by mercy. For a fine and broad introduction to this theme with an abundant bibliography, see Laffitte, *Le pardon transfiguré*.

by which everything is sustained, and in which everything ends."[3] Mercy, in its essence, describes the event through which God introduces the human being into the eternal truth of being. As such, mercy reveals a new depth of God's mysterious charity, which we have indicated up to this point with the ternary *agape*, *eros*, and *koinonia*: God's never-ending power to affirm the other, to let it be itself in union with him. God's total humility, expressed in the kenotic obedience of Christ unto death on the Cross, is, at the same time, the expression of love's sheer, inexorable power. Only this power, which wove time together with eternity, can reconcile the diastasis that man's ingratitude wedged between them. Mercy therefore reveals that divine charity "is a Mystery according to which every one of our measures and imaginations is burst open."[4] To the ultimately banal illusion of existing from himself, which forces man into a perpetually self-defeating logic of power and hatred, God incomprehensibly responds with an affirmation of the singular that renews the unity of the gift. Mercy unveils and confirms the ultimate positivity of the concrete singular because it allows the singular freely to embrace and dwell in the eternal, triune gift. Precisely because mercy is a divine prerogative, it is also a thoroughly human love that, when encountered in history, elicits the desire to conform oneself to it.

To speak of the permanence of the gift-ness of the concrete singular, that is, the unity of its own being-gift in its relation with the divine source, it is not enough to ponder its ongoing participation in being, as we attempted in the second chapter. It also calls for considering its definitive and gratuitous participation in the eternity of being. Mercy, as the final confirmation of the finite gift, has therefore theological, ontological, and soteriological dimensions. From the point of view of the triune God, the confirmation of the singular's being is a communication of his eternal love made possible by the mystery of gift in God himself, according to which God is eternally the same and eternally new. To claim that God is rich in mercy in himself does not mean, of course, that the hypostases are merciful toward each other. Rather, it indicates that the love with which the Father gathers the concrete singular to himself—in the Son's embrace of both humankind and the world through the Spirit—is eternally the same gift and eternally new. From the point of view of the concrete singular, the permanence in being has to do, on the one hand, with the singular's resurrection to the life of truth, the glorious eternity of the gift. On the other hand, it concerns the restoration of the singular's own capacity to receive and reciprocate being gratuitously. To understand this confirmation of the singular requires examining in what sense

3. Giussani, *GTSM*, 184.
4. Giussani, *USD*, 36.

mercy, as the confirmation of the finite gift, is rooted in God's own gratuity (sections 1–3). The theological grounds will shed light on the circularity between the original creative donation and the restoration of the gift (section 4). This finally will illuminate in turn the ontological and anthropological dimensions of mercy (section 5).

1. The Father's Giving

To understand how time enters into divine, eternal patience requires us to ponder more deeply what man's ingratitude means to God. While we can never give a full account of what St. Paul calls God's "foolishness" (1 Cor 1:18), contemplating this mystery helps avoid any reduction of God's mercy to a form of overlooking or forgetting evil—which is the most common and banal misunderstanding of the nature of forgiveness. Man's ingratitude to God has both subjective and objective connotations; that is, how God himself faces it and what the rejection of the gift means in itself.

To enter into the incomprehensible mystery of what ingratitude means to God, we cannot lose sight of the ever-surprising fact that the God of Jesus Christ is a God who is in love with his own creature: "For God so loved the world that he gave his only-begotten Son, that whoever believes in him should not perish but have eternal life" (John 3:16). Among the many dimensions of God's love, one is crucial for this particular question: God's love for man is a zealous love. He wants to be loved in an absolutely exclusive manner. God teaches this jealous love to the Hebrew people when he forbids them to "carve images, or fashion the likeness of anything in heaven above or on earth beneath" (Gen 20:4–5). God does not accept any shortcoming in the beloved's reciprocation of his love. His zealous love takes delight in unity with his beloved. He wants his beloved to recognize that he alone is everything, and to love him in return with an equally unconditional predilection. Marriage, as the major prophets and St. Paul make clear, is indeed a perfectly adequate image for the unity God seeks with man (Eph 5:25–27). Because of his zeal, God will not tolerate being replaced with any man-made god. God is a zealous God who accepts nothing that does not recognize the glory of his holiness. In fact, as Scripture recounts, if God seeks a nuptial union with the beloved, man's betrayal can be only adultery and harlotry (Ezek 16). His zeal reveals man's rejection as unacceptable, impure disobedience. When it goes unreciprocated, God's zealous love can also take the form of wrath (Isa 66:15–16; Luke 3:7; Rom 1:18; Rev 19:15). Whoever does not recognize him or his beloved Son, that is, whoever does not reciprocate his love, will experience the wrath of God (John 3:36).

A human lover can hardly tolerate the possibility that, rather than in him or in the common task of their life together, his beloved might find greater delight in another person or another task. All the more so, the beloved's falsity is unbearable for the God who is the ultimate principle of the being of all that is, who has bestowed on his beloved a life whose destiny is communion with God. All our intimations of God's patience cannot overshadow this fact: God will not tolerate human ingratitude. He will not have it. He who is infinite light will not stand for the shadows of evil. That, as Scripture recounts, the Father endures his children's falsity; that he has allowed grotesque ugliness to spoil the beauty he communicated to the world; that he permits his creature to put itself at the service of the flesh and to despise him who is eternally good; that his patience tolerates the fact that the world still leaves little space for the Kingdom his Son brought—these do not mean that he takes man's ingratitude lightly. He will go to the utmost to bring it to an end.

If we turn to human experience, we can see why the paradoxical unity of love and zeal that can also express itself as wrath is a necessary element of the much-needed, though undeserved, renewal of the gift. Every human beloved desires to be loved with a love that cannot bear the beloved's unfaithfulness. Every beloved is well acquainted with the joy of being loved, of loving back, and of sharing with a third the experience of being loved. Everyone who loves and is loved also knows the tragic experience of responding with ingratitude—even in the form of hate—to the one whom he loves and by whom he is loved. This ingratitude tends to provoke a twofold reaction in the beloved. Although responsible for it, the beloved loathes his own ingratitude. At the same time, also aware that he is unable to dismiss it, he tries to make it invisible by justifying it and concealing it, even in the guise of piety and friendship. Still, even when he thinks that his ingratitude has been covered up or erased, the human beloved remains mindful of the fact that he can only rest ultimately in a love that can purify the unreasonable ingratitude that he so often embraces. He seeks therefore a love that is not "yes and no." He waits to be loved by a love that is always "yes" (2 Cor 1:18–19). Only a lover who cannot bear ingratitude, who will fight it to the end, can purify it. Such a lover alone deserves to be loved. If Jesus had not chastised those who made the temple a house of trade (Mark 11:15–19), or rebuked Peter for his logic of power (Matt 16:23), or castigated James and John for their thirst for power (Matt 20:20–28), we would not know that we can rest in his love. As St. Paul's words to the Corinthians show, one can rest only in such a zealous and jealous love, regardless of how unbearable it seems. God's stance before man's ingratitude is one of wrathful intolerance, which, though feared, is perceived by the singular as an expression of true love.

God's zealous campaign against man's ingratitude does not, however, preclude the free reciprocation of the gift. God's desire to be loved back with an exclusive love, and that he turns his wrath toward burning away sin, does not force a "yes" out of man. Quite the contrary. God's refusal of man's ingratitude, rather than eliminating a gratuitous response, means precisely that he wishes to be loved back gratuitously. The command to love God and one's neighbor expresses no imposition but rather love's gratuitous nature. Only a loving, gratuitous answer is an adequate response. An absence of gratuity reveals that a response remains a denial. Finite freedom, created to respond to God, discovers its own weightiness only when faced with God's request for an unconditional, gratuitous love (John 6:67; Mark 8:29). Man grasps the greatness of his own freedom precisely because God's love is a zealous love like no other. Only such an intransigent love as his can boldly ask, "For what will it profit a man, if he gains the whole world and forfeits his life?" (Matt 16:26).

Granting that God's charity expresses itself also as a zealous love that can unleash the fullness of wrath at man's ingratitude, we cannot cast God's intolerance of sin as a form of human resentment. The God who in Jesus Christ has become flesh, one like us, the one who has created the human being in his image, is also not like us. God is and remains other: "For my thoughts are not your thoughts, neither are your ways my ways, says the Lord" (Isa 55:8). Rather than importing human categories into the Godhead to understand God's zeal, we can look at what he reveals of himself in history. Tainted by sin, human zeal tends to be self-centered, while human jealousy points to a mortal lover's unreasonable wish to be everything for the beloved. God's zeal, instead, is an expression of absolute love, that is, the zeal that seeks the beloved's life. "When God chastises his people, that is not the end of the matter," writes Daniélou, "for it is essentially not the satisfaction of retribution that he is seeking to obtain: to him, vengeance is not sweet."[5] God's punishment of human ingratitude seeks to educate man, to bring him back to the truth of himself. God's love knows no hatred and seeks no revenge.[6] If God's jealousy and zeal had sprung from resentment, Jesus could not have said from the Cross, "Forgive them, Father, for they know not what they do" (Luke 23:34). If it were a case of possessiveness, "after many of his disciples drew back and no longer walked with him" Jesus would not have asked the twelve, "Will you also go away?" (John 6:66–67).

5. Daniélou, *Lord of History*, 318.
6. Benedict XVI, *Jesus of Nazareth*, 206–8.

Pondering what our ingratitude means to God not only reveals that his loving zeal does not tolerate it and will rain down wrath to eradicate it; we also approach here the threshold of the mystery we have already touched upon. "For while it is true that God is impassible," Daniélou clarifies, "yet there is indeed in him something analogous to what we recognize as 'suffering': it is the irreducible intolerance of unfaithfulness, the impossibility of coming to terms with it. God's holiness and purity are utterly incompatible with all sin, but the most abhorrent are the sins of souls that he has chosen and reserved to himself, bestowing all his best gifts upon them."[7] No reflection on God's being can avoid coming to terms with the mystery that the God who is absolutely simple, the perfection of all perfections, is also a God whose infinite love lets man's ingratitude resonate in his own being. His action in history precludes understanding God's impassible love either as a form of stoic imperturbability or as an expression of a finite undergoing of evil. God, we mentioned earlier, "suffers" the suffering of love. Let us look at this more closely.

It is true that to consider the unity and difference between God and the world in terms of gift means asking in what sense the divine giver, and not only the receiver, is open to receiving the singular's response. This is the case, as we saw, with the very constitution of the divine hypostases. Giving and receiving are proper to each of the divine persons, albeit in a different way. Still, the world's relation to God is not simply another instance of reciprocity. The world is not God and God is not a being among beings. To elevate the created world to divine subjectivity or to lower God's being to finite singularity are sure ways to lose sight of the mystery of donation that takes place in both creation and redemption. That God can receive the world, that he wishes with unspeakable zeal to receive the finite loving response, does not mean that he lacks something the world can provide. For the God whose gratuity eludes the dialectic of freedom and necessity, the reception of the creature's loving response is not a matter of "lack" or finite "dependence" but rather a case of overabundant fullness and of a divine entrusting of himself to what is not God. That the suffering of human ingratitude embraced by the Incarnate Son mysteriously resonates in the Father does not jeopardize God's nature. This resonance of man's suffering in God bespeaks perhaps a greater mystery: absolute love can and eternally wants to be contained by what is minimal. It is fruitless to consider God and the world, or glory and humility, as contradictory poles. The God who speaks himself and reveals all of his glory to the Son is also the one who lets his glory shine on the Cross. Christ's sacrificial offer of himself does not contradict, that is, it does

---

7. Daniélou, *Lord of History*, 317.

not speak against the Father; it reveals him. To understand the relation of God and the world under the law of contradiction demands the envious view of the absolute principle as a sterile, irrelevant beginning, eternally alone with itself.

If, rather than from a dialectic of worldly power, which is what moves and sustains the logic of contradiction, we consider what man's ingratitude or gratitude means to God from the perspective of triune love itself, we see that the echo in God of the human response and of human suffering is due to the mysterious fact that God's being is overabundant gift in himself. The triune God is open to and seeks to receive the concrete singular's own gift of receiving God's eternal, unconditional love, because God eternally is tripersonal gift.[8] Receptivity and the actual reception of the singular's response are not signs of ontological incompleteness. It cannot be dismissed as a romantic, anthropomorphic analogy that fades before the rays of an enlightened, finite reason that by now should have reduced this sort of analogy to embarrassed silence. As we saw with the openness proper to the first principles required by the ontology of gift, so, *mutatis mutandis*, is God's reception of the finite response considered a perfection. Not, it bears repeating, because it adds something to God that he does not have. Rather, reception of the finite gift is a perfection, that is, it belongs to being's goodness because it expresses God's fullness through what did not previously exist. More precisely, it is a good in terms of personal indwelling, which provides a better viewpoint for considering in what the reception of the concrete singular's response consists. God does not receive a "form" or "some-thing." He receives some-one. God's absolute being is not a self-enclosed monad but rather love that has revealed itself to be a triune communion of persons. In the ineffable mystery of the *Deus Trinitas*, the Father gives all of himself without losing himself in his giving, and he is himself thanks to the eternal response of the Son. It is the Father who gives to the Son the world created in the Son's image, and the Father receives the singular's redeemed and gratuitous response uttered in the Son without ceasing to be himself. If "not losing himself" in the relation with the Son means that the Father is himself as Father of the Son, not to be "changed" by the reception of the singular's response means that God wishes to and can let his glory shine through and give life to the creature. Permitting his glory to vivify the creature entails both the distance from

---

8. God receives from the world "an additional gift, given to the Son by the Father, but equally a gift made by the Son to the Father, and by the Spirit to both. It is a gift because, through the distinct operations of each of the three persons, the world acquires an inward share in the divine exchange of life; as a result the world is able to take the divine things it has received from God, together with the gift of being created, and return them to God as a divine gift" (Balthasar, *TD*, 5:521).

the creature that allows the singular to be itself, and the radical engagement with it so that the singular, too, can be itself by dwelling in him. In God the divine life of truth, goodness, beauty, and unity moves, to adopt in this context St. Paul's expression for man's destiny, "from one degree of glory to another" (2 Cor 3:18). The God who is tripersonal love ceaselessly seeks a renewed, personal response of love. Allowing human suffering to resonate in him without himself being changed, then, is not indifference or monadic immutability in God but rather reveals the mystery of love that opens itself up to welcome the other by affirming its own ever-new and eternal being.

If receptivity—as an expression of God's omnipotent, triune love—belongs to the nature of being's goodness in that it gratuitously permits the finite singular to dwell in God's communion of love, then God's ineffable "suffering" at man's rejection should be understood in terms of his *faithfulness* to himself and to his own gift. Here again, we cannot think of suffering as a divinely passive undergoing of whatever the finite creature capriciously imposes. Christ's obedience unto death on the Cross revealed his embrace of the human passions to be an expression of his love for the Father and for man, as opposed to a simply sinful undergoing of what he would rather have avoided. As with "gift," the term "suffering" cannot be unilaterally applied to God. We already indicated that when we say that the Father is a giver, the Son is a receiver of the Father's love, and the Holy Spirit a uniting bond of this triune "gift," we do not mean the bond through which a human being gives himself to another. The Father is the unpreceded giver, the Son is the eternal receiver, and the Holy Spirit is the eternal fruit in whom the two are united and remain distinct. We, by contrast, do not know what it means to begin to give without first having been given, to participate in the reception of oneself, or to share a unifying love without beginning or end. By the same token, we cannot take our own suffering as a measure of what the creature's rejection means for God, who brought the concrete singular from nothingness and preserves it in being. We must look in the direction of his paternal, ever-new love to avoid reducing divine "suffering" to a form of human suffering. God does not remain indifferent to man's sin; he "suffers" it, because he is an eternally faithful Father. Unlike man, God does not "suffer" because of a good in which he does not share.[9] He does not undergo, connive with, or source evil. In "suffering," the Father lets the Incarnate Son's suffering reflect in him. As Origen says in the passage quoted earlier, "God bears our ways just as the Son of God bears our sufferings. The very Father is not without suffering."[10] We cannot offer any elucidation of the relation

---

9. John Paul II, *Salvifici doloris*, no. 7 (AAS 76 [1984], 206–7).
10. Balthasar, *Origen*, 122. For more on this, see Balthasar, *TD*, 5:191–246.

between God and man until we reckon with the fact that the one who is overabundant triune love neither accepts man's ingratitude nor permits it to pass by uncontested. If perfection is personal indwelling, God's ineffable "suffering" relates both to the divine giver's perception of the good that the concrete singular lacks—ultimately, dwelling in God's communion of persons—and to the giver's intolerance of unfaithfulness. God's "suffering," in fact, is coincident with the patient war he wages against man's ingratitude. In the Incarnate Logos, God causes ingratitude to face the heat of his anger so that he can bear it away. It is only thus that God can allow his own goodness to win from within man's surrender. God's inexorable intolerance of unfaithfulness and his "suffering" on account of man's deprivation of the intended good (dwelling in God's life) express themselves in history as mercy. The faithful Father unfailingly wishes to give anew. Faced with man's ingratitude, which echoes in God as unspeakable, ineffable "suffering," God forgives.

How are we to describe God's zealous love that "suffers" and is determined to change man's ingratitude? To understand the meaning of the Father's mercy we must look again at the one who "reflects the glory of God and bears the very stamp of his nature" (Heb 1:3). Drawing on our previous christological reflection, it suffices here to turn to the parable of the prodigal son (or the parable of the good father) to see that the Father's mercy means both his faithfulness and his readiness to forgive. As Ratzinger's commentary on the parable of the prodigal son, following P. Grelot's study, clarifies, "in this parable, Jesus justifies his own conduct by relating it to, and identifying it with, the Father's. It is in the figure of the father, then, that Christ—the concrete realization of the father's action—is placed right at the heart of the parable."[11]

Christ's fleshing out of the Father's merciful love reveals that the Father's gift is eternally faithful (*hesed*) to itself and ineffably compassionate (*rahamim*).[12] When Jesus recounts the parable of the two sons and the good father, his listeners can relate it to their own history. The Hebrew people's long acquaintance with God has made them familiar with his divine faithfulness (Hos 11:1–9). They have been taught "to abandon [themselves] to God's faithfulness for ever and ever" (Ps 52:8). They have been frequently told and on numerous occasions have seen that, as John Paul II clarifies, "the father is faithful to his fatherhood, faithful to the love that he had always

---

11. Benedict XVI, *Jesus of Nazareth*, 208.
12. The term "mercy," as is known, translates these two Hebrew words. See also entries for *hesed* and *raham* in Waltke, Archer, and Harris, *Theological Wordbook*, 305–7, 841–43.

lavished on his son."[13] Yet in Christ, this ever-faithful love reaches an unexpected, unforeseeable depth: God himself comes to be with them as one of them so that there is one who receives God's love and bears the Father's wrath. The Father's fidelity to himself is not a self-centered love. It does not mean that the Father focuses exclusively on carrying out his preconceived plan regardless of the rejection it meets (John 1:10–11). Rather, as the eternal love of a *father*, it is unfailingly other-centered. As the good father of the parable, the eternal Father is only concerned with the good of his Son. To be faithful to himself means that the Father never abandons his Son, nor does he allow his Son's response to remain unfulfilled. The Father remains himself because he is, so to speak, totally lost in his love for the Son.

As the parable teaches us, the prodigal son bears within himself the memory of the father's faithfulness. The father sees him depart, watches from a distance, and eagerly waits for him—so much so that upon seeing him, "he ran, and embraced him, and kissed him" (Luke 15:20). Although he lets his son go away, he remains within the son. The silence of the father's absence finally resounds in the son's memory once the clamor of false friends and the fake affections of harlots disappear, along with his inheritance. The absence of the father reminds the son of the zeal of the father's love, his tireless faithfulness. The father's silence makes the son jealous of his company; it causes him to desire it again. Had the father gone with him or refused him his inheritance, the son would not have discovered the depths of his father's mercy. The father's faithfulness brings the prodigal son back to himself, that is, to the Father who is always incomprehensibly ready to forgive (Luke 15:18–19).

In addition to faithfulness, John Paul II indicates that the Father's mercy is expressed by the availability, the readiness with which the father welcomes his prodigal son home and "even more fully by that joy, that merrymaking for the squanderer after his return, merrymaking which is so generous that it provokes the opposition and hatred of the elder brother."[14] The Father's love is not only ever-surprisingly faithful (*hesed*)—a faithfulness that also expresses itself as zealous and wrathful love; it is also compassionate (*rahamim*). His sympathy for man's ingratitude is charged with affection and understanding. To follow the Hebrew term more precisely, we could say that, contemplating man's hatred of and separation from the giving source, the Father's love is "wrenched open," just as the good Samaritan's heart is "wrenched open" (Luke 10:33). Of course, the suggestion that the Father's "womb" (*rehem*) is broken open (*rahamim*) does not imply corporeality. Yet,

---

13. John Paul II, *Dives in misericordia*, no. 6 (AAS 72 [1980], 1197).
14. Ibid., no. 6 (1196).

if we recall that "the Son is begotten not from nothing or from a substance, but from the Father's womb" (DS 526), we can say that the Father's compassionate love and understanding for humankind is the giving of himself anew, as it was always intended, in the only-begotten Son. Seeing man's suffering, the Father has compassion and sends the Son who descends so that, also as man, he may receive the Father's love, bear his unspeakable wrath, and communicate his mercy to every human being. Becoming flesh allows Jesus Christ to experience suffering. Had he not passed through the same trials as we do, he could not have been moved with pity and so communicate the Father's love. The one who experiences solitude, hunger, thirst, exhaustion, the temptation of power and disobedience, and the hate and betrayal of others, is able to have pity, to be deeply moved, to love, and to understand without limit. As Vanhoye indicates, Christ in his compassion does not take out his anger on the sinner, as we saw when the Levites carried out Moses's orders to slay the three thousand people who worshipped the golden calf (Exod 32:27), or when Phinehas pierced with a single spear-stroke the Israelite and the Midianite woman he brought as his wife (Num 25:6–12).[15] For our sake, Christ came in the likeness of sinful flesh (Rom 5:21). God "made him to be sin who knew no sin" (2 Cor 5:21) so that he could put an end to sin and let the justified sinner live anew.

Mysteriously, it is God's fidelity to his own divine fatherhood—his ineffable capacity to forgive and to understand everything—that enables the suffering caused by man's rejection of God's absolute love to resonate within him and moves him to save man. Commenting on Rembrandt's famous depiction of the father's embrace of the prodigal son, Giussani writes that "the father is in the specular position of the son: in him reverberates the son's sorrow, and hence the saved despair, the prevented destruction, the happiness that is about to rekindle."[16] Goodness triumphs in the Father, who, faithful to his love, allows his "heart to turn itself against [him], and his compassion to grow warm and tender" (Hos 11:8ff.).[17] Of course, God's "turning against himself" does not refer to a Hegelian diremption or fragmentation in God's essence, nor to a contradiction of his own original plan or, more radically, of his very self. The "turning against himself" that Hosea prophesies refers to the Paschal Mystery and to the historical event of the Cross, which Christ freely and obediently embraces. The Cross is, in fact, "the culmination of that turning of God against himself in which he gives himself in order to

15. Vanhoye, *Christ Our High Priest*, 48–49.
16. Giussani, *GTSM*, 182.
17. Benedict XVI refers to this passage in *Deus caritas est*, no. 10 (AAS 98 [2006], 226) and in Ratzinger, *Jesus of Nazareth*, 206–7.

raise man up and save him."[18] The Paschal Mystery is "the gesture of love that gives all . . . the true and final feast of reconciliation."[19] We can turn now to specify further what God's response in Jesus Christ reveals of the nature of man's ingratitude, and how his merciful response expresses in history God's mystery of an eternal, ever-fruitful beginning.

2. Restoration of Sonship

If the goal of God's creative donation is the constitution of the human being, the restoration of the gift of the concrete singular aims at reconstituting the human person. Through God's love, man is enabled to become a person, that is, to embrace the Father's infinite mercy and enter into his all-enduring patience. By personifying the Father's mercy, Jesus Christ's mission efficaciously reveals and restores the unity of the gift of the concrete singular: the permanence of the gift of the concrete singular's being is to be loved by another and to joyfully indwell and share, in the Son, the Father's eternal love.[20] Revealing the truth of love and enabling man to remain in it, Christ's sacrifice opens up the "path to true humanism," that is, he saves man's freedom and prevents the reduction of history to tragic irrelevance.[21] We can now examine the meaning of his revelatory sacrifice and then indicate in what sense it unites time with eternity.

God's intolerance of man's ingratitude brings the singular's unfaithful rejection to an end through Christ's sacrifice. It is important, however, not to conceive of this sacrifice legalistically. Ingratitude is first of all hatred of the original giver who is a triune communion of persons. Of course, man's offense is also a trespass against the law prohibiting him from eating the forbidden fruit, that is, a failure to obey the commandment to love God above everything else. Yet it is so precisely because, in breaking the law, man refuses to dwell in the personal relation with God who is all in all. This refusal is a failure to recognize God, and because this lie about God issues from man himself, only man himself can restore what his lie has broken. Neither precious objects nor animal offerings can stand in for the person's coming face to face with a zealous and merciful God. Offerings of bloody sacrifices of any kind are to no avail. They do not replace the human being.

18. Benedict XVI, *Deus caritas est*, no. 12 (AAS 98 [2006], 228).

19. Ratzinger, *Introduction to Christianity*, 128.

20. Jesus Christ re-presents in history the Father's merciful love. "Not only does Christ speak of mercy and explain it by the use of comparisons and parables, but above all, He Himself makes it incarnate and personifies it. He himself in a certain sense is mercy" (John Paul II, *Dives in misericordia*, no. 2 [1180]).

21. Benedict XVI, *Deus caritas est*, no. 9 (AAS 98 [2006], 225).

Man alone can meet God's zeal and love because what God wants is a gratuitous relation with man. Furthermore, man has to meet it with all of his life because what must be undone is man's ingratitude and the death to which it leads. Since all have fallen short of the glory of God, no human being has the virginal purity to stand before God's anger or to endure the fire of his merciful presence. Only the divine and human "yes" of Christ, more primordial than Adam and Eve's ingratitude, brings peace, that is, communion with the Father. It is "the redemption which is in Christ Jesus, whom God put forward as an expiation by his blood" (Rom 3:25) that restores the unity of man with the eternal source.

Christ takes flesh from Mary in order to see, hear, receive, and communicate the Father's love also as a man. He takes the body prepared from all eternity (Heb 10:5) so that the filthiness of the world might encounter the infinitely pure one who knows no sin. His bodily existence, therefore, both radiates the Father's light and permits its heat to burn away the filth of our ingratitude. We can be touched by God's light because his body, containing the fullness of the divinity, dissipates our darkness. When darkness meets him, his flesh does not undergo the fate of an innocent human soul exposed to human evil. An astonishing reversal takes place with the Crucified One. The unclean does not render the clean one filthy; rather, as Benedict XVI writes, "when the world, with all the injustice and cruelty that make it unclean, comes into contact with the infinitely pure one—then he, the pure one, is the stronger. Through this contact the filth of the world is truly absorbed, wiped out, and transformed in the pain of infinite love."[22] Being the Incarnate Son of the Father, Jesus Christ endures the heat and the truth of the Father's faithful love. By receiving the fire of God's zeal, Christ's death burns away the grime and decay of the world. It thus restores the relation with the Father.

We saw how the synthetic unity of the different moments of the Paschal Mystery (the last supper on Holy Thursday, the crucifixion on Good Friday, and the resurrection on Easter Sunday) reveals that Christ's sacrifice is the gift of self to the end in utter, loving obedience to the Father. To show now what his sacrifice reveals of man's ingratitude and so to see more clearly the singular's unity with the eternal Father, we need to look more closely at an event that no one can fully expound: God's silence on Holy Saturday.

The silence of Holy Saturday continues the apparent lack of response to Christ's cry of dereliction: "My God, my God, why have you forsaken me?" (Matt 27:46; Mark 15:34). As we know, with this cry, the Incarnate Logos makes his own the lamentation of the righteous, suffering man (Ps 22).

---

22. Benedict XVI, *Jesus of Nazareth*, 231.

The piercing entreaty uttered by Christ represents the entire Hebrew people with all of its tormented history. In addition to representing his people, this cry is also spoken on behalf of everyone. On the Cross, Jesus Christ represents every human being because he assumed human nature by taking flesh from Mary. More importantly, he presents all of man's suffering to God because he experiences and endures it thoroughly—more than any human could because no human nature is so united to the Godhead. The cry of dereliction expresses his enduring, out of love, the suffering of every human being. "Suffering on the Cross," says von Speyr, "Christ suffers as a man who has chosen to share humanity, with all its suffering potential, in order to make help available to every other human being."[23] When Christ cries out from the Cross, allowing the world to hear him, he does not address the Father from within his divine, personal relationship to him, but from his humanity: "here it is the man, the creature, who cries out to God. . . . The Son is forsaken."[24] Christ, forsaken on the Cross, raises the mysterious question to the Father that receives no answer.

Whoever has prayed this psalm knows, as Ratzinger indicates, that the plea for deliverance from suffering ends with the certainty that God "has not despised or abhorred the affliction of the afflicted, but has heard when he cried to him" (Ps 22:24). The ending of the psalm blossoms in the joyful conviction that "the afflicted shall eat and be satisfied" (Ps 22:26). On the Cross Christ prays with the certainty of having been heard. This certainty does not make either his cry or the Father's silence less real. The certainty of being loved does not eliminate the task of dying for everyone. It rather makes it possible. If we were to interpret Christ's certainty as psychological self-persuasion or logical necessity, the coexistence of certainty (joy) and the experience of Godforsakenness would lead to either adoptionism or atheism (God died on Good Friday). If, instead, we interpret it pneumatologically, we can say that Christ's certainty of being heard is rooted in the unity with the Father that is confirmed by the Holy Spirit, the hypostasis in whom Christ rejoices when his human glory is revealed. As the author of the epistle to the Hebrews says, Jesus Christ, "through the eternal Spirit offer[s] himself without blemish to God" (Heb 9:14). The Spirit binds him to the Father and, without breaking the divine silence, enables Christ to suffer through until everything is brought to its end. United to the Father in the Spirit, also as man, he can entrust himself to the Father's silence. The Father's silence, from this point of view, is the memory of the gift that the Son is in himself and for man (Rom 8:32).

23. Von Speyr, *Cross*, 37.
24. Ibid., 39.

VII. THE UNEXPECTED GIFT 275

Jesus Christ's cry on the Cross and the Father's silence represent the embrace of what the human being most fears: final solitude. Jesus would not have truly taken our place if he had not experienced, as a human being, this solitude that is the most rancid fruit of man's original ingratitude. Christ's loneliness on the Cross is, in this regard, a sharing in man's darkest experience: fatherlessness. The man Jesus Christ tasted on the Cross the orphanhood that Adam brought upon himself when he squandered his own sonship.[25] The original rejection generated many different forms of solitude. Betrayals of any sort leave us alone with the bitter taste of meaninglessness. Death, however, leaves us in a greater solitude. The loss of a friend, a relative, a child, or a spouse brings us closer to the hypothesis with which the possibility of our own death confronts us: utter meaninglessness seems to be what we are left with when all is said and done. Perhaps this is why losing one's father, whose task is to represent the divine origin from which we come, makes present to us the solitude that Adam and Eve felt when they were expelled from paradise. Death as such, but particularly the loss of the father, raises the doubt that there is no Father. Christ's death reveals that meaninglessness is fatherlessness. This final solitude (Godforsakenness), which grounds every human anxiety, is what, out of love, Christ embraced from within without being responsible for it.[26]

To save the old Adam, that is, to prove that orphan solitude is not the truth of the singular gift or of the Father's will, the new Adam descended to hell, the place that represents final solitude or, as Ratzinger says, "a loneliness that the word love can no longer penetrate and that therefore indicates the exposed nature of existence in itself."[27] Yet he could not have done this if he had not let his love for humankind and the Father embrace from within the solitude that the first Adam brought upon himself by returning God's love with unreasonable, loveless ingratitude. "The One, whose name is Jesus Christ, must go down into the absolute contra-diction against the sovereign majesty of the Lord, into the night of Godforsakenness and the formless chaos of hell. He must do this so as to be, and to set up, beyond anything man can expect a form to be, *the* imperishable, indivisible form, the form that clasps together God and the world in the New Eternal Covenant."[28] Just as we cannot fully tell what man's hateful rejection means to God, so we cannot describe what the silence of the Father meant for the Incarnate Logos,

---

25. John Paul II, *Dives in misericordia*, no. 5 (AAS 72 [1980], 1193–96).

26. "Anxiety" has several meanings. Here we do not interpret this category psychologically but theologically—doubt regarding God's ultimate goodness—and hence anthropologically.

27. Ratzinger, *Introduction to Christianity*, 300.

28. Balthasar, *GL*, 7:14.

to whom the Father reveals his face from all eternity. We can only indicate that this silence also means the final shouldering of the consequences of the deepest contra-diction of ingratitude: man's denial of God's love, under the illusion that he is a Father who does not fulfill his promises, and man's denial of the truth of himself, who was created to dwell in God's eternal, ever-new beginning.

It is not our concern here whether Christ's descent is best understood as a victory,[29] or as the illumination of love,[30] or as the passive descent that lets Christ's obedience shine into the region where man's disobedience condemns him.[31] In a sense, each indicates an aspect of the infinitely rich meaning of God's silence. What is crucial to see now is that Christ's sacrifice of himself on the Cross, his death, and his descent into hell are together a free handing of himself over to orphan solitude. Having handed his mother over to the beloved disciple John, and John to Mary, and having prayed his last breath, the Son enters that realm where the lie, the rejection of the gift and the paternal giver, reign. To willingly undergo death—that is, both to be offered as expiatory sacrifice and to offer himself as the sacrificial, innocent lamb—lets Christ undo from within the lie of fatherlessness. He enters hell so that the Word of love can let the Father's light shine.

The one who dies on the Cross is the one who is the Passover: it is he who, eternally coming from the Father, is always already on the way to the Father. In the midst of time, Christ is the eternal, ever-new reception and response of love to the Father. Meeting death on the Cross on his return to the Father, Jesus Christ turns death around, so to speak. Certainly death remains incomprehensible to every man until he passes through it. Yet, in light of Christ's Paschal Mystery, we can say that death is no longer the end of the human being's flight from the Father. It becomes the narrow door that grants access to him who, rich in mercy, waits for each one from all eternity. The fathers of the Church explain that by clothing Adam and Eve in skins borrowed from the animal world—that is, sexuality, mortality, and the passions—God's mercy prevents man from being united to evil forever, and hence from sliding evermore into nothingness. Death is a gift to prevent man's ingratitude from holding sway over the singular's existence.[32] Of

29. See, for example, Athanasius, *Epistola festalis* 2.7 (PG 26:1371A); Gregory of Nyssa, *Oratio catechetica magna* 23–24 (PG 45:63–67); Lateran IV, 1215 (DS 801); Lyon II, 1274 (DS 852).

30. It is through persuasion, Augustine would say, that Christ frees man. See Augustine, *De libero arbitrio* 3.10 (PL 32:1285); Augustine, *De vera religione* 16.30–31 (PL 34:134–35); Irenaeus, *Haer.* 5.21.3.

31. See Balthasar, *TD*, 5:247–69; Sara, "Descensus ad inferos."

32. Gregory of Nyssa, *Commentary on the Song of Songs*, 12.215–16; Daniélou, "Dove and the Darkness," 272.

course, it is a terrible "gift." However, Christ's death and resurrection make it clear that, although befitting man's sin, the form of death is not determined solely by the rejection at its origin. More deeply, the mystery of death is determined by the promise of the one who is eternally faithful to his fatherhood. "I will put enmity between you and the woman, and your seed and her seed: she shall crush your head, and you shall lie in wait for her heel" (Gen 3:16). The Father instills death with the memory that he will fulfill the promise of his original gift gratuitously. Before Christ's death on the Cross, however, it is hard not to perceive death as life's final stop, which leaves open the difficult question regarding the goodness of God's fatherhood. Death, to the orphan singular, is the interruption of giving, the end of time.

Jesus Christ's death on the Cross, instead, is the unconditional, reckless gift of one who, coming from the Father, returns to him. Certainly Christ's return to the Father proves victorious on the morning of Easter Sunday. Yet, as we saw, before that morning dawns, Christ's virginal love eloquently speaks of both his origin and his destination. No one could love in the way Christ does unless he comes from the Father, dwells in the Father, and returns to him. Thus, we can also say that Christ's suffering and death on the Cross opens the way back to the Father because it is a virginal sacrifice. Of course, "virginal" here does not simply mean that Christ had not been given in marriage, but rather that he is perfectly pure and never loses his relation with the Father. Throughout his obedient existence unto death, Christ recognizes the Father's goodness and loving care for all things, while also waiting on the Father to unfold his mercy in the time and way he determines. Christ is the virginal one. He is always already returning to the Father from whom he eternally proceeds. His virginal love is the gratuitous and detached affirmation of the other within his eternal coming forth from the Father and returning to dwell in him whom he never abandoned. Christ's sacrificial death and descent into hell are fruitful because virginal. Now, death, rather than marking the end of a historical human trajectory—which, underneath its ugliness, retains the seed of beauty that God planted in it—represents an entryway to the truth of love. Man's departure from God's company seemed to mean setting out for a land ravaged by fatherlessness. After the Father lets the Word be heard and seen anew on Easter Sunday, death, "the last enemy to be destroyed" (1 Cor 15:26), has lost its sting (1 Cor 15:55). Through the Holy Spirit, the crucified-risen Lord accompanies man so that he, too, who must still pass through his own death, may be brought to the Father's dwelling place.

Christ's resurrection, with its historical and meta-historical connotations, marks the victory of eternity in time. It binds time with eternity anew by renewing the Father's ever-greater gift of love. Easter Sunday reintroduces communion, the bond of peace, between God and man and thus allows the human being to receive the Father's love and reciprocate it in gratitude. Man's originary experience—which is his participation in God's love, the eternal indwelling of the three divine hypostases—teaches him that his permanence in time has to do with his being in others. Being with and in others is not secondary for the concrete singular. The search for perpetuity through work or children is an intimation of this truth, when not driven by egotistical reasons.[33] Of course, it is a fragile intimation. Children will have to face their own death, and work does not generally outlast us very long. Nonetheless, the exigence toward progeny and lasting memorials does point to something irrefutable: the unity that love generates and seeks is one of indwelling. Just as the concrete singular's present is the reception of himself from the original source through others, so his future has to do with permanence in a communion that outlasts him. If love were an emotion or an expression of the will, it could not withstand death. If, instead, it is the indwelling proper to the communion of persons, as the resurrection shows, it can conquer death. Christ's resurrection reveals love's victory over death and vanquishes our fear of an ultimate, fatherless solitude precisely because it is the victory of communion. Through Christ's suffering, death on the Cross, and resurrection, the Father's love weaves time together with eternity anew. Christ's sacrifice of himself on the Cross overcomes man's fear of death not because it is a conclusive "argument" against it, but because his sacrifice extends the Father's love all the way to hell. Before the Cross that unites heaven with earth and time with eternity, there can be no ingratitude. By extending the Father's love to the abyss of meaninglessness and to every corner of the universe, the Incarnate Logos reintroduces the human being into communion with the Father.

The reception of adoptive divine childhood, however, does not return us to the garden of Eden. The man who is seized by God's mercy is not granted an unlimited, earthly existence. To be in Christ's love is to receive the Father's love anew, to be a new creature by the mercy of God (2 Cor 5:17). Jesus Christ, resting in the sleep of death, allows his side to be pierced so that the new Eve, standing at the foot of the Cross, can be born. Through Christ's pierced side, time is permitted to be united with eternity. Whereas Eve was taken from Adam and fashioned from one of his ribs, the new Eve is generated by the blood and water flowing from Christ's pierced side, a side that is not closed up again with flesh, as was Adam's. The Church, the new Eve represented in Mary, has neither "spot nor wrinkle nor any such thing. She is holy and without blemish" (Eph 5:27). Christ's virginal sacrifice

---

33. Ratzinger, *Introduction to Christianity*, 301–10.

of himself on the Cross gives birth to a new person who will no longer be subject to death, that is, who will know no final interruption of the Father's giving, no meaningless solitude. In this way Christ's mercy represents the constitution of the human being as a person. Mercy's novelty, on the one hand, fulfills the gift of being that God already gave. On the other hand, the children of God and of the Church, having Christ as redeemer and brother, are brought to an unthinkable new level: communion with God, which one is called to enter as a spiritual body bearing the image of the man of heaven (1 Cor 15:35-49).[34] The following pneumatological reflection will enable us to grasp better the nature of this new rebirth and the unity that Christ's mercy brings about in the concrete singular.

3. The Unity of Life (I)

The triune God, who is absolute spirit and who has created the world, witnesses to the inexhaustible richness of his merciful power through the Holy Spirit. As the embrace of peace of the Father and Son and the fruit of their love, the Holy Spirit communicates God's mercy made incarnate in Christ, both within man's own spirit (John 15:26) and through all flesh. He is poured out into man's heart (Rom 5:5) so that he may see the truth of love and relinquish his own ingratitude. The Holy Spirit not only illumines the heart and the mind, he also transfigures the "flesh" so that it too may become a witness to God's merciful love: "You also are witnesses" (John 15:27). Operating at these two levels—within man and through all flesh—the Spirit of the Father and the Son effects man's unity of life. He thus constitutes the human being as a new person by introducing him into a unity of life previously unknown to him. He permits man to perceive Christ's mercy and adhere to it, while enfolding him within the arms of the Church. The Church, as the unity of redeemed humanity, is the place where God's mercy lets itself permanently be seen. The Holy Spirit, then, unifies human life by binding time with eternity, and human flesh (and with it the entire cosmos) with the body of the crucified-risen Christ, who both sits at the right hand of the Father (as head) and remains present in history through the Church (as body). The unity of life is God's renewal of the gift of being. It is thus that mercy represents the possibility of the permanence of the concrete singular's being-gift, which awaits its final confirmation through participation in the resurrection of Christ. We now examine the "bodily" dimension of

---

34. God's *agapic* love for man "demands both the Son's Cross and our conversion" (Ratzinger, *Yes of Jesus Christ*, 96).

this unity of life generated by mercy, while the final section approaches the personal dimension.

To perceive this unity more clearly, two clarifications are in order. First, the rich complexity of the gift described so far is not well served by juxtaposing the terms "objectivity" and "subjectivity" in reference to the Spirit's work through the flesh (body, world) and through man's spirit, respectively. Both the flesh (the world) and the human being are gifts given to themselves and to each other, as elucidated earlier. To think of the flesh (world, body) as "object" and of the person as "subject" is to separate them. This separation presupposes severing the ultimate giver from both instances of the concrete singular (the world and the human being) and viewing them abstractly, and, as we saw, offers an inadequate philosophical framework. It suffices now to indicate that the unity of life that mercy generates does not reside in assembling "objective" fragments, gathering "subjects" together with "objects," or manufacturing a sociological unity that is simply the sum of its "subjects." Rather, it consists in reestablishing the flow of reception and reciprocation proper to the gift, the flow of gratuitous affirmation and prayer, that binds concrete singulars with God and with each other. Since the unity of the human being with the world and God is effected in history and with the participation of the human being, we cannot think that the unity is already a fait accompli. It has a radical beginning in time (baptism) and it also unfolds in time. The Paschal Mystery does not make history redundant. Man's reception and reciprocity of God's mercy is required. Still, the more God's Spirit unifies the form of human existence, the clearer it becomes that what is gathered together was always meant to be one. From the human point of view, the renewal of unity effected by the Spirit is a gradual entering into the eternal unity with God, the world, and others that God intended from the beginning.

Second, living in a postmodern time we have the benefit of seeing that the exaltation of the subject culminating in the rejection of first principles has left the human person in the hands of "feelings." The hypertrophization of the person as subject has resulted in a time of unprecedented violence where the other is perceived as a permanent threat to one's own fragile certainties—built, for the most part, upon transient emotions. When, as we saw, the abuse of force and violence predominates, it is increasingly crucial not to lose sight of the fact that the human being can be convinced that his ingratitude is not stronger than God's mercy only if mercy comes to him through the flesh. If mercy could not be encountered historically in the figure of a man, Jesus Christ, and through those in whose unity he becomes present at every time and place, the human being could never see the goodness of being in all its breadth. If Christ's mercy did not continue to reach man through the flesh, his freedom would not be respected because it would not find itself called upon or requested. Finally, if, in addition to the Spirit's interior witness, love did not have a historical form, the temptation would remain to write off mercy as an illusion. In fact, nothing bursts man's idealistic tendencies, counters the skepticism that claims one's own ingratitude as the final word on oneself, or engages human freedom more intensely than the human encounter with the Incarnate Logos and the communion his gift of self generates.

The Holy Spirit extends Christ's mercy to every time and place by generating a dwelling place, a "new temple," as Giussani calls it.[35] The Holy Spirit, person-communion, lets the human being participate in God's gratuity by introducing him into the Church, the unity of love that is the sacramental sign of the unity of which he is the fruit and bond. Through this dwelling place, the singular enjoys God's holiness and participates in Christ's mission in the world, that is, to bind the world to the Father. The Holy Spirit, so to speak, crystallizes divine love in the Church so that whoever encounters this life is able to experience it from within and enter into its never-ending richness.

The first historical expression of this communion built by the Holy Spirit is Mary. She, Giussani writes, is the "first dwelling place of God in the world."[36] She is the first "house" chosen by God, because in her everything belongs to Christ. No space is kept in reserve. Everything is given so that Christ can take on flesh and be recognized. As such, she represents both concrete and personal sanctity. The latter because her *fiat* captures the essence of the reception and reciprocation of the gift, and the former because, since she was asked to let the Logos take flesh in her, she represents the whole Church.[37] Mary is mother of mercy, not only because "she obtained mercy in a particular and exceptional way, as no other person has," but also because she "made possible with the sacrifice of her heart her own sharing in revealing God's mercy."[38] She thus was allowed to give birth to Christ, to participate in a unique way in the Paschal Mystery, and to intercede for every human person.[39] As the dwelling place generated by the Spirit of Christ, hosting his love, Mary radiates the beauty and goodness of God's presence. Mary allows us to see that the dwelling place generated by mercy is not

---

35. Giussani, *TT*, 11–35.

36. Ibid., 15.

37. This is why Balthasar and John Paul II rightly insist on the Marian dimension of the Church. See, e.g., Balthasar, *ET*, 143–91, 315–32.

38. John Paul II, *Dives in misericordia*, no. 9 (AAS 72 [1980], 1208).

39. Balthasar, *TD*, 3:292–360.

simply a place to rest. Just as she was, it is always already poured out, given to the world.

Through his Spirit, Christ expands this first dwelling place—whose form cannot be understood without Joseph—and lets it become the Church. The complex debate about when the Church is constituted—with Mary, with the twelve apostles, on Calvary, at Pentecost—does not concern us here.[40] For our purposes—to indicate how the unity of the Church, being born from Christ's mercy, crystallizes divine love so that any human being may encounter it—it suffices to indicate that the link between the Church and Christ's mercy is first perceived in the fact that mercy is already manifested in the call that constitutes the Church (*ekklesia*). In this sense, starting from Mary, the Church takes on a further concrete form when Christ begins to live publicly with the apostles what he lives out with the Father from all eternity. Calling the twelve apostles to be with him, and then sending them, he forgives them. He introduces them—who represent the people of Israel and all the peoples of the world—into his own sonship and brings them together.[41] What unites them, then, is having been brought together by his mercy. Their life together, more than family ties or common tastes or ideas, has as its permanent source Christ, who, by calling them, forgives each one. It is already in the unity of the apostles that we begin to see something of what is confirmed at Pentecost: those who are called become whole in remaining within the bond of love uniting the Father and the Son. At Pentecost, God confirms the union of the Christians and makes it a sacramental sign of Christ's mercy, which is open to all. The Church, as the dwelling place of Christ, is the most beautiful sign of his mercy. Living her life, sharing existence with those whom Christ has forgiven and made his own, one is continuously brought to the truth of oneself. Mercy restores an unknown unity: there is, in fact, no greater unity among men than that born of forgiveness. This is primordially the case with Christ's forgiveness of those who crucify him ("Father, forgive them; for they know not what they do" [Luke 23:34]). It is this same forgiveness that Peter is taught to embrace (John 21:15–19) and to give "seventy times seven" (Matt 18:21–22), that is, without measure. The early Christian martyrs also witness to this unity in a moving way. The Christian martyr, dying for his faith, forgives the executioner who takes his very life. This unprecedented forgiveness binds the two together forever. The one putting the Christian to death understands through the martyr's forgiveness that he, the executioner, cannot escape the unity generated by the martyr's embrace of him. The unity that forgiveness

---

40. See Ratzinger, "Ecclesiology of the Constitution," 123–52.
41. Ratzinger, *Called to Communion*, 13–45.

generates is also incarnated in the daily life of those in the Church. Yet, since its source is God's mercy, the unity of Christians is greater than the sum of its members. It is a concrete, sacramental "presence" that cannot be reduced to what one lives or understands alone, no matter how often one attempts to do so. As incarnated love, to be in it means to follow a reality that remains greater than oneself and that, precisely because greater, makes the human being be human.

This unbreakable, ever-affirming unity, as it is first expressed in Mary and the apostolic communion, takes an infinite variety of forms throughout history, which may be characterized in two primary ways. The first is the family. "Family" does not simply refer to a sociological reality but rather to the sacramental family, that is, one that receives help to live out the indissoluble nature of love. Christian spouses, through their mutual and finite love, become the sign of Christ's love for them and the world. They can form and be formed in the truth of love because their fruitful union represents in a mysterious, real way the love with which Christ loves the Church (Eph 5:25–27). Through their sacramental union, their personal love becomes an objective norm, greater than themselves and their wills. As such they are called to obey this greater love in order to be true to what they feel and desire for each other. The second form of the dwelling place in which the unity of the Church is visible to all is the monastery. "Etymologically speaking, monastery," says Giussani, "is the most significant word because monastery comes from *monos*, alone, solitary, the one. Humanity's relationship with the Mystery becomes awareness, freedom, and love in the singular human being: it becomes a new 'self.' But 'monastery' also means many 'I-s' who are together. All these *monoi* express and document their being one thing alone in the Church of God."[42] It is perhaps in the "monastery" that the unity generated by mercy becomes most transparent. In marriage, the spouses' exchange of vows is a reciprocal welcoming of each other that accepts a prior having been given to each other. The spouses love each other in a prior being-called. In contrast, those who are called to dwell in Christ's love within a "monastery"—regardless of the form it takes in the history of the Church—accept being made part of Christ's form of love without choosing those with whom they are called to live. The love for the other members will be born later, as an outflowing of Christ's mercy. In both cases, however, it is the mercy of Christ that generates the memory of the Father's faithfulness through the very unity of each dwelling place. The concrete bodiliness of the dwelling place, the actual house and the other members, carries the memory of the merciful call that both generates it and constantly renews its

---

42. Giussani, *TT*, 19.

members' loving, free awareness of their union with each other, the world, and God. Therefore, the unity that God's mercy generates, and that takes the historical form of the family home or the monastery—forms in which the universality and catholicity of the Church become visible—neither flattens nor dissolves the identity of the singular. It is here in these forms that the Holy Spirit allows the person to discover his own ingratitude and to enter into the embrace of the Father's mercy. Within this dwelling place, the person is constantly called to respond to the love that renews him. Thus, rather than losing personal identity in this dwelling place, by responding to the love that regenerates it, the soul of the believer is enabled to embrace and carry everything and everyone within itself. The person becomes *anima ecclesiastica*.

United to the Father in Christ by the Holy Spirit, the communion of the Church is a sacramental one. Certainly, the Church's sacramentality is always in reference to Christ's, and her sacraments are hers only because they are Christ's, first and foremost.[43] Yet, because it is truly sacramental, the communion of the Church "is a communion of Love; it is a communion of love in Christ and with him in the mystery of the Trinity (John 17:23)."[44] While her members' obedience to the truth of love makes her nature more transparent, the Church's unity remains even if that obedience weakens. She sacramentally re-presents Christ, her head, her bridegroom.

The Church has been entrusted with the capacity to sacramentally communicate God's mercy, which she bestows through the different sacraments but also through the other concrete elements that make up her complete form. As Balthasar clarifies, Jesus Christ's mercy is present in the Church first and foremost through her very structure: the sacraments, Scripture, the wealth of Christian tradition, the dogmatic deepening of the faith, the hierarchy.[45] At the same time, it is the life itself of the Church, the living union that forms her, that represents perhaps the most existentially

---

43. The sacraments of the Church are not, as Rahner seems to contend, gestures in which and through which the Church expresses and fulfills her nature. They are the sacraments of Christ. Whereas the reflection on the sacramentality of the Church was first presented by Semmelroth and then deepened by Rahner—an emphasis that rightly found its way to the conciliar document *Lumen gentium*—the meaning of the sacraments is obfuscated by insufficient reference to Christ and the excessive weight given to a Trinitarian ontology that remains greatly influenced by both German idealism and Heideggerian phenomenology. Rahner, *Church and the Sacraments*. See also Scola, *Nuptial Mystery*; Mazza, *Mystagogy*; Mazzanti, *Teologia sponsale*; Ouellet, *Divine Likeness*. This is not the place to develop a sacramental theology. The present work could also be seen as the grounds for a further reflection on the nature of the sacrament.

44. John Paul II, *Catechesis on the Creed*, 121–24.

45. Balthasar, *TL*, 3:307–411.

persuasive, concrete aspect of love. The life of the Church is the unfolding of the sacramental belonging to Christ that generates a new culture. Through this culture, everything begins to be seen and understood in light of the mystery of the love of Christ, in whom all things hold together.

The concrete unity that the Holy Spirit, the person-gift, generates applies not only to the relationship between human beings; it also includes the world as that totality that "has been groaning in travail together until now" (Rom 8:22). When the human being welcomes divine mercy, the world begins to participate in its redemption, that is, in being united to the ultimate source. Gratitude for the gift's renewal opens the singular's eyes to rediscover the being-gift of all that exists. Now the singular, finite other is perceived for what it is, a "sacramental" sign of the *agapic* source. Through the gaze, memory, and offering of the human being, the concrete singular is allowed to dwell in the life of the divine giver.[46] Mercy, however, not only reveals to the human person his own creatureliness and the gift-ness of all that is. It also teaches the person to love and to deal with the world in a way that reflects the Logos's virginal affirmation and possession of the cosmos. The unity generated by mercy's confirmation of the gift binds the human being and the cosmos together in a non-technological way. Liberated from the lie lurking in the worldly understanding of power, art and work finally blossom as an expression of the gift and not as a manipulation or an elimination of it. They become expressive of the ever-new richness of love's triune mystery. Shifting the emphasis from the human person to the liberating union with the original giver, the Holy Spirit allows human power to become supremely creative. Man lets the original design intrinsic to the finite singular emerge and gives form to the singular by placing it at the service of expressing the glory for which it was created. The human being, in letting God's glory shine through his own work—that is, in letting his work become offering in the sense described above—realizes his own lordship over creation and permits it to be transparent to God's glory and hence to participate in the fulfillment of its own creatureliness.

The Holy Spirit introduces the singular, both the human being and other creatures, into the unity that God's mercy has regenerated gradually

---

46. This sacramentality gives full expression to the understanding of sign elucidated earlier since it indicates that the other, in its own limited way, re-presents that mystery of love from which it has been made and which has taken flesh in Mary. I draw this intuition from Schmemann, *Life of the World*. We also need to be mindful, as Colombo indicates, that sacramentality belongs fully to Christ and analogically to the Church and the cosmos. The attempt to reject positivistic readings of the cosmos should not dilute the term "mystery" (*sacramentum*) into meaninglessness. Neither should this risk prevent us from rightly indicating the "sacramentality" of the finite singular. See Colombo, *Teologia sacramentaria*, 3–61.

and organically. The confirmation of the singular gift does not eliminate history. While there are moments that do mark the transfiguration of the singular, such as the sacraments of baptism and marriage, the process of entering into the unity of God's love takes place historically. Eternity allows redeemed time to unfold in the Father's patience. The Holy Spirit takes into account the circumstances, temperament, and history of the person and, almost imperceptibly, guides him into the truth of the eternal God. Even the apostles, as we see through the descriptions of Saints Peter and Paul in the Acts of the Apostles, continue to be corrected and to change until the end of their lives. The organic growth of the person seeks to elicit the free, loving, and conscious adhesion of the singular to God's mercy. The Holy Spirit does not magically impose the Father's mercy incarnated by Christ. He changes the human being only through the person's own participation, and, since human freedom is always new, its participation is always required. Nor does the Holy Spirit change everything. Sometimes, in fact, he leaves some things broken (2 Cor 12:7–10) while, working always from within, continuing to bring the person into God's eternity. If perfection in God relates to indwelling, the purification that mercy brings to the singular introduces a new point of view from which the person learns to see his life as an ordered whole and to entrust himself to it.[47] In time, with unspeakable patience, the Holy Spirit works the unmerited change in the singular, that is, his acceptance and reciprocation of the Father's gift. The permanence of the concrete singular gift in history consists precisely in this continuous and organic reintroduction of one's entire self—that is, all of one's history, temperament, sensibility, gifts, and limitations—into God's love. While awaiting the final confirmation of his existence, the concrete singular rediscovers new depths and vistas of Christ's infinite love. The one who plumbs God's being allows the human person to taste the novelty proper to the eternality in which God is always the same and ever new.

4. The Newness of the Gift

Before we examine in what sense God's mercy reconstitutes the singular being, we need to look more closely at the circularity between the creative donation and the reconstitution of the gift. God's mercy is twofold. On the one hand, it brings an unexpected, undeserved novelty that gratuitously reconstitutes the concrete singular being. On the other hand, the novelty is new because it fulfills the original creative gift. To grasp this paradox calls for avoiding three different temptations.

---

47. Camisasca, *La casa*, 50–51.

The first has to do with the nature of the beginning. If the beginning were a perfection in which everything were contained, whatever followed it would have to be less than its source. We are already familiar with the problems this view of the beginning entails for the nature of the original giver. If we understood creation in terms of this concept of beginning, creation would be a perfect state that, once in place, would need only to be preserved. An original rejection of the gift, therefore, would mean a fall from a perfect state, and mercy the return to that original perfection. If this idea of the beginning governs our thought, then we cannot see either in what sense mercy brings about something new, or how divine forgiveness fulfills the divine originary plan "to unite all things in Christ" (Eph 1:10). If, instead, the beginning is viewed as a promise to be fulfilled, as Hegel sees it, the original gift lacks both its proper distinction from the giver and the gratuity necessary for the gift to be gift. Furthermore, in this view God's mercy appears as an instance of divine self-diffusive goodness without real novelty. If the first conception of beginning presupposes a static cosmology according to which the world is a perfectly ordered whole and the future a return to this freely abandoned state, the second rests on a more dynamic, open-ended representation of time, according to which the future represents not only the ground from which to think the present (Heidegger), but that end that will bring past and present back to nothingness.

The second temptation touches on the nature of distinction. Our contemporary scientific imagination leads us to interpret distinction in terms of separation and chronological succession. If such a distinction were made, the original donation would differ from the renewal of the creature in that it comes before and remains other than the "new creation" that Christ's gift of self merited for the singular. The first donation would remain radically independent of the second. Departing from such strict distinctions, human reason's broader task is to perceive the unity, and within this unity, to perceive its components—which, as such, do not exist independently from this unity. Thus divine mercy does not imply a denial of the original donation, but rather its fulfillment. To sever the first from the second creation, even out of a legitimate wish to preserve the novelty of the latter, signals instead an oblivion of the promise contained in the original gift, as well as of the presence of the giver in the gift. Just as distinction does not mean the separation of one from the other, so their unity does not confuse the original gift with God's forgiving. The renewal of the gift, as we have seen, is not the reiteration of the original gift.

The third temptation has to do with the nature of freedom. If freedom is understood in terms of independence, then either finite freedom will be subservient to a predetermined destiny, as Calvin suggests, or divine freedom will lack the power to call those whom the Father in his benevolence wishes to call (Eph 1:8–10). The first case leaves no room for a historical dialogue between God and man. Without history, every ingratitude is a priori removed to the realm of the divinity. On the other hand, if divine freedom is incapable of exercising divine benevolence, the human being cannot but limit transcendence within history and view eternity as innumerable, finite possibilities. If the first understanding of freedom eliminates any real salvation for the sake of preserving God's glory, the second reduces divine glory to a merely human endeavor.

To see the circularity between the original donation and the renewal of the gift effected by mercy—with beginning, unity, and freedom understood as laid out above—we need to recall that the original positivity of the singular's being is clarified and confirmed in Christ. It is crucial to see, however, that our previous claim that the Incarnate Logos is the archetype and not the prototype of gift clarifies the gift-ness of the concrete singular because it confirms it. The renewal of the gift enables us to see what was there from the beginning and not the other way around. Christ's existence, as the Pauline hymns indicate, invites us to think of time from its fulfillment and not from its chronological inception. Scripture views time in light of the end. Thus, God bestows the first gift, he creates, because from the very beginning he intends to call the human being to adoptive filiation.

The renewal of the gift in Christ, as Scotus indicates, is at the service of God's glory. It is because God wishes from the beginning to let his glory shine through the human being that the Incarnation takes place.[48] Precisely because what is at stake is the concrete singular's recognition and enjoyment of divine glory, mercy is God's unexpected, unforeseeable response to man's rejection and not simply another gift.[49] The human being could not fully enjoy God's glory without freely participating in the utter spontaneity and bottomless gratuity of God's love as hypostasized by the Holy Spirit. It is more fruitful to ponder the circularity between the original donation and its renewal in terms of Scripture than to adopt those of freedom and necessity (in the sense criticized earlier with respect to God's reception of the singular's response). Read by the Church, Scripture allows us to see that the exuberant gift of Christ's salvific death reveals the meaning of the original creation. The original gift was given because from the beginning, God wanted the concrete singular to participate in the communion of love that God is and to do so as son in the Son (Gal 4:4–7; 2 Pet 1:4). That Jesus Christ freely fulfills the original plan by obeying the Father's will in the Holy Spirit

---

48. Scotus, *Reportatio parisiensis in Sent. III*, d. 7, q. 4, in Scotus, *Minorum opera omnia*, 301–4.

49. Aquinas, *ST*, III, q. 1, a. 3.

unto the end means, therefore, that the original, creative gift "carries historically and from the beginning the mark of that orientation [towards adoptive filiation], according to which the first creation is fulfilled coincidentally with the first act that fulfills this sovereign plan."[50] The renewal of the gift, God's for-giveness, leads the human being as son to the house of the Father because it enables him to accept the Father's love after the disastrous affair with the deceitful beauty of evil. What is new, therefore, does not relate to the existence of something else but rather to God's act of making definitive the singular's indwelling in his love so that man may embrace God's mercy. This happens when, through Christ, man surrenders to the evidence that the Father's mercy is stronger than his own ingratitude. Had ingratitude and redemption not been free, God's *agapic*, overabundant love would not have been able to give what God originally intended for the singular: adoptive sonship. Mysteriously and despite itself, man's ingratitude allows him to see the extent to which being's finitization reaches. Not, again, because it makes God's redemption necessary, but because just as man's ingratitude was an expression of his real freedom, so redemption is the fruit of the infinite freedom of God's charity. In this sense, the overabundant gift of mercy grounds the very possibility of the gratuitous being given to be. Thus, there is no confusion between the original, creative gift and its renewal. Without the former, the singular's response would not be free, and without the latter, it could not be fully gratuitous. The latter is the fulfillment of the former and is itself fulfilled along with the original donation. That Christ's gratuitous and unexpected gift fulfills man's nature shows that the conclusion of history marks the fulfillment both of Christ's gift of self and of the original creation.

We can see further that mercy represents both a continuity and a discontinuity with God's donation if we recall that mercy is the historical expression of God's triune love. Because God's love is an eternal, ever-fruitful beginning, there can be such a thing as a gift that is both radically new and also simultaneously fulfills the original gift. God is eternal because he is the same God as Father, Son, and Holy Spirit. Newness in God, as we saw, resides not in the fact that something takes place that had not occurred before, but in that God is one as Father, Son, and Holy Spirit, three persons who remain eternally different from each other and eternally one. God can create anew, that is, redeem, because he is eternally a communion of persons in which each person is all that the other is and yet is other from the other two. To say that God's eternity is the ground for the historical revelation of his love as mercy does not merely affirm the Trinitarian being-gift as the condition of possibility for mercy to take place. Analogically to the way that

---

50. Bordoni, *Il Cristo*, 731.

in God newness means being other while remaining the same, mercy constitutes the human being who receives it as a new person. Thus, the nature of the renewal of the gift is for the singular to indwell God's communion while remaining himself. Mercy in-novates human nature and unites the fallen cosmos to God because it allows man to enjoy God's unfathomable life without exhausting it. What is new is a greater, deeper, and personal participation in God's being. The human person can enjoy adoptive sonship precisely because God is his eternal, ever-fruitful beginning. In other words, he can be brought ever more deeply into the ever-greatness of the relation of love that eternally binds the Father, the Son, and the Holy Spirit together without dissolving one into the other. Divine love eternally bestows perfect unity as *perichoretic* indwelling. It creates so that the concrete singular might be freely brought into this eternal, ever-new love.

From man's point of view, mercy represents a novelty because the relation with God, others, and the world is restored. Newness thus accounts for the permanence of the gift—a permanence that, since it bears within it the renewal of the gift, occurs as an event of love. For the concrete singular who rejects God's gift, "novelty" ultimately remains a tedious reiteration of his own solitude. Those who embrace God's mercy discover that thanks to the Holy Spirit, the novelty is the recurrence of the gift. The Holy Spirit does not lead the singular to a vision of another love. Rather, the Holy Spirit continuously brings the person more deeply into God's ever-greater tripersonal beginning. As Guardini writes, "In the experience of the great love, the whole world is gathered together in the I-Thou relation and whatever takes place becomes an event within this relation."[51] Within this unity of life generated by Christ's mercy, everything becomes an event precisely because everything and everyone is seen and loved in the light of God's eternal beginning, that is, in its own inexhaustible wholeness stemming from unity with the eternal source.

Another instance that helps us see the circularity between the newness of the gift brought by God's mercy and the fulfillment of the original gift is the relation between mercy and justice. I would now like to offer a few brief, and thus inevitably limited, remarks to indicate how mercy's renewal of the gift makes justice possible. We would soon reach an impasse if we uncritically accepted the current understanding of justice that, stemming from Grotius and Hobbes, considers justice first and foremost in regard to the state's regulation of social common life in its goal of the preservation of peace. Justice, in this sense, does not have to do with the human person but rather with the social order in which the state guarantees the equality of its

---

51. Guardini, *Das Wesen des Christentums*, 42.

members through procedures and the subjective determination of rights.[52] If justice is understood to preserve equality in society and to do so universally, it cannot but be viewed in dialectic opposition to mercy. Whereas mercy indicates a privilege given to someone in particular, justice defends equality of treatment for everyone. This perception of justice cannot help rebelling against the way the paternal mystery deals with us: understanding and forgiving.

Along with this cultural reduction of the meaning of justice—which shifts the emphasis from the person to society—we need to acknowledge the difficulty stemming from man's originary experience. On the one hand, it seems that justice must be upheld before mercy can enter into human relations. Indeed, the criminal should not go unpunished, and the social order needs to be respected if members are to conduct a human life. On the other hand, in the face of one's own ingratitude, one may rightly wonder whether justice is at all possible. Faithfulness to man's originary experience, however, does not simply leave us with a conundrum. It also helps us reorient our gaze to the person. It then becomes possible to discover that justice aims at the good of the person, or, more precisely, that it draws out the relationship between the person and the good. One desires to be treated justly, that is, according to one's own being and to the good for which one is made.[53] The establishment of a peaceful, ordered society—with justice for the criminal and for all—can only be the fruit of the defense of the person's relationship to the good, which is ultimately God. Once one acknowledges the good of the other, it is possible to want the good for the other. Only then does one seek to give to the other what is his due, as the classic definition of justice indicates, that is, "being" and permanence in the relation with God.[54]

The perception of the other for what he is and of his relationship to the good is precisely what mercy ensures. Mercy reveals that the human being is loved by God for who he is and that he is loved gratuitously. Justice is not therefore a first level to be secured before any talk of charity or mercy can begin. "Without gratuitousness there can be no justice in the first place."[55] It is only because, rather than denigrating the one on whom it is bestowed, mercy reveals "the unheard-of greatness of man" that people can be treated with justice.[56] Paradoxically, mercy's excessive gift alone can

---

52. Rawls, *Theory of Justice*; Rawls, *Political Liberalism*.

53. Giussani, *RS*, 113–19.

54. Homer, *Odyssey*, 14.84. See also Plato, *Republic* 331; Aristotle, *Rhetoric* 1.9; Cicero, *De finibus* 5.23; Ambrose, *De officiis* 1.24.115 (CCSL 15:41); Augustine, *Civ.* 21 (CCSL 48:688); Aquinas, *ST*, II–II, q. 58, a. 1.

55. Benedict XVI, *Caritas in veritate*, no. 38 (AAS 101 [2009], 673).

56. John Paul II, *Dives in misericordia*, no. 7 (AAS 72 [1980], 1199).

secure the equality that society needs, because only mercy affirms the being of the singular without limitation. To give the other his due is thus rooted in the infinite value of the concrete singular, for whose salvation the Father did not spare his own Son. Only in charity can one give to the other what is truly his, that without which he is not himself: his relation with the divine origin.[57] God's salvific deed in Christ is an act of justice towards man also because through his mercy he restores the human being to unity with the Father. Mercy is the personal place of origin for justice. Moreover, mercy is "a superabundance of justice."[58]

Undoubtedly, God's mercy scandalizes. Yet Christ's excessive gift, the bottomless gratuity with which he embraces the one who rejects him, is not a scandal because it is "unjust," but because it breaks open the limited measure underlying the human understanding of justice. "Am I not allowed to do what I choose with what belongs to me? Or do you begrudge my generosity?" (Matt 20:15). With this question, Jesus does not say that God's love is irrational. Rather, he shows that the scandal prompted by divine goodness expresses a guilty forgetfulness that created singularity is gift. From within original ingratitude, the human person cannot deal in full justice with his neighbor—that is, he cannot affirm the other's constitutive relationship with God in whatever he does. Just as the older son's rebellion at his father's lavish forgiveness of the prodigal son reveals his supposed obedience as an attempt to grasp through his actions what was already freely given to him, so the utter gratuitousness of the Father's love in Christ brings to light a conception of freedom that, oblivious to its own indebtedness, cultivates a desire for unlimited power. Christ's justice reveals man's misery not in order to humiliate him, but in order to allow him to be. "Mercy," says Giussani, "is a justice that re-creates because it does not conceal what I am, rather it gives me the strength of a Presence thanks to which I am reconstituted a thousand times every day."[59] After the rejection of the gift, to recognize—that is, to welcome and reciprocate—God's totality entails participating in his own unceasing and ever-surprising gratitude. Man's dignity is so elevated that he is enabled to become like the Father and "show mercy" to both the crucified-risen Son

---

57. "*Charity goes beyond justice*," says Benedict XVI, "because to love is to give, to offer from what is 'mine' to the other; but it never lacks justice, which prompts us to give to the other what is 'his,' what is due to him by reason of his being or his acting. I cannot 'give' what is mine to the other without first giving him what pertains to him in justice. If we love others with charity, then first of all we are just towards them. Not only is justice not extraneous to charity, not only is it not an alternative or parallel path to charity: justice is 'inseparable from charity,' and intrinsic to it" (Benedict XVI, *Caritas in veritate*, no. 6 [AAS 101 (2009), 644]).

58. John Paul II, *Dives in misericordia*, no. 7 (AAS 72 [1980], 1201).

59. Giussani, "Il Giubileo."

and to others (Matt 25:40).[60] Let us now examine the transformation of the concrete singular that the Holy Spirit effects in time.

5. The Unity of Life (II)

God's gratuitous re-novation of the gift that constitutes the concrete singular's being effects the unity that the singular desires by setting him within a dwelling place. We said earlier that the Holy Spirit gradually ensures through this place and through historical circumstances that the singular gratuitously receives and reciprocates the love that forgives him. Drawing on the work of Giussani, we can now approach the anthropological and ontological implications of divine mercy. Three inseparable layers reveal what it means for the concrete singular that unity is the permanence of the gift.

First, in light of God's salvific deed in history, the concrete singular perceives mercy in having been welcomed gratuitously. Through the Spirit of Christ, the human being discovers that God unexpectedly welcomes him, that he has invited him anew to be and dwell in him. Giussani contends that "mercy, in its ultimate depth, is embrace, hospitality, better, the *embrace* of the other (*diverso*)."[61] This definition of mercy, which Giussani continuously deepens throughout his life, indicates the ontological and anthropological dimensions of love: to love (as *eros-agape*, and mercy) is "to embrace the other." This embrace of the other is indeed the restoration of unity between God and the singular, and the becoming-true of the filial nature of the singular as disclosed by man's originary experience. Yet welcoming the other is most specific to the triune God: "The mystery of the Trinity is, analogically speaking, an infinite welcoming; an infinitely totalizing and infinitely gratuitous welcoming."[62] Because God's life is the eternal welcoming of the gift of the other, God first embraces the singular by overcoming in creation the distance between being and nothingness, and then the even greater distance between the being that God is and man's rejection of him. As our reflection on the Paschal Mystery showed, Jesus Christ consents to embrace the Father's wrath and bear his silence so that, by experiencing as a man a solitude no human being could endure, he may allow the Holy Spirit to witness to the Father's unfailingly faithful love for his creature. Mercy is the energy internal to love's gift that overcomes the distance of otherness.[63]

---

60. John Paul II, *Dives in misericordia*, no. 8 (AAS 72 [1980], 1205).

61. Giussani, "La *Dives in misericordia*," 157. Emphasis added. See also Giussani, *MO*, 46.

62. Giussani, *MO*, 66.

63. Giussani, "I fondamenti della condivisione," 32; Giussani, *USD*, 36.

Breaking through the solitude that the rejection of the gift introduced into God's plan for communion means returning to a vision of the whole, in which no part of the singular is left out. The Father's mercy, revealed in Christ and communicated by the Holy Spirit, is the embrace of the entire human person. This, of course, as the Fathers elucidated, requires the Logos to assume all of man. At the same time, as revelation and the Church's tradition also show, to embrace the totality of the human person is to be with him and to share all of oneself with him. God's gift of self is a sharing of all of his life with all of man. The singular who, thanks to the Holy Spirit, welcomes the Father's mercy perceives that life is communion with God. "The mystery that makes everything," Giussani said, "is communion within the Trinity."[64]

The light of the unforeseeable, ever-renewing embrace of God allows human beings to welcome each other. This welcoming, before it is something one does for the other, is a recognition of who the finite other is; that is, it is a forgiveness of the other's alterity. "Welcoming otherness is called forgiveness because to embrace the other, one first needs to forgive him. To forgive means to affirm, underneath all the waste, what is true, just, good, and beautiful in the other's being: it is to affirm the *being* of the other. Your being is greater, deeper, and more important than the thousands and thousands of sins you commit."[65] To forgive, therefore, is to affirm, to recognize the singular's being. As such, it is to assent with all of oneself to the truth of the other and to let the other be in himself and in oneself. It is, in this regard, a gratuitous obedience to the truth of the singular's being and of the communion with him to which one is called. To forgive the other, and to affirm his being, as our reflection on the circularity of religiosity and freedom

---

64. "The mystery that makes everything is communion within the Trinity. Reality, from stones all the way up to us, is an echo of this communion. Existing is the communion of God with us. Existing is God's communication to us. God is more interior to us than our own heart, our own I, than our selves. Prayer thus is the only gesture that is totally intelligent. Prayer is nothing but the realization that life is communion" (*Holy Week Exercises*, 1964. Unpublished document). More recently Giussani has stated that "the mystery of the Trinity explains further—it is not that the dogma says everything: it says something definitive about the nature of the self and of things, something of which the human mind would never have had the faintest perception or knowledge—that Being is communion. Communion should imply a plurality, pluralism. But where is unity? The greater the communion, the greater the unity. The more a relation is multiplied, the more that relation affirms itself as a profound unity. Instead, the definition of unity as isolated, as singularity, is like abandoning something in the desert; it is a fragment of something that has neither nexus nor relation; it is therefore something that has no meaning. That Being is communion explains why the more man loves, affirms the other, the more he affirms himself" (Giussani, "*Tu*," 69–70). See also his *JTE*, 69–77.

65. Giussani, *MO*, 60.

illustrated, requires acknowledging the relation between the singular and his divine source. Only when the other is let be—acknowledged, affirmed, and welcomed—in his relation with God, who is in fact the other *par excellence*, is his being-gift affirmed.[66] Ethics is ordered in light of this ontology. God's forgiveness allows the human being who lets himself be embraced by it to receive the gift of his own being and that of the others with all the vicissitudes of their historical existence. God's embrace of the singular and the latter's welcoming of other beings is a new unity. St. Paul, reflecting on the bond generated by dwelling in Christ, describes the unity into which God's mercy entrusted him: "There is neither Jew nor Greek, there is neither slave nor free, there is neither male nor female; for you are all one in Christ Jesus" (Gal 3:28). As St. Paul's existence also witnesses, mercy generates unity, but it does so through the reciprocation of the concrete singular. Only the one who lets himself be received by God is able to accept his own otherness—with respect to God and to other singulars—and to forgive others. He is thus enabled to reach in time the perfection he desires.[67]

Second, to welcome Christ's mercy means to change. God's love is powerful enough to change the human being. Through his Holy Spirit, God opens him up from within to the life God wants to share with him (Ezek 36:26). This change, being freed from ingratitude, fragmentation, and death, is neither mechanical nor instantaneous. God's light of lights slowly, and never without man's cooperation, turns man's gaze from his own sin towards the Father's unfailing love present in Christ. The singular who has embraced orphanhood, no matter how much tranquility he finds in ever-transient power or success, tends to believe that his own evil defines him. To nature's fragility in affirming being, due to its being created from nothingness, man's own ingratitude adds a tendency to cherish a strange, desolate humiliation for the shame of his sins. It is through this shame that evil persistently attempts to take hold of the singular's existence. When the Holy Spirit gives the sinner the eyes of love to look at his own ingratitude in the light of the crucified-risen Christ, the person is brought to see that the evil he generated or permitted is not greater than God's virginal love. To accept that God's love is greater is an excruciating conversion that requires the ungrateful person to let go of his own idea of perfection and of the predilection for his own coherence in responding to the original gift. The first change that mercy introduces into the singular's existence is the very desire to change. "If the human being," Giussani says, "recognizes mercy, he accepts himself and entrusts himself to Another, to the merciful

---

66. Giussani, *RVU*, 38–43.
67. Giussani, *L'alleanza*, 118.

Other, in order to change."⁶⁸ The first change of mercy is a radical re-form: rather than regret for his own failures, the human being experiences sorrow for having betrayed the one who loves him. Whereas regret is yet another outburst of orphan solitude, sorrow responds to the pain one has inflicted on another, that is, the denial of the other. The entrusting of oneself to the Father's merciful gift, his most beloved Son, therefore, "is the sorrow for oneself that is true sorrow and it is pregnant with gladness."⁶⁹ The sorrow that mercy begets in the person is neither egotistic self-pity nor desperation at one's own incapacity. It is the fruit of discovering the truth of oneself as loved. Giussani finds in the last dialogue between Jesus and Peter in John's Gospel (John 21:15–19) the clearest exemplification of this change. Rather than regret for his own threefold betrayal, Peter recognizes three times that Christ's love for him is stronger than his own sins. "He feels no more horror at what he had done, because horror sets man once more in the foreground. What imposes itself is sorrow for one's own sins, as the historic beginning of a love that waits to be recovered."⁷⁰ As a beginning that awaits recovery, the desire to change is both sorrow and gladness. Mercy, granting the certainty of the Father's faithfulness, brings the desire to change and reminds the singular that, although somehow already participating in it, he has still not reached the Father's house.

How are we to perceive the desire to change that God's gratuitous forgiveness elicits in the singular? The change that the forgiven singular longs for is not self-sufficiency or uniform coherency. Contemporary moral theories, à la Spinoza or Kant, have proved as uplifting as they are useful. The desired change, instead, is the desire to be like him who forgives the sinner. He who experiences the renewal of his own being—who, for example, becomes capable of silence and of forgiveness—sees himself and others through the one who gave his life for him. The singular not only begins to see himself and others in Jesus Christ, he also wishes to love as he is loved. Union with the one who forgives, with Jesus Christ, makes one desire that others may enjoy and taste the same delightful love that has already begun to take possession of oneself. More importantly, Giussani indicates, the one who has been forgiven yearns to be like the one who loves him. Under the light of the experience of mercy, Jesus's demand that his followers be merciful as the Father is merciful appears as the supremely desirable command (Luke 6:36). "This seems to go against common sense, but only to a certain extent, because *that* is the desire that defines the soul of the new man. Unless one

---

68. Giussani, *RVU*, 42.
69. Ibid.
70. Giussani, *GTSM*, 187; *USD*, 145.

desires to be merciful like the Father who is in heaven, one is not truly human. The question is whether we really desire it."[71]

The one who welcomes Christ's mercy and desires to be like the one whose gratuitous generosity lets him be anew, lets the sacrifice of prayer take place. Mercy's omnipotence builds upon the damaged but real freedom of the singular by allowing him to pray again.[72] Freedom's assent to the Father's mercy present in Jesus Christ through the Holy Spirit translates the desire to change into the entreaty to be changed. The singular who truly desires to be like the Father begs him to be made like him, and to be taught to deal with himself and others with the same mercy with which he himself is treated. Prayer, asking, is the truth of desire. The one who desires to reciprocate puts himself in the hands of the one who can fulfill him. He is truly himself and loves (*eros-agape*) without being afraid to enter into the joy of belonging to the one who takes delight in him. The affection for Jesus Christ, which his merciful gift of self elicits in the sinner, will be kept from withering only if the sinner asks to be like the one who loves him. Existentially, the miracle that mercy operates in the person is this prayer. In it, Christ's gift of self is welcomed and reciprocated. Giussani contends that Christ's entreaty for the Father's glory to be manifested (John 17:1) and for the miracle of unity in the world to take place (John 17:22–23) is answered above all in the one who, having been forgiven, prays.[73] We have dealt with prayer on several occasions so far. Now, faced with God's mercy in Jesus Christ, which reaches the person through the Holy Spirit, we discover that the prayer to the merciful God to be made like him is prayer's purest, most sublime, and rarest expression.

Prayer is not only the expression of freedom that has been liberated to embrace truth; it is also the fruit of the singular's poverty. The singular's unity of being is a gift given to him and gratuitously received. So it is with the permanence of that gift: it requires the poverty that recognizes that the singular's wealth is to receive himself from the eternally faithful Father and to live for him. Poverty does not mean arbitrary misery and contingency. Rather, poverty is the recognition of one's constitutive relativity to the mystery and the active availability to the paternal source. Poverty, therefore, more than the condition of possibility for mercy to effect the renewal of the singular's unity and permanence in being, is the expression of the true form of the gift. If the person continues to be unaware of his own constitutive relativity to God and of the continuous search for it, the fire of the Father's

---

71. Giussani, *GTSM*, 187. Emphasis added.
72. Giussani, *RVU*, 225.
73. Giussani, "Vita e spirito," 43.

mercy cannot purify and change ingratitude to sorrow, or transform the desire to be like him who always understands and forgives into the entreaty to be made like him.

The desire to change and the entreaty to be like the Father—that is, to be in him—emerge historically. In addition to the other ways already indicated, mercy also remains in history as education. The Father whose patience knows no end is the one who continuously educates the concrete singular to the truth of all that is. The Holy Spirit is able to bring the person into the unity of divine life and love because, both from inside and outside the person, he educates him. The Holy Spirit gratuitously, continuously removes the human being from the ingratitude where his fears hide him and introduces him into the totality proper to God's gift. The Father does not fulfill man's entreaty automatically. He educates the person in time so that the human being may deal increasingly with everyone and everything as the Father does. Education, then, means much more than obtaining an academic degree or making it through a transitional stage in life. It is the Father's capacity to teach the person to contemplate everything that exists in its gifted wholeness and to affirm and engage the world for the Father's glory. The one who is not afraid to follow the unexpected paths of Jesus Christ and who seeks continuously to be corrected is brought ever more deeply through the Holy Spirit into the very heart of being: the merciful Father.

Third, mercy, in its binding of the singular to God and to all that is, gives the human being a foretaste of eternity. "No word indicates the ultimate finishing line from which the eternal opens itself to time as much as mercy does."[74] Mercy, allowing the singular to remain in relation with the original giver, enables man to enter into the meaning of time and to discover its unity with and distinction from eternity.

Time allows us to experience love and prevents us from precipitously seizing the totality we encounter within it. We discover in time the joy of being, but we cannot detach this joy from its certain though undetermined end. Time awakens our need for a truth lived at a certain moment to remain, not simply to linger on. While a true perception and affirmation of what is takes place in time, it seems that time itself does not know how to make us dwell in it. Time, while allowing us to see the mysterious beauty shining through the richness of the world and through history, does not have the capacity to preserve this beauty within itself. This limit could lead us to say that since the goodness, the truth, and the beauty of the singulars we perceive exist within the ever-flowing stream of time, they are simply finite.

---

74. Giussani, "La fede," 1.

Some thinkers, in fact, interpret this incapacity of time as a sign that being, rather than the gift of having been given to be, is the *possibility* of being. Setting aside the passive sense of gift (having-been-given), they see in the concrete singular only the active sense (the possibility and capacity to be). They thus do not look to the present but rather to the future to illuminate the puzzling emergence of their own existence.[75] Time itself, however, prevents us from fully entrusting ourselves to this interpretation. Our desire to dwell in being—the anthropological echo of the singular's participation in *esse* through *esse commune*—attests that we constantly receive and have to receive being. Time participates in eternity. The singular's experience of time results in the yearning for the permanence of the unity of being in which time participates but which time cannot give itself. The singular waits to be confirmed in the hope that his participation in being may not only renew his existence but, in doing so, will also preserve the richness of the gift that unfolds itself as good, true, and beautiful.

It may not be immediately intuitive to think of mercy in relation to time, except, of course, in relation to the resurrection of the flesh and the entrance into the Father's house. Still, if mercy is indeed the entry of God's love into history, then it is also the truth of time. The singular's original ingratitude caused time to take on the reduced form of an enclosure. God's mercy redeems time, because it allows this limit once again to be pure relation with the source. Thanks to the Holy Spirit, mercy unifies by binding temporal being anew to the Father of Jesus Christ. This intrinsic relation between time and eternity that mercy ensures begins with the rediscovery of the present. Forgiveness, in giving us back to ourselves by restoring the relation with the merciful Father, allows us to rediscover the present. The present no longer languishes in the supporting role of a stepping-stone to more important moments, or as an empty space where we do as we will. It is instead filled with the presence of the gift's wholeness. Mercy allows the singular to perceive beings as present in time, and not as mere tools, and so to retrieve the gift of their being and their unity with the divine source for which they have been destined.

The unity of time and eternity also affects the past. Mercy does not permit anxiety, the fear that the Father is unfaithful, to wipe out what has gone before. As the fulfillment of what was originally given, mercy constitutes the memory proper to the present. This memory brings the discovery that one has always been awaited. The one who has been forgiven no longer looks at the past with nostalgia for what was lost. He rather comes to behold

---

75. The most brilliant example of this approach, as is well known, is Heidegger's *Being and Time*.

in the past, too, the richness of the gift of being and how the ensuing events led to where he now stands, in the presence of mercy. Mercy becomes the memory of the past because it redeems what took place. The past no longer threatens. It is neither a reminder of nothingness nor the burden of one's old ingratitude. Mercy enables the singular to see how his past existence, with all its crooked ways, has mysteriously brought him to rediscover the unspeakable beauty of gift's gratuity.

Mercy also prevents anxiety from reducing the future to something that simply comes and goes. The singular discovers through mercy that the future holds both the ongoing unfolding of the promise of the present gift and the coming of the one who alone can forgive him. The future is not the blank land of opportunity, but rather the unexpected arrival of the faithful giver. Mercy unites the present to the future not because it throws a bridge between them, but because it allows the present to participate in God's eternal patience. The one who has been forgiven knows that the one who was able to find him where he had hidden himself will always be able to surprise him anew with the gift of his presence. In this way, the present waits for the final fulfillment of the promise of being, that is, it asks for this fulfillment to be given. The entreaty to change, to become like the Father, is a matter of the present, not of the future. If it were attached to the future, the singular would be left back in his own hands, facing the impossible task of piecing his life together by his own feeble powers. If the entreaty did not apply to the present, strengthened with the memory of the past, the singular would have no hope. Instead, because mercy liberates the present from fear of the future, the singular discovers that the reciprocation of the gift and the longing for an answer are coincident with entrusting oneself to the one in whom all things hold together. Prayer, from this point of view, is the inchoate unity of time and eternity for which man is always on the hunt—not because prayer pulls the human being away from history, but because it enables him to dwell in its roots: eternity.

If mercy allows us to rediscover the value of the present in its unity with and distinction from the past and the future, then pondering the relation between mercy and virginity deepens the unity and distinction between time and eternity. If mercy enables the unity of the present with the eternal source, a unity that is expressed in prayer, it also reveals that the true possession of being and of people who seem constantly to escape our grasp—like Aeneas's embrace of his father in the underworld—is what we described above as virginity. If, thanks to the merciful God, time is a relation with eternity, and if man's self-awareness that takes place in time is at the service of the Father's glory, then the transient reality given to the singular becomes truly his as he lets it be. This is why, from the point of view of time, mercy and virginity are correlative terms. To the one who is forgiven, everything is given back as a gift that can finally be embraced with complete purity. Virginity allows us to see how time begins to open for us the gratuitous possession of being.

The rejection of the gift leaves the singular frustrated by the impossibility of keeping everything for himself. The ungrateful person loses what he thinks he keeps a tight grip on. As with King Midas, the singular who tries to grasp things while denying that they are given to him only reduces whatever he touches to his own narrow vision. Time will deprive him of what he owns. Mercy, however, reveals owning as possessing in gratitude—a form of possession by which, as we saw, the singular recognizes that the other is given to him and hence must be permitted to be. Mercy expresses itself also as virginity because mercy enables and educates to a possession within a detachment. Virginity, as we saw, is possession within a detachment, the affirmation of the singular simply because it is. The inseparable polarity of virginity and mercy discloses that the present receives itself continuously from the Father, who awaits the singular and lets him live in the present so that he can slowly learn the infinite fruitfulness of the Father's presence. Therefore, when viewed in the light of mercy, time does not deprive us of what we hold dear (ourselves, the beloved other, the world, and life itself with all its beauty). It rather reminds us that our possession is true because it is given to us. Whatever belongs to us, even the fruit of our own work, is ours because it is given to us and asks to be offered without delay to the one of whose charity it speaks. Paradoxically, "things and people belong, in me, to Another."[76] Virginal love affirms the other in its relation to the mystery and lets the other be. The detachment proper to love's never-ending gratuity ensures another important aspect: the future is not collapsed into the present, nor is eternity reduced to time. Time, and the present, patiently wait to receive from the paternal giver whatever he wishes to bestow at the fullness of time. Mercy allows the singular a foretaste of eternity, not by eliminating time but by bestowing on him a ray of love's final form. It is the sheer exuberance and newness of divine mercy that bring about this radically new way of receiving and reciprocating the gift, which Christianity calls virginity.[77]

---

76. Giussani, *TT*, 88.

77. Obviously, that mercy allows the singular to remain in the present, to affirm and to own with a gratuitous detachment the gift that he yearns to receive eternally, does not mean that the distinction between the states of life elucidated earlier is blurred. It is indeed the case that whoever encounters Christ's mercy experiences his fruitful virginity and hence has a foretaste of the deathlessness and virginity proper to him. Yet, the one called to live virginally is asked to dwell in Christ's fruitful virginity and remains in

If mercy allows us to see in what sense eternity renews time by allowing it to remain in the life proper to the gift, and by enabling the person to own what is given without demanding or raising a claim to it, it also educates the person in the certainty that the *goal* of all that exists is absolutely positive. This claim, of course, does not *eo ipso* transform evil into good. The singular that has rejected the gift needs to be redeemed and so needs time for God's mercy to change him. Still, in light of the unity of eternity with time that mercy introduces in history, we can say that regardless of whatever one might have done or might do, "it is certain that God cannot wipe out any good action—not even one—made by man. Because if the nature of being is love, even one single human action can defend whole lives."[78] Apart from the experience of mercy, this understanding of human action could seem appallingly unjust, a conception, in other terms, that does not give evil its adequate weight. Nevertheless, Giussani continues, "The mystery overcomes our measure; the mystery rests on the gap open between what the human being is and his actions, between what is conscious and what is objective of his action: only God can save this disproportion."[79]

The existence of evil should not deceive us into thinking that the rejection of the gift—expressed in ever more subtle and pervasive ways—defines the singular. The singular, given to himself, does not have the capacity to cast himself into nothingness. He can work destruction in history, which he does, but he cannot undo being altogether. Furthermore, the presence of evil, as John Paul II says, has a historical limit: Jesus Christ.[80] Mercy, however, is not simply a "limit," like a pier that blocks waves from ships anchored in the harbor. It is the love powerful enough to make all things new. "Mystery as mercy remains the last word also on every ugly possibility of history. In its evident piety, mercy is the most irresistible embrace of the Being, source, goal, and nature of every being.... This is Mystery's ultimate embrace, against which man—even the one who is furthest away, the most perverse, darkened, gloomiest one—cannot oppose anything, no objection: he can only desert this Mystery [of mercy], and in so doing he deserts himself and his own good. Mercy remains the last word even on every ugly possibility of history."[81]

---

it—by grace—in a way that will be given to those who have not been called to this state of life only at the end of time.

78. Giussani, *GTSM*, 189.
79. Ibid.
80. John Paul II, *Memory and Identity*, 1–30.
81. Giussani, *USD*, 49.

The experience of mercy, in giving the human being a real and unimaginable taste of longed-for unity with the Eternal, promises a final, irrevocable denial of any division. Since the solitude and ingratitude through which mercy pierces are those of death, then mercy, which is the presence and company of the crucified-risen One in the communion he continually generates, colors the ontological desire to be like the Father and to remain in being with hope for the resurrection of one's bodily self. The redeemed singular being hopes for the resurrection, that is, for that unity with the merciful God that affirms in a loving embrace the singular other and all that is. Just as the Holy Spirit confirms the divine gift in itself, so mercy, in allowing us to taste the eternity for which the singular gift is created, promises the unity intended by God from the beginning, which is always new. In history, the presence of the gift renewed is perceived as the dawn of a life that has already begun but still waits to reach all its eternal luminosity. The new, definitive beginning that the eschaton represents for the concrete singular leads him to enjoy communion with the one who, from all eternity, awaits him. In history, the resurrection promised by the merciful God continuously deepens and intensifies the ontological question. It does not silence it. Just as it strengthens and solicits freedom's response, so mercy does not allow reason to content itself with its own limited comprehension of the mystery of being. The singular's participation in divine love—without diminishing either God, *ipsum esse subsistens*, or the finite creature, whose being, eternally affirmed, will remain itself—abides as ever-greater wonder before God's inexhaustible gift of being and its luminous glory that alone is able to gather each singular being to itself.

Envoi

Contemplating the mystery of birth and our own originary experience invited us to acknowledge that the nature and unity of the singular being is gift, given to itself in order to recognize and adhere to the mystery of God, the *agapic* giver. The existence of the concrete singular reflects at every level—from the dual unity of its being to its action—its constitutive being-gift. Failing to heed the call to affirm himself and the world as gift by gratuitously recognizing that God is everything, the created singular human being attempted to grasp at a greater delight by conceiving himself from and for himself, rather than letting the promise of the gift become true in time. In so causing the irruption of nothingness, that is, in separating the gift from its *logos*, the concrete singular introduced disunity where communion was intended, and transience in the place of eternity. The singular, however, is not abandoned. His ingratitude does not silence the memory of the Father's faithfulness, and, in the midst of the sorrow it inflicts and the havoc it raises, evil—despite itself—causes the singular to recognize the need to welcome the gratuitous and unexpected confirmation of his own existence from the paternal mystery that begets every being.

Expressing anew in history his eternal, ever-fruitful beginning, God overturns the lie of the rejection of the gift through the long-awaited but unforeseeable event of the Incarnation. Wishing to give again, God discloses the ever-greater beauty and delight of the life proper to the gift: to be a person within the communion of being, to indwell love's eternal communication of itself. Christ reveals that the gift of being is a sharing in the *agapic* fullness of the triune act of being, which is eternally open for the concrete singular to participate in it as other. Assuming human nature and giving himself to the end, the crucified-risen Lord sends, with the Father, the Holy Spirit, the unifying memory of God's gratuitous gift. God thus renews the concrete singular and welcomes it again in the eternal, ever-fruitful beginning that he is. Rather than flattening the gift into an alogical equivocity or a mute univocity, the hypostatic union mysteriously discloses that the concrete singular gift, as *other* than God, is a most welcome participant in the sheer, gratuitous life that the Father constantly generates. God's triune communion of love offers to every concrete singular being the possibility of being and remaining in the eternal beginning that God is.

In the one who welcomes the icon of the Father's mercy and begins to live for him who makes the singular be, the unexpected restoration of the gift represents the beginning of a new culture, a new way of thinking and living that reflects the nature of being-gift and that shapes history according to this most beautiful light. The contemplation of gift as the form of being's unity and of this unity's permanence yields a new culture. Let us, to conclude, offer a few brief remarks on the nature of this culture.

Culture is the multifaceted, historical expression of life perceived and lived in light of the ultimate affirmed by a given people. Throughout its various forms—artistic, culinary, intellectual, ritual, sociological, architectural, et cetera—a culture offers to those who live within it, and who continue to shape it, the meaning of the whole. Culture is the historical expression of a people's religiosity. "The truly cultured person," writes Giussani, "is one who understands the *link* that binds one thing to another and all things to each other."[1] As our account of the circularity of freedom and religiosity pointed out, the human person always affirms something as the ultimate meaning of the whole and understands every singular in its light. Human reason and man's finite freedom can recognize and embrace this meaning; but they cannot not create it.[2] The ultimate is given to be recognized. As Ratzinger explains, "No one can understand the world at all, no one can live his life rightly, so long as the question about the Divinity remains unanswered. Indeed, the very heart of the great cultures is that they interpret the world by setting in order their relationship to the Divinity."[3]

The new culture that the ontology and theology of gift yields in history, precisely because it takes its bearings from the revelation of the truth of being in Jesus Christ, responds more deeply to man's natural religiosity. It is Christ's person, the archetype of gift, that represents the ultimate

---

1. Giussani, *JTE*, 20.

2. While noting the urgency of the question whether religion is a positive force, Ratzinger reminds us that "we must face *doubts about the reliability of reason*. For in the last analysis, even the atomic bomb is a product of reason, just as the breeding and selection of human beings in the laboratory have also been thought out by reason" (Benedict XVI, *Values*, 36–37).

3. Ratzinger, *Truth and Tolerance*, 65; Ratzinger, *Crisis of Cultures*. See also his "Meeting with Representatives from the World of Culture" (address given at Collège des Bernardins, Paris, France, September 12, 2008) (AAS 100 [2008], 721–30).

explanation of the gift-ness of reality. "The rationality that saves the universe from absurdity is not an abstract idea or a mechanism but *a person*: Jesus Christ."[4] If the cultured person is the one who is able to account for the relationship binding the singular with the universal, culture can be seen as the fruit of the ongoing work of "comparison between the truth of [Christ's] person and life in all its implications."[5] Culture is thus the historical, social, and multifaceted expression of the recognition of the gift that forms the unity of being and its permanence as it is disclosed by Christ.

To acknowledge that gift is the form of being's unity also implies that the cultural expression of the nature of being is always a limited, historical one, which is a priori open to other such expressions. The relation established with these others is governed by the dynamism of being, that is, the gift of self that affirms the other and lets the other be itself within the unity. To read this definition of culture and its unity as integralism, then, would misunderstand the ontology and theology of gift under consideration here. The culture that is born from recognition of the gift-ness of being is not the ideological exaltation of a singular as the meaning of the whole, which inevitably begets violence and war. "Properly understood," Schindler writes, "integralism is a program for effecting a (religious) unity, or wholeness, arbitrarily and through relations of power. Such an integration will by definition exclude those who do not share the same arbitrary relation to God: integralism is the progenitor of sectarianism."[6] Confusing with integralism the unity and the permanence of the gift of being that culture expresses in history betrays a positivistic conception of religion, one that, however sincerely pious it may be, relegates God to the outskirts of the intelligent order. Integralism, not seeing the intrinsic relation between gift and *logos*, deprives the gift of any presence of the giver in its interiority and denies the gratuity of their unity. The corrective to an integralist, ideological way of thinking is to take Christ, the concrete universal, as one's starting point. In Christ, "all the fullness of deity dwells bodily" (Col 2:9). The new culture generated by Christ's renewal of the singular gift does not exalt a particular as the meaning of the whole, nor does it perpetuate a partial worldview.[7] The encounter with the historical presence of Jesus Christ through his ecclesial communion generates a new person, the baptized, whose spirit is called to constantly deepen and change in order to enter into Christ's *nous* (Rom 12:1). When it drifts away from Jesus Christ and the dwelling place that sacramentally

---

4. Giussani, *JTE*, 20.
5. Ibid., 21.
6. D. L. Schindler, "Religious Sense," 93.
7. Giussani, *GTSM*, 152.

represents him, this culture tends to relinquish its universality and catholicity into the hands of divisive, sectarian ideologies. Within the Church, instead, the conversion required to welcome Christ's gift is a *meta-nous*, a radical change of mind that consists in acquiring the filial mind of Christ, that is, the mind of one whose being is eternally from and for the Father. In this way, the new creature, rather than conceiving of himself as being from and for himself, permits himself to be introduced by the Holy Spirit into the truth of the gift of his being and thus collaborates in bringing to perfection the Father's work in history.[8] Whatever he does is marked by this inherited filiality. The person who is aware of his own renewed gift-ness, and so lives with and for the giver in communion with others, creates a culture that is organic or native to the world's own being—a culture, that is, that can assist the ideal that the sign carries within itself, an ideal that culture suggests to the singular, on toward his fulfillment.

The culture that Christ makes possible is the *logiken latreia*, a spiritual worship (Rom 12:1). As such, it is both the perception, from within Christ and inasmuch as he allows it, of how things come together in the mystery of God (Rom 12:2; Eph 1:10), which is also the nuptial mystery of Christ and the Church (Eph 5:32), and the gratuitous offering of all of oneself. By indwelling him who appeared in the likeness (*schemata*) of man, Giussani insists, every thought (*schema*) is prevented from becoming empty: "Things are made of Christ and the only scheme is the design of the Father, which has a name: Christ."[9] In him, every thought takes on its proper light. Whereas the mentality that rejects the ontology and theology of gift adopts a logic of power as its *logos*—understood in the sense criticized earlier—and so renounces both the vision and the grateful possession that accompany the renewal of the gift, the new culture that stems from this renewal is the offering of oneself—an offering that is, as we saw, the apex of rationality and love, on the one hand, and the fulfillment of oneself, on the other.

Giussani calls ecumenism (*oikumene*) the full and organic development of the culture born from God's gift of self in Christ. Ecumenism "indicates that the Christian gaze vibrates with an impetus that makes it capable of exalting all the good that is in whatever it encounters."[10] Yet this good is perceived as good because "it is recognized as part of that design whose actualization has been revealed in Christ and whose final fulfillment begins

---

8. "Who lives not for himself but for God's 'Thou' is a non-egocentric self; he is rather a self who affirms the gratuity of the creative Mystery, one who belongs to the unity that originates in Baptism, unity of oneself and with others" (Giussani, *GTSM*, 148–49).

9. Ibid., 154.

10. Ibid., 157.

in the history of his mysterious Body."[11] Ecumenism, therefore, is not tolerance or a humanly produced unity. It is "the receiving again and again from the other as other, while respecting his otherness," that is, acknowledging the other's participation in the Father's design.[12] Just as the new culture has its origin in the person of Jesus Christ announced by the Church, so ecumenism begins with the event of the Incarnation of the Father's mercy. This love is the truth made visible (John 14:6) in history and, through the Holy Spirit, remains present in it (Matt 28:20). Within this love the value of a singular can be properly seen in its inexhaustible wholeness and is eternally affirmed.

The ecumenical gaze, rather than simply tolerating the other, loves and welcomes the other, precisely in its otherness. Whoever is attached to the whole that reveals itself in the concrete universal (John 1:14), along with the renewal of his own nature, also receives the truly critical gaze that can "recognize the emergence and the importance of a small particular over all its misery and strangeness."[13] The logic of power issuing from the rejection of the gift seeks to find the limit of the created singular and then reductively define it apart from any relation to God, thus as ultimately finite. This logic presents itself as objective, equanimous, and reasonable, criteria that are in themselves valuable. Yet if not understood in the relativized sense indicated earlier, these criteria would end up emphasizing in the other the constitutive finitude that one sees and rejects in oneself. If not viewed from within its intrinsic relation with the giving, paternal source, the perception in the other of "what is not" does not seek the affirmation of the other's alterity but rather goes after alterity's annihilation. By contrast, the logic of the gift, whose power and exuberance appear in the eucharistic sacrifice of Christ, is able to grasp and affirm unconditionally the frequently hidden value of alterity: "'things' true value can be found only by him who has the perception of being and goodness, who lets being emerge and be loved, without obliterating, severing, closing or denying; true critique is not hostility towards things but love of them."[14] The person whose existence has been renewed by God's gratuitous gift is called to live patiently with this tension: on the one hand, he does not know the form of the final fulfillment and destiny of each concrete singular; on the other hand, dwelling in the life that God's Spirit communicates, he is brought to see in ever-new and deeper ways that

11. Giussani, *NFT*, 32.

12. Ratzinger, *Church, Ecumenism, and Politics*, 136. The Catholic task of attempting to reconstruct unity with Orthodoxy, Protestantism, and Judaism is also a persistent note in Giussani's ecclesial work. See Camisasca, *Don Giussani*, 87–95.

13. Giussani, *NFT*, 35.

14. Giussani, *GTSM*, 158.

"the positivity with which Being made the participated being is an ultimate positivity for any participated being."[15] Without knowing the final form of this positivity, he still remains certain that "God our Savior desires all men to be saved and to come to the knowledge of the truth" (1 Tim 2:3–4).

The *oikumene* that the renewal of the gift generates, Giussani indicates, assigns us a precious task: "test everything; hold fast to what is beautiful (*to kalon katejete*)" (1 Thess 5:21). The affirmation of the gift-ness of being, in its inexhaustible truth and beauty, enables the human being to participate in God's unifying embrace of all that is. "Images of unsuspected possibilities for repairing ruined houses and for building new ones (Isa 58:12) are born from beauty."[16] It is precisely by affirming the beauty of the concrete singular gift that human beings enjoy the possibility of contributing to the restoration of what is given to be. God's love gratuitously calls the human person to participate in his own being and his own glory. He asks the person who reciprocates his ever-new love to collaborate in the radiation of its beauty. By enjoying and dwelling in God's ever-surprising communion of being and light, to the extent that this communion is given to him in history, the concrete singular receives and hands on anew this love that makes all things be themselves in the unity with the giver of all that is.

---

15. Giussani, *NFT*, 35.
16. Giussani, *GTSM*, 160.

Bibliography

Aeschylus. *Oresteia*. Translated by Richmond Lattimore. Chicago: University of Chicago Press, 1991.
Anatolios, Khaled. *Athanasius: The Coherence of His Thought*. New York: Routledge, 2005.
Anaxagoras. *The Fragments of Anaxagoras*. 2nd ed. International Pre-Platonic Studies 4. Sankt Augustin: Academia Verlag, 2005.
Anderson, Carl, and José Granados García. *Called to Love: Approaching John Paul II's Theology of the Body*. New York: Doubleday, 2009.
Aquinas, Thomas. *Aquinas on Creation: Writings on the "Sentences" of Peter Lombard, Book 2, Distinction 1, Question 1*. Translated by Steven E. Baldner and William E. Carroll. Toronto: Pontifical Institute of Mediaeval Studies, 1997.
———. *In duodecim libros Metaphysicorum Aristotelis expositio*. Edited by M. R. Cathala and R. M. Spiazzi. Turin: Marietti, 1950.
———. *In librum beati Dionysii De divinis nominibus expositio*. Edited by C. Pera. Turin: Marietti, 1950.
———. *In quator libros Sententiarum*. Vol. 1 of *S. Thomae Aquinatis opera omnia*, edited by R. Busa. Stuttgart-Bad Cannstatt: Frommann-Holzboog, 1980.
———. *Quaestiones disputatae de potentia Dei*. Turin: Marietti, 1965.
———. *Quaestiones disputatae de veritate*. Vol. 1. Turin: Marietti, 1964.
———. *Sancti Thomae de Aquino Opera omnia*. Editio altera retractata. Rome: Commissio Leonina, 1882–.
———. *Summa contra gentiles*. Vols. 22.1, 22.2, 22.3 of *Sancti Thomae de Aquino Opera omnia*. Leonine ed. Rome, 1882.
———. *Summa theologiae*. Turin: Marietti, 1962.
Aristotle. *Analytica posteriora*. Vol. 1. London: Oxford University Press, 1955.
———. *Categories. On Interpretation. Prior Analytics*. Translated by H. P. Cooke and Hugh Tredennick. Cambridge: Harvard University Press, 2002.
———. *Metaphysics*. Translated by Joe Sachs. Santa Fe, NM: Green Lion, 2002.
———. *Metaphysics, Books I–IX*. Translated by Hugh Tredennick. Cambridge: Harvard University Press, 2003.
———. *Metaphysics, Books X–XIV, Oeconomica, Magna Moralia*. Translated by Hugh Tredennick and G. Cyril Armstrong. Cambridge: Harvard University Press, 1990.
———. *Nicomachean Ethics*. Translated by Harris Rackham. Cambridge: Harvard University Press, 2003.
———. *Physics, Books I–IV*. Translated by P. H. Wicksteed and F. M. Cornford. Cambridge: Harvard University Press, 1996.

———. *Physics, Books V–VIII*. Translated by P. H. Wicksteed and F. M. Cornford. Cambridge: Harvard University Press, 2000.

———. *Posterior Analytics. Topica*. Translated by Hugh Tredennick and E. S. Forster. Cambridge: Harvard University Press, 2004.

Athanasius. *Athanasius: Selected Works and Letters*. Vol. 4 of *Nicene and Post-Nicene Fathers, Second Series*. Edited by Philip Schaff and Henry Wace. Peabody, MA: Hendrickson, 1994.

———. *On the Incarnation: The Treatise* De Incarnatione Verbi Dei. Crestwood, NY: St. Vladimir's Seminary Press, 1998.

———. *The Orations of S. Athanasius against the Arians*. Ancient and Modern Library of Theological Literature. London: Griffith, Farran, Okeden, & Welsh [1889?].

Augustine. *De civitate Dei*. In PL 41.

———. *De libero arbitrio*. In PL 32.

———. *De Trinitate*. In *Aurelii Augustini opera*. CCSL 50–50a. Turnhout: Brepols, 1968.

———. *De vera religione*. In PL 34.

Balthasar, Hans Urs von. *Bernanos: An Ecclesial Existence*. Translated by Erasmo Leiva-Merikakis. A Communio Book. San Francisco: Ignatius, 1996.

———. *Cosmic Liturgy: The Universe according to Maximus the Confessor*. Translated by Brian E. Daley. A Communio Book. San Francisco: Ignatius, 1988.

———. *Does Jesus Know Us? Do We Know Him?* Translated by Graham Harrison. San Francisco: Ignatius, 1983.

———. *Epilogue*. Translated by Edward T. Oakes. San Francisco: Ignatius, 2004.

———. *Explorations in Theology*. Translated by A. V. Littledale and Alexander Dru. 4 vols. San Francisco: Ignatius, 1989.

———. *The Glory of the Lord: A Theological Aesthetics*. Translated by Oliver Davies. 7 vols. San Francisco: Ignatius, 1982.

———. *Love Alone Is Credible*. Translated by D. C. Schindler. San Francisco: Ignatius, 2004.

———. *New Elucidations*. Translated by Mary Theresilde Skerry. San Francisco: Ignatius, 1986.

———. *Origen, Spirit and Fire: A Thematic Anthology of His Writings*. Translated by Robert J. Daly. Washington, DC: Catholic University of America Press, 1984.

———. *Theo-drama: Theological Dramatic Theory*. Translated by Graham Harrison. 5 vols. San Francisco: Ignatius, 1988.

———. *Theo-logic: Theological Logical Theory*. Translated by Adrian J. Walker and Graham Harrison. 3 vols. San Francisco: Ignatius, 2000–2005.

———. *A Theology of History*. A Communio Book. San Francisco: Ignatius, 1994.

———. *Unless You Become Like This Child*. Translated by Erasmo Leiva-Merikakis. San Francisco: Ignatius, 1991.

———. *You Crown the Year with Your Goodness*. Translated by Graham Harrison. San Francisco: Ignatius, 1989.

Bandow, Doug, and David L. Schindler. *Wealth, Poverty, and Human Destiny*. Wilmington, DE: ISI, 2003.

Barnes, Michel René. "De Régnon Reconsidered." *Augustinian Studies* 26.2 (1995) 51–80.

Barth, Karl. *Church Dogmatics*. Study ed. London: T. & T. Clark, 2009.

Basil the Great. *On the Holy Spirit*. Translated by David Anderson. Crestwood, NY: St. Vladimir's Seminary Press, 2001.

Beckett, Samuel. *Waiting for Godot*. Translated by Dougald McMillan and James Knowlson. The Theatrical Notebooks of Samuel Beckett 1. London: Faber & Faber, 1993.

Benedict XVI. *Caritas in veritate*. San Francisco: Ignatius, 2009.

———. *Church Fathers: From Clement of Rome to Augustine; General Audiences, 7 March 2007–27 February 2008*. San Francisco: Ignatius, 2008.

———. *Deus caritas est*. San Francisco: Ignatius, 2006.

———. *Jesus of Nazareth, Part Two: Holy Week: From the Entrance into Jerusalem to the Resurrection*. Translated by Philip J. Whitmore. San Francisco: Ignatius, 2011.

———. *Values in a Time of Upheaval*. Translated by Brian McNeil. San Francisco: Ignatius, 2006.

Bergson, Henri. *Essai sur les données immédiates de la conscience*. Paris: Alcan, 1889.

Berkeley, George. *Three Dialogues between Hylas and Philonous*. New York: Oxford University Press, 1998.

Bernanos, Georges. *The Diary of a Country Priest*. Translated by Pamela Morris. New York: Doubleday, 1974.

———. *La liberté, pour quoi faire?* Paris: Gallimard, 1953.

Bernard of Clairvaux. *On the Song of Songs: Sermones in cantica canticorum*. London: Mowbray, 1952.

Berry, Wendell. *The Way of Ignorance and Other Essays*. Berkeley: Shoemaker & Hoard, 2005.

Bieler, Martin. *Befreiung der Freiheit: Zur Theologie der stellvertretenden Sühne*. Freiburg: Herder, 1996.

———. "Causality and Freedom." *Communio: International Catholic Review* 32.3 (2005) 407–34.

———. *Freiheit als Gabe: Ein schöpfungstheologischer Entwurf*. Freiburg: Herder, 1991.

———. "Meta-anthropology and Christology: On the Philosophy of Hans Urs von Balthasar." *Communio: International Catholic Review* 20.1 (1993) 129–46.

Blondel, Maurice. *L'action (1893)*. Paris: Presses Universitaires de France/Quadrige, 1993.

Boff, Leonardo. *Trinity and Society*. Translated by Paul Burns. Theology and Liberation Series. Maryknoll, NY: Orbis, 1988.

Bonaventure. *Breviloquium*. Translated by Dominic V. Monti. Works of St. Bonaventure 9. St. Bonaventure, NY: Franciscan Institute, 2005.

———. *Collationes in Hexaemeron*. Translated by José de Vinck. Vol. 5 of *The Works of Bonaventure*. New York: St. Anthony Guild, 1970.

Bordoni, Marcello. *Gesù di Nazaret, Signore e Cristo: Saggio di cristologia sistematica*. 3 vols. Rome: Herder/Università Lateranense, 1982–1986.

———. *Il Cristo annunciato dalla Chiesa*. Vol. 3 of *Gesù di Nazaret, Signore e Cristo: Saggio di cristologia sistematica*. Rome: Herder/Università Lateranense, 1985.

Bouyer, Louis. *The Spirit and Forms of Protestantism*. Translated by A. V. Littledale. Westminster, MD: Newman, 1956.

Brague, Rémi. *Aristote et la question du monde: Essai sur le contexte cosmologique et anthropologique de l'ontologie*. Paris: Presses Universitaires de France, 1988.

Brito, Emilio. *Hegel et la tâche actuelle de la christologie*. Translated by Th. Dejond. Paris: Lethielleux, 1979.

Brown, Colin, editor. *The New Dictionary of New Testament Theology*. 3 vols. Grand Rapids: Regency Reference Library, 1982.

Bruaire, Claude. *L'affirmation de Dieu: Essai sur la logique de l'existence*. Paris: Le Seuil, 1964.

———. "L'être de l'esprit." In *L'univers philosophique*, edited by André Jacob, 34–38. Paris: Presses Universitaires de France, 1987.

———. *L'être et l'esprit*. Paris: Presses Universitaires de France, 1983.

———. *Le droit de Dieu*. Paris: Aubier, 1974.

———. *Philosophie du corps*. Paris: Le Seuil, 1968.

———. *Pour la métaphysique*. Paris: Fayard, 1980.

Bulgakov, Sergei. *The Bride of the Lamb*. Translated by Boris Jakim. Grand Rapids: Eerdmans, 2002.

———. *The Comforter*. Translated by Boris Jakim. Grand Rapids: Eerdmans, 2004.

———. *La luce senza tramonto*. Translated by Maria Campatelli. Rome: Lipa, 2002.

———. *The Lamb of God*. Translated by Boris Jakim. Grand Rapids: Eerdmans, 2008.

Burtt, Edwin Arthur. *The Metaphysical Foundations of Modern Physical Science: A Historical and Critical Essay*. London: Routledge, 1932.

Calvin, John. *Institutes of the Christian Religion*. Translated by Henry Beveridge. Grand Rapids: Eerdmans, 1997.

Camisasca, Massimo. *Don Giussani: La sua esperienza dell'uomo e di Dio*. Tempi e figure 55. Cinisello Balsamo (Milan): San Paolo, 2009.

———. *La casa, la terra, gli amici: La Chiesa nel terzo millennio*. Dimensioni dello spirito. Cinisello Balsamo (Milan): San Paolo, 2011.

Caputo, John D. "Commentary on Ken Schmitz; 'Postmodernism and the Catholic Tradition.'" *American Catholic Philosophical Quarterly* 73.2 (1999) 253–59.

———. *Heidegger and Aquinas: An Essay on Overcoming Metaphysics*. New York: Fordham University Press, 1982.

Caputo, John D., and Michael J. Scanlon, editors. *God, the Gift, and Postmodernism*. Indianapolis: Indiana University Press, 1999.

Cervantes, Miguel de. *Don Quixote*. Translated by Edith Grossman. New York: HarperCollins, 2003.

Césarée, Basile de. *Contre Eunome suivi de Eunome Apologie*. Translated by Bernard Sesboüé. Vol. 2. Paris: Cerf, 1982.

Chapelle, Albert. *Hegel et la religion*. 3 vols. Paris: Éditions Universitaires, 1964.

Cicero, Marcus Tullius. *Cicero's Five Books De finibus: Concerning the Last Object of Desire and Aversion*. Translated by Samuel Parker. London: Lackington, Allen, 1812.

———. *De senectute, De amicitia, De divinatione*. Translated by William Armistead Falconer. Cambridge: Harvard University Press, 1964.

Claudel, Paul. *The Satin Slipper, or the Worst Is Not the Surest*. Translated by John O'Connor. London: Sheed & Ward, 1932.

———. *The Tidings Brought to Mary: A Mystery*. Translated by Louise Morgan Sill. New Haven: Yale University Press, 1916.

Coda, Piero. *Dalla Trinità: L'avvento di Dio tra storia e profezia*. Vol. 1 of *Per-corsi di Sophia*. Rome: Città Nuova, 2011.

———. *Il negativo e la Trinità: Ipotesi su Hegel*. Rome: Città Nuova, 1987.

———. *L'altro di Dio: Rivelazione e kenosi in Sergej Bulgakov*. Rome: Città Nuova, 1998.

Colombo, Giuseppe. *Teologia sacramentaria*. Milan: Glossa, 1997.

Congar, Yves. *Je crois en l'Esprit Saint*. Paris: Cerf, 1997.

———. "Le Père: Source absolue de la divinité." *Istina* 25 (1980) 236–46.

Daniélou, Jean. "The Dove and the Darkness in Ancient Byzantine Mysticism." In *Man and Transformation: Papers from the Eranos Yearbooks*, edited by Joseph Campbell, 270–96. New York: Pantheon, 1964.
———. *The Lord of History: Reflections on the Inner Meaning of History*. Translated by Nigel Abercrombie. Chicago: H. Regnery, 1958.
Derrida, Jacques. *The Gift of Death*. Translated by David Wills. Chicago: University of Chicago Press, 1995.
———. *Given Time: 1. Counterfeit Money*. Translated by Peggy Kamuf. Chicago: University of Chicago Press, 1992.
———. *Margins of Philosophy*. Translated by Alan Bass. Chicago: University of Chicago Press, 1982.
———. *Of Grammatology*. Translated by Gayatri Chakravorty Spivak. Baltimore: Johns Hopkins University Press, 1997.
Desmond, William. *Being and the Between*. Albany: State University of New York Press, 1995.
———. *Beyond Hegel and Dialectic: Speculation, Cult, and Comedy*. Albany: State University of New York Press, 1992.
Dunn, James D. G. *Jesus Remembered*. Vol. 1 of *Christianity in the Making*. Grand Rapids: Eerdmans, 2003.
Duns Scotus, John. *Joannis Duns Scoti doctoris subtilis, ordinis minorum opera omnia*. Editio nova/juxta editionem Waddingi XII tomos continentem a patribus Franciscanis de observantia accurate recognita. Vol. 23. Paris: Apud Ludovicum Vivés, 1891.
Durand, Emmanuel. *La périchorèse des personnes divines: Immanence mutuelle, réciprocité et communion*. Vol. 243 of *Cogitatio fidei*. Paris: Cerf, 2005.
Durrwell, François-Xavier. *Jésus Fils de Dieu dans l'Esprit Saint*. Paris: Desclée, 1997.
———. *Le Père: Dieu en son mystère*. Paris: Cerf, 1987.
Eccles, John C. *Evolution of the Brain: Creation of the Self*. New York: Routledge, 1989.
Epicurus. *The Essential Epicurus: Letters, Principal Doctrines, Vatican Sayings, and Fragments*. Translated by Eugene Michael O'Connor. Buffalo, NY: Prometheus, 1993.
Fabro, Cornelio. "Dall'essere di Aristotele allo 'esse' di Tommaso." In *Mélanges offerts à Etienne Gilson, de l'Académie française*, 227–47. Toronto: Pontifical Institute of Mediaeval Studies, 1959.
Feuerbach, Ludwig. *The Essence of Christianity*. Translated by George Eliot. New York: Harper & Row, 1957.
Firestone, Shulamith. *The Dialectic of Sex: The Case for Feminist Revolution*. New York: Morrow, 1974.
Forschner, Maximilian. *Die stoische Ethik: Über den Zusammenhang von Natur-, Sprach-, und Moralphilosophie im altstoischen System*. 2nd ed. Darmstadt: Wissenschaftliche Buchgesellschaft, 1995.
Foucault, Paul-Michel. *The Archeology of Knowledge*. Translated by Alan Sheridan. New York: Vintage, 1972.
———. *The Order of Things*. Translated by Alan Sheridan. New York: Vintage, 1970.
Gadamer, Hans-Georg. *Truth and Method*. Translated by Joel Weinsheimer and Donald Marshall. 2nd ed. New York: Continuum, 1989.
Gasché, Rodolphe. *The Tain of the Mirror: Derrida and the Philosophy of Reflection*. Cambridge: Harvard University Press, 1986.

Geiger, L.-B. *La participation dans la philosophie de s. Thomas d'Aquin*. 2nd ed. Paris: J. Vrin, 1953.
Gilson, Etienne. *L'être et l'essence*. 3rd ed. Paris: J. Vrin, 1994.
Giuliodori, Claudio. *Intelligenza teologica del maschile e del femminile: Problemi e prospettive nella rilettura di von Balthasar e P. Evdokimov*. Rome: Città Nuova, 1991.
Giussani, Luigi. *Alla ricerca del volto umano*. Milan: Rizzoli, 1995.
———. *At the Origin of the Christian Claim*. Translated by Viviane Hewitt. Montreal: McGill-Queen's University Press, 1998.
———. *Avvenimento di libertà: Conversazioni con giovani universitari*. Milan: Marietti 1820, 2002.
———. "Esperienza cristiana e potere." *Tracce: Litterae Communionis* 6 (1986) 17–19.
———. "I fondamenti della condivisione." *Tracce: Litterae Communionis* 2 (1991) 31–34.
———. "Il Giubileo e la vita." *Tracce: Litterae Communionis* 11 (1999) 1–12.
———. *Il miracolo dell'ospitalità: Conversazioni con le Famiglie per l'Accoglienza*. Casale Monferrato, Alessandria: Piemme, 2003.
———. *Il rischio educativo: Come creazione di personalità e di storia*. Turin: SEI, 1995.
———. *Il tempo e il tempio: Dio e l'uomo*. Milan: Rizzoli, 1995.
———. *Is It Possible to Live This Way? An Unusual Approach to Christian Existence*. 3 vols. Montreal: McGill-Queen's University Press, 2007–2009.
———. *The Journey to Truth Is an Experience*. Translated by John Zucchi. Montreal: McGill-Queen's University Press, 2006.
———. *L'alleanza: Volume 1 dagli Esercizi spirituali*. Milan: Jaca, 1979.
———. *L'autocoscienza del cosmo*. Milan: Rizzoli, 2000.
———. *L'esperienza*. Milan: Gioventù Studentesca, pro manuscripto, 1963.
———. *L'io, il potere, le opere: Contributi da un'esperienza*. Genoa: Marietti 1820, 2000.
———. *L'uomo e il suo destino: In cammino*. Genoa: Marietti 1820, 1999.
———. "La *Dives in misericordia* nella testimonianza e nell'esperienza di C.L." In *"Prima lettura della* Dives in misericordia*." Atti del Convegno internazionale di Collevalenza (26–29 novembre, 1981)*. Collevalenza, Perugia: L'amore Misericordioso, 1982.
———. "La fede è un cammino dello sguardo." *Tracce: Litterae Communionis* 9 (1995) 1–12.
———. *La libertà di Dio*. Milan: Marietti 1820, 2005.
———. "Mistero e segno coincidono." In *Affezione e dimora*, 241–301. Milan: Rizzoli, 2001.
———. *Morality: Memory and Desire: A Spirituality of the Moral Life*. Translated by K. D. Whitehead. San Francisco: Ignatius, 1986.
———. "Ogni cosa: Mistero e segno." *Tracce: Litterae Communionis* 6 (1999) 1–16.
———. "Paternità ed appartenenza: Un'esperienza personale." *Tracce: Litterae Communionis* 9 (1999) 1–4.
———. "Per lo sviluppo della dimensione culturale dell'esperienza cristiana." *Tracce: Litterae Communionis* 7 (1978) 39–40.
———. *Porta la speranza*. Genoa: Marietti 1820, 1997.
———. "Quella prima carezza che ti segna la strada." *Il Sabato* 52 (1982) 27.
———. *The Religious Sense*. Translated by John Zucchi. Montreal: McGill-Queen's University Press, 1997.

---. *The Risk of Education: Discovering Our Ultimate Destiny*. Translated by Rosanna M. Giammanco Frongia. New York: Crossroad, 1996.

---. *Se non fossi tuo, mio Cristo, mi sentirei creatura finita*. Supplement, *Tracce: Litterae Communionis* 8 (1997).

---. "Seminario con Msgr. Luigi Giussani (6 gennaio 1984)." *Annuario teologico* (Milan: Istra-Edit) (1985) 131–35.

---. *Si può (veramente?!) vivere così?* Milan: Rizzoli, 1996.

---. *Si può vivere così? Uno strano approccio all'esistenza cristiana*. 2nd ed. Milan: Rizzoli, 2007.

---. *"Tu" (o dell'amicizia)*. Milan: Rizzoli, 1997.

---. *Un avvenimento di vita, cioè una storia: Interviste e conversazioni con Luigi Giussani*. Rome: Il Sabato, 1992.

---. "Vita e spirito del sacerdote cattolico." *30 Giorni* 11 (1993) 37–43.

---. *Vivendo nella carne*. Milan: Rizzoli, 1998.

---. *Why the Church?* Translated by Viviane Hewitt. Montreal: McGill-Queen's University Press, 2001.

Giussani, Luigi, Stefano Alberto, and Javier Prades. *Generare tracce nella storia del mondo: Nuove tracce d'esperienza cristiana*. 3rd ed. Milan: Rizzoli, 1998.

Granados García, José. *La carne si fa amore: Il corpo, cardine della storia della salvezza*. Siena: Cantagalli, 2010.

---. *Los misterios de la vida de Cristo en Justino Mártir*. Rome: Editrice Pontificia Università Gregoriana, 2005.

Grant, George Parkin. "Faith and the Multiversity." In *Collected Works of George Grant: Vol. 4, 1970–1988*, edited by Arthur Davis and Henry Roper, 607–39. Toronto: University of Toronto Press, 2009.

---. "Time as History." In *Collected Works of George Grant: Vol. 4, 1970–1988*, edited by Arthur Davis and Henry Roper, 3–78. Toronto: University of Toronto Press, 2009.

Gregory of Nazianzus. *Faith Gives Fullness to Reasoning: The Five Theological Orations of Gregory Nazianzen*. Edited by Frederick W. Norris. Translated by Lionel Wickham and Frederick Williams. Supplements to *Vigiliae Christianae* 13. New York: Brill, 1991.

---. *On God and Christ: The Five Theological Orations and Two Letters to Cledonius*. Translated by Frederick Williams and Lionel Wickham. Crestwood, NY: St. Vladimir's Seminary Press, 2002.

Gregory of Nyssa. *Commentary on the Song of Songs*. Translated by Casimir McCambley. Brookline, MA: Hellenic College Press, 1987.

---. *Dogmatic Treatises*. Translated by H. A. Wilson. Edited by Philip Schaff and Henry Wace. In vol. 5 of *Nicene and Post-Nicene Fathers*. Peabody, MA: Hendrickson, 1999.

---. *The Life of Moses*. Translated by Abraham J. Malherbe and Everett Ferguson. New York: Paulist, 1978.

Greshake, Gisbert. *Der dreieine Gott: Eine trinitarische Theologie*. Freiburg: Herder, 1997.

Grotius, Hugo. *De iure belli ac pacis libri tres: In quibus ius naturae et gentium item iuris publici praecipua explicantur*. Aalen, Germany: Scientia, 1993.

Guardini, Romano. *Das Ende der Neuzeit: Ein Versuch zur Orientierung/Die Macht: Versuch einer Wegweisung.* Mainz: Matthias Grünewald; Paderborn: Schöningh, 1989.

———. *Das Wesen des Christentums: Die menschliche Wirklichkeit des Herrn.* Mainz: Matthias Grünewald; Paderborn: Schöningh, 1991.

———. *The End of the Modern World.* Translated by Frederick D. Wilhelmsen. Rev. ed. Wilimington, DE: ISI, 1998.

———. *The Spirit of the Liturgy.* Translated by Joanne M. Pierce. New York: Crossroad, 1998.

Hales, Alexander of. *Doctoris irrefragabilis Alexandri de Hales Ordinis minorum Summa theologica.* Ad Claras Aquas (Quaracchi) prope Florentiam: ex typographia Collegii s. Bonaventurae, 1924.

Hart, Kevin. *Counter-Experiences: Reading Jean-Luc Marion.* Notre Dame: University of Notre Dame Press, 2007.

Hauerwas, Stanley. *Suffering Presence: Theological Reflections on Medicine, the Mentally Handicapped, and the Church.* Notre Dame: University of Notre Dame Press, 1986.

Healy, Nicholas J. *The Eschatology of Hans Urs von Balthasar: Being as Communion.* Oxford: Oxford University Press, 2005.

Hegel, Georg W. F. *The Consummate Religion.* Translated by Robert F. Brown and Peter Crafts Hodgson. Vol. 3 of *Lectures on the Philosophy of Religion.* Berkeley: University of California Press, 1984–1987.

———. *Encyclopedia of the Philosophical Sciences (1830) Together with the Zusätze.* Translated by William Wallace and A. V. Miller. 3 vols. Oxford: Clarendon, 1975–2004.

———. *Phenomenology of Spirit.* Translated by A. V. Miller. Oxford: Oxford University Press, 1977.

———. *Science of Logic.* Translated by A. V. Miller. Amherst, NY: Humanity, 1969.

———. *Vorlesungen über die Geschichte der Philosophie.* 4 vols. Hamburg: Meiner, 1984–1987.

———. *Wissenschaft der Logik.* Philosophische Bibliothek 375–77, 385. Hamburg: Meiner, 1986.

Heidegger, Martin. *Being and Time.* Translated by Joan Stambaugh. Albany: State University of New York Press, 1996.

———. *Beiträge zur Philosophie (Vom Ereignis).* Vol. 65 of *Gesamtausgabe: III. Abteilung: Unveröffentlichte Abhandlungen.* Frankfurt: Vittorio Klostermann, 2003.

———. *The Concept of Time.* Translated by William McNeill. Oxford: Blackwell, 1992.

———. *Contributions to Philosophy (From Enowning).* Translated by Parvis Emad and Kenneth Maly. Bloomington: Indiana University Press, 1999.

———. *Gesamtausgabe.* 90 vols. Frankfurt: Vittorio Klostermann, 1975–.

———. *Identity and Difference.* Translated by Joan Stambaugh. Chicago: University of Chicago Press, 2002.

———. "Letter on Humanism." In *Basic Writings: From Being and Time (1927) to the Task of Thinking (1964),* edited by David Farrell Krell, 213–65. New York: HarperCollins, 1993.

———. "On the Essence and Concept of Φυσις in Aristotle's *Physics* B, 1." In *Pathmarks,* edited by William McNeill, 183–230. Cambridge: Cambridge University Press, 1998.

———. *On Time and Being*. Translated by Joan Stambaugh. New York: Harper & Row, 1972.

———. *Pathmarks*. Edited by William McNeill. Cambridge: Cambridge University Press, 1998.

———. "The Question Concerning Technology." In *Basic Writings: From Being and Time (1927) to the Task of Thinking (1964)*, edited by David Farrell Krell, 307–41. New York: HarperCollins, 1993.

———. *Supplements: From the Earliest Essays to "Being and Time" and Beyond*. Edited by John van Buren. Albany: State University of New York Press, 2002.

———. *Zur Sache des Denkens*. Vol. 14 of *Gesamtausgabe: I. Abteilung: Veröffentlichte Schriften 1910–1976*. Frankfurt: Vittorio Klostermann, 2007.

Hénaff, Marcel. *Le prix de la vérité: Le don, l'argent, la philosophie*. Paris: Seuil, 2002.

Heraclitus of Ephesus. *Fragments: The Collected Wisdom of Heraclitus*. Translated by Brooks Haxton. New York: Viking, 2001.

Hobbes, Thomas. *Leviathan, or the Matter, Form, and Power of a Commonwealth, Ecclesiastical and Civil*. London: John Bohn, 1839.

Homer. *The Odyssey of Homer*. Translated by Richmond Alexander Lattimore. New York: Harper Colophon, 1975.

Hyppolite, Jean. *Logic and Existence*. Translated by Leonard Lawlor and Amit Sen. Albany: State University of New York Press, 1997.

Irenaeus of Lyons. *St. Irenaeus of Lyons against the Heresies*. Translated by Dominic J. Unger. Ancient Christian Writers 55–. New York: Newman, 1992.

Ivánka, Endre von. *Plato christianus: Übernahme und Umgestaltung des Platonismus durch die Väter*. Einsiedeln: Johannes, 1964.

James, William. *The Varieties of Religious Experience: A Study in Human Nature*. New York: Collier, 1973.

Jeremias, Joachim. *The Eucharistic Words of Jesus*. Translated by Norman Perrin. New York: Scribner, 1966.

———. *New Testament Theology*. Translated by John Bowden. London: SCM, 1971.

———. *The Prayers of Jesus*. Philadelphia: Fortress, 1978.

John Paul II. *The Church: Mystery, Sacrament, Community: A Catechesis on the Creed*. Boston: Pauline, 1998.

———. *Dives in misericordia*. Boston: Pauline, 1980.

———. *Dominum et vivificantem*. Boston: Pauline, 2003.

———. *Evangelium vitae*. Boston: Pauline, 1995.

———. *Familiaris consortio*. Boston: Pauline, 1981.

———. *Fides et ratio*. Boston: Pauline, 1998.

———. *Man and Woman He Created Them: A Theology of the Body*. Translated by Michael Waldstein. Boston: Pauline, 2006.

———. *Memory and Identity: Conversations at the Dawn of a Millennium*. New York: Rizzoli, 2005.

———. *Redemptor hominis*. Boston: Pauline, 1979.

———. *Salvifici doloris*. Boston: Pauline, 1984.

Johnson, Elizabeth A. *She Who Is: The Mystery of God in Feminist Theological Discourse*. New York: Crossroad, 1992.

Jonas, Hans. *The Gnostic Religion: The Message of the Alien God and the Beginnings of Christianity*. 3rd ed. Boston: Beacon, 2001.

———. *Organismus und Freiheit: Ansätze zu einer philosophischen Biologie.* Göttingen: Vandenhoeck & Ruprecht, 1973.
———. *The Phenomenon of Life: Toward a Philosophical Biology.* Evanston, IL: Northwestern University Press, 2001.
———. "Toward a Philosophy of Technology." In *Philosophy of Technology: The Technological Condition: An Anthology*, edited by Robert C. Scharff and Val Dusek, 191–204. Malden, MA: Blackwell, 2003.
Kant, Immanuel. *Critique of Practical Reason.* Translated by Werner S. Pluhar. Indianapolis: Hackett, 2002.
———. *Critique of Pure Reason.* Translated by Norman Kemp Smith. Boston: Palgrave Macmillan, 2003.
———. *Foundations of the Metaphysics of Morals.* Translated by Lewis White Beck. Edited by Robert Paul Wolff. Bobbs-Merrill Text and Commentary Series 7. Indianapolis: Bobbs-Merrill, 1969.
———. *Religion within the Limits of Reason Alone.* Translated by Theodore M. Greene and Hoyt H. Hudson. New York: Harper Torchbooks, 1960.
Kierkegaard, Søren. *The Concept of Anxiety: A Simple Psychologically Orienting Deliberation on the Dogmatic Issue of Hereditary Sin.* Translated by Reidar Thomte and Albert B. Anderson. Kierkegaard's Writings 8. Princeton: Princeton University Press, 1980.
Konrad, Michael. *Tendere all'ideale: La morale di Luigi Giussani.* Milan: Marietti 1820, 2010.
Ladaria, Luis F. "Dios Padre en Hilario de Poitiers." *Estudios trinitarios* 24 (1990) 443–79.
———. *El Dios vivo y verdadero: El misterio de la Trinidad.* Salamanca: Secretariado Trinitario, 1998.
———. *La Trinità, mistero di comunione.* Translated by Marco Zapella. Milan: Paoline, 2004.
Laffitte, Jean. *Le pardon transfiguré.* Paris: L'Emmanuel/Desclée, 1995.
Lawler, Michael G. *What Is and What Ought to Be.* New York: Continuum, 2005.
Le Guillou, Marie-Joseph. *Le mystère du Père: Foi des apôtres, gnoses actuelles.* Paris: Fayard, 1973.
Leibniz, Gottfried W. *Die philosophischen Schriften von G.W. Leibniz.* Edited by C. I. Gerhardt. Vol. 7. Olms: Hildesheim, 1965.
Lonergan, Bernard J. F. *Insight: A Study of Human Understanding.* Vol. 3 of *Collected Works of Bernard Lonergan.* 5th ed. Toronto: University of Toronto Press, 1992.
López, Antonio. "Divine Revelation." In *Catholic Engagement with World Religions: A Comprehensive Study*, edited by Karl J. Becker and Ilaria Morali, 230–43. New York: Orbis, 2010.
———. "Eternal Happening: God as an Event of Love." *Communio: International Catholic Review* 32.2 (2005) 214–45.
———. "The Reasonableness of an Event that Awakens Love." *Communio: International Catholic Review* 34.4 (2007) 585–615.
———. "Restoration of Sonship: Reflections on Time and Eternity." *Communio: International Catholic Review* 32.4 (2005) 682–704.
———. *Spirit's Gift: The Metaphysical Insight of Claude Bruaire.* Washington, DC: Catholic University of America Press, 2006.
Louth, Andrew. *Maximus the Confessor.* New York: Routledge, 1996.

Lubac, Henri de. *Catholicism: Christ and the Common Destiny of Man*. Translated by Lancelot C. Sheppard and Elizabeth Englund. San Francisco: Ignatius, 1988.
———. *The Drama of Atheist Humanism*. Translated by Edith M. Riley and Anne Englund Nash. San Francisco: Ignatius, 1995.
———. *History and Spirit: The Understanding of Scripture According to Origen*. Translated by Anne Englund Nash. San Francisco: Ignatius, 2007.
———. *La révélation divine*. Paris: Cerf, 1983. Lyotard, Jean-François. *The Postmodern Condition: A Report on Knowledge*. Translated by Geoff Bennington and Brian Massumi. Theory and History of Literature 10. Minneapolis: University of Minnesota Press, 1999.
Mansion, Suzanne. *Le jugement d'existence chez Aristote*. 2nd ed. Louvain: Éditions de l'Institut supérieur de philosophie, 1976.
Marion, Jean-Luc. *Being Given: Toward a Phenomenology of Givenness*. Translated by Jeffrey L. Kosky. Stanford: Stanford University Press, 2002.
———. *Reduction and Givenness: Investigations of Husserl, Heidegger, and Phenomenology*. Translated by Thomas A. Carlson. Evanston, IL: Northwestern University Press, 1998.
Marx, Karl, and Friedrich Engels. *Werke*. Berlin: Dietz, 1961–1974.
Mauss, Marcel. "Essai sur le don: Forme et raison de l'échange dans les sociétés archaïques." In *Sociologie et anthropologie*, 145–279. Paris: Presses Universitaires de France/Quadrige, 1999.
Maximus the Confessor. *The Disputation with Pyrrhus of Our Father among the Saints Maximus the Confessor*. Translated by Joseph P. Farrell. South Canaan, PA: St. Tikhon's Seminary Press, 1990.
———. *Maximi Confessoris Quaestiones ad Thalassium*. Corpus Christianorum, Series Graeca 7 and 22. Turnhout: Brepols, 1980.
———. *On the Cosmic Mystery of Jesus Christ: Selected Writings from St. Maximus the Confessor*. Translated by Paul M. Blowers and Robert Louis Wilken. Crestwood, NY: St. Vladimir's Seminary Press, 2003.
Mazza, Enrico. *Mystagogy: A Theology of Liturgy in the Patristic Age*. Translated by Matthew J. O'Connell. New York: Pueblo, 1989.
Mazzanti, Giorgio. *Teologia sponsale e sacramento delle nozze: Simbolo e simbolismo nuziale*. Nuovi saggi teologici 54. Bologna: Edizioni Dehoniane, 2001.
Milbank, John. *Being Reconciled: Ontology and Pardon*. London: Routledge, 2003.
———. "Can a Gift Be Given? Prolegomena to a Future Trinitarian Metaphysics." *Modern Theology* 11 (1995) 119–61.
Millán Puelles, Antonio. *Léxico filosófico*. Madrid: Rialp, 1984.
Moltmann, Jürgen. *The Trinity and the Kingdom of God: The Doctrine of God*. Translated by Margaret Kohl. Minneapolis: Fortress, 1993.
Montini, Giovanni B., and Luigi Giussani. *Sul senso religioso*. Milan: Rizzoli, 2009.
Mouroux, Jean. *The Christian Experience: An Introduction to Theology*. Translated by George Lamb. New York: Sheed & Ward, 1954.
———. "Eros et Agape." *La vie intellectuelle* 14 (1946) 23–38.
———. *L'expérience chrétienne: Introduction a une théologie*. Paris: Éditions Montaigne, 1952.
Murray, John Courtney. *We Hold These Truths: Catholic Reflections on the American Proposition*. Lanham, MD: Sheed & Ward, 2005.

Nédoncelle, Maurice. *La réciprocité des conscience: Essai sur la nature de la personne.* Paris: Éditions Montaigne, 1942.
———. *Personne humaine et nature: Etude logique et métaphysique.* Paris: Éditions Montaigne, 1963.
———. *Vers une philosophie de l'amour et de la personne.* Paris: Aubier, 1957.
Nichols, Aidan. *Say It Is Pentecost: A Guide through Balthasar's Logic.* Washington, DC: Catholic University of America Press, 2001.
Nietzsche, Friedrich. *The Portable Nietzsche.* Translated by Walter Kaufmann. New York: Penguin, 1976.
———. *The Will to Power.* Translated by Walter Kaufmann and R. J. Hollingdale. New York: Random House, 1967.
Nygren, Anders. *Agape and Eros.* Library of Religion and Culture. New York: Harper Torchbooks, 1969.
Ockham, William of. *Quodlibetal Questions.* Translated by Alfred J. Freddoso and Francis E. Kelley. Yale Library of Medieval Philosophy. New Haven: Yale University Press, 1991.
———. *Scriptum in librum primum Sententiarum.* Vols. 1–3 of *Opera theologica.* St. Bonaventure, NY: Franciscan Institute, 1967.
Oliver, Simon. *Divine Motion: Physics and Theology.* London: Routledge, 2005.
———. "Motion According to Aquinas and Newton." *Modern Theology* 17.2 (2001) 163–99.
Orbe, Antonio. "*Gloria Dei vivens homo*: Análisis de Ireneo, *Adv. Haer.* IV, 20, 1–7." *Gregorianum* 73.2 (1992) 205–68.
O'Regan, Cyril. *The Heterodox Hegel.* Albany: State University of New York Press, 1994.
Origen. *Commentary on the Gospel according to John.* Translated by Ronald E. Heine. Fathers of the Church 80, 89. Washington, DC: Catholic University of America Press, 1989.
———. *Homilies on Genesis and Exodus.* Translated by Ronald E. Heine. Fathers of the Church 71. Washington, DC: Catholic University of America Press, 1982.
———. *The Song of Songs: Commentary and Homilies.* Ancient Christian Writers 26. New York: Newman, 1956.
Oster, Stefan. *Mit-Mensch-Sein: Phänomenologie und Ontologie der Gabe bei Ferdinand Ulrich.* Freiburg: Karl Alber, 2004.
Ouellet, Marc. *Divine Likeness: Toward a Trinitarian Anthropology of the Family.* Translated by Philip Milligan and Linda M. Cicone. Ressourcement. Grand Rapids: Eerdmans, 2006.
Owens, Joseph. *The Doctrine of Being in the Aristotelian "Metaphysics."* 3rd ed. Toronto: Pontifical Institute of Mediaeval Studies, 1978.
Pannenberg, Wolfhart. *Systematic Theology.* Translated by Geoffrey William Bromiley. 3 vols. Grand Rapids: Eerdmans, 1991–1998.
Pérez-Soba Díez del Corral, Juan. "*Amor es nombre de persona*" (I, q. 37, a. 1): Estudio de la interpersonalidad en el amor en santo Tomás de Aquino. Theses ad doctoratum in s. theologia. Rome: Pontificia Universitá Lateranense, 2001.
Perrin, Norman. *The Kingdom of God in the Teaching of Jesus.* New Testament Library. Philadelphia: Westminster, 1963.
Pickstock, Catherine. *After Writing: On the Liturgical Consummation of Philosophy.* Oxford: Blackwell, 1998.

Pinckaers, Servais. *The Sources of Christian Ethics*. Washington, DC: Catholic University of America Press, 1995.
Plato. *Alcibiades*. In *Complete Works*, edited by John M. Cooper, 557–95. Indianapolis: Hackett, 1997.
———. *Apology*. In *Complete Works*, edited by John M. Cooper, 17–36. Indianapolis: Hackett, 1997.
———. *Republic*. In *Complete Works*, edited by John M. Cooper, 971–1223. Indianapolis: Hackett, 1997.
———. *Sophist*. In *Complete Works*, edited by John M. Cooper, 235–93. Indianapolis: Hackett, 1997.
———. *Timaeus*. In *Complete Works*, edited by John M. Cooper, 1224–91. Indianapolis: Hackett, 1997.
Plotinus. *Enneads*. Translated by A. H. Armstrong. 7 vols. Cambridge: Harvard University Press, 1988.
Prieto, Antonio. "*Eros* and *Agape*: The Unique Dynamics of Love." In *The Way of Love: Reflections on Pope Benedict XVI's Encyclical* Deus Caritas Est, edited by Livio Melina and Carl A. Anderson, 212–26. San Francisco: Ignatius, 2006.
Pseudo-Dionysius. *The Divine Names*. In *The Complete Works*, 47–131. New York: Paulist, 1987.
Rahner, Karl. *The Church and the Sacraments*. Translated by W. J. O'Hara. Quaestiones disputatae 9. New York: Herder & Herder, 1964.
———. "Dogmatic Reflections on the Knowledge and Self-Consciousness of Christ." In *Later Writings*, vol. 5 of *Theological Investigations*, translated by Karl H. Kruger, 193–215. Baltimore: Helicon, 1966.
———. "Experience of Self and Experience of God." In *Theology, Anthropology, Christology*, vol. 13 of *Theological Investigations*, translated by David Bourke, 122–32. New York: Crossroad, 1975.
———. *More Recent Writings*. Vol. 4 of *Theological Investigations*. Translated by Kevin Smyth. Baltimore: Helicon, 1966.
———. "The Theology of the Symbol." In *More Recent Writings*, vol. 4 of *Theological Investigations*, translated by Kevin Smyth, 221–52. Baltimore: Helicon, 1966.
Rahner, Karl, and Joseph Ratzinger. *Offenbarung und Überlieferung*. Freiburg: Herder, 1965.
Ratzinger, Joseph. *Behold the Pierced One*. Translated by Graham Harrison. San Francisco: Ignatius, 1986.
———. *Called to Communion*. Translated by Adrian J. Walker. San Francisco: Ignatius, 1996.
———. *Christianity and the Crisis of Cultures*. Translated by Brian McNeil. San Francisco: Ignatius, 2006.
———. *Church, Ecumenism, and Politics: New Endeavors in Ecclesiology*. Translated by Michael J. Miller et al. San Francisco: Ignatius, 2008.
———. "The Ecclesiology of the Constitution *Lumen gentium*." In *Pilgrim Fellowship of Faith: The Church as Communio*, edited by Stephan Otto Horn and Vincent Pfnür, 123–52. San Francisco: Ignatius, 2005.
———. *The Feast of Faith: Approaches to a Theology of the Liturgy*. Translated by Graham Harrison. San Francisco: Ignatius, 1986.
———. "Freiheit und Bindung in der Kirche." In *Die Grundrechte des Christen in Kirche und Gesellschaft. Akten des IV. Internationalen Kongresses für Kirchenrecht*, edited

by Niklaus Herzog, Eugenio Corecco, and Angelo Scola, 37–52. Freiburg: Herder, 1981.

———. "The Holy Spirit as *Communio*: Concerning the Relationship of Pneumatology and Spirituality in Augustine." *Communio: International Catholic Review* 25.2 (1998) 324–39.

———. *"In the Beginning...": A Catholic Understanding of the Story of Creation and the Fall*. Translated by Boniface Ramsey. Grand Rapids: Eerdmans, 1995.

———. *Introduction to Christianity*. Translated by J. R. Foster. San Francisco: Ignatius, 2004.

———. *Jesus of Nazareth: From the Baptism in the Jordan to the Transfiguration*. Translated by Adrian J. Walker. New York: Doubleday, 2007.

———. "Man between Reproduction and Creation: Theological Questions on the Origin of Human Life." *Communio: International Catholic Review* 16.2 (1989) 197–211.

———. *A New Song for the Lord: Faith in Christ and Liturgy Today*. Translated by Martha M. Matesich. New York: Crossroad, 1996.

———. "The Paschal Mystery as the Core and Foundation of Devotion to the Sacred Heart." In *Towards a Civilization of Love: A Symposium on the Scriptural and Theological Foundations of the Devotion to the Heart of Jesus*, edited by Mario Luigi Ciappi, 145–65. San Francisco: Ignatius, 1985.

———. *Principles of Catholic Theology: Building Stones for a Fundamental Theology*. San Francisco: Ignatius, 1987.

———. *The Spirit of the Liturgy*. Translated by John Saward. San Francisco: Ignatius, 2000.

———. "Truth and Freedom." *Communio: International Catholic Review* 23 (1996) 16–35.

———. *Truth and Tolerance: Christian Belief and World Religions*. Translated by Henry Taylor. San Francisco: Ignatius, 2004.

———. *The Yes of Jesus Christ: Spiritual Exercises in Faith, Hope, and Charity*. Translated by Robert Nowell. New York: Crossroad, 2005.

Ratzinger, Joseph, and Hans Urs von Balthasar. *Mary: The Church at the Source*. Translated by Adrian J. Walker. San Francisco: Ignatius, 2005.

Rawls, John. *Political Liberalism*. Expanded ed. Columbia Classics in Philosophy. New York: Columbia University Press, 2005.

———. *A Theory of Justice*. Rev. ed. Cambridge: Belknap Press of Harvard University Press, 1999.

Régnon, Théodore de. *Études de théologie positive sur la Sainte Trinité*. 4 vols. Paris: Victor Retaux, 1892–1898.

Richard of St. Victor. *The Twelve Patriarchs. The Mystical Ark. Book Three of the Trinity*. Translated by Grover A. Zinn. New York: Paulist, 1979.

Richardson, William J. *Heidegger: Through Phenomenology to Thought*. 4th ed. Perspectives in Continental Philosophy 30. New York: Fordham University Press, 2003.

Ricoeur, Paul. *Le mal: Un défi à la philosophie et à la théologie*. Paris: Labor et Fides, 1996.

Rossetti, C. Lorenzo. "La perichoresi: Una chiave della teologia cattolica." *Lateranum* 72.3 (2006) 553–75.

Rotenstreich, Nathan. *From Substance to Subject: Studies in Hegel.* The Hague: Martinus Nijhoff, 1974.
Rougemont, Denis de. *L'amour et l'Occident.* Éd. définitive. Paris: Plon, 1972.
Rousseau, Jean-Jacques. "Of the Social Contract." In *Classics of Modern Political Theory,* edited by Steven M. Cahn, 420–85. Oxford: Oxford University Press, 1997.
Sachs, Joe. *Aristotle's Physics: A Guided Study.* New Brunswick: Rutgers University Press, 2008.
Sachs, John R. "Deus semper major—Ad majorem Dei gloriam: The Pneumatology and Spirituality of Hans Urs von Balthasar." *Gregorianum* 74.4 (1993) 631–57.
Sallust. *Catiline's War, The Jugurthine War, Histories.* Translated by A. J. Woodman. New York: Penguin Classics, 2008.
Sani, Roberto. "L'educazione tra rischio e libertà." In *Sperare nell'uomo: Giussani, Morin, MacIntyre e la questione educativa.* Edited by Giorgio Chiosso. Turin: SEI, 2009.
Sara, Juan. "*Descensus ad inferos,* Dawn of Hope: Aspects of the Theology of Holy Saturday in the Trilogy of Hans Urs von Balthasar." *Communio: International Catholic Review* 32.3 (2005) 541–72.
Sartre, Jean-Paul. *Being and Nothingness: An Essay on Phenomenological Ontology.* Translated by Hazel E. Barnes. New York: Philosophical Library, 1956.
———. *Les mains sales: Piecè en sept tableaux.* Paris: Gallimard/Folio, 1948.
Scheffczyk, Leo. *Die Heilsverwirklichung in der Gnade: Gnadenlehre.* Vol. 6 of *Katholische Dogmatik.* Aachen: MM Verlag, 1998.
Schelling, Friedrich W. J. *The Ages of the World.* Translated by Jason M. Wirth. Albany: State University of New York Press, 2000.
———. "Einleitung in die Philosophie der Offenbarung." In vol. 5 of *Ausgewählte Schriften.* Frankfurt: Suhrkamp, 1985.
———. *Philosophie der Offenbarung 1841/42.* Edited by Frank Manfred. Frankfurt: Suhrkamp, 1977.
Schindler, David C. *Hans Urs von Balthasar and the Dramatic Structure of Truth: A Philosophical Investigation.* New York: Fordham University Press, 2004.
———. "'Wie kommt der Mensch in die Theologie?': Heidegger, Hegel, and the Stakes of Onto-theo-logy." *Communio: International Catholic Review* 32.4 (2005) 637–68.
Schindler, David L. "The Embodied Person as Gift and the Cultural Task in America: Status Quaestionis." *Communio: International Catholic Review* 35.3 (2008) 397–431.
———. *Ordering Love: Liberal Societies and the Memory of God.* Grand Rapids: Eerdmans, 2011.
———. "The Religious Sense and American Culture." In *A Generative Thought: An Introduction to the Works of Luigi Giussani,* edited by Elisa Buzzi, 84–102. Montreal: McGill-Queen's University Press, 2003.
Schleiermacher, Friedrich. *The Christian Faith.* Edited by H. R. Mackintosh and J. S. Stewart. Philadelphia: Fortress, 1976.
———. *On Religion: Speeches to Its Cultured Despisers.* Translated by Richard Crouter. 2nd ed. Cambridge: Cambridge University Press, 1996.
Schlier, Heinrich. *Der Römerbrief: Kommentar.* Herders theologischer Kommentar zum Neuen Testament 6. Freiburg: Herder, 1977.
———. *Grundzüge einer paulinischen Theologie.* Freiburg: Herder, 1978.
Schmemann, Alexander. *For the Life of the World: Sacraments and Orthodoxy.* Crestwood, NY: St. Vladimir's Seminary Press, 2002.

Schmitz, Kenneth L. "Created Receptivity and the Philosophy of the Concrete." *The Thomist* 61.3 (1997) 339–71.
———. *The Gift: Creation.* Milwaukee: Marquette University Press, 1982.
———. "Human Nature, History, and the Transcendental Character of Being." In *Scholasticism in the Modern World: The American Catholic Philosophical Association; Proceedings for the Year 1966*, edited by F. McLean, 124–34. Washington, DC: Catholic University of America Press, 1966.
———. "Postmodernism and the Catholic Tradition." *American Catholic Philosophical Quarterly* 73.2 (1999) 233–52.
———. *The Recovery of Wonder.* Montreal: McGill-Queen's University Press, 2005.
———. "Substance Is Not Enough. Hegel's Slogan: From Substance to Subject." In *The Metaphysics of Substance*, vol. 61 of *Proceedings of the American Catholic Philosophical Association*, edited by Daniel O. Dahlstrom, 52–68. Washington, DC: Catholic University of America Press, 1987.
———. *The Texture of Being: Essays in First Philosophy.* Edited by Paul O'Herron. Studies in Philosophy and the History of Philosophy. Washington, DC: Catholic University of America Press, 2007.
Schoonenberg, Piet J. A. M. *The Christ: A Study of the God-Man Relationship in the Whole of Creation and in Jesus Christ.* Translated by Della Couling. New York: Herder & Herder, 1971.
Schürmann, Reiner. *Heidegger on Being and Acting: From Principles to Anarchy.* Translated by Christine-Marie Gros. Bloomington: Indiana University Press, 1990.
Scola, Angelo. "Esperienza cristiana e teologia: Note introduttive." In *Questioni di antropologia teologica*. Rome: Mursia, 1997.
———. "Esperienza, libertà e rischio." In *Un pensiero sorgivo: Sugli scritti di Luigi Giussani*. Genoa: Marietti, 2004.
———. *Identidad y diferencia: La relación hombre-mujer.* Madrid: Ediciones Encuentro, 1989.
———. *The Nuptial Mystery.* Translated by Michelle K. Borras. Grand Rapids: Eerdmans, 2005.
Seneca, Lucius Annaeus. *Seneca's Letters to Lucilius.* Translated by Edward Phillips Barker. Oxford: Clarendon, 1932.
Sesboüé, Bernard. *Jésus-Christ dans la tradition de l'Eglise: Pour une actualisation de la christologie de Chalcédoine.* Paris: Desclée, 1982.
Sharkey, Michael, editor. *International Theological Commission: Texts and Documents, 1969–1985.* San Francisco: Ignatius, 1989.
Sheehan, Thomas. "*Kehre* and *Ereignis*: A Prolegomenon to *Introduction to Metaphysics*." In *A Companion to Heidegger's* Introduction to Metaphysics, edited by Richard Polt and Gregory Fried, 3–16, 263–74. New Haven: Yale University Press, 2001.
———. "A Paradigm Shift in Heidegger Research." *Continental Philosophy Review* (formerly *Man and World*) 34 (2001) 183–202.
Sokolowski, Robert. *The God of Faith and Reason: Foundations of Christian Theology.* Washington, DC: Catholic University of America Press, 1995.
Spaemann, Robert. "Ende der Modernität?" In *Philosophische Essays*, 232–60. Stuttgart: Philipp Reclam, 1994.
Speyr, Adrienne von. *The Cross: Word and Sacrament.* Translated by Graham Harrison. San Francisco: Ignatius, 1983.

———. *The Farewell Discourses: Meditations on John 13–17*. Translated by E. A. Nelson. Vol. 3 of *John*. San Francisco: Ignatius, 1987.

———. *Kostet und seht: Ein theologisches Lesebuch*. Edited by Hans Urs von Balthasar. Einsiedeln: Johannes, 1988.

———. *The Word Becomes Flesh: Meditations on John 1–5*. Translated by Lucia Wiedenhöver and Alexander Dru. Vol. 1 of *John*. San Francisco: Ignatius, 1994.

———. *The World of Prayer*. Translated by Graham Harrison. San Francisco: Ignatius, 1985.

Spinoza, Baruch. *Ethics*. Translated by George H. R. Parkinson. Oxford: Oxford University Press, 2000.

Splett, Jörg. *Die Trinitätslehre G. W. F. Hegels*. Symposion: Philosophische Schriftenreihe 20. Freiburg: Karl Alber, 1965.

Stock, Gregory. *Redesigning Humans: Our Inevitable Genetic Future*. New York: Houghton Mifflin, 2002.

Tertullian. *Adversus Praxean liber: Tertullian's Treatise against Praxeas*. Translated by Ernest Evans. London: SPCK, 1948.

Testori, Giovanni. *Il senso della nascita: Colloquio con don Luigi Giussani*. Milan: Rizzoli, 1980.

Tilliette, Xavier, and Giuseppe Riconda. *Del male e del bene*. Rome: Città Nuova, 2001.

Torrance, Thomas F. *The Christian Doctrine of God: One Being Three Persons*. Edinburgh: T. & T. Clark, 1996.

Tossou, Kossi K. Joseph. *Streben nach Vollendung: Zur Pneumatologie im Werk Hans Urs von Balthasars*. Freiburg: Herder, 1983.

Turek, Margaret M. *Towards a Theology of God the Father: Hans Urs von Balthasar's Theodramatic Approach*. New York: Peter Lang, 2001.

Ulrich, Ferdinand. *Der Mensch als Anfang: Zur philosophischen Anthropologie der Kindheit*. Freiburg: Johannes, 1970.

———. *Homo abyssus: Das Wagnis der Seinsfrage*. 2nd ed. Freiburg: Johannes, 1998.

———. "The Unity of Life and Death in the Word of Life." *Communio: International Catholic Review* 28 (2001) 99–111.

Vanhoye, Albert. *Let Us Confidently Welcome Christ Our High Priest: Spiritual Exercises with Pope Benedict XVI*. Translated by Joel Wallace. Herefordshire, UK: Gracewing, 2010.

———. *Our Priest Is Christ: The Doctrine of the Epistle to the Hebrews*. Rome: Editrice Pontificio Istituto Biblico, 1977.

———. *Structure and Message of the Epistle to the Hebrews*. Rome: Editrice Pontificio Istituto Biblico, 1989.

Velde, Rudi A. te. *Participation and Substantiality in Thomas Aquinas*. New York: Brill, 1995.

Villalmonte, Alejandro de. "El Padre: Plenitud fontal de la deidad." In *San Bonaventura 1274–1974*, 221–42. Grottaferrata (Rome): Coleggio S. Bonaventura, 1974.

Walker, Adrian J. "Personal Singularity and the *Communio Personarum*: A Creative Development of Thomas Aquinas' Doctrine of *Esse Commune*." *Communio: International Catholic Review* 31.3 (2004) 457–79.

Wallace, William A. *The Modeling of Nature: Philosophy of Science and Philosophy of Nature in Synthesis*. Washington, DC: Catholic University of America Press, 1996.

Waltke, Bruce K., Gleason Leonard Archer, and R. Laird Harris. *Theological Wordbook of the Old Testament*. Chicago: Moody, 1990.

Weil, Simone. *The Simone Weil Reader*. Edited by George Andrew Panichas. New York: McKay, 1977.

Weinandy, Thomas. *The Father's Spirit of Sonship: Reconceiving the Trinity*. Edinburgh: T. & T. Clark, 1995.

Weiner, Annette B. *Inalienable Possessions: The Paradox of Keeping-While-Giving*. Berkeley: University of California Press, 1992.

Welte, Bernhard. *Auf der Spur des Ewigen: Philosophische Abhandlungen über verschiedene Gegenstände der Religion und der Theologie*. Freiburg: Herder, 1965.

Whitehead, Alfred North. *Process and Reality: An Essay in Cosmology*. Corrected ed. Edited by David Ray Griffin and Donald W. Sherburne. New York: Free Press, 1978.

———. *Symbolism: Its Meaning and Effect*. New York: Capricorn, 1959.

Widdicombe, Peter. *The Fatherhood of God from Origen to Athanasius*. Oxford: Clarendon, 1994.

Wippel, John F. *The Metaphysical Thought of Thomas Aquinas: From Finite Being to Uncreated Being*. Washington, DC: Catholic University of America Press, 2000.

Wittgenstein, Ludwig. *Philosophical Investigations*. Oxford: Blackwell, 1958.

Wojtyła, Karol. *The Acting Person*. Translated by Andrzej Potocki and Anna-Teresa Tymieniecka. Boston: Reidel, 1979.

Index of Names

Aeschylus, 60n32
Alexander of Hales, 64, 65n44
    Alfarabi, 193n6
Ambrose, 291n54
Anatolios, Khaled, 194n8
Anaxagoras, 222n72
Anderson, Carl, 11n2
Anselm, 181, 205n44
Aquinas, Thomas, xiii, 17, 38–39,
    44, 60–66, 69–71, 74–88,
    96–103, 111n43, 112,
    114n49, 126n77, 127n80,
    128, 138n101, 140n104,
    152–57, 160n43, 161, 165,
    195nn11–13, 198n22,
    202n26, 211nn55–56,
    212, 215n66, 219, 222n75,
    239n39, 254, 255n66,
    288n49, 291n54
Archer, Gleason, 269n12
Aristotle, x, 17, 47n82, 51n1, 60,
    63n40, 69–76, 82, 84–89,
    96–99, 102, 108–11, 116n55,
    291n54
Athanasius, 184, 194–97, 234n20,
    276n29
Augustine, 38, 39n62, 62n36, 71n64,
    81n100, 116n55, 117n60,
    131n86, 136, 140, 157n27,
    163, 191n1, 195n11, 197n16,
    212n60, 219, 220n70,
    222, 233, 234–37, 239n39,
    246n56, 276n30, 291n54
Avicenna, 193n6

Balthasar, Hans Urs von, xi, 14n5,
    23, 30, 31n46, 36, 39n61, 78,
    81n103, 95, 102n7, 113n47,
    118nn62–63, 128n81,
    144n117, 150–55, 160n39,
    162–66, 173, 178, 181,
    183, 188n107, 192nn2–5,
    197n17, 201n25, 209–12,
    214n63, 215–18, 230n7,
    236–40, 244, 245n52, 246,
    250–53, 267n8, 268n10,
    275n28, 276n31, 281n37,
    284
Bandow, Doug, 55n11
Barnes, Michel René, 220n70
Barth, Karl, 160n41, 225n79
Basil the Great, 148n1, 195n11,
    230nn2–3, 232n11, 233n14,
    234n20, 237n35
Baudelaire, Charles 56–58
Beckett, Samuel, 54n7, 117n56
Benedict XVI, x, 24n27, 39n61, 66–
    68, 207n47, 265n6, 269n11,
    271–73, 291n55, 292n57,
    306n2
Bergson, Henri, xiii, 116n52
Berkeley, George, 94
Bernanos, Georges, 128, 144n117
Bernard of Clairvaux, 236
Berry, Wendell, 55n11
Bieler, Martin, 14n5, 102n6, 151n10,
    153, 160n41, 167n59
Blondel, Maurice, 25n28
Boehme, Jakob, 205n43
Boethius, 71n64, 221n71
Boff, Leonardo, 225n77

330 INDEX OF NAMES

Bonaventure, 65n46, 171, 192n3, 195n11, 212n60, 214–15, 222n75, 239n39, 244
Bordoni, Marcello, 148n2, 160n41, 162n46, 164n50, 289n50
Bouyer, Louis, 193n7
Brague, Rémi, 60n33
Brito, Emilio, 203n34
Brown, Colin, 168n63
Brown, David, 220n70
Bruaire, Claude, xi, xii, 81n103, 91–98, 117, 156, 197n20, 213, 245, 256n67
Bulgakov, Sergei, 45, 139, 140, 143n116, 160–66, 197–201, 220n70, 227n81, 234, 256n67
Burtt, Edwin Arthur, 102n6

Calvin, John, 42n70, 287
Camisasca, Massimo, 286n47, 309n12
Caputo, John, 53n4, 54n9, 104n12, 107n24, 111
Cervantes, Miguel de, 101n4
Chapelle, Albert, 202, 204n40, 206n46
Cicero, Marcus Tullius, 131n85, 291n54
Claudel, Paul, 120, 193
Coda, Piero, 201n25, 204n39, 205n43, 227n81
Colombo, Giuseppe, 285n46
Congar, Yves, 191n1, 245n52
Cyril of Alexandria, 173, 180

Damascene, John, 222
Daniélou, Jean, 265, 266, 276n32
Dante, vi
de Lubac, Henri. See Lubac, Henri de
Derrida, Jacques, 8, 12n3, 53–63, 71n62, 94, 98, 104n12, 117
Descartes, René, 21n18, 97n143
Desmond, William, 62, 137
Dunn, James, 162n46

Duns Scotus, John, 193n6
Durand, Emmanuel, 225n77
Durrwell, François-Xavier, 235n27

Eccles, John, 116n52
Eckhart, Meister, 220n70
Engels, Friedrich, 117n56
Epicurus, 131n85
Eunomius, 195, 218

Fabro, Cornelio, 75n79, 103n8, 111
Feuerbach, Ludwig, 115n51
Fichte, Johann Gottlieb, 205n43, 251
Firestone, Shulamith, 42n71
Forschner, Maximilian, 115n51
Foucault, Paul-Michel, 57n21

Gadamer, Hans-Georg, 11n1, 18n13
Gasché, Rodolphe, 54n9, 58
Geiger, L.-B., 75n79, 103n8
Gilson, Etienne, 69n58, 75nn79–80, 76, 78, 193n7
Giuliodori, Claudio, 63n39
Giussani, Luigi, xi, xii, 9, 14, 20–29, 33–41, 49, 81n103, 121–35, 141–48, 164n50, 172n70, 175n72, 184–90, 251, 252n61, 261–62, 271, 281, 283, 291n53, 292, 293–310
Godelier, Maurice, 12n3
Granados García, José, 11n2, 33n49, 231n8
Grant, George, 43, 242n44
Gregory of Nazianzus, 149n5, 191n1, 197n16, 230n2, 233nn12–13, 236n34
Gregory of Nyssa, 20n17, 45, 100, 118, 158, 168n62, 195n11, 276n29, 276n32
Gregory the Great, 240
Grelot, Pierre, 269
Greshake, Gisbert, 225n78
Grotius, Hugo, 18n11, 290
Guardini, Romano, xi, 134n90, 144–46, 164n50, 290

INDEX OF NAMES 331

Harris, Robert, 269n12
Hart, Kevin, 113n46
Hauerwas, Stanley, 136n94
Healy, Nicholas J., 155n21
Hegel, Georg W. F., x, 5, 8, 18,
    46n81, 50–51, 61, 83, 84,
    88–92, 96, 105n13, 108,
    110n36, 114, 120n65, 135–
    37, 191, 201–17, 220n70,
    271, 287
Heidegger, Martin, xii, 12, 18, 44,
    46–49, 53n6, 54, 56, 59, 61,
    91, 104–17, 121, 283n43,
    287, 299n75
Hénaff, Marcel, 54n10
Henry, Paul, 201n24
Henry of Ghent, 193n6
Heraclitus, 108, 112n44, 113
Hilary of Poitiers, 221
Hobbes, Thomas, 116, 290
Homer, 291n54
Husserl, Edmund, xii, 42, 105n13,
    112n46
Hyppolite, Jean, 205n41

Irenaeus of Lyons, 61n34, 137n99,
    140, 149n7, 185n96, 207n48,
    230n4, 230n6, 231n8,
    276n30
Ivánka, Endre von, 60n33

James, William, 42
Jeremias, Joachim, 167, 177nn74–75
John Paul II, 6, 11, 33n49, 94n133,
    96n142, 136n94, 161,
    162n45, 186, 187n101,
    190n110, 197n18, 210n53,
    214, 215n64, 231, 236n33,
    261, 268–70, 272n20,
    275n25, 281nn37–38,
    284n44, 291n56, 292n58,
    293n60, 302
Johnson, Elizabeth, 42n71, 225n77
Jonas, Hans, 12, 102n6, 107n23,
    116n52, 137n99
Joyce, James, 54n7

Kant, Immanuel, 80, 89n124,
    96n141, 116, 119, 121,
    137n98, 205n44, 296
Kierkegaard, Søren, 71, 117n56
Konrad, Michael, 21n18

LaCugna, Catherine, 220n70
Ladaria, Luis, 191n1, 198n21,
    212n61, 213n8, 235n27
Laffitte, Jean, 261n2
Lafont, Guy, 220n70
Lawler, Michael, 26
Le Guillou, Marie-Joseph, 192, 193,
    220n70
Leibniz, Gottfried, 155
Locke, John, 72n64
Lonergan, Bernard, 17n10
López, Antonio, ix–xiii, 91n128,
    94n131, 160n41, 162n46,
    171n66, 248n58
Lossky, Vladimir, 220n70
Louth, Andrew, 158n30, 179n78,
    179n80
Lubac, Henri de, 20n17, 38, 123n72,
    210n53, 214n63 Lubich,
    Chiara, 227n81
Luther, Martin, 67n53, 192n5
Lyotard, Jean-François, 53

Mackey, James, 220n70
Malet, Andre, 220n70
Mansion, Suzanne, 74n77
Marion, Jean-Luc, xii, 12n3, 104n12,
    107, 108n25, 112n46
Marx, Karl, 117n56
Mauss, Marcel, ix, 12n3, 54, 95
Maximus the Confessor, 140n104,
    148, 149n4, 157–59, 178–81
Mazza, Enrico, 284n43
Mazzanti, Giorgio, 284n43
Milbank, John, ix, 12n3, 54n9,
    137n98
Millán Puelles, Antonio, 97n143
Moltmann, Jürgen, 196n14, 225n79
Montini, Giovanni, 21n19

Mouroux, Jean, xi, 16n7, 20n16, 21n19, 63n39
Murray, John Courtney, 117n57

Nédoncelle, Maurice, 28n42, 166
Nichols, Aidan, 238n36
Nietzsche, Friedrich, 54n6, 117n56, 118
Nygren, Anders, 67n53

Ockham, William of, 70, 116n54, 192, 193n7
O'Donnell, John, 220n70
Oliver, Simon, 43n72
Orbe, Antonio, 185
O'Regan, Cyril, 61
Origen, 68–69, 123, 159–60, 196, 199, 214, 268
Oster, Stefan, 54n8
Ouellet, Marc, 284n43
Owens, Joseph, 71n62, 72, 74, 75n79, 82n106

Paissac, Henri, 220n70
Pannenberg, Wolfhart, 225n78
Pelagius, 115n51
Pérez-Soba Díez del Corral, Juan, 63n39
Perrin, Norman, 176, 177n74
Picasso, Pablo, 54n7
Pickstock, Catherine, 59n31
Pinckaers, Servais, 116n54
Plato, 15, 45, 60–65, 72, 108, 205nn42–43, 291n54
Plotinus, 45n77, 60, 63, 171
Pollock, Jackson, 54n7
Prieto, Antonio, 63n39
Pseudo-Dionysius, 24n26, 69n57, 140n104
Pyrrhus, 178

Rahner, Karl, 22n23, 26n32, 37n57, 162n46, 171n67, 181, 284n43

Ratzinger, Joseph, 16n7, 29n45, 69n59, 116n55, 121n66, 134n90, 144n118, 149, 160–67, 181n90, 183n92, 188n107, 214nn62–63, 234, 269–82, 306–9
Rawls, John, 117n57, 291n52
Régnon, Théodore de, 220n70
Richard of St. Victor, xiii, 239–43
Richardson, William, 105n14
Ricoeur, Paul, 136n94
Riconda, Giuseppe, 136n94
Rosmini, Antonio, 227n81
Rossetti, C. Lorenzo, 225n77, 247n57
Rotenstreich, Nathan, 89
Rougemont, Denis de, 63n39
Rousseau, Jean-Jacques, 116n55

Sachs, Joe, 72n64, 72n69
Sachs, John R., 238n36
Sallust, 66n51
Sani, Roberto, 21n18
Sara, Juan, 276n31
Sartre, Jean-Paul, 54n6, 71, 115n51, 118
Saussure, Ferdinand de, 56
Scanlon, Michael, 53n4, 54n9
Scheffczyk, Leo, 116n51
Schelling, Friedrich, 170, 205n43, 228, 247
Schindler, David C., 95n137, 105n14
Schindler, David L., 55n11, 78, 82n105, 96n142, 307
Schleiermacher, Friedrich, 19
Schlier, Heinrich, 142–43
Schmemann, Alexander, 285n46
Schmitz, Kenneth, 42, 43n72, 51n1, 60n33, 78–82, 92, 102n6, 104n12, 109n32, 203n32, 215n65
Schoonenberg, Piet, 148n2
Schrag, Calvin, 12n3
Schürmann, Reiner, 105n14, 107n24, 108, 110n37
Scola, Angelo, 21n18, 33n49, 63n39, 284n43

INDEX OF NAMES   333

Semmelroth, Otto, 284n43
Seneca, Lucius Annaeus, 12n3, 131n85
Sergius of Constantinople, 178
Sesboüé, Bernard, 148n2
Shakespeare, William, 137n97
Sharkey, Michael, 165n53
Sheehan, Thomas, 105n14, 106
Sokolowski, Robert, 60
Spaemann, Robert, 18n12, 19
Speyr, Adrienne von, 165, 208n49, 209n49, 216, 253n62, 253n64, 274
Spinoza, Baruch, 61n34, 136, 139, 202n30, 254, 296
Splett, Jörg, 204n40
Stambaugh, Joan, 106n18
Stock, Gregory, 29n45

Tertullian, 191n1
Testori, Giovanni, 29n44
Tilliette, Xavier, 136n94
Torrance, Thomas, 225n79
Tossou, Kossi K. Joseph, 238n36
Tracy, David, 53
Turek, Margaret, 201n25

Ulrich, Ferdinand, xi, 31, 78, 81n103, 84, 150, 156n23, 170n64, 218, 248n58

Vanhoye, Albert, 181n90, 271
Velde, Rudi te, 103n8
Villalmonte, Alejandro de, 191n1

Walker, Adrian, 81n103, 179, 180, 239n38
Wallace, William A., 102n6
Waltke, Bruce, 269n12
Weil, Simone, 140, 143
Weinandy, Thomas, 235n27
Weiner, Annette, 12n3, 54n10
Welte, Bernhard, 160n41
Whitehead, Alfred North, 11n1, 46n80
Widdicombe, Peter, 194n8
Wippel, John, 75nn79–81, 79nn90–91, 80n91, 82, 88n122
Wittgenstein, Ludwig, 56, 57n21
Wojtyła, Karol, 11n2

Index of Subjects

Abba, 167, 169, 178, 230n7, 256
abiding, 47, 200, 212, 234. See also in; indwelling; *perichoresis*
abseity, 223
abstraction, x, 70, 71, 101
acceptance, 135, 286; of gift of oneself, 78, 119, 122, 128, 134
accident, 63n37, 70–72, 79–80, 82, 85, 87–90, 94, 96–98, 140, 234, 256
act, xii–xiii , 2, 4–7, 18, 45n76, 61, 62, 70, 72, 80, 82, 88, 96n141, 98, 105, 117, 127, 129, 131, 134, 142, 157, 162, 226n80, 228–30, 238, 240, 246–47, 250, 256, 305; capacity to, 100; creative act, 77, 81–82, 130, 153, 155; creation and, 92, 153; open principle and, 77–85, 112, 214–18, 226; first act, 70, 76–79, 83–85, 99–100, 289; form and, 72–77,101; as received (first act), 70, 77–81, 83–84, 99, 118, 260, 289; as reception and reciprocation (second act), 77, 79, 100–101, 110n36, 118. See also operation.
action, x, 4, 7, 24–25, 30, 44, 47, 52n1, 62n37, 93, 98, 115, 119–21, 123, 127, 128, 139–46, 164, 179–80, 192–93, 203, 302, 305; as affirmation of mystery of being, 129–30;

as communication of love, 128–34; as gift of self, 129; gift-form of, 100–101; God and, 69n58, 76n84, 209n50, 214–18, 229, 254, 266; passive, 214–18; as reception (first act), 77–85, 118–19
actuality, 46, 72–73, 76, 80, 84n114, 97n143, 111, 114
adseity, 94, 223. See also substance; concrete singular
affection, 15, 40, 131, 182, 187, 270, 297
affirmation: of being's gift-ness, 157–59; creation *ex nihilo* as, 65, 155; in giving to others 129–30; love and, 189; mercy as, 262; in originary experience, 22–23; sacrifice as, 175–76, 189–90; of self, 146, 242; virginity and, 189, 301
agape, 59–70, 79, 85, 114, 138, 172, 211, 213–14, 217, 223–24, 253–54, 262, 293; creation and, 68–70; katalogical movement of, 67–70; reciprocation of gift and, 120–22. See also communion; *eros*; *koinonia*
aition, 102, 104, 109. See also cause
aletheia, 102, 104, 110–15, 121–22. See also truth
alterity, 23–24, 32, 104, 113, 156, 294, 309

INDEX OF SUBJECTS 335

analogy, 161–62, 236–37, 267; *analogia atributionis*, 152; *analogia entis* (analogy of being), 23, 36, 151–52, 154, 162; *analogia libertatis*, 36; *analogia personarum*, 36; *analogia proportionalitatis*, 152; Christ and, 154–55
anarchy, 52–59
anxiety, 170, 275, 299–300
apophaticism, 151, 220n70, 221, 261
arche, 5, 52, 102, 104, 109–10, 143. *See also* origin, ultimate
Arianism, 243
art, 17, 53, 54n7, 133, 285
asymmetrical reciprocity, xi, 31, 132; of *esse* and essence, 81–83
autexousia, 31, 100, 119, 144, 173, 179. *See also* freedom
availability, 84–85, 177, 229, 254–55, 270, 297
awareness, 12, 16, 21, 24, 26, 28, 42, 44, 67, 90, 98, 122, 126, 128–29, 133–35, 145, 163–68, 171, 197, 203, 219, 240, 283–84, 300
axioms, 104n11, 114n50, 192n5

baptism, 163, 231, 280, 286, 308n8
beauty, 12, 23–24, 47, 64–66, 68, 116, 119, 123, 133, 138, 171, 174, 191, 196, 199–200, 252, 264, 268, 277, 281, 289, 298, 300–301, 305, 310
becoming, 33, 44–45, 61, 90, 94–95, 98, 100n3, 126–27, 139, 153, 201, 206, 211
begetting, 27, 29, 34, 49, 79, 155–57, 171, 173, 176, 186, 191, 196–99, 203, 209–13, 215–16, 227–28, 233
beginning, xiii, 2–7, 11, 26, 45–46, 60, 109, 117, 123, 133, 142, 163, 296–303; eternal, 206, 214–18, 224–26, 243n48, 245–49, 261, 287–90, 305–6; nature of the, 272–79, 286

being: in Aristotle, 71–76, 82, 84n114, 85–86; in Aquinas, 74–88, 96n141, 99; as communion, 32, 91–92, 218–27, 294; event of, 108, 153; gift-character of, 13–14, 18, 23–24, 94; mercy and, 288–89, 302; positivity of, 1, 6, 32, 40, 51, 70, 76, 117, 148, 154, 207, 228, 248, 310. *See also esse*
belonging, 5, 18, 23–24, 32, 47–48, 51, 76, 85, 94, 96, 102, 105–6, 111, 123, 172, 186, 189, 208, 241, 243, 249, 285, 297; See also *Ereignis*
benevolence, divine, 139, 288,
birth, mystery of, 1–6, 26, 28–29, 34, 96, 100, 112, 156, 159, 173, 205, 259, 279, 281, 305
body, x, 1–2, 6, 13, 29, 45n76, 59, 66, 78, 96–99, 138, 159, 161, 174–75, 181–83, 187, 200, 210, 232, 254n65, 273, 279–80, 309; gift of self and, 103, 119; nuptial, 33; prayer and, 167; sacrifice and, 190; threefold poverty of, 103–4.
bonum, 63–65, 102, 171. *See also* good

causality, 18, 70–81, 102–15
cause, 17, 62n37, 69, 72, 80, 82, 88n122, 100, 102–16, 140, 151
celibacy, 185n98, 187. *See also* virginity
Chalcedon, Council of, 149, 151
change, 62, 86–87, 92–94, 100–2, 110, 132, 145, 157, 181, 193, 286, 295–300
charity, x, 88n122, 132, 161, 187, 240, 248, 250–51, 262, 265, 289, 291–92
child, 2, 29–34, 59, 118, 125, 132, 166, 197, 242, 275
childhood, 32–34, 48, 68, 278

336 INDEX OF SUBJECTS

choice, ix, 24, 40, 100n3, 116, 122, 124, 127, 141, 179–80, 251, 255. See also freedom
Christology, x, 7, 26, 150, 160, 164n50, 166, 230n5,
Church, x–xi, 140, 159–63, 175, 182, 278–85, 288, 308–9
circularity, 6–7, 24n27, 58, 72, 84n114, 117, 129, 150, 186, 196, 208–9, 230n5; of creative donation and reconstitution of gift, 286–90; of love and gift, 64–65, 234–38, 252, 256, 259, 263, 286; of religiosity and freedom, 175, 294–306
circumincession, 216. See also *perichoresis*
co-eternality, 201–12, 248–49
communication, 33, 97, 98, 118n63, 121, 128–31, 169, 241–43, 245, 305; of *esse*, 63, 69, 75–82, 100–104, 114, 137–38, 156, 215, 262; in God, 63–65, 172–76, 199, 201, 211n57, 218, 223, 226–27, 240n39, 250, 255
communion: being as, 32, 91–92, 219–28, 294; of beings, 24, 51n1, 92, 132, 260; Body of Christ as, 182; built by Holy Spirit, 280–85; comparison, 36, 40, 124–25; gift of self and, 176; restoration of, 272–78; Trinitarian, 191–92, 196, 219–27. See also *agape*; *eros*; *koinonia*
communio personarum, 220–27
compassion, God's, 214, 271
concrete singular, x; becoming and, 127, 138; defined, 51n1; as dual unity, 44, 81–84; as gift, 46, 47, 259–62; as given to itself, 70–77, 119–22; historical existence of, 44; as irreducible to origin, 61–62; ontological structure of, 70–99; permanence of, 259–62, 278–80, 286, 293–99; as relation, 44, 61–62, 85, 92–93, 277–78; restoration of, 272–79; time and, 259–62; unity of, 51–99, 259–61, 272–79; wholeness of, 77, 113
condignus, 240–41
condilectus, xiii, 241–44
confirmation: gift and, 4, 29, 91, 200, 249, 254, 260–63, 279, 285–86, 305; Holy Spirit and, 157, 206, 208–9, 213, 237. See also mercy
Constantinople, Third Council of, 149
contradiction, 6, 41, 58, 61, 83–85, 90, 120n65, 143, 178, 192, 198, 204–7, 267, 271
conversion, 41, 93, 98, 177, 193n7, 244, 279n34, 295, 308. See also change
creation (*ex nihilo*), xi, 3, 52, 59–65; vs. begetting, 155–57, 194–95; in Christ, 20, 38n59, 155–57, 288–89; hypostatic union and, 223–24; as love, 65, 222–23, 153–54; redemption and, 287–89
creativity, 145
creatureliness, 23, 94n133, 140–43, 147, 158, 285
Cross, 6, 84, 154–55, 159–60, 163–64, 167, 172–75, 177, 180–81, 183–84, 186–90, 194, 203–5, 208–9, 214, 221, 230–31, 236–37, 261–62, 265–66, 268, 271, 274–79
culture, 35, 42–43, 52, 54, 93, 145, 186, 221, 285, 306–9

Da-sein, 18, 105–6, 111
death, 34–35, 45n76, 49, 55–56, 61, 87, 91, 97, 121, 137, 139, 144, 154, 160, 163, 167–68, 172–73, 177, 180–81, 183, 190, 199, 200, 203–4, 207–9,

218, 230, 248, 257, 259–62, 268, 273, 275–79, 288, 295, 303
delight, 64–65, 67, 90, 119, 170, 175, 190, 236, 239, 243, 263–64, 297, 305. *See also* fruition
denial of gift, 34, 45, 48, 56, 67, 83, 87, 99, 119, 136–37, 139, 141–42, 144–47, 171, 187, 190, 203–4, 238, 241–42, 247, 260–61, 265, 276, 287, 296, 303
dependence, 19, 28n41, 29n43, 31–34, 76–77, 83, 88n120, 92–93, 114, 117, 122, 135, 127, 167–68, 172, 207, 246, 266. *See also* obedience; freedom
descent into hell, 160, 276–77
desire, ii, 3, 5, 13, 15, 17, 20, 24, 36n52, 38n59, 45, 65–67, 101, 104, 163, 172, 176, 180, 183–86, 189–90, 193, 217, 221n71, 256, 262, 265, 270, 283, 292; change and, 295–300; freedom and, 115, 120–26, 134; prayer and, 296–97
detachment, 34, 151, 186–87, 255, 301. *See also* virginity
différence, 58
difference, xiii, 2; as availability, 83–84; creation and, 59–62, 153–57; vs. evil, 137–38; innertrinitarian, 208–15, 217–18, 239–45; reciprocation of gift and, 120–22, 213
dignity, human, xi, 20, 214, 220, 240, 292
disobedience, 141, 263, 271, 276
distinction, 6, 21, 48–49, 51n1, 113, 150–52, 157, 163n47, 167, 206, 215, 218, 242–43, 247, 249, 287, 298, 300–301. *See also* real distinction
Donum doni, 209, 213, 229, 233–38
drama, 8, 25, 200

dual unity: of *eros* and *agape*, 69–70, 121, 172, 224; of essence and *esse*, 1, 3, 44, 84–85, 102, 105, 154, 155, 157, 215; of gift and *logos*, 25–27, 36–37, 41
dwelling place, 29, 60, 114, 133, 151n11, 258, 277, 281–84, 293, 307. *See also* home
dynamic, of gift, 229, 245–46

Easter Sunday, 181, 273, 277
economy, x–xi, xiv, 54–55, 70, 192, 200, 203, 206, 215, 218, 221n71, 230, 232, 234, 250; logic of, 54–59
ecumenism, 308–9
education, 31, 134–135, 186; mercy as, 298
egotism, xiii, 67–68, 239, 241
eidos, 71, 92, 97, 110. *See also* form
ek-stasis, 68–69
embrace. *See* welcoming
emeth, 102, 104, 112, 114–15, 121–22. See also *aletheia*; truth
encounter, 6, 8, 11, 13, 16–17, 19, 22–23, 26, 28, 35–39, 56, 64, 92, 95–96, 102–3, 116, 124, 166, 212, 219, 247, 273, 281–82, 298, 307
energeia, 42, 71–72, 98
Enlightenment, 40, 115
ens, 76, 79–80, 97, 154, 157; *commune*, 79n90
entelecheia, 42–44, 72, 88, 90, 110, 114, 123, 175
Entity, 8, 23, 51n1, 58, 71–72, 74–75, 82, 97, 195. See also *ousia*
equality, 33, 131, 137, 173, 217–18, 229, 290–92
equivocity, 71n62, 151, 154, 305
Ereignis, 47–49, 57, 59, 104–7, 111–13. *See also* event
Er-fahrung. *See* experience
eros, 60, 65–70, 84–85, 114, 120–21, 138, 172, 174, 189, 207–8, 223–24, 253, 262, 293, 297. See also *agape*; *koinonia*

INDEX OF SUBJECTS

esse: as act, 76; in Aristotle, 71–74; in Aquinas, 74–77, 79; as gift, 70–77, 156–57; of Christ, 150–59; creation *ex nihilo* and, 74–85, 153–57; communication of, 69, 75, 82, 100, 103–4, 114, 129; fourfold dimensionality (*esse ab, per se, ad*, being with), 78; fullness of, 112; as mode of revealing, 112; quasi-unity of, 80–81, 113

esse, divine, 64, 77, 80–81, 86, 153, 154, 156, 164, 168, 192n3, 218, 221–22, 242–43, 246–47. See also *ipsum esse subsistens*

esse commune, 79–81, 113, 121, 130, 153–54, 157, 207, 299; as non-subsistent, 84, 103, 138, 153, 156, 259

essence, x, xiii, 1–7, 44, 46, 52, 56, 85–96, 102–116, 127, 157, 193n6, 212n60, 219, 222–29, 243, 271; existence and, 70–85, 153–54

eternity, 44–48, 245–49, 259–61; time and, 4, 44, 170–71, 259–61, 277–78, 298–302; truth of, 170; the singular and, 298–302

Eucharist, 161, 166–67, 175, 181–83

event, xii, 2, 18–19, 28–29, 37, 41, 47–49, 57–59, 104–8, 112, 125–26, 148–49, 153–54, 159–62, 173, 185, 210n53, 215, 225, 245, 262, 271, 273, 290, 305, 309. See also *Ereignis*

ever-greatness, God's, 128, 151, 219, 251, 258, 290

evidence, 26–28, 32, 34, 37n55, 38, 40, 44, 102, 124, 142, 289

evil, 78, 135–47, 152–53, 295, 302. See also fatherlessness

excess, 239–42, 244, 248

existence: essence and, 70–85, 153–54; as gift, 75–85. See also *esse*

experience 11–50; fragmentation of, 52–59, 145–46. See also judgment; originary experience

experior, 14

faithfulness, 38, 177, 224, 261, 268–70, 283, 291, 296, 305

family, 28, 32, 35, 52, 115–16, 204, 282–84

father, 1–2, 27, 30–31, 63n41, 83, 120, 182, 191, 194–95, 205, 217, 269–71, 275, 300

Father, God the, 191–227; as absolute person, 191, 194–96, 212; gift of self, 199–215, 238–39; gratitude of, 216; mercy of, 260–72; monarchy of, 212, 225; as origin of communion, 191–92, 225–26; receptivity of 216–17, 267–68; as relative person, 196; relation to Son and Spirit, 212–18

fatherhood, divine, 141–42, 151, 163–64, 191–92, 194, 216, 220, 225, 231, 247n57, 269, 271, 277; as perfection in God, 194–95; revelation and, 196–97, 199

fatherhood, human, 30–32

fatherlessness, 141, 275–77. See also evil

filiality, 32–33, 220–21, 154, 250, 254, 308

filiation, 8, 148–50, 158–60, 163–64, 171, 194, 288–89

finitude, 31, 47, 207–8, 259; bodiliness and, 2, 96; event and, 106–07; evil and, 137–39, 238–40; as relation, 2, 151–52,

forgiveness, 57, 176–77, 261, 263, 282, 287, 292, 294–96, 299. *See also* mercy
form, 3–6, 11, 13–14, 24, 28, 32, 33–34, 36, 40–42, 52, 63, 65–78, 81–82, 89–92, 94, 97–98, 101, 103, 105, 107, 109–10, 113, 116, 119, 121, 126, 129, 131–135, 141, 143, 145, 148, 150, 152, 155, 158–65, 171–73, 179, 183, 185–90, 201, 210, 215, 221, 228–30, 232, 245, 246, 254, 260–61, 267, 275, 280–85, 296–97, 301, 306–7, 309–10
fragmentation, 4, 52–59, 131, 145, 147, 171, 260, 271, 295
freedom, 40–41; choice and, 127–28; Christ's, 177–80; as comparison with destiny, 123–24, 306–7; divine, 69, 118, 151, 192–93, 197–98, 211, 217–18, 229, 247, 250–53, 288; of the gift, 31, 114; in Giussani, 122–28; human, 115–22, 224–25, 250–52, 265, 286, 292; infinite and finite, 117–18, 192–193, 250–52, 287–89; liberated by Christ, 173, 175–80; in Maximus the Confessor, 178–81; as ontological satisfaction, 122–23; power and, 144–45, 192–94, 217–18; in prayer, 134–35, 167; as reception and reciprocation of the gift, 118–21; as recognition of God, 125–28; reductions of, 115–16, 126–27; religiosity and, 121–28, 135, 175–76, 306. *See also* obedience; dependence
friendship, 33, 66n51, 130–31, 135, 172, 176, 204n38, 232, 236, 264

fruitfulness, 97, 121, 132, 151n11, 162, 181, 190, 229, 236, 240n39, 242–43, 258, 301
fruition, 64, 90; as availability, 255; as expression of communion, 236; in God, 64, 212, 224, 226, 243; in Holy Spirit, 231, 242–43
future, 29, 43–44, 46–50, 56, 91, 170–171, 247, 249, 259, 278, 287, 299–301

generation, 160n39, 194–195, 197–200, 203, 211, 215–16, 235–36, 243. *See also* begetting
gift: absolute, 135, 155, 157, 209n52, 210, 214, 224, 249, 251; active and passive senses of, 90–91, 114, 145, 180, 299; at anthropological level, x, 31, 47, 51–52, 78, 92, 106, 148, 181; Christ as archetype of, 6–7, 151, 288, 307; communion, existing only in, 28–30, 91–92, 222–23, 294; in Derrida, 54–59, 94; dynamic of, 32, 229; elements of, 29, 228–29, 244; *esse* and, x, 7, 12, 16, 23, 25, 44, 47, 71, 77–85, 128–30, 157, 218; freedom of, 31, 114, 115–21, 250–53; as form of unity, 3–4, 245–46, 306–10; as given to itself, 33–34, 36, 46, 50, 62, 70, 78–79, 85–86, 90–91, 96, 120, 124, 128, 138, 144, 152n13, 259, 305; in God, 228–58; goodness and, 12; gratuity of, 32, 70, 183–90, 249–59; in Heidegger, 44–50; historical and eternal dimensions of, 169–70; *logos* of, 25, 72, 305, 307–8; love and, 64–70; main characteristics of, 28–35;

gift (*continued*)
as noun vs. verb, 46; as ontological principle, 4–5, 231–58; originary experience and, 11–12; paradoxical structure of, 59; personified in Holy Spirit, 233–38; and presence of giver, 87, 120, 171, 176, 235, 241, 287, 307; purpose of (indwelling), 104, 113, 223, 290; received, only as, xii–xiii, 25–26, 31, 50, 86, 88, 92, 98, 99, 118, 120, 125, 130, 135, 140, 170, 221n57, 223, 239, 241, 252, 297; rejection of, 8, 34, 135–47, 164, 172, 175–76, 181, 259–60, 263–72, 276, 287, 292, 294, 301–2, 309; restoration of, 272, 286–93; as revealing synthesis, 5, 11–12; spirit and, 93–94, 210–11, 245–46; substance (*ousia*) and, 85–96; as task, 37, 98, 101, 119, 137, 249; truth of, 31–32, 35, 44, 46, 60, 117, 121, 124, 128, 131, 164, 250, 275, 308

gift of self, 67, 77, 96, 128–35, 98, 100, 117, 119, 120–22, 125, 128–35, 144, 148–90, 199–201, 208–11, 218–19, 224, 226–27, 229–30, 232, 241, 245, 249, 253, 258, 273, 281, 287, 289, 294, 297, 307–8

giver, x, xii, 2–4, 6–8, 29–31, 33–36, 38, 45–47, 67, 68, 87, 99, 151, 172, 176, 183, 191–227, 229, 235, 241–44, 280, 285, 287, 298, 300, 305, 307–8, 310

giving, ix; in God (*see* gift: in God); as including receiving, 32–34, 78–85, 228–29; as paradoxical, 59–60; recognition of God and, 17, 125–28

glory, 103, 133, 141–42, 169, 174, 182, 185, 191–93, 196–99, 210, 214, 218, 227, 230–32, 255–58, 263, 266–69, 273–74, 285, 288, 297–98, 300, 303, 310

God: as communion of love, 8, 68, 126, 148, 196, 219–27, 235–37, 268, 284, 288, 306; dialogue in, 172, 196–97, 255–58; fatherhood of, 31, 141–42, 151, 163–64, 191–92, 216, 231, 247n57, 271, 277; participation in, 80, 103, 223, 259, 278, 290; personality of, 64, 210–218; suffering of, 214–15, 266–69; as ultimate origin, 2–3, 17, 27, 31, 34, 40, 194–96, 247–49

good, the, 23, 43, 55, 63–66, 73, 78, 87, 104, 115–16, 131, 136, 139–40, 162, 178–79, 185, 227, 269–70, 291, 308. See also *bonum*

Good Friday, 181, 200, 203, 216, 273–74

gratitude, 31, 55, 119, 134, 143, 173, 181, 216–17, 238, 253–54, 257–58, 267, 278, 285, 292, 301

gratuity, x, 32, 34, 184–90; *agape* and, 59, 213, 252–53; arbitrariness and, 251; availability and, 254–55; in Derrida, 54; in God, 229, 241–45, 249–58; as grounded in creation, 59; motherhood and, 30–32; prayer and, 255–58; recognition and, 251–53; of redemption, 176–90, 260–61, 287–93; unity and fecundity and, 251

ground, xiii, 4, 7, 18–19, 25, 39, 41, 54, 59, 104n11, 105–7, 116, 137–41, 182, 192, 210, 219,

224–26, 238–39, 244, 247,
255, 287, 289

happiness, 36–37, 123, 126, 271
hate, 144, 176, 185, 264, 271
heart, the, xi–xii, 188, 200, 257, 270, 271, 279, 281; as complex of needs, 36, 39–40; as criterion, 124–25
hierarchy, 195n11, 198n22, 217–18, 284. *See also* order; *taxis*
historical existence, 1–2, 20, 34, 44, 104, 119, 130, 158, 160, 165, 189, 228, 256, 295
historicity, 14, 91, 91, 114
history, 8, 11–12, 18n13, 22n23, 24, 42–50, 53, 60, 71, 97–98, 106n21, 112, 126, 133, 139n102, 141–43, 162–63, 170–71, 184, 190, 206, 247, 255, 260, 272, 280–81, 285–86, 302, 305–6
Holy Saturday, 273
Holy Spirit, x, xiii, 228–58; anonymity of, 247; breath, image of, 245–46; changing human person, 285–86, 290, 295–98; and Church, 281–85; as communion, 281–86; as confirmation of gift, 213–14; in economy of salvation, 160, 229–32; as excess, 239–45; as fruit, 244–45; in Hegelian system, 205–9; kenosis of, 201n25, 206, 209; as memory, 246–49; mission of, 229–34, 242–45; securing unity and difference, 213–14, 226–27, 230–31, 243–44, 246–49; as Spirit of love, 197n17, 209, 232; as Spirit of truth, 192n3, 210–12, 232; relation to Father and Son, 229–34, 238–45; unifying human life, 279–86. *See also* gratuity
home, 29–32, 34, 131–32, 270, 284. *See also* dwelling place; work

homelessness, 30, 133. *See also* technology
homoousion, 194
humanism, 53, 113, 121, 272
hypostases, 63, 156, 192, 196–98, 202, 209, 211–15, 217, 219, 221–25, 227, 231, 233–34, 238, 244–45, 251–54, 262, 266, 278
hypostatic union, 6, 8, 150, 152–55, 157–58, 160, 169, 179, 186, 223, 306

idea. *See* form
idealism, x, xii, 18, 22, 201, 284
identity, logic of, 143, 217, 248
ideology, 21, 24, 27, 41, 184
image, 7, 20, 22, 31, 33, 45, 96, 128, 130, 140, 157–58, 179, 184, 189, 193, 196n15, 197n19, 208n45, 219, 223, 243n48, 244, 246, 248–49, 254, 263, 265, 267, 279,
imago Dei, 157, 219–20, 256
imperfection, 67, 78–79, 83, 135, 138
"in," 222–23, 234. *See also* indwelling
Incarnation, the, x–xi, 27, 149, 152–54, 157–60, 171, 184, 223, 256, 288, 305, 309
indissolubility, 4
indwelling, 4, 62, 66, 68, 92–95, 115, 167, 221–26, 248, 251–52, 267–69, 278, 286; hypostatic union and, 149; renewal of concrete singular gift and, 182, 289–90, 308; of subhuman and human (asymmetrical), 94–96. *See also perichoresis*
ingratitude, 142–43, 146, 229, 232, 238–39, 257–60, 262–73, 275–76, 278–81, 284, 288–89, 291–92, 295, 298–303, 305
integralism, 307
interiority, 23, 93–94, 216, 226, 307

ipsum esse subsistens, 75, 80–81, 88, 103n8, 112, 114, 121, 207, 215, 239, 303

jealousy, 63n41, 140n107, 141, 229, 241, 254, 265
Jesus Christ, 148–90, 230–33, 239, 245–46, 274–75, 277–78, 307–8
judgment, 39–40, 42, 188
justice, x, 36–37, 123, 133, 177, 221; mercy and, x, 290–92

kenosis, 149, 160, 164, 166, 173–74, 188, 201–4, 206, 209, 213
kerygma, 162–63
kinesis, 106, 110. See also movement
knowledge, 12, 15, 17–19, 24, 42, 70, 73–74, 89, 93–94, 117, 136, 164–66, 168, 202, 210, 294n64, 310; in God, 154, 224, 252–53; judgment as, 39; love and, 39–40, 126, 240n39, 252, 257; as recognition, 125–26
koinonia, 60, 68–69, 85, 91, 121, 223, 262. See also *agape*; communion; *eros*

Lateran Council, Fourth, 219
letting be, 90, 216–17, 251
lie, 29, 45, 66, 91, 119, 140–41, 171, 174–75, 190, 258, 272, 276–77, 285, 305. See also denial of gift
limitedness, 137–38. See also finitude
logic, 90, 198, 202, 208, 221n71, 267; of economy, 54–59, 113n46; of gift, 33, 35, 54, 95, 143, 177, 309; of identity, 61, 143, 217; of power, 174, 217, 226, 262–64, 308–9
logos: Aristotelian form and, 76, 81; of concrete singular, 5, 16, 22–23, 25–27, 35, 102, 305, 307; love and (*eros* and *agape*), 64, 66–72, 97, 115, 120, 128, 133, 143, 197, 211, 305
Logos, xiii, 6, 8, 14, 27, 149–59, 161–62, 164–71, 173–74, 180–81, 186, 194–97, 210, 214, 223, 226, 230, 233, 244–46, 254, 256, 259, 269, 273, 275, 278, 281, 288, 294. See also Jesus Christ; Word
loneliness, 2, 275. See also solitude
love, 36–37; absolute, 241–45; dynamic and static aspects of, 222; essential in God, 221–27; gift and, 62–70, 233–45; God as mystery of, 70–77; God's for man, 264–72; the Good and, 63–64; historical form of, 280–81, 284; Holy Spirit as, 234–38; as indwelling, 277–78, 289–90; knowledge and, 239–40, 252–53, 288–89; perfection of, 67–68, 79, 238–45; prayer and, 257; of self, 143, 242; zeal and, 264–66

making, 133, 215; human, 13, 24, 61, 103; technological, 30, 108, 113, 132–33
Manicheism, 238
manipulation, 12, 18, 20, 23, 29, 51n1, 144, 146, 250, 285
marriage, xi, 33, 35, 187, 277; sacramentality of, 186, 263, 283, 286
Mary, x, 7, 125, 159, 161, 163, 166, 173, 175, 188–89, 231, 254, 256; and communion, 27–74, 276, 278, 28–83, 285n46
mastery. See nature: mastery over
memory, 5, 12, 21, 24, 33, 48, 51n1, 55–56, 96, 119, 125–26, 128, 131, 143–44, 170, 182, 186, 189, 277, 283; Holy Spirit as, 228–51, 270, 274, 285, 299–300, 305

mercy, x, 159, 176–77, 230, 263, 269n12, 309; anthropological and ontological dimensions of, 261–62; bodily dimension of, 279–80; changing human person, 282; coming through the flesh, 276–77, 280; as constitution of person, 279, 286, 290; as historical expression of God's love, 215, 221, 232, 255, 269–72, 289; justice and, 290–92; as mystery, 261; nature of, twofold, 286–88; novelty and, 288; singular's reception of, 262; time and eternity and, 261–62, 278, 298–302; unity of life and, 183, 185, 189, 282–84, 292–96, 303, 306; virginity and, 187, 188, 301; as welcoming, 280, 281, 285, 297. *See also* forgiveness

methodology, 14, 74n77, 194; analogy, 23, 36, 151–52, 154, 161, 162n45, 223, 236, 237n36, 267; anthropology, 6–7, 12, 14n5, 20, 37n57, 41, 44, 47, 67, 104n11, 112, 117, 147, 224, 230n5; Christology, 8, 26, 148–49, 160–63, 171n67, 197n17, 223, 269; circularity, 6–7, 24n27, 58, 64–65, 69n59, 72, 84n114, 117, 129, 150, 175, 186, 196, 208–9, 230n5, 234, 252, 256, 259, 263, 286, 288, 290, 294, 306; economy and theology, relation of, xi, 54–55; historical-critical, xiii, 159; integral mode of being (esp. of concrete singulars), 5–6, 59, 148; metaphysics, xi–xiii, 6–7, 17–18, 23, 46, 48, 70, 77n86, 79n90, 105, 108, 112, 136, 198, 218; paradox, 7, 58, 118, 121, 123, 127, 165, 183, 198, 220, 286; theology and philosophy, relation of, xi, 6–8, 60, 84, 109, 149, 150, 155, 191, 192n3, 202–3, 256n67

mission(s), 154–55, 159, 161–68, 174, 177, 178, 188, 229–33, 272, 281

monastery, 132, 283–84

Monotheletism, 178

morality, 6, 23n43

morphe, 71. *See also* form

mother, 1, 2; as sign of gratuity, 30–31

motherhood, 31–32

motion, 43

movement, 2, 24n26, 41–48, 55–63, 67–68, 83–84, 89–110, 114–16, 127, 136, 138–53, 159–62, 201–9, 217, 222, 244–46, 249, 255

mystery, 1–8, 13–17, 20–29, 48–49, 63–69, 97, 98, 157–73, 187, 191–98, 208, 263, 266–85, 291–97, 302–8; gift and, 29, 33–41, 78, 81, 86, 87, 91, 102, 108, 112, 118–42, 148–52, 220, 223, 228–30, 248–56, 259–62

nature, 11–14, 109; human, 37–38, 94, 121–22, 124–25, 179–81, 289–90; grace and, 31–38, 287–91; mastery over, 12–14, 18–21, 43–44, 115–16, 132, 174, 280–81, 285–86

necessity, 86–87; in Aristotelian ontology, 73–76; God and, 198–99, 228–29, 239–341, 250–51; of singular beings, 70

needs, original, 36–41, 124n75; freedom and, 122–25

negativity: Hegelian, 83–85, 89–90, 110n36, 117–18, 135, 201–9; positive sense of, 201n26, 214–18, 248–49

INDEX OF SUBJECTS

Nestorianism, 179
newness, 7, 79; in God, 289–91; permanence of gift and, 134, 289–91, 301
nihil, 17, 61, 81, 91, 139. *See also* nothingness
nihilism, fatherlessness and, 275–79
nominalism, 192–93
non-contradiction, law of, 198–99
non-subsistence, 45, 84, 103–4, 138, 153–54, 156, 259
nothingness, 59–62, 70, 155–56, 202–8; irruption of, 8, 139–40, 238. *See also* evil
nous, 93–94, 197, 256, 307. *See also* spirit
novelty, 7, 41, 87, 133, 143–44, 194–95, 247–49; beginning and, 287; Christ, brought by, 149–50; mercy and, 261, 279, 287–90; as unity of identity and difference, 148, 287–90
nuptiality, 33, 128, 161–63, 221, 250, 263, 308. *See also* body

obedience, 163–64, 166, 172–74, 268, 276, 284
object, 280
observation, 24
offering, 182–85, 256–58, 260–61, 308
One, the, 60–68, 171–72, 217, 226
ontological difference, 44, 96, 105–6, 122, 150, 155–57, 171, 224
onto-theology, 18, 70, 106–9
operation, 100, 115–22
order (in Godhead), 212–14, 217–18, 224–26, 234–36, 244–45. *See also* hierarchy; *taxis*
origin: the body and, 97, 115; concrete singular and, 44, 61–62, 85–86, 90–92, 118–19, 127; of human action, 142; mystery of birth and, 1–2, 30–31, 156; originary experience and, 12–13, 17, 21–24, 27, 35–37, 102, 124; postmodernity and, 53–59
origin, ultimate, 30–31; as cause, 17, 102–115; entrustment to, 33–35; the Father as, 8, 27, 156, 168–69, 191–227, 249–51; God as, 2, 27; as ultimate meaning, 37, 127
original solitude, 2, 11n2
originary experience, 8, 11–50, 121, 187, 305; causality and, 113; content of, 14–16; in Giussani, 21–28, 33, 35–41, 124–33; God's love and, 277–78; justice and, 291; meaning of "originary", 11–14; as revealing unity, 39–40, 94–95; twofold dimension, 14
orphanhood, 141–42, 226, 275–77, 295–96
otherness, 203, 208, 216–17. *See also* alterity
ousia, 71–77, 85–96

paradox, 7, 58; in structure of gift, 59–60, 121
participation, 218; in being, 46, 66, 262; in divine *esse*, 80–81, 114–15, 184–90, 250–51, 262, 289–90; in giving, 77–85; human work as, 132–33
Paschal Mystery, 149, 181–200, 271–72, 276, 293
passive action, 214–18
passivity, 78–79; activity and, 214–18; in God, 214–17; ontological, 215–16
past, the, 47–50, 252; mercy and, 299–301
paternal giver, 103, 114–15, 151; as mystery, 36. *See also* Father, God the
peiraw, 14–15
penia, 61, 65
Pentecost, 282
perichoresis, 221–27, 247n57

permanence, 4; of concrete singular gift, 259–60, 262–63, 278, 279, 286; of divine gift, 238–49; subsistence and, 90–91
perseity, 85–96, 223; as absolute and relative, 86–88; bodily, 96–99, 103; dependence and, 92–93, 260
person, 64, 220n70, 222–72, 305–6, 310; divine, 194–95, 210–14, 220, 243–44, 254; in Hegel, 201–4, 212–20; human, reconstitution of, 6, 11–15, 19–23, 28–41, 94–96, 100–103, 129–35, 272–79, 285–86, 289–92
phenomenology, 18–19, 42
philosophy: Heidegger and, 105–9; theology and, xi, 6–8, 60, 84, 109, 149–50, 155, 191, 192n3, 202–3, 256n67
physics, 12–13
play, 52, 56–57, 119
pneuma, 93–94, 197, 256. *See also* spirit
pneumatology, 229–31, 244–45
poiesis, 109–10, 144
poros, 61, 65–66
positivism, 3, 86, 163, 307
possession, 133–34, 184–90, 300–301
postmodernism, 51–59, 280–81; narrative in, 53–58
potency, 46, 72–76, 83–85, 110
poverty, 5–6, 65–67, 208n49; of gift, 35, 95–99, 116, 132–33, 154, 173; in Hegel, 201–9; prayer and, 297–98
power, 13, 40n65, 93–94, 109–10, 113–14, 193, 215; Christ's, 174–78; divine, 187–94, 217–18; evil and, 143–47; logic of, 174, 226, 308–10; restoration of, 176, 285–86; unity and, 53, 93–94
prayer, 128, 131, 134, 183, 255–58, 294n64, 297; of Christ, 151, 166–72, 181–85, 255–58, 297, 300; desire and, 296–97, 300–301; gift and, 134–35, 151, 167–72; in God, 254–58; mercy and, 297, 300; as offering, 182–83, 185, 256–58; poverty and, 297–98; as unity of time and eternity, 300–301
presence, 23–28, 283; as alterity, 23–24; being as, 23, 46–50, 54–62, 105; as belonging, 23–24, 47–48, 171–72; in God, 81, 104, 192, 248–49, 299–303; as relational category, 110–12, 170–71
presencing, 46–49; causality and, 104, 108–15
present, the, 46–50, 91, 98, 169–70, 182, 259–60; in Derrida's distinction from gift, 56–58; rediscovery of, 299–301
principle, open, 82–85, 214, 226n80
processions, 161, 198, 212, 217–20, 225, 239–40, 250–51; missions and, 254; psychological model of, 250
prodigal son, parable of, 269–72, 292
progress, 18, 29, 43, 52, 116
promise, 46, 121, 260, 287; cut short by evil, 138–42; death and, 277; fulfillment of, 221, 232, 254, 275–77, 300–303; future as, 48–50
Protestantism, 19, 192–94
punishment, 265, 272–79

quality, 96–98
quantity, 96–97
quiddity, 85–86

rationality, 307–8
real distinction, 73–77, 85–91, 212, 222, 225, 229

reason, 18, 36–41; affection and, 40–41, 182; freedom and, 24, 27–28, 40–41, 115–18, 121–22, 187, 250, 251n60; prayer and, 167–71, 182; task of, 287; technological, 18, 52–53, 250; ultimate meaning and, 306–8

receiving: concrete singular's, 44, 77–79, 85–99, 118–28, 135–36, 249, 254–55, 301; in Derrida, 54–55; freedom and, 121–28; in God, 169–76, 212–16, 228–29, 238–59, 266–73; as including giving, 33–34, 77–79, 228–29; in love, 65–70; in originary experience, 16, 19, 33–34; prayer and, 134–35; recognition of God and, 126

reception, ix–x, xiii; of children, 31–32; Christ's, 166, 273–78; of contrary qualities, 85–88; denial of, 135–47, 259; first act and, 77–85, 259–60; of gift of oneself, 1, 7, 32, 44, 77–88, 97, 118–47, 216, 242, 278–82; in God (see receiving: in God); of mercy, 280–82; of others, 96–99, 119; as response, 32; second act and, 100–147, 259–60; spirit and, 93–94

receptivity: of Father, 216–17, 267–68; as perfection of being, 267–68

reciprocation: Christ's, 163–84, 211n57, 212–13, 238–40, 244–46, 254–55; in Derrida, 54–59; evil and, 135–47, 193–94; the Father and, 208, 212–18, 238–40, 244–46; first act and, 77–78; freedom and, 100–101, 115–22, 141–47, 193–94; of gift of oneself, 7, 32–34, 59, 99–147, 259–60, 310; as gift of self, 128–35, 176–77, 183–84; Holy Spirit and, 228–29, 238– 55; of mercy, 262–67, 277–78, 280–82, 285–86, 292–301; nature of gift and, 119–28, 222–27, 238–39; in *perichoresis*, 222–27, 252–55; second act and, 99–147, 259–60; reception as, 119; recognition as, 125–26, 175–76

recognition, 50, 122–28, 134, 139, 141–42; as dialogue with God, 126–27; freedom and, 125–28; in God, 251–53; of God, 288, 293–94; as sacrifice of thanksgiving, 175–76

reddition, 156–57, 213–14

redemption, 146n122, 164, 232, 272–79; creation and, 287–93; gratuity of, 149, 174–90, 260, 287–93

regret, 296

rejection of gift, 135–47, 172–76, 181, 259–60, 263–72, 275–76, 287, 292–94; as not definitive of concrete singular, 301–3

relation: analogical, 51n1, 68–69, 137–38, 151–52, 212–16; category of, 85–96; constitutive, 3, 64, 84–85, 88, 92–94, 114, 169–70, 189, 191–92, 210–18, 222–24, 297–98; spiritual, 92–94, 119, 196–97, 222–24

relativism, 19

religiosity, 40n65; freedom and, 121–28, 135, 146–47, 175, 294–95, 306

renewal of gift, 7–8, 259–61, 264, 285, 308–10; Holy Spirit and, 279–80; original donation and, 287–93. See also mercy

response, xii, 1–2, 22–23, 31–38, 59–61, 67, 98–101, 120–21, 127–30, 157, 161–62, 199–

200, 208, 220, 261, 265–72, 288–89, 303; availability and, 254–55; Christ's, 172–84, 254–55, 272–79; in God, 211–18, 226–28, 244–47, 253–54; prayer as, 172, 181; virginity and, 186–90
responsibility: in Derrida, 55; as freedom, 123–24; as gift, 32
restoration, 185, 250–51, 260–63, 272–79, 295, 306
resurrection, 174, 183, 200, 205–6, 213–13, 277–79, 299, 303
revelation, 39n61; causality and, 104–15; divine, 60, 63–64, 68, 113–14, 137n100, 162–63, 191–92, 196–99, 220–21, 230n7, 236, 294
risk, 15, 34, 77–78

sacramentality: of Church, 162, 284–85; of marriage, 282–83
sacrifice, 175–76; Christ's, 160, 174–76, 181, 186, 189–90, 231, 272–73, 276–78; in Hegel, 204–8; virginity and, 189–90, 277–79
sanctity, 281–82
Satan, 139–41
second act, 77–78, 100–101, 110n36, 118, 126–28, 178–80, 259–60. *See also* operation
self-determination, 101, 117, 126–28, 178–79; evil and, 140; Hegelian, 110n36, 136–37, 202–4, 206
self-possession, 78, 101, 118, 211n58, 237
self-presentation: of being, 21–22, 41; of truth, 28, 112
service: Christ's, 174–75, 182; and power, 144–46
sexual difference, 33
sign, 23–27, 30–32, 59, 81, 123, 285n46; concrete singular as, 21, 47, 128, 285; as dual unity of gift and *logos*, 35–41, 307–8; failure to recognize, 142–43; vs. symbol, 25–26
silence, God's, 270–76, 293
simplicity, God's, 219
sin, 147, 268; Christ and, 180–81, 200, 215, 271, 273, 277, 295; vs. freedom, 141–42, 265; Holy Spirit and, 221, 232; ingratitude as, 142–44, 259–61, 272–79, 295; original, 140–41, 143
social order, 290–93
solitude, 271–79, 290, 293–94, 296
sonship, adoptive, 31, 162, 164–68, 200, 247n57, 255, 282, 289; intended in creation, 289–90; restoration of, 272–79. *See also* filiation
sorrow, 296–98
source, 2–6, 24–27, 32–34, 39, 45, 48, 50, 59–62, 69, 78–79, 81, 85–87, 90–92, 98–99, 102–9, 113–14, 117–22, 128–35, 137–47, 167, 191–92, 194–98, 210, 212–13, 228, 246, 249, 273, 285, 290. *See also* origin
space, 54–58
spiration, 191, 196–99, 209–14, 227, 245n52, 247n57, 234–35, 251
spirit: absolute, 61, 83–84, 89, 110n36, 136, 201–13, 279; gift-character of being and, 92–94, 211, 97–99; God as, 103, 196–97; *nous*, 93–94, 197, 256, 307; *pneuma*, 93–94, 197, 256; relation and, 92–93, 245–46
structural disproportion, 14, 35–41
subject, 280–81; in Derrida, 53–59
subjectivity, 51n1, 58–59, 95
sublation, 89, 136–37, 202–6
subordinationism, 198n22, 212
subsistence, 91–94

subsisting relations, 87n122, 201n26, 210–14
substance, 5–6, 46, 71, 74–76, 85–96, 97n143, 103, 193n7, 195–98, 217, 221n71, 223–26, 234, 239n39, 244–45, 254, 271; in Aquinas, 74–77, 96n141, 100n1, 215n66; in Hegel, 88–90, 136, 202n30; subhuman, 94–96. *See also* perseity
suffering, 136–137; of God, 173–81, 200, 209, 214–15, 266–79
summa caritas, 64, 234–45, 247, 252
superabundance, 95, 247, 292
symbol, 26, 171n67

task, 49, 190; gift as, 37, 101, 119; possible in Christ, 150, 157–59; power and, 144–45; work as specific, 132–35
taxis, 46, 211, 224, 235, 244. *See also* order; hierarchy
techne, 108–9, 144–45
technology, 12, 29–30, 43, 52–54; in Heidegger, 108–11; power and, 29–30, 144–45; work and, 131–33, 145–47, 285–86
telos, 22, 24, 26, 30, 32, 90–92, 119, 123–24, 127, 141–42, 153, 230n5
temptation, 140–41; of Christ, 177–78
thanksgiving, 175–76, 183. *See also* gratitude
theological difference, 155–57, 209, 224, 239–45
thou, 27, 121–22, 166, 233, 253n64, 290, 308n8
time, 3–5, 29, 42–50, 69, 106n20; in Derrida, 54–59; eternity and, 45, 164–72, 171n66, 247–49, 259–63, 272, 276–81, 286–88, 298–302; experience and, 42–50; gratuity and, 259–61; as history, 42–43;

mercy and, 298–303; prayer and, 298–302; as promise, 45, 142, 261, 299–303; unified givenness of, 49–50; vow and, 129–30
tolerance, 308–9
totalitarianism, 41, 52–53
totality: gift and, 21, 34, 46, 87n121, 90, 98, 129–31, 181–82, 208, 238–39; need for 16, 37–38, 140–42, 294; in postmodern thought, 53–54, 202n30,
tradition, 48–49, 98
transcendentals, the, 23, 39, 64–65, 119, 171, 191–92, 192n3, 210
Trinity, 32, 81n100, 192n5, 195–96, 293–94; as communion of love, 168–69, 202–03, 218–27, 235–38, 254; *taxis*, 211, 235, 244; theological accounts of, 219–22; unity and difference in, 156–57, 197n20, 199–218, 223–24, 242–45, 289–90
tripersonal gift, 228–29, 238–49, 251, 253, 268
truth, ii, 17–19, 28, 112, 187, 275–78, 294; the Church and, 279, 282–86; education in, 297–98; freedom and, 115–17, 121–28; gift and, 31–32, 35–37, 60, 121, 170–71, 308–10; innertrinitarian relations as, 172–74, 192, 210–14, 232, 234. *See also* transcendentals

unbegotten, Father as, 194–95, 210
unity: action and, 100–101, 128–35, 141–42, 214–18; of being and time in eternity, 3–5, 42–50, 169–72, 245–49, 259–303; bodily dimension of, 96–99, 96n142, 96n143, 279–86; breaking of, 4, 41, 52–59, 135–47, 259–60;

Christ's revelation of, 148–90, 220–23; as communion, 7, 66–70, 167–72, 182, 191–92, 218–27, 277–79, 281–86, 294, 294n64; of concrete singular, 3–8, 11–14, 25–26, 44–50, 51–99, 81–85, 113, 249, 259–303; culture and, 306–8; ecumenism and, 308–9; *esse* and, 79–85, 89–94, 105–6, 113, 152–59, 246–47; Eucharistic, 172–90; fruitfulness and, 236–51; with God, 27, 35–50, 121, 181–90, 206, 272–303; gratuity and, 54–55, 58–70, 183–90, 228–29, 238–63; in Hegel, 201–214; Holy Spirit and, xiii, 192n3, 228–58, 279–86, 293–99; of human life, 12–14, 32–35, 130 , 279–86; incarnated in Church, 279–85; love and, 63–70; mercy and, generated by, 259–303; objectified in a third, 65–68, 169, 189, 192n3, 223–27, 238–45; ontological, 1–8, 21–23, 39–41, 44–46, 69–99, 96n142, 150–59, 285, 293–95; originary experience and, 11–50; *perichoretic*, 221–27, 236–38, 252, 289–90; as permanence of gift, 3–4, 149, 245–49, 258–303, 306–7; postmodernity and, 51–60; in prayer, 134–35, 167–72, 257, 297–98, 300–301; restoration of, 149, 158–59, 172–90, 257–58, 259–303; substantial, 85–96, 242–43; through reciprocation, 121, 212–13; trinitarian, 7, 211n57–58, 218–27, 236; as tripersonal gift, xiii, 167–72, 192n3, 199–258, 267–68; virginity and, 67–68, 185–90, 300–301; work and, 131–34
unity and difference, 32, 44–50, 287; in Christ, 148–62, 167; in creation *ex nihilo*, 59–62, 153–54; evil and, 136–39; Holy Spirit and, 231–32, 239–43; as newness, 289; in recognition of God, 125–26; specific to love, 65–68; substance and, 88–96; trinitarian, 197n20, 198n22, 199–227, 239–43
univocity, 151, 154
unmoved mover, 60, 68, 72–73, 172

violence, 53n3, 146, 280–81, 307
virginity, 185–90; as affirmation, 189, 300–301; mercy and, 300–301; sacrifice and, 189, 277–79; time and, 300–301; as total gift of self, 189–90; as witness, 186–87
vocation, 195
vow, 129–31, 283

wealth, 5, 6, 35, 65, 98, 115, 132, 164, 173, 211, 218, 248n58, 284, 297
welcoming, 23, 130, 283, 293–95
whole, the 3, 5–8, 20, 21, 23–24, 36, 39, 40n65, 47n82, 290, 306–7. *See also* concrete singular: wholeness of
will, 20, 43–44, 172–73, 177–80, 181n89, 198–99, 211–12, 250–51, 254–56
witness: Holy Spirit as, 210, 217, 226–27, 229, 231–32, 245n52, 246–47, 279, 293; virginity and, 186–87
wonder, 23, 85–87, 100, 132–33, 197, 233; in Heidegger, 107, 113
Word, the, 98; creation and, 93, 156–57; of Father, 171–72,

Word, the (*continued*)
of Father (*continued*)
211, 228, 243–48, 251–52, 276–77; Holy Spirit and, 243–48, 251–52; Incarnate, 152–53, 159–64. *See also* Logos

work, human: as act of love, 131–34; bodiliness and, 145; Christ's (*ergon*), 175–77; as gift, 119, 285–86; as giving further, 33–34; power and, 144–46; as transfiguration of reality, 132

world 12, 38, 59–62, 92–93, 129, 131–34, 179, 306; God and, 84–85, 103, 113, 154–59, 161–62, 173, 206, 213n62, 223, 240, 247, 260–67, 273, 290; unity of, 167 183, 249, 280–87, 297

worship, 308

wrath, 223, 263–66, 270–71, 293

youth, 32

zeal, 263–73

www.ingramcontent.com/pod-product-compliance
Lightning Source LLC
Chambersburg PA
CBHW032012300426
44117CB00008B/1001